# International Legal Theory and the Cognitive Turn

# International Legal Theory and the Cognitive Turn

*Edited by*

ANNE VAN AAKEN

*Chair of Law and Economics, Legal Theory, Public International Law and European Law (Humboldt Professor 2018–23) and Co-Director of the Institute of Law and Economics, University of Hamburg, Germany*

MOSHE HIRSCH

*Emilio Von Hofmannsthal Chair in International Law and Co-Director of the International Law Forum, Hebrew University of Jerusalem, Israel*

OXFORD
UNIVERSITY PRESS

OXFORD
UNIVERSITY PRESS

Great Clarendon Street, Oxford, OX2 6DP,
United Kingdom

Oxford University Press is a department of the University of Oxford. It furthers the University's objective of excellence in research, scholarship, and education by publishing worldwide. Oxford is a registered trade mark of Oxford University Press in the UK and in certain other countries.



Published in the United States of America by Oxford University Press
198 Madison Avenue, New York, NY 10016, United States of America

British Library Cataloguing in Publication Data

Data available

Library of Congress Control Number: 2025930596

ISBN 9780198909262

DOI: 10.1093/9780198909293.001.0001

Printed and bound by
CPI Group (UK) Ltd., Croydon, CR0 4YY

MIX
Paper | Supporting responsible forestry
FSC® C013604

The manufacturer's authorised representative in the EU for product safety is Oxford University Press España S.A. of El Parque Empresarial San Fernando de Henares, Avenida de Castilla, 2 – 28830 Madrid (www.oup.es/en or product.safety@oup.com). OUP España S.A. also acts as importer into Spain of products made by the manufacturer.

*In memory of Uta-Marie Stinnes-van Aaken, Paul van Aaken, and Ben Stolk*

# Preface and Acknowledgements

This book grew out of the editors' participation in several research workshops focused on the cognitive and behavioural dimension of international law, and fruitful discussions on fascinating interactions between new cognitive studies and a variety of international legal issues. It struck us that while the findings of cognitive and behavioural research work are making inroads into international law literature, their implications for the theoretical foundations of international law have largely been explored only in a rudimentary fashion. Being convinced that cognitive and behavioural studies generate valuable insights for international legal thought, and that they interact with international law theories in diverse manners, we set out to fill this gap. We aimed, together with a group of scholars, to systematically analyse if, to what extent, and how new insights gained from cognitive sciences studies influence some principal theoretical approaches to international law. We were lucky to find outstanding scholars who were ready to take on the challenging task of analysing various interrelationships between cognitive-behavioural literature and distinct international law theories. We believe that this joint endeavour brings some new insights to various theories of international law and may advance a constructive dialogue between the two fields and between distinct theories.

The workshop held at the inspiring Warburg House of the University of Hamburg (in March 2023) enabled all participants to receive valuable feedback on their draft chapters, to engage in meaningful discussions on some issues resurfacing in multiple chapters, to learn a lot from one another, and to enjoy numerous social encounters.

Doing research is a profoundly creative and productive endeavour that sometimes helps to deal with difficult times. Sofia Stolk's father, Ben Stolk, attended the workshop and did beautiful drawings that sensitively captured some unique scenes. We were extremely sad to learn that he passed away on 11 October 2023; we profoundly share in Sofia's pain. The drawing presented on the page following this Preface was done by Ben Stolk during the workshop. In addition, Anne van Aaken's father, Paul van Aaken, passed away unexpectedly in May 2024, during the final stage of editing this book. Her mother, Uta-Marie Stinnes-van Aaken, her beloved Mamuschka, passed away peacefully in September 2024 after a long illness. This book is therefore dedicated to the memory of Uta-Marie Stinnes-van Aaken, Paul van Aaken, and Ben Stolk, in deep gratefulness and with love.

Many people have contributed in one way or another to the long process of writing and editing this book. We are indebted to Robert Cavooris (acquisitions editor, public international law), Lisa Butts (the previous project editor), and

Rebecca Lewis (the current project editor) at Oxford University Press who believed in the project since its inception, encouraged us to pursue it, and accompanied us on the journey. We are also grateful to the OUP production team and to Ohad Abrahami who competently and skilfully assisted us in editing the book's chapters. Many thanks also go to the anonymous reviewers of the book proposal whose comments were very helpful.

We are particularly indebted to the Alexander von Humboldt Foundation for funding support provided for the workshop, as well as the open-source publication. Our gratitude goes out to Anne van Aaken's secretary, Sonia Mestre, for taking on the administrative organization of the workshop, as well as to the research assistants—Katharina Luckner, Raphael Maesschalk, and Magdalena Benjamin—who also greatly assisted us in organizing the workshop. Special thanks are also owed to Dr Sophie Duroy, Dr Anne Dienelt, and Dr Lys Kulamayil, who provided insightful and helpful comments on several papers presented at the workshop.

Finally, and above all, we owe a great debt of gratitude to each contributor to this volume who joined us in this intellectually challenging (but rewarding) journey.

H.B. '23
Ben

# Contents

# Abbreviations

| | |
|---|---|
| BIT | bilateral investment treaty |
| CACJ | Central American Court of Justice |
| CAT | Communication Accommodation Theory |
| CBM | confidence-building measure |
| CBP | Customs and Border Protection |
| CCJ | Caribbean Court of Justice |
| CICC | Coalition for the International Criminal Court |
| CLS | critical legal studies |
| CoPs | communities of practice |
| EBCG | European Border and Coast Guard Agency |
| ECtHR | European Court of Human Rights |
| EU | European Union |
| FATF | Financial Action Task Force |
| IACtHR | Inter-American Court of Human Rights |
| ICC | International Criminal Court |
| ICJ | International Court of Justice |
| ICL | international criminal law |
| IIA | international investment agreement |
| IL | international law |
| IR | international relations |
| ISDS | investor-state dispute settlement |
| ITLOS | International Tribunal for the Law of the Sea |
| JCPOA | Joint Comprehensive Plan of Action |
| MCA | Multiple Correspondence Analysis |
| NAFTA | North American Free Trade Agreement |
| NGO | non-governmental organization |
| OECD | Organisation for Economic Co-operation and Development |
| RSD | refugee status determination |
| SATRC | South African Truth and Reconciliation Commission |
| SDGs | Sustainable Development Goals |
| TJ | transitional justice |
| TLP | transnational legal process |
| TWAIL | Third World Approaches to International Law |
| UN | United Nations |
| UNGA | United Nations General Assembly |
| UN GGE | United Nations Group of Governmental Experts |
| VCLT | Vienna Convention on the Law of Treaties |
| WTO | World Trade Organization |

# Contributors

**Anne van Aaken** (Dr iur and MA Economics) is Chair for Law and Economics, Legal Theory, Public International Law and European Law, University of Hamburg (2018–2023 Alexander von Humboldt Professor). Previously, she was professor at St. Gallen University and Senior Researcher at two Max Planck Institutes. Anne was Vice-President of ESIL and chaired the EUI Research Council. She has taught in the US, Europe, Africa, Asia, and Latin America, is general editor of JIDS and has served as a member of the editorial boards of AJIL, EJIL, International Theory, and JIEL. She has been consultant for the IBRD, OECD, UNCTAD, and the UN. Her over 100 publications concentrate on international law and behavioural economics/psychology and legal theory.

**Kanad Bagchi** is a postdoctoral fellow at the Amsterdam Center for International Law, University of Amsterdam. Before that, he was a research fellow at the Max Planck Institute for Comparative Public Law and International Law in Heidelberg. His recent publications include 'Depoliticizing Money: How the International Monetary Fund Transformed Central Banking', Journal of International Economic Law (2024) and 'Marxist Approaches to International Law: An Outline' (Max Planck Institute for Comparative Public Law and International Law 2022 and forthcoming in OpenRewi Textbook on Public International Law).

**Daniel Bodansky** is Regents' Professor at Arizona State University's Sandra Day O'Connor College of Law. He served as Climate Change Coordinator at the U.S. State Department from 1999–2001. He is the author of the award-winning books, *The Art and Craft of International Environmental Law* (2nd edition co-authored with Harro van Asselt, OUP 2024) and *International Climate Change Law* (co-authored with Jutta Brunnée and Lavanya Rajamani, OUP 2017). He is a member of the Council on Foreign Relations and a graduate of Harvard (AB), Cambridge (MPhil), and Yale (JD).

**Tomer Broude** is Dean of the Faculty of Law at the Hebrew University of Jerusalem, and Bessie and Michael Greenblatt, QC, Chair of Public and International Law at the Faculty of Law and Department of International Relations. He holds bachelors degrees from the Hebrew University and a Doctoral degree from the University of Toronto Faculty of Law. He specializes in public international law and international economic law; and particularly in international trade and investment, human rights, dispute settlement, development, and cultural diversity. He has served as Academic Director of the Minerva Center for Human Rights at the Hebrew University of Jerusalem, and Vice-Dean of the Faculty of Law.

**Salvatore Caserta** is an Associate Professor of Sociology of Law and International Law at the Faculty of Law in the University of Copenhagen. He specializes in sociology of globalization, the sociology of the legal profession, international courts and international dispute resolution, and public international law. His publications have appeared in leading European and American law journals, such as Leiden Journal of International Law, Duke Journal of Comparative and International Law, Human Rights Law Review, American

Journal of International Law, and Law & Contemporary Problems. He is a member of iCourts, the Centre of Excellence for International Courts.

**Harlan Grant Cohen** is Professor of Law at Fordham University School of Law. Previously, he was the Gabriel M Wilner/UGA Foundation Professor in International Law at the University of Georgia School of Law. Cohen is a member of the Board of Editors of the American Journal of International Law and Vice President of the American Society of International Law (ASIL). He has previously served as Chair of the ASIL International Legal Theory Interest Group.

**Veronika Fikfak** is an Associate Professor in International Law and International Relations at University College London School of Public Policy; and a co-Director of the UCL Institute for Human Rights. She is the author of more than fifty publications; and has won several prizes, including the British Academy Rising Stars award, the ICON Society Best Paper Prize (Special Mention), and the ASIL Dispute Settlement Best Paper Prize. She has secured more than €5 million in research funding, including an ERC Starting Grant, an ERC Consolidator Grant, and a Humboldt Senior Research Fellowship. She is a managing editor of the American Journal of International Law Unbound and sits on the Board of the European Society of International Law. She also serves as a judge ad hoc at the European Court of Human Rights.

**Moshe Hirsch** is the Emilio Von Hofmannsthal Professor of Law at the Hebrew University of Jerusalem. A significant part of his publications involves theoretical and interdisciplinary research that draws, inter alia, on sociological literature, social-cognition studies, political economy, and international relations theory. His recent publications include International Law's Invisible Frames-Social Cognition and Knowledge Production in International Legal Processes (co-edited with Andrea Bianchi, OUP 2021); 'Cognitive Sociology, Social Cognition and Coping with Racial Discrimination in International Law', EJIL (2019); and 'The Sociological Perspective on International Law', in Jeffrey L Dunoff and Mark A Pollack (eds), *International Legal Theory: Foundations and Frontiers* (CUP 2022).

**Robert Howse** is the Lloyd C Nelson Professor of International Law at NYU School of Law. He received his BA in philosophy and political science with high distinction, as well as an LLB, with honours, from the University of Toronto, where he was co-editor in chief of the Faculty of Law Review. He also holds an LLM from the Harvard Law School. He has been a visiting fellow at the London School of Economics and visiting professor at Harvard Law School, Tel Aviv University, Hebrew University of Jerusalem, the University of Paris 1 (Pantheon-Sorbonne), Tsinghua University, and Osgoode Hall Law School in Canada and taught in the Academy of European Law, European University Institute, Florence.

**Regina Jefferies** is an Assistant Professor at Western Washington University and Adjunct Lecturer at the University of New South Wales Faculty of Law. Jefferies is also an attorney admitted to the bar in the United States, with more than a decade of experience in the practice of immigration and human rights law. She has published articles in leading academic journals such as Globalizations, the Melbourne University Law Review, and the Brooklyn Journal of International Law.

**Ian Johnstone** is a Professor of International Law at The Fletcher School, Tufts University. He served as Interim Dean from 2018 to 2019 and Academic Dean from 2013 to 2015. Prior to joining Fletcher, Johnstone worked in the Executive Office of the United Nations

Secretary-General. His most recent books include *Building an International Cybersecurity Regime: Multistakeholder Diplomacy* (co-editor 2023); *Talking International Law: Legal Argumentation Outside the Courtroom* (Co-editor 2021); and *Law and Practice of the United Nations* (co-author, 3rd edn, 2016). A citizen of Canada, he holds an LLM degree from Columbia University and JD and BA degrees from the University of Toronto.

**Shiri Krebs** is a Professor of Law at Deakin University and Director of the Centre for Law as Protection. She is also the elected Chair of the Lieber Society on the Law of Armed Conflict, an affiliate scholar at Stanford University Center for International Security and Cooperation (CISAC), and co-lead of the Australian Government Cyber Security Cooperative Research Centre (CSCRC) Law and Policy Theme. In 2024, she was appointed Visiting Legal Fellow at the Australian Government Department of Foreign Affairs and Trade (DFAT). Her research is funded by several research grants, including an Australian Research Council DECRA fellowship and an Alexander von Humboldt Senior Research Fellowship.

**Mikael Rask Madsen** is a Professor of European Law and Integration, at the Faculty of Law, University of Copenhagen, and director of iCourts, Centre of Excellence for International Courts. Trained as both a lawyer and a sociologist, his research focuses on international law and institutions, and the evolution of the legal profession. He is the author of numerous books and articles, including International Court Authority, Oxford University Press, co-edited with KJ Alter and LR Helfer and 'Sovereignty, Substance, and Public Support for European Courts' Human Rights Rulings,' American Political Science Review, co-authored with J Mayoral, E Voeten, and A Strezhnev.

**Daniel Peat** is Assistant Professor of Public International Law at the Grotius Centre for International Legal Studies at Leiden Law School. He is Academic Coordinator of the Advanced LLM on International Dispute Settlement and Arbitration and Director of the Leiden International Administrative Law Clinic. Previously, Daniel worked at the International Court of Justice and completed his PhD at the University of Cambridge. His book *Comparative Reasoning in International Courts and Tribunals* (CUP 2019), was awarded the ESIL Book Prize 2020. He is on the Editorial Board of the Leiden Journal of International Law and the Advisory Board of the International Community Law Review.

**Shreya Shankar** is a PhD researcher in Hamburg University, Germany. She has a background in public international law and forensic psychology. She is specifically interested in understanding the ways in which human emotion, cognition, and identity interact with transitional justice, human rights law, and international humanitarian law. She has previously worked in the NGO space, on issues of indigenous peoples' rights, education, and access to medical care.

**Sofia Stolk** is Assistant Professor in International Law, Vrije Universiteit Amsterdam and Associate Fellow, Asser Institute, The Hague. She is co-founder of the Legal Sightseeing platform (https://www.legalsightseeing.org). Her recent publications include 'Courtroom 600: The (Virtual) Reality of Being There', International Criminal Law Review (2021, with Renske Vos); 'Building (of) the International Community: A History of the Peace Palace through Transnational Gifts and Local Bureaucracy', London Review of International Law (2022, with Tanja Aalberts); and 'Law in Concrete: Institutional Architecture in Brussels and The Hague', Law and Humanities (2020, with Renske Vos).

**Arun Mohan Sukumar** is an Assistant Professor at the Institute of Security and Global Affairs, Leiden University. He is an international lawyer by training, with a PhD in international relations and MA in Law and Diplomacy from the Fletcher School, Tufts University; and a bachelor's in law (BA LLB) from NALSAR University of Law, India. Arun was previously a post-doctoral research fellow at The Hague Program on International Cybersecurity at Leiden University. He is the co-editor of *Building an International Cybersecurity Regime: Multistakeholder Diplomacy* (Edward Elgar Publishing 2023) and *Responsible Behaviour in Cyberspace: Global Narratives and Practice* (Publications Office of the European Union 2023).

**Ruti G Teitel** is the Ernst C Stiefel Professor of Comparative Law, and a co-director of the Center for International Law at New York Law School, where she chairs the Institute for Global Law, Justice, and Policy. She is one of the world's leading experts on international human rights and a thought-leader of transitional justice. She is the author of a wide body of work, including three books: *Globalizing Transitional Justice* (2014), *Humanity's Law* (2011), *Transitional Justice* (2002), and *The Justice Archive: Transitional Justice and Digital Memory in the London Review of International Law* (2023). She is the founding co-chair of the American Society of International Law Interest Group on Transitional Justice and Rule of Law and a life member of the Council on Foreign Relations.

# Introduction

## International Legal Theory and the Cognitive Turn

*Anne van Aaken and Moshe Hirsch*

### 1. Introduction

Significant changes in social sciences often herald changes in legal theory, including in international legal theory. In light of the cognitive turn in social sciences, this volume seeks to explore the implications of this 'turn' for international legal theories. One might ask: what do cognitive studies have to do with international legal theory? Humans operate cognitive processes in their minds and international legal theory is traditionally about states and inter-governmental organizations, which do not have cognition; and states and international organizations are rather legal constructs which have been legally ascribed power and the authority to act. Yet, behind these legal entities are decision-making individuals[1] who employ cognitive processes to respond to events taking place in their (legal) environment. Perceptions of reality by international law decision-makers (including national policy-makers and international adjudicators) affect their assessments of ongoing factual and normative developments, decisions regarding adequate responses, and interpretations of existing legal rules (and the development of new ones). Cognitive processes that shape legal decision-makers' perceptions are often susceptible to diverse biases. Thus, this book is premised on the assumptions that first, human cognition affects the perceptions and behaviour of real-world international law decision-makers and, second, that cognitive processes matter in how international law is formed, interpreted, implemented, and theorized. The following chapters set out to unearth if and how implicit or explicit assumptions about human cognition are present in different international legal theories, as well as if and how these theoretical approaches can be informed and potentially modified by cognitive studies.

The book is also situated within the broader turn of international legal scholarship to interdisciplinary studies. This turn is on the rise,[2] reflecting an increasing

[1] See, eg, Tamar Megiddo, 'Methodological Individualism' (2019) 60 Harvard International Law Journal 219. See also Anne Peters and Tom Sparks (eds), *The Individual in International Law, The History and Theory of International Law* (OUP 2024).

[2] See, eg, Jeffrey L Dunoff and Mark A Pollack, 'Reviewing Two Decades of IL/IR Scholarship: What We've Learned, What's Next' in Jeffrey L Dunoff and Mark A Pollack (eds), *Interdisciplinary Perspectives on International Law and International Relations: The State of the Art* (CUP 2013) 626.

Anne van Aaken and Moshe Hirsch, *Introduction* In: *International Legal Theory and the Cognitive Turn*.
Edited by: Anne van Aaken and Moshe Hirsch, Oxford University Press. 
DOI: 10.1093/9780198909293.003.0001

recognition of the valuable insights drawn from neighbouring disciplines—prominently history,[3] (political) philosophy,[4] political science, international relations,[5] economics,[6] sociology,[7] and psychology[8]—to international legal scholarship. These and other perspectives present certain assumptions about human behaviour. Some international legal theories are explicit about their cognitive-behavioural assumptions, such as rational choice approaches. Others, such as positivism, political philosophy, or sociological perspectives, have largely been less explicit about the cognitive-behavioural aspects of their 'models of man'.[9]

Cognitive and behavioural studies are making inroads into the international law literature[10] and international policy-making,[11] yet their implications for international legal theory remain under-explored. This book aims to fill this gap by systematically analysing if, to what extent, and how new insights gained from cognitive sciences influence some principal theoretical approaches to international law. We hope to take a significant step towards a more methodological and comprehensive analysis of cognitive elements included (implicitly or explicitly) in various international law theories. We believe that the cognitive turn in neighbouring disciplines (see further below) provides scholars with research and theoretical tools for building bridges between diverse 'models of man'[12] and distinctive approaches to international law.[13] We hope that this endeavour will also contribute to shedding light on some underlying implicit assumptions of international law theoretical perspectives, desirable for constructive exchanges between the proponents of different theories.

This Introduction proceeds as follows: after the introduction of the 'cognitive turn' and its basic assumptions (Section 2), we briefly address some central

[3] See, eg, Alexander Orakhelashvili, 'The Relevance of Theory and History: The Essence and Origins of International Law' in Alexander Orakhelashvili (ed), *Research Handbook on the Theory and History of International Law* (2nd edn, Edward Elgar 2020) 2.

[4] See, eg, 'Introduction' in Samantha Besson and John Tasioulas (eds), *The Philosophy of International Law* (OUP 2010) 1.

[5] See, eg, Dunoff and Pollack (n 2).

[6] See, eg, Andrew Guzman, *How International Law Works: A Rational Choice Theory* (OUP 2008) 3 et seq; Joel P Trachtman, *The Economic Structure of International Law* (Harvard UP 2008) 1.

[7] See, eg, Moshe Hirsch and Andrew Lang, 'Introduction' in Moshe Hirsch and Andrew Lang (eds), *Research Handbook on the Sociology of International Law* (Elgar 2018) 1.

[8] See, eg, Anne van Aaken and Tomer Broude, 'The Psychology of International Law: An Introduction' (2020) 30 EJIL 1225.

[9] Herbert A Simon, *Models of Man: Social and Rational—Mathematical Essays on Rational Human Behavior in a Social Setting* (Wiley 1957) 1.

[10] See, eg, van Aaken and Broude (n 8); Andrea Bianchi and Moshe Hirsch, 'International Law's Invisible Frames: Introductory Insights' in Andrea Bianchi and Moshe Hirsch (eds), *International Law's Invisible Frames: Social Cognition and Knowledge Production in International Legal Processes* (OUP 2021) 1; as well as many other publications in different fields of international law.

[11] Lauren Manning and others, *Behavioural Science around the World: Volume II—Profiles of 17 International Organizations* (World Bank 2020) 12.

[12] Simon (n 9).

[13] Some of the following chapters highlight certain tensions between cognitive-behavioural studies and international legal theories; see, eg, Chapter 12 by Kanad Bagchi in this volume; Chapter 4 by Shiri Krebs in this volume.

terminological issues and tenets of cognitive and behavioural studies. As elaborated in Section 3, cognitive and behavioural studies constitute two streams in cognitive sciences; they share substantial commonalities and the differences between them are often a matter of emphasis and general orientation. Section 4 exposes some key concepts of cognitive-behavioural studies, such as the dual-process model, heuristics, cognitive biases, and prospect theory. Section 5 discusses various interactions between cognitive-behavioural studies, international law, and some prominent properties of international legal theories; and calls for further research in this intellectually challenging field. Section 6 provides brief summaries of the book's chapters.

## 2. The Cognitive Turn and Human Cognition

Although the roots of cognitive science can be traced to ancient Greek philosophy,[14] its genesis as a collaborative endeavour of multiple disciplines lies in the 1950s, and most prominently in the Symposium on Information Theory held at the Massachusetts Institute of Technology (MIT) in 1956. The organizational origins of the 'cognitive revolution' are widely dated to the mid-1970s, particularly to the establishment of the journal *Cognitive Science* (1977) and the founding of the *Cognitive Science Society* (1979). The Sloan Foundation's support had a catalytic effect on the field and cognitive science became an institutionalized part of the intellectual landscape in the late 1970s.[15]

People are commonly exposed to large amounts of stimuli, and cannot deeply internalize and process all information in the brain. Some cognitive mechanisms are employed to reduce, interpret, and store certain incoming information in the memory.[16] These selective and interpretative processes are influenced by mechanisms relating to the particular features of the incoming information itself ('bottom-up' mechanisms—from the external environment to perception in the brain), as well as mechanisms pertaining to patterns of prior knowledge ('top-down' mechanisms—from pre-existing patterns to perception in the brain).[17] Top-down processes include cognitive 'schemas' that are organized clusters of existing

[14] On the 'prehistory' of cognitive science, see José Luis Bermúdez, *Cognitive Science: An Introduction to the Science of the Mind* (3rd edn, CUP 2020) 15 et seq.

[15] Howard E Gardner, *The Mind's New Science: A History of the Cognitive Revolution* (Basic Books 1985) 3–5, 35–38; George A Miller, 'The Cognitive Revolution: A Historical Perspective' (2003) 7 Trends in Cognitive Sciences 141 at 141–43; William Bechtel, Adele Abrahamsen, and George Graham, 'Cognitive Science: History', *International Encyclopaedia of the Social & Behavioral Sciences* (2001) 2154; Bermúdez (n 14) 15.

[16] See, eg, Michael SA Graziano and Taylor W Webb, 'The Attention Schema Theory: A Mechanistic Account of Subjective Awareness' (2015) 6 Frontiers in Psychology 3.

[17] Hans Eysenck and Mark Keane, *Cognitive Psychology* (7th edn, Psychology Press 2015) 98– 99, 101, 125; Graziano and Webb (n 16) 3–4. See also Perry Hinton, *The Perception of People* (Routledge 2016) 18–21.

knowledge about the world, events, people, or actions; for example, a schema containing information about the expected sequence of events in a restaurant or a schema indicating relationships between various pieces of information (eg between parts of the body). Not only do schemas embody generalized structures of existing knowledge but they also constitute lenses through which people perceive and process new information.[18] Schemas influence, for example, patterns of attention or the formation of new memories.[19]

Various kinds of schemas have been studied by scholars from different disciplines, prominently the 'habitus' analysed by Pierre Bourdieu,[20] 'frames' examined in the psychological and behavioural literature,[21] and sociological scholarship.[22] The Bourdieusian concept of habitus refers to general and durable socially produced cognitive structures ('dispositions') that are deeply internalized (largely below the conscious level), often embedded in bodily operations that generate people's practices and constitute the basis for the perception and appreciation of human experiences.[23]

Discussion of the above mental processes and structures led to the fundamental idea that reverberates in numerous cognitive studies: that people do not directly sense their physical environment; and that cognitive processes *mediate between* sensory input from the external environment and human behaviour. Thus, cognitive processes (like attention or categorization) and structures (such as schemas) construct *mental representations* in people's minds that organize our knowledge and expectations about various social objects in our environment.[24]

The book's chapters address both individual and social ('relational') aspects of cognitive-behavioural processes. It is worth emphasizing that *analytically*, individual and social levels of cognitive processes and their effects can be separately explored. An individual-level examination generally focuses on the particular decision-maker's cognitive processes (including heuristics and biases), often

[18] Paul DiMaggio, 'Culture and Cognition' (1997) 23 Annual Review of Sociology 263 at 269; Eysenck and Keane (n 17) 284–85, 436; Kathleen Galotti, *Cognitive Psychology: In and Out of the Laboratory* (6th edn, SAGE 2018) 195–98. See also Hinton (n 17) 31.

[19] See, eg, Karen Cerulo, 'Mining the Intersections of Cognitive Sociology and Neuroscience' (2010) 38 Poetics 115, 125–26.

[20] On the concept of 'habitus', see Chapter 10 by Mikael Rask Madsen and Salvatore Caserta in this volume; Chapter 9 by Moshe Hirsch in this volume.

[21] On framing in psychological and behavioural studies, see Section 4. For a behavioural discussion of 'frames' in international law, see Anne van Aaken and Jan-Philip Elm, 'Framing in and through Public International Law' in Andrea Bianchi and Moshe Hirsch (eds), *International Law's Invisible Frames: Social Cognition and Knowledge Production in International Legal Processes* (OUP 2022) 35.

[22] Erving Goffman, *Frame Analysis: An Essay on the Organization of Experience* (Northeastern UP 1974) 21, 10.

[23] Pierre Bourdieu, 'Structures, Habitus, Practices' in *The Logic of Practice* (Stanford UP 1990) 52 at 52 et seq; Omar Lizardo, 'The Cognitive Origins of Bourdieu's Habitus' (2004) 34 Journal for the Theory of Social Behaviour 375, 393–94. The concept of 'frame' is discussed in Section 4.

[24] See, eg, Susan T Fiske and Shelly E Taylor, *Social Cognition: From Brains to Culture* (4th edn, Sage 2021) 12, 17; Martha Augoustinos, Iain Walker, and Ngaire Donaghue, *Social Cognition* (3rd edn, Sage 2015) 20–21; Paul Thagard, *Mind: Introduction to Cognitive Science* (2nd edn, MIT Press 2005) 4.

backgrounding socio-cultural or contextual processes. A social-level analysis emphasizes cognitive patterns shared by people belonging to a particular social group[25] (such as patterns of attention or collective memory), frequently relegating to the background differences between individuals.[26] Individual and social analyses of human cognition complement one another and we would like to caution the reader that the boundaries between these analytical fields are porous and fluid. We submit that individuals' cognitive processes and related behavioural patterns very often involve some combination of individual and social elements.

## 3. Cognitive and Behavioural Studies: Terminology, Overlap, and Nuances

*Cognitive science*[27] is the interdisciplinary study of the mind and the diverse mental processes involved in acquiring, processing, and storing information, as well as judgements and decision-making processes.[28] These cognitive processes include attention, categorization, interpretation, framing, memory, learning, language, problem-solving, and reasoning (which are often intertwined with emotions).[29] Cognitive science aims to explain how people accomplish a wide range of mental tasks, such as problem-solving, understanding other people's behaviour, and acquiring new concepts. Cognitive studies also endeavour to explain when and why mental processes sometimes fall short.[30] Cognitive processes have long been studied by cognitive psychologists and neuroscientists.

Labelling of the cognitive field can depend on the faculty where the research work is conducted and where it is published. Cognitive studies are dubbed in some social sciences *behavioural economics* or, when applied to legal analysis, *behavioural law and economics*.[31] As discussed below, the border between

[25] See, eg, on interactions between 'social proof' and cognitive processes, Chapter 7 by Regina Jefferies in this volume.

[26] See, eg, Moshe Hirsch, 'Cognitive Sociology, Social Cognition and Coping with Racial Discrimination in International Law' (2019) 30 EJIL 1319, 1324 et seq.

[27] The term 'cognitive science' refers here primarily to *human* cognition as addressed in the 'social cognition' literature (a branch of psychology) which is mainly focused on how people make sense of other people and themselves. See, eg, Fiske and Taylor (n 24) 1.

[28] Gardner defines cognitive science 'as a contemporary, empirically based effort to answer long-standing epistemological questions—particularly those concerned with the nature of knowledge, its components, its sources, its development, and its deployment' Gardner (n 15) 6.

[29] On the fundamental interactions between cognition and emotion, see, eg, Jonathan Haidt, *The Righteous Mind* (Penguin 2012) 33 et seq; Fiske and Taylor (n 24) 415 et seq. and Alessia Celeghin and others, 'Basic Emotions in Human Neuroscience: Neuroimaging and Beyond' (2017) 8 Fontiers in Psychology 1, 2, on the relationship between cognition and basic emotions (fear, anger, joy, sadness, surprise, and disgust). On emotions in international law, see Anne Saab, 'Emotions and International Law', 10(3) ESIL Reflections (2021) and Susan Bandes and others (eds), Research Handbook on Law and Emotion (Edward Elgar 2021).

[30] See, eg, Thagard (n 24) 3 et seq.

[31] Eyal Zamir and Doron Teichman, *Behavioral Law and Economics* (OUP 2018) 7 et seq.

behavioural[32] and cognitive studies is blurred, and the difference between them is largely often a matter of emphasis.[33] Daniel Kahneman, a cognitive psychologist who won the Nobel Prize in economics, deplores but admits that: '[l]ike it or not, it is a fact of life that economics is the only social science that is generally recognized as relevant and useful by policy makers'.[34] The reason for economics being perceived as more relevant to policy-makers than cognitive psychology, he speculates, may be a book based on cognitive psychology by another Nobel Prize laureate in economics (Richard Thaler), together with a well-known legal scholar (Cass Sunstein),[35] which has influenced national policy-makers worldwide.[36] But given that economics has long been premised on the rational choice model, the rational assumption continues to serve widely as a benchmark in behavioural economics literature (and to some degree also in psychological social cognition studies). Behavioural economics thus primarily explores the impact of cognitive and motivational factors on individual decision-making (not confined to market transactions), highlighting deviations from the rational choice paradigm ('heuristics' and 'biases') and examining under which conditions such deviations occur.[37]

Cognitive and behavioural studies share substantial commonalities (including some basic assumptions) and they overlap extensively. The distinctions between the two fields are often a matter of emphasis or general orientation, and here we only mention some of these nuances. While cognitive studies are more orientated to exploration of internal processes in the human mind (like attention or memory), behavioural studies are generally more concerned with externally observable behaviour. Behavioural studies are typically more policy-orientated, frequently aimed at designing intervention programmes to attain socially desirable objectives (notably aimed at correcting certain biases). As for links with other disciplines, cognitive studies draw considerably on the social psychology and neuroscience literature, while behavioural studies draw more often on experimental psychology and game theory, as well as economics. Both cognitive and behavioural

[32] We follow the definition of behavioural science offered by Hallsworth: 'In its broadest sense, [behavioural science is] a discipline that uses scientific methods to generate and test theories that explain and predict the behaviour of individuals, groups and populations. … Behavioural science is different from "the behavioural sciences", which refers to a broader group of any scientific disciplines that study behaviour.' Michael Hallsworth, 'A Manifesto for Applying Behavioural Science' (2023) 7 Nature Human Behaviour 310, 311.

[33] Cognitive psychology often appears in the literature under the heading of 'behavioural economics'.

[34] Daniel Kahneman, 'Foreword' in Eldar Shafir (ed), *The Behavioral Foundations of Public Policy* (Princeton UP 2013) vii.

[35] Richard H Thaler and Cass R Sunstein, *Nudge: Improving Decisions About Health, Wealth, and Happiness* (Yale UP 2008).

[36] Cass R Sunstein, Lucia A Reisch, and Julius Rauber, 'A Worldwide Consensus on Nudging? Not Quite, But Almost' (2018) 12 Regulation & Governance 3.

[37] Whereas some experts regard deviations from rational choice as detrimental and thus aspire to 'debias' such deviations (see, eg, Christine Jolls and Cass R Sunstein, 'Debiasing through Law' (2006) 35 JLS 199), others view them more favourably (see, eg, Gerd Gigerenzer and Peter M Todd, *Simple Heuristics That Make Us Smart* (OUP 1999)). All agree that the rational choice theory does not accurately describe human decision-making.

studies to a certain degree take the rational individual as a benchmark in positive inquiry and sometimes draw on normative decision theory (how should people decide were they to act rationally);[38] but the benchmark of the rationality assumption is more pronounced in behavioural literature (especially with regard to decisions deviating from the rational choice model).[39] Since the two spheres overlap substantially and are often intertwined, we frequently refer to them as 'cognitive-behavioural' studies.

International practice has recently turned to behavioural science[40] and international institutions are paying increasing attention to insights drawn from cognitive-behavioural studies. The United Nations (UN) has stated that behavioural science is crucial for achieving its mandate, inter alia, with regard to the Sustainable Development Goals (SDGs).[41] This UN practice followed the World Bank, which devoted its World Development Report 2015 'Mind, Society, and Behavior' to the potential employment of insights gained from behavioural literature to promote economic development. Other international organizations have also followed suit.[42]

The cognitive-behavioural field is fundamentally interdisciplinary. Gardner explains in his renowned book on the history of the cognitive revolution that 'cognitive scientists harbor the faith that much is to be gained from interdisciplinary studies'.[43] In its early stages of development, cognitive science involved at least six disciplines (psychology, linguistics, neuroscience, computer science, anthropology, and philosophy),[44] and at present, experts from numerous disciplines (including biology, neuroscience, economics, and sociology) explore a variety of aspects of cognitive processes and their consequences for human behaviour. Bermúdez concludes about the pluralistic nature of the field that '[i]n fact very few academic areas are not relevant to the study of the mind in some way'.[45]

[38] On the assumption of rationality in social cognition and behavioural decision theory, see Fiske and Taylor (n 24) 227–29. On the rational choice model in behavioural literature, see n 37.

[39] See Chapter 8 by Anne van Aaken and Tomer Broude in this volume.

[40] The term behavioural science as understood by the UN is broadly defined by António Guterres (UN Secretary-General) as follows: 'Behavioural science refers to an evidence-based understanding of how people actually behave, make decisions and respond to programmes, policies, and incentives.' UNSG, *Behavioural Science—Guidance Note* (2021) 1. The UN has established a behavioural insights unit.

[41] As explained, cognitive science 'can contribute to combating poverty, improving public health and safety, preventing and managing crisis, promoting gender and economic equality, tackling corruption, strengthening peacebuilding and all the SDGs. At the same time, it is being used to make the public sector more efficient and holds potential in this area for the UN. UN entities are strongly encouraged to invest in behavioural science and work in a connected and collaborative interagency community to realise its tremendous potential to achieve impact'. Guterres (n 40) 4. See also Adam Oliver, *The Origins of Behavioural Public Policy* (CUP 2017) 108.

[42] This trend is prominent with regard to UN agencies, but also discernable in many other international institututions. For an overview, see Manning and others (n 11).

[43] Gardner (n 15) 6.

[44] George A Miller, 'The Cognitive Revolution: A Historical Perspective' (2003) 7 Trends in Cognitive Sciences 141, 143.

[45] Bermúdez (n 14) xxiii.

## 4. Some Key Concepts in Cognitive-Behavioural Studies

Humans frequently come across large volumes of information, but they possess limited cognitive capacity to process such data. To cope with this influx of information from diverse channels, people resort to automatic processes and heuristics, thus often succumbing to various cognitive biases. The brain's dual-process model has been widely accepted in cognitive science.[46] Cognitive processes involve different levels of awareness, and cognitive-behavioural studies make a distinction between *automatic and deliberate processes.* Automatic cognitive processes ('System 1') can occur below the level of consciousness, while deliberate thought ('System 2')[47] demands consciousness. Automatic cognition involves rapid, effortless, and unintentional processes of information, essentially activating some well-learned sets of associations or responses that have developed through the repeated activation of memory (often involving emotions). Deliberate cognition involves slow, well-thought-out, and measured cognitive processing.[48] Although most of our thoughts and behaviours tend to be automatic or have automatic components,[49] people tend to overestimate the extent to which their thoughts control actions and the extent they *can* control their thoughts.[50] When engaged in deliberate thought, people may reject and override their automatically activated biases.[51] Such deliberate processes are mentally effortful, requiring, for example, constant re-evaluation of existing assessments and correcting biases, thus necessitating more cognitive resources.[52]

While rational choice theory assumes that people perceive outcomes in absolute terms (expected utility), the well-established *prospect theory*[53] posits that

[46] Jonathan St BT Evans, 'In Two Minds: Dual-Process Accounts of Reasoning' (2003) 7 Trends in Cognitive Sciences 454. On the dual-process model in neuroscience, see Matthew D Lieberman, 'Social Cognitive Neuroscience: A Review of Core Processes' (2007) 58 Annual Review of Psychology 259. On dual-process cognition in international relations and international law, see, eg, Chapter 3 by Ian Johnstone and Arun Mohan Sukumar in this volume.

[47] Rational choice theory has focused solely on System 2, while neglecting System 1 and other relevant factors that are relevant to human decision-making but difficult to grasp or quantify (such as emotions).

[48] See, eg, Daniel Kahneman, *Thinking Fast and Slow* (Farrar, Straus and Giroux 2012) 20 et seq; Fiske and Taylor (n 24) 35 et seq; Galotti (n 18) 90–93.

[49] T Wheatley and DM Wegner, 'Automaticity of Action, Psychology of' in *International Encyclopedia of the Social and Behavioral Sciences* (2001) 991. See also Stanislas Dehaene, *Consciousness and the Brain* (Penguin Books 2014) 13.

[50] Fiske and Taylor (n 24) 65. See also Dehaene (n 49) 47, 79–80.

[51] Cerulo (n 19) 117. See also Augoustinos (n 24) 113.

[52] Gordon Moskowitz, *Social Cognition: Understanding Self and Others* (1st edn, Guilford Press 2005) 224. See also Margo Monteith, Anna Woodcock, and Jill E Gulker, 'Automaticity and Control in Stereotyping and Prejudice' in Donal E Carlston (ed), *The Oxford Handbook of Social Cognition* (OUP 2013) 74, 81.

[53] Prospect theory has long been used in international relations literature to explain state behaviour: Jack S Levy, 'Prospect Theory and International Relations: Theoretical Applications and Analytical Problems' (1992) 13 Political Psychology 283; James Davis (ed), *Psychology, Strategy and Conflict* (Routledge 2013) 5.

individuals assess their loss and gain in an asymmetric manner. People ordinarily perceive outcomes as either gains or losses and feel losses more strongly than equivalent gains. Losses and gains are defined in relation to some reference point—usually (but not invariably) the status quo or an entitlement. Generally, a loss counts more than a gain (explaining 'loss aversion') and actors seek out or focus on risks when considering the domain of losses ('loss frame').[54] Loss aversion also adds to the significance of *default rules* which, as opt-in or opt-out rules, alter the behaviour of actors (including states);[55] although according to rationalist assumptions, default rules should not exhibit such a strong influence on decisions. The *endowment effect*, namely the tendency to place a higher value on objects and entitlements that people already have (compared with objects and entitlements they do not yet have), may also inhibit efficient transactions and negotiations, and thus often hinders international cooperation.[56] Viewing compromises as losses can also impede cooperation. People's subjective confidence in their judgements is reliably greater than the objective accuracy of these judgements; and like the 'fundamental attribution error'[57] (as well as the above 'loss aversion'), this tends to produce more hawkish decisions in international conflictual situations.[58]

*Framing effects* similarly violate the rationalist axiom of 'descriptive invariance'. A framing effect exists 'when different ways of describing the same choice problem change the choices that people make, even though the underlying information and choice options remain essentially the same'.[59] This phenomenon is called equivalence framing, and it is pervasive; eg, when a choice is described as a loss rather than a gain, people decide differently. Many experiments have explored these effects,[60] including in public goods games, a sub-field of game theory modelling (which includes, inter alia, strategic interaction in international relations). Framing plays a subtler role when a given problem description influences the decision-maker's choice (mostly unconsciously) with regard to how to address a broader problem. This happens primarily by making certain aspects of an

[54] Tomer Broude and Caroline Henckels, 'Not All Rights Are Created Equal: A Loss–Gain Frame of Investor Rights and Human Rights' (2021) 34 LJIL 93.

[55] Default rules also matter greatly in international law (including the analysis of sources); see Anne van Aaken, 'Behavioral International Law and Economics' (2014) 55 Harvard International Law Journal 421; Jean Galbraith, 'Treaty Options: Towards a Behavioral Understanding of Treaty Design' (2013) 53 Virginia Journal of International Law 309.

[56] Daniel Kahneman, Jack L Knetsch, and Richard H Thaler, 'Experimental Tests of the Endowment Effect and the Coase Theorem' (1990) 98 Journal of Political Economy 1325.

[57] The fundamental attribution error refers to the tendency to attribute other people's behaviour to their personal attitudes and motivations rather than to external influences and constraints; see, eg, Zamir and Teichman (n 31) 68–69.

[58] Daniel Kahneman and Jonathan Renshon, 'Hawkish Biases' in Trevor Thrall and Jane K Cramer (eds), *American Foreign Policy and the Threat of Fear: Threat Inflation since 9/11* (Routledge 2009) 79.

[59] Richard Cookson, 'Framing Effects in Public Goods Experiments' (2000) 3 Experimental Economics 55. On different theories about framing, see Tore Ellingsen and others, 'Social Framing Effects: Preferences or Beliefs?' (2012) 76 Games and Economic Behavior 117, 118.

[60] ibid.

information set more salient, to the detriment of other aspects of the information set ('issue framing'). Frames influence beliefs, and beliefs in turn influence behaviour.[61] Specific examples abound: framing ultimatum games[62] as a product of resource scarcity generates higher offers and fewer rejections.[63] Framing negotiations as taking place in an international (rather than a business) context tends to trigger enhanced cooperative behaviour.[64] And supposedly, reframing a perceived zero-sum game (e.g. in a security context) as a positive-sum game can increase cooperation.[65] Framing thus seems to be highly important for understanding how states' decision-makers *perceive* the game. Do they think they face a prisoner's dilemma situation when engaging with climate change treaties or rather do they perceive it as a stag hunt game ('assurance game')? Their respective framing is likely to lead to divergent approaches to negotiations as well as institutional design.[66]

The well-known *confirmation* bias is relevant to numerous international legal situations.[67] This bias refers to the tendency to search for, interpret, favour, and recall information in a way that confirms or supports one's prior beliefs or values.[68] Thus, people display this bias when they select information that supports their previous views, underestimating or ignoring contrary information, or when they interpret ambiguous evidence as supporting their existing attitudes.

Cognition is also relevant for strategic interaction. *Behavioural game theory* combines insights from economics, psychology, and cognitive science to study strategic decision-making; it focuses on the motivational aspects of behaviour, motivated cognition,[69] and social preferences, especially in public goods games.[70]

[61] Martin Dufwenberg, Simon Gächter, and Heike Hennig-Schmidt, 'The Framing of Games and the Psychology of Play' (2011) 73 Games and Economic Behavior 459.

[62] In this experiment, the proposer makes an offer concerning how to share a fixed amount, which the recipient can accept or reject. If the recipient rejects the offer, both get nothing. According to the rational choice model, a proposer would offer the smallest monetary unit, and the recipient would accept it. Yet experiments do not attain this result. François Cochard and others, 'Social Preferences across Different Populations: Meta-Analyses on the Ultimatum Game and Dictator Game' (2021) 90 Journal of Behavioural and Experimental Economics 101613.

[63] Colin F Camerer, *Behavioral Game Theory: Experiments in Strategic Interaction* (Princeton UP 2003) 75.

[64] Richard J Eiser and Kum Kum Bhavnani, 'The Effect of Situational Meaning on the Behaviour of Subjects in the Prisoner's Dilemma Game' (1974) 4 European Journal of Social Psychology 93.

[65] Brian Skyrms, *The Stag Hunt and the Evolution of Social Structure* (CUP 2004).

[66] On the impacts of framing the prisoner's dilemma in a particular manner, see Chapter 1 by Daniel Peat in this volume.

[67] See, eg, Shiri Krebs, 'The Invisible Frames Affecting Wartime Investigations: Legal Epistemology, Metaphors, and Cognitive Biases' in Andrea Bianchi and Moshe Hirsch (eds), *International Law's Invisible Frames: Social Cognition and Knowledge Production in International Legal Processes* (OUP 2021) 124, 132–33.

[68] See, eg, Raymond S Nickerson, 'Confirmation Bias: A Ubiquitous Phenomenon in Many Guises' (1998) 2 Review of General Psychology 175, 175–90.

[69] On motivated reasoning in behavioural economics, see, eg, Zamir and Teichman (n 31) at 58 et seq.

[70] Applying public goods scholarship to international interactions assumes that some international fields or situations (such as environmental ones) constitute 'public goods'. An analysis of such public goods can explain factors upholding social order in a non-centralized setting. For details, see Anne van Aaken, 'Behavioral Aspects of the International Law of Global Public Goods and Common Pool

Behavioural game theory questions whether other players assume purely self-interested behaviour, or whether fairness perception plays any role in social interactions. Repeated findings suggest that individuals systematically engage in collective action to provide public goods or commons without any external authority enforcer,[71] and the outcomes are labelled as 'better than rational'.[72] Such outcomes occur where reciprocity, reputation, and trust can help to overcome the strong temptations of short-run self-interest.[73] These experiments suggest that rationalist theories may be faulted for neglecting: (1) reciprocity *stricto sensu*, (2) the distinction between (perceived) fair and unfair sanctions, (3) altruism, spitefulness, and preferences for equality, (4) the role of trust and communication, (5) the intentions ascribed to the other players, and (6) the type of actor. Furthermore, it has been suggested that these factors are 'probably relevant in all domains in which voluntary compliance matters'.[74] These experimental studies are clearly relevant for international legal theory.

The intergroup relations literature reveals the significant effects of *social identity* on individuals' cognitive processes and behaviour.[75] Humans strive to belong to social groups and have the tendency to differentiate themselves through group membership.[76] As famously shown by Tajfel and his colleagues, the mere perception of belonging to two distinct groups is sufficient to provoke intergroup responses by ingroup members.[77] Empirical studies have persuasively demonstrated that once people identify with a particular social group, they are likely to provide ingroup members preferable treatment.[78] People's cognitive processes (such as interpretation) are affected by their identity,[79] and identity can trigger automatic processes.[80] Generally, ingroup members are more likely to be perceived

Resources' (2018) 112 AJIL 67. On the ultimatum game and the dictator game, see also Dufwenberg, Gächter, and Hennig-Schmidt (n 61).

[71] Elinor Ostrom, 'A Behavioral Approach to the Rational Choice Theory of Collective Action' (1998) 92 American Political Science Review 1, 2.
[72] Leda Cosmides and John Tooby, 'Better Than Rational: Evolutionary Psychology and the Invisible Hand' (1994) 84 American Economic Review 327.
[73] Ostrom (n 71) 3; Carsten KW De Dreu, Jörg Gross, and Angelo Romano, 'Group Formation and the Evolution of Human Social Organization' (2024) 19 Perspectives on Psychological Science 320.
[74] Ernst Fehr and Bettina Rockenbach, 'Detrimental Effects of Sanctions on Human Altruism' (2003) 422 Nature 137.
[75] On social identity in feminist studies, see Chapter 5 by Veronika Fikfak in this volume.
[76] Marilynn Brewer, *Intergroup Relations* (2nd edn, Open UP 2003, repr 2009) 103, 20; Fiske and Taylor (n 24) 54–55. See also Jan Stets and others, 'Getting Identity Right' (2020) 37 Advances in Group Processes 191. With regard to primates, see Frans de Waal, *The Bonobo and the Atheist* (WW Norton 2013).
[77] Henri Tajfel and John C Turner, 'The Social Identity Theory of Intergroup Behaviour' in Stephen Worchel (ed), *Psychology of Intergroup Relations* (Hall 1986) 7, 9.
[78] Walter Stephan and Cookie W Stephan, *Intergroup Relations* (Routledge 1996) 92–93; Brewer (n 76) 43 et seq.
[79] On interactions between social identity, perception of space, and experience of justice, see Chapter 11 by Sofia Stolk in this volume.
[80] Fiske and Taylor (n 24) 54–55.

as trustworthy, cooperative, peaceful, and honest; whereas outgroup members are often perceived as untrustworthy, competitive, quarrelsome, and dishonest.[81] Behavioural and neuroscientific studies shed light on intergroup conflict and explain what factors can mitigate or enhance conflict[82] (such as environmental stress).[83]

## 5. The Cognitive Turn and International Legal Theory

The cognitive-behavioural turn in social science has spawned innovative research work in disciplines neighbouring international law (notably municipal law, international relations, and political science) and it is gaining traction in international legal scholarship.[84] The formation, interpretation, and implementation of international law interact with diverse cognitive-behavioural processes. There are differences in how international legal decision-makers (including national policymakers and international adjudicators)[85] perceive, interpret, and assess new information that affects their judgement and normative behaviour.[86] Mental processes employed by legal decision-makers can be swayed by an array of biases. The development of international legal concepts is frequently influenced by prevalent cognitive structures (such as schemas, frames, or habitus).[87]

While cognitive-behavioural studies attract increasing attention among international law scholars, their impact on the theoretical foundations of international law has only been explored in a rudimentary fashion.[88] Exploring the interactions between cognitive-behavioural studies and international law may assist researchers in addressing two (closely interrelated) questions: the first concerns the effects of cognitive-behavioural processes on *real-world* legal decision-makers,

[81] Brewer (n 76) 51. See also Fiske and Taylor (n 24) 58.

[82] Carsten KW De Dreu and others, 'Prosociality as a Foundation for Intergroup Conflict' (2022) 44 Current Opinion in Psychology 112.

[83] Carsten KW De Dreu, Jörg Gross, and Lennart Reddmann, 'Environmental Stress Increases Out-Group Aggression and Intergroup Conflict in Humans' (2022) 377 Philosophical Transactions of the Royal Society B 20210147.

[84] See, eg, van Aaken (n 55); Tomer Broude, 'Behavioral International Law' (2015) 163 University of Pennsylvania Law Review 1099; Galbraith (n 55); Moshe Hirsch, 'Social Cognitive Studies, Sociological Theory, and International Law' in Andrea Bianchi and Moshe Hirsch (eds), *International Law's Invisible Frames: Social Cognition and Knowledge Production in International Legal Processes* (OUP 2021) 15–34; Harlan Grant Cohen and Timothy Meyer (eds), *International Law as Behavior* (CUP 2021).

[85] With regard to international arbitrators, see Franck and others, 'Inside the Arbitrator's Mind' (2017) 66 Emory Law Journal 1115.

[86] On this assumption in international relations scholarship, see Rose McDermott, *Political Psychology in International Relations* (Michigan UP 2004); Robert Jervis, *Perception and Misperception in International Politics* (Princeton UP 1976); James W Davis, *Terms of Inquiry: On the Theory and Practice of Political Science* (Johns Hopkins UP 2005).

[87] On 'schemas' and 'habitus', see Section 3.

[88] Anne van Aaken, 'Experimental Insights for International Legal Theory' (2019) 30 EJIL 1237.

and the second relates to the impact of such cognitive-behavioural factors on international law *theoretical approaches*. As for the latter, with few exceptions, international legal theory has scarcely addressed the cognitive-behavioural (often implicit) assumptions of their own approaches, frequently relying tacitly on a self-interested rational choice model. In light of the increasing incorporation of cognitive-behavioural insights in the international law literature and practice, there is a notable gap in scholarship regarding the impact of these developments on international legal theories.

Leading scholars have already discussed some distinctive properties and objectives of international law theories,[89] and we will not rehearse these enlightening discussions. In keeping with the cognitive theme of this book, we propose viewing different international law theories as distinctive perspectives or sets of cognitive lenses. Significant international legal fields (such as international criminal law) or events (like the conclusion of a major treaty or a blatant violation of international law) exhibit numerous features associated with various theoretical approaches. From every geographical or intellectual location, the international legal field is perceived differently. Each theoretical perspective offers its own unique set of lenses, directing our *attention* to the role of particular factors operating in a multi-dimensional field; and relegating to the background (or filtering out) certain other factors present in the field. Each international legal theoretical perspective can also be considered as a cognitive schema, leading its proponents to *organize* abundant legal information differently and *interpret* pertinent items of information distinctively.

International legal theories can be analysed along numerous parameters. The following parameters are not exhaustive. Thus, for example, such theories often present explanatory and/or normative perspectives, yet without always drawing a clear epistemological line between those very different operations. Theoretical perspectives can also be descriptive or explanatory, including rational choice and sociological approaches, as well as some streams in international relations theory. Explanatory theories often concern cause–effect relationships, seeking to explain how and why legal actors behave as they do. The constructivist approach to international law[90] also falls into this category, as well as some streams in Third World Approaches to International Law (TWAIL)[91] and feminist perspectives[92] in international law theory (prominently with regard to arguments concerning *who* benefits from certain legal rules). Given that cognitive processes are significantly involved in international legal decision-making, cognitive science is clearly

[89] See, eg, Andrea Bianchi, *International Law Theories* (OUP 2016) 3 et seq; Jeffrey L Dunoff and Mark A Pollack, 'Introduction to International Legal Theory' in Jeffrey L Dunoff and Mark A Pollack (eds), *International Legal Theory: Foundations and Frontiers* (CUP 2022) 3 et seq.

[90] See Chapter 3 by Ian Johnstone and Arun Mohan Sukumar in this volume.

[91] See Chapter 4 by Shiri Krebs in this volume.

[92] See Chapter 5 by Veronika Fikfak in this volume.

relevant for such theories as it can either support or undermine causal accounts presented by these legal theories.

Other international legal theory approaches, such as positivism,[93] highlight descriptive[94] and analytical arguments (though they also include certain explanatory ones). Cognitive-behavioural studies are relevant to the descriptive and analytical dimensions of these international legal theories. Other theoretical perspectives underline normative arguments, such as liberalism[95] (in international relations theory) and Marxist[96] or feminist approaches[97] to international law. They can be based on ideology and occasionally include analysis and criticism of power imbalances and resulting structures in international law. For these perspectives, cognitive-behavioural studies are clearly relevant for the descriptive and explanatory premises of these *normative* approaches, for example the assumption that humans are fundamentally social, self-interested, or rational. A cognitive-behavioural inquiry can examine whether the particular assumptions underlying these theories reflect real-world decision-makers, and can support or criticize the validity of resulting normative arguments derived from these approaches. Cognitive-behavioural studies may also be employed to devise practical strategies to address undesirable patterns highlighted by a particular critical perspective (eg strategies aimed at coping with gender discrimination) or in the design of transitional justice institutions.[98]

International law theories also differ with respect to the above-mentioned level of analysis (individual and social)[99] and the weight they accord to actors or structures. As for the latter distinction, theories focusing on actors differ with respect to whether they view the state (or other legal entities) exclusively as a unitary actor (whereby individuals may come in as a means to analyse states),[100] or whether they break up the 'black box' state and examine internal processes. Given that international law is a social phenomenon, virtually all these approaches involve to some extent certain assumptions highlighted in (social) psychology and sociological

[93] On international legal positivism and cognitive studies, see Chapter 1 by Daniel Peat in this volume.

[94] Hart deemed his famous concept of law 'an essay in descriptive *sociology*', designed to further the understanding of law, coercion, and morality as different but related to social phenomena. Herbert LA Hart, *The Concept of Law* (OUP 1961) 'Preface' vi. To the best of our knowledge, the international legal theoretical literature does not yet offer systematic and comprehensive analysis of descriptive *cognitive psychology or sociology* aimed at understanding the interactions between international law, cognitive-behavioural processes, and motivations. For a general discussion of these issues in legal analysis, see Anne van Aaken, 'The Concept of Law Revisited: A Psychological Approach to Legal Theory' in Christoph Bezemek, Michael Potacs, and Alexander Somek (eds), *Vienna Lectures on Legal Philosophy, Volume 2* (Hart 2020).

[95] On liberal normative theories of international law, see Chapter 6 by Robert Howse in this volume.

[96] See Chapter 12 by Kanad Bagchi in this volume.

[97] See Chapter 5 by Veronika Fikfak in this volume.

[98] See Chapter 13 by Ruti G Teitel and Shreya Shankar in this volume.

[99] See Section 2 above.

[100] See Meggido (n 1).

literatures: they often resort to some kinds of (at least implicit 'common-sense') assumptions about human behaviour and the interaction between humans and their environment, including social and normative-legal environments. At times, international law theories indirectly resort to social psychological and sociological studies; for example, when analysing authority or legitimacy (eg how these significant factors are constructed and perceived). And significantly, these theories differ concerning the role they attribute to cognitive process, rationality, and systematic deviations therefrom.

As discussed above, each international legal theory can be considered as a distinctive set of cognitive lenses, affecting patterns of attention to, interpretation and organization of, and knowledge pertaining to, international law. This book does not endeavour to cover all international legal theories but rather to shed light on the cognitive-behavioural dimension of some major theoretical approaches to international law. The authors of the following chapters engage, in different ways, with the question of how new insights gained from cognitive-behavioural sciences are reflected (or not) in, or are likely to affect, a particular international legal theory. While such systematic explorations are still at a relatively early stage (and may well be challenged in later studies), we hope that this volume will encourage more scholars and policy-makers to engage with vital questions pertaining to interactions between cognitive-behavioural studies and the theoretical foundations of international law.

## 6. The Chapters

We are grateful to all the authors for taking up the intellectual challenge and exploring the significance of cognitive-behavioural studies for the respective international legal theories. The readers are invited to make up their own mind on how far the cognitive turn contributes to international legal theoretical debates.

**Daniel Peat** takes a refreshing look at how cognitive-behavioural studies can impact positivism. He challenges a caricature idea of positivism as a theory that is formalist, voluntarist, state-centric, and detached from morals. This, he argues, no longer accords with the prevalent conception of the theory in much of the literature. For Peat, the principal challenge to positivism comes from experimental jurisprudence, a nascent body showing that the general public fails to recognize a source-based concept of law. The reliance on cognitive-behavioural studies, which follows the emerging experimental philosophy research, also challenges positivists to explain why their view is to be preferred over the so-called 'folk' concept of law. Given that positivism is an analytic take on international legal theory, the chapter also argues that analytical approaches may benefit from cognitive-behavioural studies.

**Harlan Grant Cohen and Daniel Bodansky** examine the interaction between legal realism and cognitive-behavioural studies. They start from the premise that legal realism and cognitive-behavioural studies share an interest in studying empirically how individuals think and behave. Focusing on the actual people who practise, argue about, interpret, and implement international law is essential for explaining how international law works. The two approaches can thus mutually enrich one another; marrying legal realism's empiricism and pragmatism with cognitive-behavioural studies' rigour can be powerful and seductive. Yet, in sharpening each other's focus, legal realism and cognitive-behavioural studies may also amplify each other's blind spots. Considering related critiques of both legal realist and cognitive scientific approaches to international law that emphasize instrumentalism at the expense of normativity, this chapter reaffirms the importance of legal realism's characteristic pluralism, openness, and capacity for self-critique. Those values, the chapter argues, can provide a path forward for a partnership between legal realism and cognitive-behavioural studies that remains true to the objectives and values of both.

**Ian Johnstone and Arun Mohan Sukumar** examine how cognitive studies can inform and augment constructivist approaches to international law. Their central argument is that research into the working of the human mind and intergroup relations helps to explain how the institutional environment in which rules are developed and interpreted shapes the legal positions of states. The chapter reflects on how cognitive studies can help to explain the argumentative behaviour of government officials and other international actors associated with a particular type of 'community of practice', namely interpretative communities. It identifies avenues for improving the design of legal regimes and institutions to address biases and heuristics associated with individual and group decision-making, and emphasizes the importance of mechanisms that stimulate reasoned deliberation (as opposed to purely intuitive and/or 'automatic' cognition in global governance institutions). A case study of cybersecurity regime-building is used to highlight both the value and limitations of cognitive studies in understanding international legal argumentation and interpretation.

**Shiri Krebs** explores the potential contribution of cognitive-behavioural science to critical approaches to international law. She asks whether cognitive and behavioural science can provide meaningful insights to inform and advance critical approaches to international law, and vice versa: can insights from critical international law studies contribute to cognitive-behavioural approaches to international law? To answer these questions, this chapter briefly explores the disciplinary boundaries of international law critique. It then considers the main areas of tension—and consolidation—between critical and cognitive-behavioural approaches to international law, suggesting three pathways for their engagement and contribution: a theoretical contribution, a methodological refinement, and a disciplinary self-reflection. To demonstrate this potential for engagement, Krebs proposes developing a cognitive-behavioural critique of international law that builds on insights from both critical theory and cognitive-behavioural science. Such a critique, she argues, can account for both systemic biases in the design and application of international law, and the individual-based cognitive limitations that support, enable, and entrench bias and domination in the international legal system.

**Veronika Fikfak**'s chapter addresses certain interactions between feminist approaches to international law and cognitive-behavioural studies. Generally, feminist studies have sought to provide scholars with a critical analysis of international law. In particular, they have aimed to show how existing structures, processes, and methodologies of international law marginalize women by failing to take into account their lives and experiences. In many respects, this literature has argued for a need for women to be represented in the international legal community, including on judicial and arbitration panels; and for their different voices to be heard in diverse international law forums. These calls have yielded great changes in law and in the composition of judicial panels. Yet, as Fikfak argues, behavioural and psychological sciences can add further insights to feminist studies: they can illuminate why and how discrimination arises; to what extent the biases that drive discrimination are unconscious; and how insidious they are. Insights drawn from these sciences can help us understand better how and why discrimination and structural inequality endure.

**Robert Howse** investigates the extent to which cognitive-behavioural science can be applied to liberal normative theories of international law. Although these theories constitute a fundamentally normative endeavour, he argues that a fundamental aspect of the liberal normative theory of international law is the 'bottom-up' approach, which roots governance and obligation in the interests and rights of individuals as reflected through representative democratic institutions. In focusing on individuals, in relation to social and political institutions, the common ground between normative liberal theory and cognitive science and social science concerns the unit of analysis. Howse thus explores, in a preliminary fashion, some areas where there could be a fruitful encounter between liberal normative theories of international law and cognitive-behavioural studies: the relevance of altruism in human behaviour for the possibilities of liberal global justice with a redistributive element, the relationship of perceptions of shared values to the possibility of international legal cooperation among liberal states, the influence of group affiliation and bias on how states and societies are viewed as 'liberal', and in the case of commercial liberalism (free trade), how 'friend-shoring' (as opposed to non-discriminatory multilateralism) is supported by studies on whom individuals trust as trading partners and why.

**Regina Jefferies**' chapter focuses on the 'transnational legal process' (TLP) theory and examines how the conceptual framework offered by this perspective affects our understanding of the role of individuals in making (or changing), interpreting, and enforcing international law. The chapter argues that the relational human connection inherent in TLP theory provides the basis for an exploration of how cognitive-behavioural studies might bring additional clarity to under-described aspects of TLP. Jefferies outlines an approach aimed at hypothesizing and empirically studying TLP's behavioural assumptions, with a particular emphasis on the concepts of 'norm internalization' and 'transnational legal substance'. Cognitive sociology and cognitive psychology provide a means for expounding the who, how, and why of 'norm internalization' and the process by which 'transnational legal substance' is produced. Three case studies draw upon international refugee law and illustrate how cognitive-behavioural science might enrich our understanding of how individual behaviour interfaces with transnational legal processes (including the development of international law in this sphere).

**Anne van Aaken and Tomer Broude** chart the development from the rational choice paradigm (also used by realism and institutionalism) to the behavioural paradigm in the economic analysis of law. International law was one of the last areas of law to be analysed by economic theory. Economic analysis of international law was also late in turning from rational choice theory to cognitive-behavioural science. Yet, it has progressed rapidly, accelerated also because international practice has turned to behavioural science. They highlight different ways in which behavioural insights can be, and are, used in international theoretical inquiries. When behavioural science is applied within the state-to-state context, law-making and compliance as governance mechanisms need to be re-theorized. Yet, the cognitive-behavioural approach faces challenges in respect of the unit of analysis as well as the hitherto strict focus on methodological individualism. Van Aaken and Broude suggest some ways forward, including moving to a more social psychological approach. They also submit that the cognitive-behavioural approach can build bridges in respect of the 'models of man' used between the strictly rationalist theories and constructivism, as well as critical approaches.

**Moshe Hirsch's** chapter is focused on cognitive-sociological analysis of international law. The chapter argues that while the conventional sociological approach to international law principally explores society's influence on decision-makers' *behaviour* and vice versa (eg via social norms), the recent cognitive-sociological analysis of international law largely highlights the influence of society on legal decision-makers' *perception* of reality (via cognitive processes like attention or memory). Cognitive-behavioural studies influence the sociological approach to international law in many ways and Hirsch highlights four major implications of these studies: (i) cognitive studies show that social groups guide not only individuals' behaviour but also the mental process through which individuals perceive and comprehend their environment; (ii) cognitive-behavioural studies turn the spotlight onto the unconscious layer of social influence and indicate that socio-cognitive patterns often become a blind spot; (iii) new cognitive-sociological literature is significantly influenced by Bourdieu's critical scholarship, thus gravitating towards a critical analysis of international law; and (iv) cultural-cognitive writings tend to underline legal pluralist features in international legal theory and project an image of the international legal community as profoundly fragmented along socio-cognitive lines.

The chapter by **Mikael Rask Madsen and Salvatore Caserta** explores the concept of 'international judicial habitus' through the lens of Pierre Bourdieu's sociological theory, particularly focusing on its relevance to international legal theory and practice. Using this concept, the chapter seeks to unveil the under-explored cognitive and embodied dimensions of international law. The authors emphasize the internalization of social environments into unconscious dispositions and how it guides the behaviour of legal actors, notably international judges. By examining international judges as embodiments of the 'cognitive unconscious', the chapter highlights how international judicial practices are influenced by social and cognitive structures. Madsen and Caserta also examine how the notion of the habitus, particularly when coupled with other tools of the Bourdieusian arsenal (ie field, symbolic power, and capital), constitutes a central tool for scholars engaging in international legal theories, particularly with regard to making practices of the international judiciary intelligible.

**Sofia Stolk**'s chapter explores the interplay between cognitive studies and critical legal geography. Drawing on literature on spatial cognition and behavioural geography, Stolk investigates how space can shape our perception, understanding, and appreciation of international law and (in)justice. The chapter specifically discusses how spatial cognitive studies can complement the critical legal geography perspective on the everyday (re)production of systemic patterns of inclusion and exclusion in international law. The chapter takes the courthouse design of the International Criminal Court as a case study to illustrate the points of connection between the two fields as well as the limits of their convergence.

**Kanad Bagchi**'s chapter aims at bringing together two different traditions of thought, namely Marxism and cognitive-behavioural studies, into a singular conversation. The chapter highlights the 'uneasy' relationship between the two traditions, especially with respect to their epistemological and methodological commitments, as well as their radically different ways of approaching questions of justice, emancipation, and the role of law within it. After situating these approaches within the discourse of international law, Bagchi argues that Marxism usefully brings three sets of propositions to cognitive-behavioural studies, namely the importance of ideology, the influence of history in determining preferences and intentions, and, finally, a critical reflection on the empiricist and voluntarist assumptions of the field. This might open up space for cognitive-behavioural approaches to supplement a Marxist structural inquiry, through situating individual agency and freedom while being mindful of the limits of the legal form.

The chapter by **Ruti G Teitel and Shreya Shankar** presents the 'four pillars' of transitional justice (TJ) together with memorialization, an analysis of the genealogy of the evolution of this field, and an examination of various potential interactions between cognitive-behavioural studies and TJ processes. The chapter argues that while TJ theory involves psychological and cognitive processes, the TJ scholarship has yet to meaningfully incorporate the results of empirical findings and theoretical insights drawn from cognitive-behavioural studies. More specifically, Teitel and Shankar analyse how existing cognitive schemas impact expectations regarding truth commissions, the influence of witnesses' memories on criminal prosecutions, the influence of group identity on the perception of reparations, and how certain framing may affect guarantees of non-repetition. The discussion of these four issues is accompanied by some suggestions concerning the design of TJ processes, as well as some observations regarding the potential limitations of using cognitive-behavioural literature to shape TJ processes. The analysis offered of the specific links between TJ pillars and cognitive-behavioural studies should be read as examples of a broad range of possible interrelationships between these two fields.

# 1

# Positivism and the Cognitive Turn

*Daniel Peat*[*]

## 1. Introduction

Of all the strands of international legal theory that exist in contemporary international law scholarship, one might have thought that the cognitive turn would impact positivism the most. Cognitive-behavioural studies—which, in line with the editors of this volume, I define to be the 'interdisciplinary study of the mind and the diverse mental process involved in acquiring, processing, and storing information, as well as judgements and decision making processes'[1]—challenge the objectivity that many of us conceive to be the very basis of positivist legal thought. Cognitive and motivational biases, heuristics, framing, and heterogenous styles of reasoning, we might think, all take us further away from the positivist ideal of the objective ascertainment of whether a rule is legally valid or not.

In this chapter, however, I want to paint a different picture. The caricature of classical positivism that many of us hold in our heads—as a theory that is formalist, voluntarist, state-centric, and detached from morals—no longer accords with the modern conception of the theory that is prevalent in much of the literature (if, indeed, it ever did). Instead, modern international legal positivists challenge the classical notion of positivism, attempting to reconcile the theory with the plurality of actors and relative normativity now encountered in contemporary international law. They integrate insights from other influential schools of thought, such as post-modernism and critical legal studies, to reflect more accurately the process of law identification than their classical predecessors. The result is a broad church of theorists that, whilst differences amongst them are rife, gather around the relatively modest proposition that the validity of law is source- and not merit-based.

The question that I address in this chapter is how the cognitive turn might be said to affect this somewhat nebulous group of theorists. In Section 2, I outline what I understand by positivism, describing the classical formulations of the theory in international legal thought and its modern variants. In this narrative, the work of Hans Kelsen and HLA Hart plays an important role,[2] and I return to

* Thanks to Dan Bodansky and the editors of this volume for their helpful comments on previous drafts of this chapter.

[1] See Anne van Aaken and Moshe Hirsch's Introduction to this volume, at 5.

[2] cf Jörg Kammerhofer, 'Hans Kelsen in Today's International Legal Scholarship' in Jean d'Aspremont and Jörg Kammerhofer (eds), *International Legal Positivism in a Post-Modern World* (CUP 2014) 97.

Daniel Peat, *Positivism and the Cognitive Turn* In: *International Legal Theory and the Cognitive Turn*.
Edited by: Anne van Aaken and Moshe Hirsch, Oxford University Press. © Daniel Peat 2025.
DOI: 10.1093/9780198909293.003.0002

the relatively sophisticated, nuanced picture that both authors painted, to which, in some ways, modern positivists have reverted. Despite the diversity of ideas that exist under the positivist rubric, I conclude the section by identifying some common threads amongst the theories and try to pick apart the descriptive and normative claims made.

Section 3 addresses how the cognitive turn might challenge and complement positivist theories in two relatively modest ways. The first is by calling into question the objectivity that some classical positivists consider that individuals should exercise in the identification of the law; that is to say, in determining whether a norm is a legal rule. Whilst this indeed poses a challenge for the descriptive claims of positivists, I suggest that the normative goals of positivism might benefit from taking on board the lessons of cognitive and behavioural studies. The second way in which the cognitive turn interacts with positivism is in respect of the interpretative process, which many positivists themselves recognise to be jurisgenerative. Here, insights from the cognitive sciences may help put empirical flesh on the theoretical bones of modern positivist thought.

Section 4 moves to address what I consider to be a more fundamental challenge for positivism. Work in the nascent field of experimental jurisprudence explores what is referred to as the 'folk' concept of law; that is, the concept of law that is held by the public at large. Experiments have explored whether such a concept necessarily integrates moral considerations, if such a concept is cross-cultural, and what kind of structure the concept of law might be. The results from these experiments suggest that the premises of the positivist project—namely, to describe a univocal concept of law that is source-based—may be misplaced.

Cognitive-behavioural studies have the potential both to refine the descriptive claims of positivist theories and to nuance their normative arguments. Yet understanding how this should be done requires careful reflection on what positivist theory aims to achieve and, as a corollary, the appropriate role of legal theory.

## 2. What Is Positivism?

Positivism is—and has been for a long time—characterised as the dominant paradigm in international law.[3] Many of us teach our students that (with some exceptions) the sources of international law are found in Article 38 of the Statute of the International Court of Justice, and that the principle underpinning those sources is state consent.[4] Yet, this view of positivism is rejected in much of the current

[3] Jean d'Aspremont, 'International Legal Positivism' in Jeff L Dunoff and Mark A Pollack (eds), *International Legal Theory: Foundations and Frontiers* (CUP 2022) 73.

[4] See, eg, Malcolm N Shaw, *International Law* (9th edn, CUP 2021) 59; James Crawford, *Brownlie's Principles of Public International Law* (9th edn, OUP 2019) 18 ('The formally recognized sources of international law are reflected in Article 38 of the Statute of the International Court of Justice'); Jean Combacau and Serge Sur, *Droit international public* (8th edn, Montchrestien 2008) 42; Hilary

international law scholarship as reflecting poorly the diversity of legal actors and norms that inhabit the international legal universe, and overemphasising the importance of state consent.[5] In its place, a new 'international legal positivism' has flourished,[6] with modern positivists attempting to attenuate the descriptive claims of classical positivism whilst simultaneously adhering to the latter's normative goals. The result is a diverse contemporary positivist literature that rejects many of the tenets that are commonly associated with classical positivism, such as determinacy of rules and voluntarism. Despite this evolution, certain common themes can be discerned: in particular, the importance of the source of a legal rule as opposed to its merit for the question of validity.[7] In this section, I give an overview of the two strands of the classical version of positivism and how those claims have been revised by modern variants of the theory. Note that the section focusses on positivist thought within international legal scholarship; it addresses positivism in general jurisprudence insofar as those theories are relevant to international law scholarship.[8]

## 2.1. Classical positivism

Attempting to define positivism is a difficult, if not impossible, task. The positivist theories that were advanced in the late nineteenth and twentieth centuries shared, to be sure, some characteristics, but many diverged on salient points more than they converged.[9] For the purposes of this chapter, two strands of classical positivist thought in international legal scholarship can be distinguished.[10] The first is what

Charlesworth, 'Law-Making and Sources' in James Crawford and Martti Koskenniemi, *The Cambridge Companion to International Law* (CUP 2012) 188–89.

[5] Jean d'Aspremont and Jörg Kammerhofer, 'Introduction: The Future of International Legal Positivism' in Jean d'Aspremont and Jörg Kammerhofer (eds), *International Legal Positivism in a Post-Modern World* (CUP 2014) 4–5; Devika Hovell, 'The Elements of International Legal Positivism' (2022) 75 Current Legal Problems 71, 74. The classical perspective is still alive and well in literature published in other languages; see, eg, Olivier Corten, *Méthodologie du droit international public* (UBlire 2017) 47 ('Un grand nombre d'auteurs considèrent ainsi que le droit international est le produit de la volonté des Etats. Dans leur optique, chacune des sources formelles du droit ne renvoie qu'à un accord entre Etats souverains: accord écrit et explicite (traités, droit dérivé des organisations internationales), ou accord informel (coutume, principes généraux de droit').

[6] See in particular Jörg Kammerhofer, *Uncertainty in International Law: A Kelsenian Perspective* (Routledge 2010); Jean d'Aspremont, *Formalism and the Sources of International Law: A Theory of the Ascertainment of Legal Rules* (OUP 2011); Jean d'Aspremont and Jörg Kammerhofer (eds), *International Legal Positivism in a Post-Modern World* (CUP 2014) and contributions therein.

[7] Andrea Bianchi, *International Law Theories: An Inquiry into Different Ways of Thinking* (OUP 2016) 41.

[8] cf Hovell (n 5) 72. cf Chapter 2 by Daniel Bodansky and Harlan Cohen in this volume.

[9] For a comprehensive overview of early positivist theories, see Roberto Ago, 'Positive Law and International Law' (1957) 51 AJIL 691.

[10] cf Michael W Reisman, 'Lassa Oppenheim's Nine Lives' (1994) 19 Yale Journal of International Law 255, 258.

I will call the strict variant of classical international legal positivism,[11] a theory that is characterised by voluntarism and state-centrism, and which has the objective identification of international rules as its goal. The second strand of classical positivism shares this goal but places less weight on the consent of states as the core criterion for the identification of the law.

One of the clearest statements of the strict variant of classical international legal positivism was, somewhat ironically, written at the end of the twentieth century. Steven Ratner and Anne-Marie Slaughter characterised the school of thought as follows:

> Positivism summarizes a range of theories that focus upon describing the law as it is, backed up by effective sanctions, with reference to formal criteria, independently of moral or ethical considerations. For positivists, international law is no more or less than the rules to which states have agreed ... Positivism also tends to view states as the only subjects of international law, thereby discounting the role of nonstate actors. It remains the lingua franca of most international lawyers, especially in continental Europe.[12]

The roots of this strand of classical positivist thought in international law scholarship are often traced to the early twentieth century, and, in the English-language literature, to the work of Lassa Oppenheim.[13] Oppenheim was born near Frankfurt in 1858[14] and taught law in Freiberg and Basel before moving to London in 1895. Upon relocating to the United Kingdom, Oppenheim taught at the London School of Economics before taking up the Whewell Chair of International Law at Cambridge in 1908.[15] The first edition of Oppenheim's treatise, *International Law*, published in 1905/06, cemented his place in the international law academy and remains the work for which he is still best known.[16]

[11] d'Aspremont and Kammerhofer (n 5) 5.

[12] Steven R Ratner and Anne-Marie Slaughter, 'Appraising the Methods of International Law: A Prospectus for Readers' (1999) 93 AJIL 291, 293.

[13] This is not to say that Oppenheim was the first to advance positive thought in international law scholarship. Continental European scholars, such as Dionisio Anzilotti and Heinrich Triepel, adopted positivist positions pre-dating Oppenheim. For an overview of late nineteenth- and early twentieth-century positivist thought, see Ago (n 9).

[14] Mathias Schmoeckel, 'The Internationalist as a Scientist and Herald: Lassa Oppenheim' (2000) 11 EJIL 699.

[15] Benedict Kingsbury, 'Legal Positivism as Normative Politics: International Society, Balance of Power and Lassa Oppenheim's Positive International Law' (2002) 13 EJIL 401, 404–05. Oppenheim's personal library was so vast when he emigrated that even the British Foreign Office borrowed books from him; Schmoeckel (n 14) 700.

[16] See Reisman (n 10) 256 (referring to Oppenheim's *International Law* as 'the premier modern treatise in English'). For an excellent biography, see Mathias Schmoeckel, 'Lassa Oppenheim (1858–1919)' in Jack Beatson and Reinhard Zimmerman (eds), *Jurists Uprooted: German-Speaking Emigré Lawyers in Twentieth Century Britain* (OUP 2004).

Following his predecessor at Cambridge, John Westlake,[17] Oppenheim was strident in his division of law from non-legal considerations, such as morality. In his view, '[w]hatever we think of the value of a recognized rule—whether we approve or condemn it, whether we want to retain, abolish, or replace it—we must first of all know whether it is really a recognized rule of law at all, and what are its commands'.[18] Whilst he acknowledged the importance of natural law in laying the foundations for international law, he steadfastly refused that it had any role to play in determining contemporary international law: in his words, '[w]e know now-a-days that it is impossible to find a law which has its root in human reason only and is above legislation [ie treaties] and customary law',[19] these two sources being the only manner in which Oppenheim thought the common consent of states could be manifested.[20]

The central tenets of Oppenheim's approach—separation of law from morals, apolitical description as a scholarly goal, voluntarism, and state-centrism—laid down the foundations for what is often considered to be classical international legal positivism. That is not to say, however, that Oppenheim was agnostic about positivism himself. For Oppenheim, the 'science of international law' was a means to achieve certain ends, those being stable international relations, the peaceful settlement of disputes, and the regulation of war.[21] Positivism was, for him, simply the best way to achieve these goals.[22]

In the latter half of the twentieth century, positivist thought became increasingly linked to voluntarism, following Oppenheim's theory, as well as that of earlier continental scholars, such as Triepel and Anzillotti.[23] Prosper Weil is often heralded as the vanguard of this stream of classical positivist thought.[24] But he stood in good company, particular amongst authors of a certain kind of treatise that aimed to provide an overview of contemporary international law as it stood at that time.[25]

[17] Schmoeckel (n 14) 710.

[18] Lassa Oppenheim, 'The Science of International Law: Its Task and Method' (1908) 2 AJIL 313, 314–15.

[19] ibid 329. cf Lassa Oppenheim, *International Law*, vol. 1 Peace (1st edn, Longmans, Green and Company 1906) 92 ('We know nowadays that a Law of Nature does not exist. Just as the so-called Natural Philosophy had to give way to real natural science, so the Law of Nature had to give way to jurisprudence, or the philosophy of positive law. Only a positive Law of Nations can be a branch of the science of law').

[20] Oppenheim (n 19) 21.

[21] Oppenheim (n 18) 314. For an elaboration of the normative agenda behind Oppenheim's work, see Kingsbury (n 15).

[22] Reisman notes that Oppenheim's positivism was 'curiously theoretical' in that he cited only 54 cases and incidents in the 594 pages of his first volume; Reisman (n 10) 265.

[23] See Giorgio Gaja, 'Positivism and Dualism in Dionisio Anzilotti' (1993) 3 EJIL 123; Bruno Simma and Andreas Paulus, 'The Responsibility of Individuals for Human Rights Abuses in Internal Conflicts: A Positivist View' (1999) 93 AJIL 302, 304.

[24] See Prosper Weil, 'Towards Relative Normativity in International Law?' (1983) 77 AJIL 413, 420 ('states are at once the creators and the addressees of the norms of international law ... [a]bsent voluntarism international law would no longer be performing its functions').

[25] Reisman (n 10) 258, referring to Georg Schwarzenberger, *International Law* (3rd edn, Stevens and Sons 1952) as an example.

This tradition endures to this day by the primacy given in textbooks to Article 38 of the International Court of Justice (ICJ) Statute (the first three enumerated sources of which are based on state consent) as an authoritative description of the sources of international law.[26] Outside the realm of textbooks, however, few self-professed positivists adhere to this strict voluntarist conception of international law.[27]

At the time of Oppenheim's death, another German-speaking jurist, Hans Kelsen, had just been promoted to the position of full professor of public and administrative law at the University of Vienna.[28] Although Kelsen was to become an important figure in the movement, it was only from 1933 onwards, when he moved to the Institut des Hautes Etudes Internationales in Geneva from the University of Cologne, that his attention shifted from the relations between domestic and international law to positive international law.[29] Kelsen, like Oppenheim, was concerned with separating law from the morals or the law of nature: in his words, 'the purity of the theory is to be secured against the claims of the natural law theory, which ... takes legal theory out of the realm of positive legal norms and into the realm of ethico-political postulates'.[30] But he was also concerned to distinguish the study of law—or rather the identification of legal rules (what he called the 'cognition of law')—from the study of its formation or a normative analysis of what the law should be.[31] The former, he argued, was the proper domain of a jurist, not the latter.[32]

The main ideas of the theory that Kelsen laid down in the *Pure Theory of Law* (*Reine Rechtslehre*), *General Theory of Law and State*, and other works are well known. His principal argument was that legal normativity flows from a so-called *Grundnorm*; a basic norm that is 'a hypothesis of juristic thinking, the fundamental condition under which our juristic propositions are possible'.[33] The basic

[26] See, eg, Andrew Clapham, *Brierly's Law of Nations* (OUP 2012) 54; Hugh Thirlway, 'The Sources of International Law' in Malcolm D Evans (ed), *International Law* (4th edn, OUP 2014) 94–95.

[27] Although see Alexander Orakhelashvili, *The Interpretation of Acts and Rules in Public International Law* (OUP 2008) 53 ('from the viewpoint of the character of international law, where State consent is the principal basis of legal obligations, positive law can only be described as the law laid down through the consent and agreement of the actors that are entitled to create rules of international law').

[28] Nicoletta Bersier Ladavac, 'Hans Kelsen (1881–1973) Biographical Note and Bibliography' (1998) 9 EJIL 391, 392.

[29] ibid 392.

[30] Hans Kelsen, *Hauptprobleme der Staatsrechtslehre* (2nd edn, JCB Mohr 1923, repr Aalen: Scientia, 1960) v; cited in Hans Kelsen, *Introduction to the Problems of Legal Theory: A Translation of the First Edition of the Reine Rechtslehre or Pure Theory of Law* (Clarendon 1997) introduction.

[31] See Hans Kelsen, *General Theory of Law and State* (Harvard UP 1945) xiv ('When this doctrine is called the "pure theory of law", it is meant that it is being kept free from all the elements foreign to the specific method of a science whose only purpose is the cognition of law, not its formation. A science has to describe its object as it actually is, not to prescribe how it should be or should not be from the point of view of some specific value judgments').

[32] Jörg Kammerhofer, 'Hans Kelsen in Today's International Legal Scholarship' in Jean d'Aspremont and Jörg Kammerhofer (eds), *International Legal Positivism in a Post-Modern World* (CUP 2014) 85. See Kelsen (n 30) v (the pure theory of law 'is to be secured against the claims of a so-called "sociological" point of view, which uses the methods of the causal sciences to appropriate the law as a part of nature').

[33] Hans Kelsen, *Principles of International Law* (Rinehart and Co 1952) 412.

norm identifies who or what within a legal system is competent to make laws, and hence functions as the 'wellspring of a linear notion of law, where law follows in a chain of validity from this originating source'.[34] Importantly, the basic norm is hypothesised by the legal scholar, 'intellectually presupposed' and content-free,[35] thus freeing the normativity of the law from 'the need for an ultimate extra-legal foundation of the law'.[36] This means that one need not explain the sources of international law in terms of the explicit or tacit consent of states, a view that he rejected;[37] indeed, he considered that the voluntarist approach begged the question why consent itself was the source of legal normativity. Instead, for Kelsen, the legal normativity of customary international law flows from the hypothesised basic norm, and it is upon the customary norm of *pacta sunt servanda* that the legal normativity of treaties is based.[38]

Classical international legal positivism has often been characterised as state-centric, voluntarist, formalist, and concerned with separating law from non-legal elements, such as morality and political ideology.[39] This has a certain ring of truth when it comes to the first, strict variant of positivism that I described above. However, as a general proposition, some of these claims are overstated.[40] For example, the consent of states is often identified as 'the' characteristic associated with the classical view.[41] However, whilst forming the basis of certain positivist theories that fall within the first strand of thought, consent was certainly not a necessary condition for Kelsen's pure theory of law.[42] Moreover, whilst descriptions of classical international positivist thought often portray those theories as purporting to be neutral, many authors themselves were relatively clear that they considered positivism to be the best theory of law to pursue the goals they imputed to the international order.[43] These theories thus blend both descriptive and normative aspirations, claiming that the source-based identification of the law is both how rules

[34] Hovell (n 5) 79. Note that Kelsen considered the normativity of domestic legal systems to rest on conformity to a principle of international law—the principle of effectiveness. He hence considered the basic norm that underpinned international legal systems to be the ultimate source of validity for domestic legal systems; Kelsen (n 33) 414–15.

[35] Jochen von Bernstorff, *The Public International Law Theory of Hans Kelsen: Believing in Universal Law* (CUP 2011) 164.

[36] ibid.

[37] Kelsen (n 33), 311–13.

[38] ibid 314.

[39] See Simma and Paulus (n 23) 303–05; Christian J Tams and Antonios Tzanakopoulos, 'Use of Force' in Jean d'Aspremont and Jörg Kammerhofer (eds), *International Legal Positivism in a Post-Modern World* (CUP 2014) 500–02. cf Hovell (n 5) 74.

[40] See in particular Hovell (n 5); Jörg Kammerhofer, 'International Legal Positivism' in Samantha Besson and others (eds), *The Oxford Handbook of the Theory of International Law* (OUP 2016) 411 ('The best that can be said about this narrative is that it is not utterly wrong').

[41] Simma and Paulus (n 23) 303.

[42] Jean d'Aspremont, 'Herbert Hart in Today's International Legal Scholarship' in Jean d'Aspremont and Jörg Kammerhofer (eds), *International Legal Positivism in a Post-Modern World* (CUP 2014) 144–46.

[43] Hovell (n 5) 100–01.

*are* identified in practice and how they *should* be identified. Understanding these intertwined goals is important when thinking about how cognitive and behavioural studies might challenge or complement those theories.

For the purposes of this chapter, three commonalities of classic international positivist theories are of note.[44] First, many of the authors share the same theoretical goal; that is, the identification of legal rules ('legal cognition'[45] or 'law ascertainment').[46] Second, classical international positivists consider that the identification of legal rules should be separate from what they perceived to be extra-legal considerations, such as morality, political ideology, and religion. Third, and relatedly, they consider that the source of a legal norm, and not the merit of that norm, is the basis of legal validity.[47]

## 2.2. Modern international legal positivism

Over the past twenty-five years, modern authors, in attempting to revitalise positivism, have taken up the mantle of classical positivism, nuancing (or abandoning completely) the strict voluntarist and state-centric claims made by some earlier authors.[48] In this section, I focus on those that explicitly identify themselves as positivists whilst acknowledging that many (if not most) contemporary international lawyers probably implicitly subscribe to some tenets of positivism.

Self-identified 'modern' international legal positivists acknowledge the diversity of actors involved in the creation of international law, the indeterminacy of legal rules,[49] and the political nature of the formation, identification, and application of international law.[50] Whilst their goal is to provide a descriptive account of international law that better accords with contemporary reality, their approaches echo

[44] cf Frauke Lachenmann, 'Legal Positivism' in *Max Planck Encyclopedia of Public International Law* (2011) (saying that the lowest common denominator of positivist thought is separation of *lex lata* from *lex ferenda*).

[45] d'Aspremont (n 42) 144.

[46] Jean d'Aspremont, 'The Multidimensional Process of Interpretation: Content-Determination and Law-Ascertainment Distinguished' in Andrea Bianchi, Daniel Peat, and Matthew W Windsor (eds), *Interpretation in International Law* (OUP 2015).

[47] Kammerhofer, 'International Legal Positivism' (n 40) 410. Note here that I use 'source' rather than 'form' as the identifying characteristic of positivism. As Gardner points out, formal validity is also consistent with certain conceptions of natural law, such as Lon Fuller's theory of legality; see John Gardner, '5 ½ Myths about Positivism' (2001) 46 American Journal of Jurisprudence 199.

[48] Some authors note the continued importance of state consent but recognise that it is not the sole source of legal normativity in contemporary international law; see Simma and Paulus (n 23); Theodore Christakis, 'Human Rights from a Neo-Voluntarist Perspective' in Jean d'Aspremont and Jörg Kammerhofer (eds), *International Legal Positivism in a Post-Modern World* (CUP 2014) 423.

[49] Indeed, the indeterminacy of legal rules was already recognised by some classical positivists; see the text cited at n 96.

[50] For a good overview of modern engagement with positivism, see the contributions in Jean d'Aspremont and Jörg Kammerhofer (eds), *International Legal Positivism in a Post-Modern World* (CUP 2014). For some examples of developed 'modern' international positivist theories, see Benedict Kingsbury, 'The Concept of "Law" in Global Administrative Law' (2009) 20 EJIL 23; d'Aspremont (n 6).

some of the tenets of classical international positivist thought; namely, that law and morality are not necessarily coextensive and that the source of a norm is important to determine legal validity.[51]

Several modern international legal positivists engage with the work of another mid-twentieth-century legal philosopher, HLA Hart, in their attempts to re-invigorate positivist thought.[52] A brief overview of Hart's theory is hence useful to understand some strands of modern international positivism. HLA Hart was elected to the chair of jurisprudence at Oxford in 1952, delivering undergraduate lectures from that time that would be published later as his *The Concept of Law* in 1961.[53] Hart was not particularly concerned with international law; indeed, his treatment of the topic has been criticised as inadequate, broadly indifferent,[54] and 'an afterthought'.[55] The absence of courts of compulsory jurisdiction, a legislature, and centrally organised sanctions on the international plane meant that, for Hart, 'the rules for states resemble that simple form of social structure, consisting only of primary rules of obligation, which, when we find it among societies of individuals, we are accustomed to contrast with a developed legal system'.[56] Whilst I won't address this claim,[57] suffice to note that international lawyers contest the validity of Hart's position in light of the development of the international legal system over the past half-century.[58]

The core of Hart's theory is that legal systems are composed of primary and secondary rules, the most important of the latter being the rule of recognition,[59] a conventionally accepted norm that specifies the criteria for legal validity and according to which primary legal rules are identified by officials.[60] Whilst Hart was himself sceptical that a rule of recognition did exist in international law, the idea

[51] cf Patrick Capps, 'International Legal Positivism and Modern Natural Law' in Jean d'Aspremont and Jörg Kammerhofer (eds), *International Legal Positivism in a Post-Modern World* (CUP 2014) 218; Bianchi (n 7) 41.

[52] See, eg, Kingsbury (n 50); d'Aspremont (n 42); David Lefkowitz, 'H.L.A. Hart: Social Rules, Officials, and International Law' in David Lefkowitz, *Philosophy and International Law: A Critical Introduction* (CUP 2020); David Lefkowitz, 'What Makes a Social Order Primitive? In Defense of Hart's Take on International Law' (2017) 23 Legal Theory 258.

[53] Tony Honoré, 'H.L.A. Hart: Some Biographical Notes', Jurisprudence in Oxford <www.law.ox.ac.uk/research-and-subject-groups/jurisprudence-oxford/hla-hart> accessed 21 June 2023.

[54] Jeremy Waldron, 'International Law: "A Relatively Small and Unimportant" Part of Jurisprudence?' in Luís Duarte d'Almeida, James Edwards, and Andrea Dolchetti (eds), *Reading HLA Hart's 'The Concept of Law'* (Hart 2013) 211.

[55] ibid 209.

[56] HLA Hart, *The Concept of Law* (2nd edn, Clarendon 1994) 214.

[57] The basis of Hart's critique—comparing the international legal system to the benchmark of domestic legal systems—was itself criticised as the 'modern state conception' of a legal system by Oona Hathaway and Scott Shapiro; Oona Hathaway and Scott Shapiro, 'Outcasting: Enforcement in Domestic and International Law' (2011) 121 Yale Law Journal 252, 268–70.

[58] See, eg, Kingsbury (n 50) n 15; Sean D Murphy, 'The Concept of Law' (2009) Proceedings of the Annual Meeting (ASIL) 165, 169; Waldron (n 54).

[59] The other secondary rules being those of change and adjudication; Hart (n 56) 95–99.

[60] Hart (n 56) 100–17. On the conventional nature of the rule of recognition, see Andrei Marmor, 'The Conventional Foundations of Law' in Andrei Marmor, *Social Conventions: From Language to Law* (Princeton UP 2009) 155–75.

that there are conventionally accepted criteria for the determination of law—that need not, but may, refer to considerations of morality[61]—is one that has taken hold in the field.[62]

In the context of the present chapter, the most important way in which some modern positivist writings diverge from their classical predecessors is their acceptance that identification of the law is not and cannot be objective. In the words of Jean d'Aspremont and Jörg Kammerhofer,

> [t]here is ... an awareness among many [modern international positivist] authors that positivism, even one not wedded to the doctrines of voluntarism, objectivity and determinacy, cannot, from a theoretical point of view, sustain itself on its own terms ... meaning cannot be internally generated and kept immune from normative choices and epistemic biases.[63]

This approach harnesses the insights provided by post-modern thought, such as the hermeneutic theory of Hans-Georg Gadamer,[64] as well as those of critical scholars within the international law academy, such as Martti Koskenniemi.[65] By conceding that the identification of law is subjective, however, modern international positivists are left with relatively few claims that tie them to their classical antecedents. Indeed, perhaps the most that could be said is that modern international legal positivists, like their classical predecessors, reject any necessary link between law and morality, and, relatedly, consider the source—not the merit—of rules to be the basis of legal validity.[66] What modern international positivists are missing, however, is a clear account of how this subjectivity is exercised in practice, and whether commonalities might exist within the population. It is on these points that cognitive-behavioural studies might play a role.

## 3. Positivism in Practice: Does the Cognitive Turn Challenge the Tenets of Positivism?

At first sight, the objectivity presupposed by certain strands of positivism and insights from the cognitive turn might seem to be inherently antagonistic. In this

[61] Hart (n 56) 250. See further Andrei Marmor, 'The Separation Thesis and the Limits of Interpretation' (1999) 12 Canadian Journal of Law and Jurisprudence 135.

[62] See, eg, Kingsbury (n 50) 29; d'Aspremont (n 42) 136 et seq.

[63] d'Aspremont and Kammerhofer (n 5) 17.

[64] Hans-Georg Gadamer, *Truth and Method* (Bloomsbury 1975, tr J Weinsheimer and DG Marshall 2013). See, eg, Gleider Hernández, 'Interpretation' in Jean d'Aspremont and Jörg Kammerhofer (eds), *International Legal Positivism in a Post-Modern World* (CUP 2014) 319.

[65] Martti Koskenniemi, *From Apology to Utopia: The Structure of International Legal Argument* (CUP 2006).

[66] cf Kammerhofer (n 40) 410; Capps (n 51) 218; Bianchi (n 7) 41–42.

section, however, I suggest that the latter may play a relatively modest role in relation to much of the international positivist literature in two different ways.[67] First, classical international legal positivism emphasises objectivity and neutrality in law identification, something that studies from the behavioural sciences have consistently shown to be illusive. However, whilst the cognitive-behavioural studies challenge the descriptive claim of classical positivist theories (*this is how law is identified*), I suggest that the normative goal of those theories (*this is how law should be identified*) may actually be furthered by having a solid understanding of how individuals' behaviour as a starting point. Furthermore, with descriptive claims of objective identification of the law largely absent from modern theories of international positivism, insights from the cognitive social sciences do not challenge the main premises of those theories but rather offer an additional layer of nuance regarding human cognition and decision-making. This relates to the second manner in which I suggest the cognitive-behavioural studies may complement modern positivist theories by shedding light on how processes of interpretation occur in practice.

### 3.1. Objectivity in law identification

One of the main goals of all forms of positivist thought is to identify the law. As noted above, despite their differences, classical forms of positivism considered that this task was undertaken objectively, leaving aside the biases, political preferences, and moral standards of the law determiner (whether they be a scholar or an official). However, the idea of the objective identification of a norm—one that is divorced from all extraneous influences—is anathema to much of the work in the behavioural social sciences. Suffice here to mention two strands of literature that are relevant.

The first is that prior beliefs necessarily affect our cognition of new facts.[68] When we are confronted with new information, we have a tendency to assimilate that information to our pre-existing beliefs so as to avoid the uncomfortable feeling engendered by being forced to revise those beliefs in light of the new information (so-called 'cognitive dissonance').[69] This is referred to in the behavioural

[67] I note that it has also been suggested that psychological factors may explain the use of soft law on the international plane, which I do not address in this chapter; see Tomer Broude and Yahli Shereshevsky, 'Explaining the Practical Purchase of Soft Law: Competing and Complementary Behavior Hypotheses' in Harlan Grant Cohen and Tim Meyer (eds), *International Law as Behavior* (CUP 2021) 98–127.

[68] See Brian Rathbun, *Reasoning of State; Realists, Romantics and Rationality in International Relations* (CUP 2019) 20; Robert Jervis, *Perception and Misperception in International Politics* (2nd edn, Princeton UP 2017) xlix–l.

[69] See Chapter 3 by Johnstone and Sukumar in this volume. This 'uncomfortable feeling' is referred to in the literature as cognitive dissonance. The work on cognitive dissonance stems from Leon Festinger's studies in the late 1950s; see Leon Festinger, *A Theory of Cognitive Dissonance* (Stanford UP 1957). For one of the foundational studies on motivated reasoning and confirmation bias, see PC Wason, 'On the Failure to Eliminate Hypotheses in a Conceptual Task' (1960) 12 Quarterly Journal of Experimental

economics literature as 'confirmation bias'.[70] The literature on the role of prior beliefs finds parallels in the cognitive sociology concept of schemata, which highlights that new information is processed through the lens of an individual's pre-existing experiences and beliefs.[71]

An example of the role of prior beliefs in the processing of new information is provided by political scientist David Redlawsk.[72] Redlawsk conducted an experiment on ninety-nine individuals, in which they acted as voters in a mock US presidential primary election. Participants could access information about the fictional candidates throughout the experiment and were asked to vote for a candidate at the end of the experiment. Redlawsk found that subjects took longer to process new information that was incongruent with their prior beliefs about candidates, as they were 'actively counter-arguing the information, developing reasons why it is wrong or should otherwise be ignored in an attempt to explain it away'.[73] Furthermore, the subjects engaged in a biased information search, looking for information that confirmed their opinion of favoured candidates whilst neglecting to search for information that may change their opinion of disliked candidates.[74]

Perhaps the clearest manner in which the role of prior beliefs challenges the descriptive claim of classical positivist theory is in relation to customary international law.[75] Custom is traditionally thought of as being evidenced by settled state action taken in the belief of legal obligation (*opinio juris*).[76] If one wants to induce the existence of a rule of custom, therefore, one must determine whether states acted a certain way in pursuance of their desire to conform to legal obligation. However, the literature in international relations has shown that the perception of a state's

Psychology 129. In the context of behavioural international relations, see Robert Jervis, *Perception and Misperception in International Politics* (2nd edn, Princeton UP 2017) xlix–l; Philip E Tetlock, *Expert Political Judgment: How Good Is It? How Can We Know?* (New edn, Princeton UP 2017) 128.

[70] For an overview of the work on motivated reasoning, see Roland Bénabou and Jean Tirole, 'Mindful Economics: The Production, Consumption, and Value of Beliefs' (2016) 30 Journal of Economic Perspectives 141.

[71] See Andrea Bianchi and Moshe Hirsch, 'International Law's Invisible Frames: Introductory Insights' in Andrea Bianchi and Moshe Hirsch (eds), *International Law's Invisible Frames: Social Cognition and Knowledge Production in International Legal Processes* (OUP 2021) 2–3. See also Cristina Bicchiei and Peter McNally, 'Shrieking Sirens: Schemata, Scripts, and Social Norms. How Change Occurs' (2018) 35 Social Philosophy and Policy 23, 26–27; Paul DiMaggio, 'Culture and Cognition' (1997) 23 Annual Review of Sociology 263.

[72] David P Redlawsk, 'How Cognition or Cool Consideration? Testing the Effects of Motivated Reasoning on Political Decision Making' (2002) 64 The Journal of Politics 1021.

[73] ibid 1040.

[74] ibid.

[75] For an exploration of the 'False Consensus Effect' and 'False Uniqueness Effect' biases in the context of customary international law, see Ryan M Scoville, 'Egocentric Bias in Perceptions of Customary International Law' in Harlan Grant Cohen and Tim Meyer (eds), *International Law as Behavior* (CUP 2021), 74–97.

[76] For the locus classicus of this formulation, see *North Sea Continental Shelf* (FRG/Denmark; FRG/Netherlands), Judgment (1969) *ICJ Reports* 3, para 77.

intention is indissoluble from our prior beliefs about that state.[77] If we have a prior belief that a state is law-conforming, for example, we may be more likely to see that state's actions as an assertion of a latent rule of custom than those of a state we perceive to be deviant, despite that practice being in principle 'worth' the same.[78]

The second strand of literature which challenges the descriptive claim of classical positivism relates to framing. The term 'framing' has been used in different ways across disciplines;[79] I understand the term to refer to 'when different ways of describing the same choice problem change the choices that people make, even though the underlying information and choice remain essentially the same'.[80] The literature makes a distinction between 'equivalency' from 'issue' framing, which is useful for our purposes.[81] The former refers to the well-known behavioural economics literature, and to prospect theory in particular. According to prospect theory,[82] individuals view gains and losses in relation to a reference point and are inherently loss averse.[83] Whether a decision is framed in terms of gains or losses, therefore, makes a difference to the outcome: when presented with a choice framed in terms of gains, individuals will take the risk-averse option, whereas, when presented with a choice framed in terms of losses, they will be more likely to be risk-seeking.[84] Issue framing, on the other hand, 'refer[s] to situations where, by emphasizing a subset of potentially relevant considerations, a speaker leads individuals to focus on these considerations when constructing their opinions'.[85] Individuals' attitudes to trade policy, for example, have been found to be

[77] See, eg, Karen Yarhi-Milo, *Knowing the Adversary: Leaders, Intelligence, and Assessment of Intentions in International Relations* (Princeton UP 2014) 21; Jervis (n 68).

[78] On customary international law and cognitive-behavioural studies, see Chapter 4 by Krebs in this volume.

[79] Alex Mintz, Nicolas A Valentino, and Carly Wayne, *Beyond Rationality: Behavioral Political Science in the 21st Century* (CUP 2022) 66.

[80] Richard Cookson, 'Framing Effects in Public Goods Experiments' (2000) 3 Experimental Economics 55.

[81] James N Druckman, 'Political Preference Formation: Competition, Deliberation, and the (Ir)relevance of Framing Effects' (2004) 98 American Political Science Review 671 at 672; Anne van Aaken and Jan-Philip Elm, 'Framing in and through Public International Law' in Andrea Bianchi and Moshe Hirsch (eds), *International Law's Invisible Frames: Social Cognition and Knowledge Production in International Legal Processes* (OUP 2021) 36.

[82] Daniel Kahneman and Amos Tversky, 'Prospect Theory: An Analysis of Decision under Risk' (1979) 47 Econometrica 263.

[83] Daniel Kahneman, 'Maps of Bounded Rationality: Psychology for Behavioral Economists' (2003) 93 American Economics Review 1449, 1457.

[84] See Amos Tversky and Daniel Kahneman, 'The Framing of Decisions and the Psychology of Choice' (1981) 211(4481) Science 453. Tversky and Kahneman is based on the following vignette: 'Imagine that the United States is preparing for the outbreak of an unusual Asian disease, which is expected to kill 600 people. Two alternative programs to combat the disease have been proposed. Assume that the exact scientific estimates of the consequences of the programs are as follows: If Program A is adopted, 200 people will be saved; If Program B is adopted, there is a one-third probability that 600 people will be saved and a two-thirds probability that no people will be saved' (choice is framed as gains); 'If Program A is adopted, 400 will die; If Program B is adopted, there is a one-third probability that nobody will due and a two-thirds probability that 600 people will die' (choice is framed as losses).

[85] Druckman (n 81) 672.

influenced by how those policy issues are introduced;[86] labelling a counterparty in an experimental game as a 'partner' or 'opponent' has significant effects on trust between the parties;[87] and framing the prisoner's dilemma game as an experiment on economic bargaining, international negotiations, or interpersonal behaviour impacts participants' cooperation.[88]

Framing effects are in tension with the objectivity presupposed by classical legal positivism, with issue framing being particularly relevant. Classical positivism assumes that the situatedness of the individual does not affect their decision-making with regard to the identification of law. However, it would be easy to think how framing might change an individuals' judgement about whether a norm qualifies as law. If an individual confronts the same choice—for example, whether nascent state practice has crystallised into custom—within the context of litigation, amicable diplomatic correspondence, or the activities of a non-governmental organisation, one would think that the circumstances may have a bearing on the outcome. Needless to say, in the real world, it would be hard to test whether framing has an impact on law identification; however, laboratory studies under controlled conditions might help us to understand its influence.

My argument in this section has so far focussed on the descriptive claim of classical international legal positivism. However, cognitive-behavioural sciences may usefully complement the normative argument for positivism. The gist of this argument is that it is *desirable* for law identification to occur without biases (cognitive or otherwise) to be brought to bear on the process. However, to understand how the effect of such biases might be effectively counteracted, it is a prerequisite to know the biases to which individuals are susceptible. Studies have shown, for example, that domestic judges are influenced by what should be irrelevant factors that relate to the amount of compensation awarded, such as the amount of compensation claimed by the complainant.[89] Understanding that this 'anchoring effect' and other cognitive biases exist allows those that adhere to the normative goal of positivism—that law identification should be undertaken objectively and neutrally—to think constructively about how rules, procedures, and institutions might be designed to counteract those biases and hence pursue this goal.[90]

[86] Michael J Hiscox, 'Through a Glass and Darkly: Attitudes toward International Trade and the Curious Effects of Issue Framing' (2006) 60 International Organization 755. See further Anne van Aaken and Jurgen Kurtz, 'Beyond Rational Choice: International Trade Law and the Behavioral Political Economy of Protectionism' (2019) 22 Journal of International Economic Law 601, 616–19.

[87] Terence Burnham, Kevin McCabe, and Vernon L Smith, 'Friend-or-Foe Intentionality Priming in an Extensive Form Trust Game' (2000) 43 Journal of Economic Behavior and Organization 57.

[88] J Richard Eiser and Kum-Kum Bhavnani, 'The Effect of Situational Meaning on the Behaviour of Subjects in the Prisoner's Dilemma Game' (1974) 4 European Journal of Social Psychology 93.

[89] Gretchen B Chapman and Brian H Bornstein, 'The More You Ask for the More You Get: Anchoring in Personal Injury Verdicts' (1996) 10 Applied Cognitive Psychology 519.

[90] See, eg, Jan-Philip Elm, 'Behavioral Insights into International Arbitration: An Analysis of How to De-Bias Arbitrators' (2016) 27 American Review of International Arbitration 1. For overviews of the operation of cognitive biases and heuristics in the judicial and arbitral context, see Chris Guthrie, Jeffrey J Rachlinkski, and Andrew J Wistrich, 'Inside the Judicial Mind' (2000) 86 Cornell Law Review 777;

Insights from the cognitive-behavioural sciences may both challenge and complement classical international legal positivism, but what about the modern variant? As noted above, modern authors recognise that the indeterminacy of language and the situatedness of the decision-maker inevitably colour the decision outcome: 'the legal system cognised by positivism is itself bound to be generative and constitutive of the world according to certain frameworks determined by choices and biases'.[91] In this respect, modern international legal positivists share much in common with legal realists and critical legal studies scholars, who have for a long time recognised the inherently subjective nature of law identification and application.[92] In doing so, modern international legal positivism is certainly in line with insights from the cognitive social sciences. What the latter can offer the former, however, is more detailed accounts of which psychological processes have been found to affect decision-making, the scope conditions necessary for these effects to come into play, and evidentiary support for theoretical assertions drawn from post-modernist critical thought. Insights from the cognitive turn and modern international legal positivism complement each other's goal of providing a more descriptively accurate account of the process of law identification.

## 3.2. Objectivity in law interpretation

Whilst law identification was, and still is, the central edifice of both classical and modern positivist theories, renewed scholarly interest in interpretation in the recent past gives us cause to question how that process might interact with the cognitive turn in international law.[93] The orthodox view associated with positivist approaches to interpretation is that the process is one of 'discovering' or 'discerning' the meaning of an already-identified rule, as if meaning were an objective fact existing in the ether, waiting to be plucked from the air by the interpreter.[94] Yet, this point of view—very much like the strict voluntarist conception of classical positivism—is not widely held.[95] Instead, many classical and modern positivist authors recognise the jurisgenerative and subjective character of the interpretative

Susan D Franck and others, 'Inside the Arbitrator's Mind' (2016) 66 Emory Law Journal 1115. As an example of anchoring from the domestic context, see the proposal to reform the US Federal Sentencing guidelines to lessen the anchoring effect on sentencing judges in Mark W Bennett, 'Confronting Cognitive "Anchoring Effect" and "Blind Spot" Biases in Federal Sentencing: A Modest Solution for Reforming a Fundamental Flaw' (2014) 104 The Journal of Criminal Law and Criminology 489.

91 d'Aspremont and Kammerhofer (n 5) 17.

92 See Chapter 3 by Cohen and Bodansky in this volume.

93 See, eg, Ingo Venzke, *How Interpretation Makes International Law: On Semantic Change and Normative Twists* (OUP 2012); Andrea Bianchi, Daniel Peat, and Matthew W Windsor (eds), *Interpretation in International Law* (OUP 2015).

94 See Hernández (n 64) 322–24.

95 Although see Orakhelashvili (n 27) 309.

process,[96] arguing that the interpretative process itself at least partially constitutes the 'meaning' of a rule. Indeed, even the drafters of the 'rules' of interpretation enshrined in Articles 31 to 33 of the Vienna Convention on the Law of Treaties (VCLT) acknowledged that the goal of interpretation was not, and could not be, a mechanical search for a determinate meaning.[97] Moreover, some scholars question the distinction between law identification and interpretation by noting that the identification of a rule is *in itself* an interpretative process, in particular in relation to rules of customary international law.[98] However, regardless of one's view of the extent of the interpretative process, insights from the cognitive turn may help to shed light on how individuals exercise their discretion when interpreting, exploring why they place weight on certain materials in the interpretative process. Two examples illustrate this point.

First, within the framework of the Vienna Convention rules on interpretation, the preparatory work of a treaty is meant to play a secondary role, used only if the elements enumerated in Article 31 result in ambiguity or absurdity or to confirm a meaning that results from those elements. However, experience suggests that the preparatory work plays a significantly more important role in the practice of interpretation.[99] The question is whether the rules on interpretation in any way constrain interpreters' recourse to the preparatory work of a treaty. To explore this question, Yahli Shereshevsky and Tom Noah conducted experimental work to study how exposure to the preparatory work of a treaty affected interpretation,[100] finding that the VCLT provisions moderated but did not eliminate lay people's reference to the preparatory work, whereas experts' recourse to preparatory work was

[96] See Hart (n 56) 144–45; Kelsen, *Reine Rechtslehre* (2nd edn 1960) 348–49 ('[i]n all these cases the law to be applied only provides a frame, within which there is more than one possibility of application. Any act that stays within this margin and gives the frame a possible sense is legal.... If "interpretation" is to be understood as epistemic ascertainment of the meaning of the object to be interpreted, the result of a legal interpretation can only be the ascertainment of a frame (which is the law to be interpreted) and thus the cognisance of multiple possibilities [of meaning], which are possible within the frame'), cited in Jörg Kammerhofer, 'Positivist Approaches and International Adjudication', *Max Planck Encyclopedia of International Procedural Law*, para 16.

[97] See, eg, 'Third Report on the Law of Treaties by Sir Humphrey Waldock' (1964) II YBILC 5, 54, para 6; 'Sixth Report on the Law of Treaties by Sir Humphrey Waldock' (1966) II YBILC 94, para 1. See further Daniel Peat, 'Disciplining Rules? Compliance, the Rules of Interpretation and the Evaluative Dimension of Articles 31 and 32 of the VCLT' (2022) 69 Netherlands International Law Review 221.

[98] See Duncan B Hollis, 'The Existential Function of Interpretation in International Law' in Andrea Bianchi, Daniel Peat, and Matthew W Windsor (eds), *Interpretation in International Law* (OUP 2015), 78–110; Jean d'Aspremont, 'The Multidimensional Process of Interpretation: Content-Determination and Law-Ascertainment Distinguished' in Andrea Bianchi, Daniel Peat, and Matthew W Windsor (eds), *Interpretation in International Law* (OUP 2015), 111-130. Although cf Panos Merkouris, 'Interpreting Customary International Law: You'll Never Walk Alone' in Panos Merkouris, Jörg Kammerhoffer, and Nora Arajärvi (eds), *The Theory, Practice and Interpretation of Customary International Law* (CUP 2022) 347-369.

[99] See Julian D Mortenson, 'The *Travaux* of *Travaux*: Is the Vienna Convention Hostile to Drafting History?' (2013) 107 AJIL 780, 783–84.

[100] Yahli Shereshevsky and Tom Noah, 'Does Exposure to Preparatory Work Affect Treaty Interpretation? An Experimental Study on International Law Students and Experts' (2018) 28 EJIL 1287.

eliminated by a prohibition on such use. This experiment demonstrates that, despite widespread scepticism in the literature about the capacity of rules to constrain an interpreter, 'rules can actually affect treaty interpretation'.[101]

A second example comes from my own work. In a study on the use of comparative law in treaty interpretation, I noticed a correlation between the use of comparative law and the character of the treaty provision that was being interpreted; the former was often used if the latter had a vague, 'standard'-like character, such as fair and equitable treatment, the right to a fair trial, or necessity.[102] As the use of comparative law falls outside the scope of the elements specified in Articles 31 and 32 of the VCLT, the courts and tribunals I surveyed were not legally obliged to look at that as an element in the interpretative process, so why did they? Drawing on findings from social psychology, I explored whether the use of comparative law might be linked to individuals' aversion to large choice sets,[103] analysing judgments of the Grand Chamber of the European Court of Human Rights over a period of twenty-five years. The findings suggested a correlation between the use of comparative law and the character of the legal norm being interpreted, supporting the idea that the interpretative practice may be partially motivated by psychological factors.[104]

## 4. Positivism and Folk Law

The previous sections have examined how lessons from the cognitive and behavioural social sciences may challenge or complement classical and modern international positivist thought. But another, different challenge comes from the nascent field of experimental jurisprudence.[105] Experimental jurisprudence and its older sibling, experimental philosophy, harness experimental methodologies to explore philosophical questions. Like other fields that form part of the cognitive turn, experimental jurisprudence aims to explore how individuals' mental concepts, processes, and perceptions diverge from those present in the literature. And whilst the field is new, some findings are of particular interest to positivist thought.

Despite their many stripes, the idea underpinning positivist thought is that there is an identifiable, unitary concept of law within a legal system. This may be objectively verifiable (as per classical positivism) or it may be coloured by the law-identifier's own experiences and biases (as per modern international legal

[101] ibid 1310.

[102] Daniel Peat, *Comparative Reasoning in International Courts and Tribunals* (CUP 2019) 217–18.

[103] Daniel Peat, 'The Tyranny of Choice and the Interpretation of Standards: Why the European Court of Human Rights uses Consensus' (2021) 53 New York University Journal of Law and Politics 381.

[104] ibid 426–27.

[105] For an overview of experimental jurisprudence, see Kevin Tobia, 'Experimental Jurisprudence' (2022) 89 University of Chicago Law Review 735.

positivism). Positivist theories have become widespread at least partially because they are thought to resonate with the general public's conception of the law.[106] But recent studies in experimental jurisprudence complicate this picture. These studies explore the 'folk' concept of law; that is, the concept of law held by those outside the realm of philosophy of law. In particular, the studies explore whether the folk concept of law is separable from considerations of morality, and, relatedly, what conceptual structure law takes in people's mental representation of the concept.

The folk concept of law is relevant to the present discussion for two reasons. First, it constitutes the general public's prior beliefs regarding what law is. As noted in Section 3.1, cognitive-behavioural studies have shown that prior beliefs inevitably colour our cognition of new facts.[107] Insofar as a legal system utilises a concept of law that diverges from the folk concept, then, this system needs to overcome the cognitive effect of the folk concept of law to secure acceptance of its own concept. Understanding whether and how legal systems do this is important to comprehend the (effective) operation of law within a community. Secondly, the folk concept of law engages with positivist theory because—insofar as the folk concept is not co-extensive with a positivist conception of law—it places the burden on positivists to explain why the value of the positive theoretical alternative outweighs the costs of divergence from the folk concept of law.[108] Positivists might argue, for example, that their theory best serves the maintenance of the international order or peaceful relations,[109] or some other value. But the point is that it would be incumbent on positivist scholars *to make* this normative argument for positive theory rather than to claim simply that their theory should be preferred due to its descriptive superiority.

One of the earlier studies on the topic explored whether the folk concept of law mapped onto the procedural natural law theory of Lon Fuller.[110] Fuller, in his *The Morality of Law*, argued that rules needed to fulfil eight procedural requirements of 'legality', such as promulgation, generality, and non-retroactivity, to qualify as law.[111] Donelson and Hannikainen conducted experiments on 242 lay people and 73 legal professionals to test whether consistency with Fuller's eight principles is required of legal rules in the abstract and if they thought that actual laws conformed

[106] Mark Greenberg, 'The Moral Impact Theory of Law' (2014) 123 Yale Law Journal 1288 at 1297–98. As noted above, this is not to say that positivist theories have no normative agenda, but rather to say that they cannot solely be (normative) theories of law identification; ie, they must have some descriptive basis. On the normative nature of international legal positivist theories, see Hovell (n 5) 100–01.

[107] See text at nn 68 to 79.

[108] Brian Flanagan and Ivar R Hannikainen, 'The Folk Concept of Law: Law Is Intrinsically Moral' (2022) 100 Australasian Journal of Philosophy 165, 167.

[109] See, eg, Oppenheim (n 18) 314; Hans Kelsen, 'Essential Conditions of International Justice' (1941) 35 ASIL Proceedings 70, 73.

[110] Raff Donelson and Ivar R Hannikainen, 'Fuller and the Folk: The Inner Morality of Law Revisited' in Tania Lambrozo and others (eds), *Oxford Studies in Experimental Philosophy, vol. 3* (OUP 2020), 6–28.

[111] Lon L Fuller, *The Morality of Law* (rev edn, Yale UP 1969).

to the principles. The results showed that there was no widespread support for Fuller's principles, but participants were more likely to agree with Fuller's theory if framed in abstract, rather than concrete, terms.[112] This led to the suggestion that the concept of law itself may work on different levels: in the abstract, the folk concept may conform to some of the principles proposed by Fuller, whilst, in more concrete situations, the procedural natural law considerations seemed to play a lesser role in the folk concept of law.[113] The results of a subsequent study echoed these findings.[114]

Further studies have explored whether a rule—in particular, a legal rule—is a 'dual character' concept.[115] This idea, which is imported from experimental philosophy, is that there are certain social concepts that have 'two independent sufficient criteria for application, one descriptive and the other normative'.[116] Take the concept of a scientist, for example. We might say that a person is a scientist if they conduct experiments, analyse data, develop theories, and write scientific papers.[117] But what if they hate their job, don't care about their work, and dream of being a novelist? It would make sense to say that, whilst they might be a scientist in a *technical* (ie descriptive) sense, they are not a *true* scientist (ie in a normative sense).[118]

In a recent study,[119] the authors conducted seven experiments on lay people and law graduates that were designed to test whether the folk concept of law is dual character, a 'mixed' concept that combines normative and descriptive elements,[120] or a concept in which morality does not necessarily play a role. Several experiments presented participants with so-called over- and under-inclusion cases: the former are cases in which a person is in violation of the text of the rule but not the purpose underpinning that rule; the latter are the opposite. Wearing brand new shoes inside someone's house might, for example, breach a rule against shoes inside the house, but it would not offend the (presumptive) purpose of that rule—to keep the house clean (an over-inclusion case).[121] Conversely, if a person entered the house with muddy bare feet, they would not breach the 'no shoes' rule but they

112 Donelson and Hannikainen (n 110) 24.

113 ibid 24. This hypothesis was supported by another study on the character of a rule; see Noel Struchiner, Ivar R Hannikainen, and Guilherme dFCF de Almeida, 'An Experimental Guide to Vehicles in Parks' (2020) 15 Judgement and Decision-Making 312, 326.

114 Flanagan and Hannikainen (n 108).

115 This comes from Joshua Knobe, Sandeep Prasada, and George E Newman, 'Dual Character Concepts and the Normative Dimension of Conceptual Representation' (2013) 127 Cognition 242.

116 Guilherme dFCF de Almeida, Noel Struchiner, and Ivar R Hannikainen, 'Rule Is a Dual Character Concept' (2023) 230 Cognition 105259, 3.

117 Knobe, Prasada, and Newman (n 115) 243.

118 ibid 244.

119 de Almeida, Struchiner, and Hannikainen (n 116).

120 Unlike dual character concepts, for which they are each individually sufficient to qualify something as a member of a group, *both* descriptive and normative elements need to be fulfilled in cases of mixed character concepts; ibid 3.

121 ibid 9.

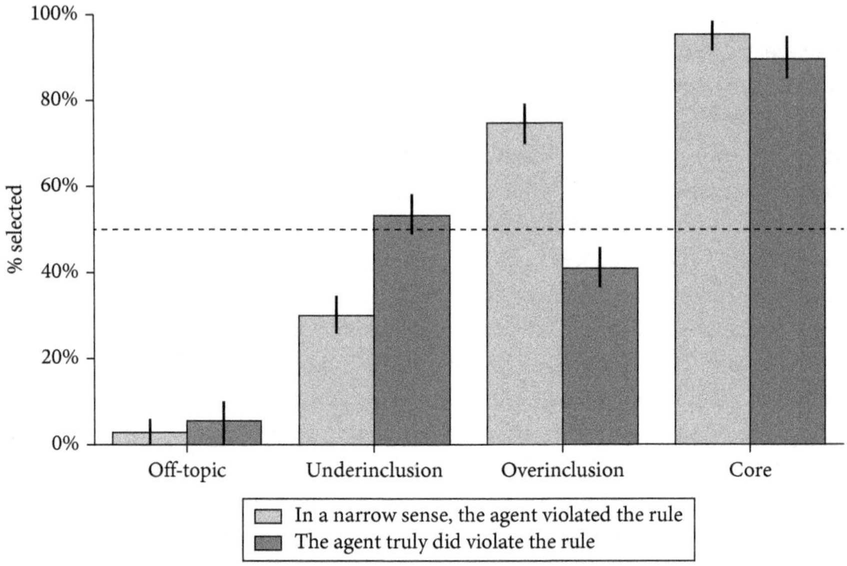


**Figure 1.1** A bar chart which shows that participants distinguished between two different ways in which they considered that a legal rule had been violated.
Source: Reprinted from de Almeida, Struchiner, and Hannikainen, 'Rule Is a Dual Character Concept' (n 116) with permissions from Elsevier.

would certainly defeat its purpose (an under-inclusion case). If a rule were a dual character concept, then one would be able to say that there is one sense in which the 'no shoe' rule has been broken, but another sense in which it has not.

To be clear, I acknowledge that positivist theories may account for such under- and over-inclusion cases by admitting the possibility of teleological interpretation of a rule. For example, a positivist may recognise that an action which offended the telos of the rule is still considered to be a legal violation even if not expressly covered by the text of the provision.[122] However, these experiments call into question positivist theories in a different way: by challenging the very idea that there is *one concept* of law within a legal system and suggesting instead the conceptual plurality of the (folk concept of) law.

A dual character folk concept of law was the only conceptual structure that corresponded with the results of the seven experiments. As shown in Figure 1.1, the majority of participants thought that in under-inclusion cases, the agent violated the rule in the narrow sense but did not 'truly' violate the rule, and, in over-inclusion cases, vice versa. This shows that participants could identify two distinct ways in which a rule could be violated.

[122] See Frederick Schauer, 'A Critical Guide to Vehicles in the Park' (2008) 83 New York University Law Review 1109 at 1129–30.

The findings from the nascent field of experimental jurisprudence pose two challenges for positivism. First, they question the distinction that both classical and modern positivists draw between the source of a legal rule and its merits. As noted above, some modern international law positivists recognise that consideration of morality *may* form part of the criteria for law if accepted by society.[123] But they maintain that this need not necessarily be the case. Findings from experimental jurisprudence challenge that by suggesting that there are at least some ways in which the concept of a legal rule *inherently* rest on the merits of its content, even if we are just talking about the normative criteria of the concept (ie what it means to be *truly*, as opposed to technically, law). Indeed, one study found that 64.4 per cent of participants rejected the notion that identification of the law was completely divorced from considerations of morality.[124] Positivists might respond to this by arguing that they aim to provide description of how law is identified in the 'technical' (ie descriptive) as opposed to 'true' (ie normative) sense of the term. However, studies suggest that it is unclear whether the term 'law' is considered as separate from morality even in the descriptive sense of the concept.[125] In any case, the findings from experimental jurisprudence shift the burden to positivists to explain why their concept of law diverges from the folk concept of law by denying *any* role for morality.

Second, positivists approach the concept of law as if it were a unitary concept: positivist theories attempt to describe, by reference to its source, what a legal rule *is*. The issue raised by experimental jurisprudence is that a 'legal rule' might mean several things to the same person; not just different kinds of legal rule, but different conceptions of a legal rule itself. Positivism must take into account this conceptual plurality—and how it is addressed within a legal system—in order to make any claim to descriptive accuracy. Engaging with law as a dual character concept would seem to be more in line with the mental image held by the folk, and provides an avenue via which positivism might complement both natural law theories and insights from the cognitive-behavioural sciences.

## 5. Conclusion

To explore how the cognitive turn affects positivist thought is a challenging task. Positivism is a 'broad church' and any attempt to generalise about its core claims will inevitably fail to capture the nuances of individual theories. In this chapter, I have tried to synthesise some of the points on which positivist theories converge

[123] See, eg, Jules L Coleman, 'Incorporationism, Conventionality, and the Practical Difference Thesis' (1998) 4 Legal Theory 381; Jules L Coleman, 'Negative and Positive Positivism' (1982) 11 Journal of Legal Studies 139; Hart (n 56) 250.

[124] Flanagan and Hannikainen (n 108) 175.

[125] ibid.

and to explore how these might be challenged or complemented by the cognitive social sciences.

I suggest that interaction between international legal positivism and cognitive-behavioural studies may happen in three different ways. First, the cognitive turn challenges the objectivity presupposed by certain strands of classical positivist theory with regard to the identification of the law. Conversely, these insights may help nuance the normative claims of positivists as well as complement modern positivists' descriptive claims by helping theorists to identify concrete ways in which psychological processes bring cognitive biases, heuristics, and social dynamics to bear on the identification of the law. Second, I suggest that even modern positivists, who accept the subjective nature of interpretation, may profit from lessons drawn from the cognitive social sciences. Insights from the cognitive turn may help us to understand the extent to which the rules of interpretation constrain an interpreter and why certain interpretative approaches are adopted.[126] Finally, both classical and modern strands of positivism would benefit from engaging with findings coming out of the nascent field of experimental jurisprudence, in particular those regarding the conceptual structure of legal rules held by members of the public and the role of morality in law identification.

[126] See further Anne van Aaken, 'The Cognitive Psychology of Rules of Interpretation in International Law' (2021) 116 AJIL Unbound 258.

# 2

# Close Relations

## International Legal Realism and Cognitive-Behavioral Studies

*Harlan Grant Cohen and Daniel Bodansky*

### 1. Introduction

Legal realism has a somewhat different relationship to the cognitive and behavioral sciences than other legal theories. Other legal theories make explicit or implicit assumptions about human cognition and behavior in an effort to describe, explain, conceptualize, or justify law—assumptions that developments in cognitive and behavioral sciences can support or challenge, prompting reconsideration, refinement, or even rejection of a theory. In contrast, legal realism does not make cognitive or behavioral assumptions of its own that could be confirmed or challenged by cognitive-behavioral studies. It is less a legal theory than an orientation or perspective on law. Karl Llewelyn famously described its American variant as a "movement in thought and work about law" rather than a "school."[1] The same is true of international legal realism, which describes an approach to law that is empirical and pragmatic rather than formalist and dogmatic. Committed to viewing law as a social phenomenon, legal realism not only embraces but also commands empirical study of its actual operation. It seeks to investigate all of the factors at work in the legal process—both those internal to the law (that is, doctrine) and those external to the law, such as politics, ideological beliefs, social structure, and cognitive processes. It is thus open to any empirical evidence—including cognitive and behavioral findings—about "how law obtains meaning, operates, and changes through practice."[2]

This sets up a different set of challenges from other legal theories in pairing the two. International legal realism and cognitive-behavioral study of international law largely amplify rather than challenge each other. Legal realism encourages and is a consumer of the type of empirical analysis that cognitive-behavioral studies produces; cognitive-behavioral studies feed off a belief that its advances can improve

[1] Karl Llewellyn, 'Some Realism about Realism: Responding to Dean Pound' (1931) 44 Harvard L Rev 1222.

[2] Gregory Shaffer, 'Legal Realism and International Law' in Jeffrey L Dunoff and Mark Pollack (eds), *International Legal Theory: Foundations and Frontiers* (CUP 2022) 82.

Harlan Grant Cohen and Daniel Bodansky, *Close Relations* In: *International Legal Theory and the Cognitive Turn*.
Edited by: Anne van Aaken and Moshe Hirsch, Oxford University Press.
 DOI: 10.1093/9780198909293.003.0003

the law. The marriage of the two can be quite powerful. The two might work together both to bring a critical eye to international law and institutions and to suggest tools for debiasing and improving their operation.

But in sharpening each other's focus, legal realism and cognitive-behavioral studies may also amplify each other's blind spots. Two interrelated sets of common criticisms of both legal realist and cognitive scientific approaches to international law stand out: (a) managerialism and (b) realism/attitudinalism. The former, focused on the instrumentalism of both approaches, raises questions about international law's autonomy. The latter, focused on their shared naturalism, raises questions about international law's normativity and authority.

This chapter proceeds as follows: Section 2 briefly describes international legal realism and its relation to philosophical realism, international relations realism, and the different variants of domestic legal realism: in particular, American and Scandinavian legal realism. Section 3 discusses the relationship between international legal realism and cognitive-behavioral studies. Section 4 then explores two common challenges that both international legal realism and cognitive-behavioral studies raise.

## 2. What Is International Legal Realism?

The term "realist" has quite different meanings in different fields. In philosophy, realism refers to a theory of ontology—namely, that the abstract entities, objects, and/or properties we know or perceive (numbers, beauty, justice, chairs, atoms, stars, and so forth) really exist, "independent of anything anyone happens to say or think about the matter."[3] Examples of philosophical realism include Plato's theory of forms, which holds that universals such as beauty and justice exist; the commonsense view that everyday objects such as tables and chairs exist independent of the human mind; and the view of many if not most scientists that their theories describe a real world composed of things and properties such as atoms, stars, electromagnetism, and gravity.

By contrast, in political science, realism refers to a specific theory of international politics, namely that states are the principal actors in international relations, that they are motivated by a desire for security and power, and that international politics is a zero-sum gain, in that an increase in power for one state means a loss of power by others.[4] Political science realists include Thucydides, Hobbes, EH Carr, Hans Morgenthau, and Kenneth Waltz.

[3] Alexander Miller, 'Realism', *The Stanford Encyclopedia of Philosophy* (December 13, 2019) <https://plato.stanford.edu/entries/realism>.

[4] Jack Donnelly, *Realism and International Relations* (CUP 2000). It is beyond the scope of the discussion here, but international relations realists have often built off behavioral assumptions. Hans Morgenthau argued "that politics, like society in general, is governed by objective laws that have their roots in human nature." Hans Morgenthau, *Politics among Nations: The Struggle for Power and Peace*

Legal realism is quite different from either philosophical or international relations realism.[5] It is defined not by any particular substantive views but rather by a common approach that rejects formalism and urges the empirical study of law and the use of law to advance progressive social policy.[6] Individual legal realists may have specific theories of the law, but that isn't what brings them together. Rather, what unites them is a critical perspective, a commitment to empiricism, a focus on the legal process rather than on rules, a watchful eye toward politics and bias, and an instrumental belief that law should be shaped to serve societal goals.[7] Legal realism is the instantiation of these general attitudes.

Legal realism comes in several variants. *American legal realism*[8] was a movement that began in the late nineteenth century and emerged as a force in the early twentieth century, which brought together a disparate group of scholars, practitioners, and judges with different theories of law. Some scholars have tried to reconstruct their theories.[9] But they were defined more by what they were "against rather than what they were for."[10] The particular object of their ire was the dominant, formalist approach to law in the nineteenth-century United States that has come to be known as "classical legal thought": the theory that law is an autonomous, formal system consisting of a few fundamental principles from which the

(5th edn, Knopf 1978) 4–5. Thucydides famously attributed state action to "fear, honour, and interest." Thucydides, *The Peloponnesian War* (Random House 1982) 44.

[5] Some see links between legal realism and international relations realism, suggesting that legal realism's skepticism about formalism inspired skepticism about law's force in international relations; see Martti Koskenniemi, *The Gentle Civilizer of Nations: The Rise and Fall of International Law 1870–1960* (CUP 2001) 475–76; that legal realism's focus on power relations inspired international relations realism's rejection of all *but* power relations—see Richard H Steinberg and Jonathan M Zasloff, 'Power and International Law' (2006) 100 AJIL 64, 71–72; that legal realism's pragmatism continues to inspire more rationalist explanations of law—see Harlan Grant Cohen, 'Are We (Americans) All International Legal Realists Now?' in Chiara Giorgetti and Guglielmo Verdirame (eds), *Whither the West? Concepts on International Law in Europe and the United States* (CUP 2021) 33–52; or simply that international legal realism is a mask worn by international relations realists who want to sound respectable in legal circles. The two approaches, however, are quite distinct. Legal realism is fundamentally committed to the power of law as a social phenomenon, while international relations realism denies its force as anything but mirage. For fuller discussion, see Afroditi Giovanopoulou, 'Pragmatic Legalism: Revisiting America's Order after World War II' (2021) 62 Harvard Intl LJ 325, 351–53.

[6] See Heikki Pihlajamaki, 'Against Metaphysics in Law: The Historical Background of American and Scandinavian Legal Realism Compared' (2004) 52 Am J Comp L 469; Gregory S Alexander, 'Comparing the Two Legal Realisms—American and Scandinavian' (2002) 50 Am J Comp L 131.

[7] See, eg, Brian Z Tamanaha, 'Legal Realism in Context' in Elizabeth Mertz, Stewart Macauley, and Thomas W Mitchell (eds), *The New Legal Realism: Translating Law-and-Society for Today's Legal Practice* (CUP 2016) 147.

[8] See generally William W Fisher, Morton J Horwitz, and Thomas A Reed (eds), *American Legal Realism* (OUP 1993).

[9] See, eg, Brian Leiter, 'American Legal Realism' in Dennis Patterson (ed), *The Blackwell Companion to Philosophy of Law and Legal Theory* (Wiley-Blackwell 2010) 249–66.

[10] Stewart Macauley, 'The New Versus the Old Legal Realism: "Things Ain't What They Used to Be"' [2005] Wisconsin L Rev 365, 369. They had "one common bond," Jerome Frank observed: "a skepticism as to some of the conventional legal theories." Jerome Frank, *Law and the Modern Mind* (6th edn, Coward-McCann Inc 1949) viii.

answers to legal questions can be deduced.[11] The legal realists rejected as "transcendental nonsense"[12] this view that legal rules determine legal outcomes and sought to unmask the "rule-fetishism"[13] that they believed dominated classical legal thought and was being used at the time to justify conservative politics. They sought to demonstrate that the legal rules that supposedly required conservative outcomes are, in fact, indeterminate.[14] Legal outcomes (at least in hard cases) are always influenced by social, psychological, political, and/or moral thinking. American legal realists sought to uncover these extra-legal factors that help determine how judges actually decide cases—for example, their political ideology, psychological biases, or sociological background. And this critique, in turn, suggested a program going forward. Legal rules can and should be interpreted to promote social, political, and/or moral progress. For American legal realists, law requires an attention to real-world outcomes, a commitment to empirical testing and retesting, and a goal of improvement.

By contrast, *Scandinavian legal realists* such as Axel Hägerström, Karl Olivecrona, and Alf Ross were more philosophically oriented. They sought to "demystify" and "naturalize" the law by ridding it of metaphysical concepts such as rights, duties, and obligations, replacing these concepts with a scientific account of law that explains empirically the relationship between law and behavior and that reconceptualizes rights, duties, and obligations in terms of the attitudes of legal actors.[15]

Finally, *"new" legal realists* such as Stewart Macauley[16]—and their international law counterparts such as Greg Shaffer[17]—are the descendants of the "law and society" movement, which grew out of American legal realism but is distinct.[18] Like their forebears, the new legal realists are critical of legal formalism and view law instrumentally. However, in contrast to the earlier generation of American legal realists, they are more empirically minded and seek to study the law from the bottom up in order to understand, pragmatically, how it actually operates in society and how it can be reformed in order to serve social ends.[19]

[11] See generally William M Wiecek, *The Lost World of Classical Legal Thought: Law and Ideology in America, 1886–1937* (OUP 1998). Legal realism was part of a larger reaction to formalism in the early twentieth century. See Morton White, *Social Thought in America: The Revolt against Formalism* (Beacon Press 1957).

[12] Felix Cohen, 'Transcendental Nonsense and the Functional Approach' (1945) 2 R General Semantics 82.

[13] Frank (n 10) 295.

[14] Leiter (n 9).

[15] Jes Bjarup, 'The Philosophy of Scandinavian Legal Realism' (2002) 18 Ratio Juris 1.

[16] See Macauley (n 10).

[17] Greg Shaffer, 'The New Legal Realist Approach to International Law' (2015) 28 Leiden J Intl L 189.

[18] Elizabeth Mertz, 'Introduction: New Legal Realism: Law and Social Science in the New Millennium' in Elizabeth Mertz, Stewart Macauley, and Thomas W Mitchell (eds), *Translating Law-and-Society for Today's Legal Practice* (2016) 1–26.

[19] The American legal realists of the 1920s and 1930s, although championing the empirical study of law, did relatively little empirical work themselves. As Holmes said, with typical pungency, "I have little

If we had to sum up the differences between the three groups, American legal realists were (and still are) defined by their approach to legal practice and reasoning, Scandinavian legal realists by their naturalist philosophy, and new legal realists by their social scientific orientation.

Although we focus at times in this chapter on American legal realism, we will consider international legal realism in its broadest, most generic sense, defined by only a few common features.

- A critical perspective that is skeptical (but not necessarily dismissive) of the degree to which rules determine outcomes.
- A desire to understand how international law "really" works, which leads to empiricism.
- A focus on the international legal process and the actors within it.
- An instrumental orientation, interested in how the law can better serve social ends.

We believe that widening the aperture in this manner is appropriate when we consider international legal realism. American and Scandinavian legal realism as movements have passed and are mainly of historical interest. New legal realism is alive and well but has relatively few international practitioners. In contrast, legal realism of the more generic kind described above permeates the international legal academy and profession, at least in the United States, and has considerable influence.[20] We include under its umbrella not only self-styled legal realists such as Greg Shaffer but also many others, such as Abram Chayes, Michael Reisman, Monica Hakimi, and ourselves. Like their American legal realist ancestors, they are bound together more by their general attitude or approach than by any particular theoretical account of international law. Instead, they are omnivorous in their methods, ready to analyze international law at the level of the individual, the professional group, or the state, to the extent useful in developing a better understanding of international law's operation. A few international legal realists are sociolegal scholars with a rigorous empirical method. But most draw on anecdotal evidence, citing a few examples to illustrate their points. To the extent they engage with more rigorous empirical scholarship, it is as consumers rather than producers.

doubt that it would be good for my immortal soul to plunge into [facts] ... but I shrink from the bore." Quoted in Macauley (n 10) 372.

[20] See Cohen (n 5).

## 3. The Relation of International Legal Realism to Cognitive-Behavioral Studies

As a result of international legal realism's overall orientation, it relates to cognitive-behavioral studies differently from other legal theories. We define cognitive-behavioral studies, as the editors of this volume do, as "the interdisciplinary study of the mind and the diverse mental processes involved in acquiring, processing and storing information, as well as judgments and decision-making processes,"[21] and include work done across a range of fields and under different titles including neurology, psychology, and behavioral law and economics. In general, cognitive-behavioral studies can relate to legal theory in either of two ways, depending on whether a legal theory addresses the same types of questions as the cognitive and behavioral sciences or different ones.

First, like cognitive-behavioral studies, some legal theories (eg rational choice and constructivism) address explanatory questions to which empirical evidence is relevant. They seek to understand the causes and effects of beliefs and behavior, to explain how and why individuals relate to legal arguments and the law. For these legal theories, cognitive-behavioral studies can help confirm or undermine their empirical claims.[22]

Other legal theories such as positivism[23] and natural law ask conceptual and normative questions about what law is and should be and use analytic and interpretive methods to answer these questions. These legal theories are best understood to be in conversation across a divide with cognitive science, since they ask different questions and use different methods. Each brings insights to the other from the "outside." Legal theory can identify potentially important phenomena that cognitive science had not focused on and might test, to see whether they are associated with observable cognitive processes: for example, the internal point of view; the "logic of consequences" versus the "logic of appropriateness"; and the role of sanctions versus rewards in influencing behavior. Conversely, cognitive science might prompt legal theorists to refine or revise their theories. Is there an internal point of view and, if so, how does it work cognitively?[24] Do individuals consider moral beliefs in answering legal questions? Do different people apply different concepts of law, acting in some cases as Holmesian bad men, "who care only for the material consequences" of violating the law,[25] in others as Hartian internalizers,[26] and in

[21] Anne van Aaken and Moshe Hirsch's Introduction to this volume, Section 3.

[22] See Chapter 8 by Anne van Aaken and Tomer Broude in this volume and Chapter 3 by Ian Johnstone and Arun Mohan Sukumar in this volume.

[23] See Chapter 1 by Daniel Peat in this volume.

[24] cf Daniel Peat, 'Perception and Process: Towards a Behavioural Theory of Compliance' (2022) 13 J Intl Dispute Settlement (2022) 190–92.

[25] Oliver Wendell Homes, 'The Path of the Law' (1897) 10 Harvard L Rev 457, 459.

[26] HLA Hart, *The Concept of Law* (OUP 1961).

still others as moral absolutists?[27] In addressing questions such as these, cognitive science and legal theory could productively be in conversation with one another (as is already true of cognitive science and metaethics[28]), even though they are fundamentally different disciplines.

The relationship of international legal realism and cognitive-behavioral studies is much closer than either of these two types of relationships. Like rational choice and constructivism, legal realism is concerned less with conceptual or normative questions than with descriptive and explanatory ones. But unlike rational choice and constructivism, it does not put forward any particular explanatory theory. Instead, international legal realism is pragmatic and pluralist. It is open to any approach, including cognitive science, that can help explain how legal norms emerge, gain meaning, and have effects. It can thus incorporate cognitive science directly into its analysis.

Historically, the relationship of the American variant of legal realism and cognitive science was particularly close. Like legal realists today, the American legal realists of the 1920s and 1930s wanted to lift the obscuring curtain of legal doctrine and reveal the judges, lawyers, and other actors operating the machine. They wanted to unveil the social, psychological, and political factors that actually drive legal arguments and outcomes.[29] And they wanted to understand what effects law actually has. Their object was as much to critique those hiding behind legal formalisms to push a conservative agenda as it was to encourage more empirically grounded approaches to the law. Once revealed, prior assumptions could be tested, and fresh empirical analyses of the law and its effects could, in turn, provide stronger foundations for the law going forward.

The focus of American legal realists on the role of individual actors and on empiricism led them naturally to cognitive science. As one historian comments, "To the early legal realists, psychology seemed to open up unlimited avenues of inquiry and it is hardly surprising that they were profoundly influenced by its novel insights."[30] As early as 1927, shortly after his appointment as dean of Yale Law School, Robert Hutchins brought a psychologist to Yale to help him understand

[27] cf Steven L Winter, 'Contingency and Community in Normative Practice' (1991) 139 U Pennsylvania L Rev 963.

[28] See, eg, Patricia S Churchland, *Braintrust: What Neuroscience Tells Us about Morality* (Princeton UP 2011); Walter Sinnott-Armstrong, *Moral Psychology*, 5 vols. (MIT Press 2007–17). For example, neuroscience has been used to study which parts of the brain are activated by Kantian versus utilitarian reasoning. See Joshua D Greene, 'The Cognitive Neuroscience of Moral Judgment and Decision Making' in Jean Decety and Thalia Wheatley (eds), *The Moral Brain: A Multidisciplinary Perspective* (MIT Press 2015) 197.

[29] Hence, American legal realists would have embraced the two premises of this book 'that first, human cognition affects the perceptions and behaviour of real-world international law decision-makers and second, cognitive processes matter for how international law is interpreted, conceived, and theorized'. Van Aaken and Hirsch (n 21) 1.

[30] Simon N Verdun-Jones, 'The Jurisprudence of Jerome N Frank: A Study in American Legal Realism' [1974] Sydney L Rev 180, 181.

the psychology of evidence, and they subsequently co-authored a series of articles seeking to apply the relevant psychological literature to various evidentiary problems.[31]

Many of the leading American legal realists tried to incorporate psychological insights into their work. Underhill Moore's research drew on behavioralism, while Judge Joseph Hutcheson emphasized the importance of the "hunch" in judicial decision-making—"that intuitive flash of understanding that makes the jump-spark connection between question and decision"[32]—a phenomenon we would now call "fast," System 1 thinking, which is instinctive and unconscious, as opposed to the "slow," deliberative, conscious, System 2 thinking characteristic of doctrinal legal analysis.[33] But among the American legal realists, cognitive science is most clearly implicated by Jerome Frank's psychological approach to legal decision-making, which focused on a variety of cognitive processes, including perception, memory, and bias. In a strikingly modern passage, Frank wrote in the preface to the revised edition of *Law and the Modern Mind*:

> The trial court's "finding" of the fact involves a multitude of elusive factors: First, the [fact-finder] ... must learn the facts from the witnesses; and witnesses, being humanly fallible, frequently make mistakes in observation of what they heard, or in their recollections of what they observed, or in their court-room reports of their recollections. Second, the trial judges or juries, also human, have prejudices—often unconscious, unknown even to themselves—for or against some of the witnesses, or the parties to the suit, or the lawyers.
>
> Those prejudices, when they are racial, religious, political, or economic, may sometimes be surmised by others. But there are some hidden, unconscious biases of trial judges or jurors, such as for example, plus or minus reactions to women, or unmarried women, or red-haired women, or brunettes, or men with deep voices or high-pitched voices, or fidgety men, or men who wear thick eyeglasses, or those who have pronounced gestures or nervous tics—biases of which no one can be aware.[34]

At the time Frank and the other American legal realists wrote, cognitive science was still in its infancy, dominated by behavioralism and psychoanalysis. Developments since then undermine some of Frank's specific arguments. Frank believed that cognitive processes are "highly idiosyncratic" and "cannot be formulated as uniformities or squeezed into regularized 'behavior patterns'"[35] and that

[31] John Henry Schlegel, 'American Legal Realism and Empirical Social Science: From the Yale Experience' (1979) 28 Buffalo L Rev 459, 480.

[32] Quoted in Verdun-Jones (n 30) 182.

[33] Daniel Kahneman, *Thinking Fast and Slow* (Farrar, Straus, and Giroux 2011).

[34] Frank (n 10) x–xi.

[35] ibid xi.

attempts to develop a legal science were "fatuous."[36] He would no doubt be surprised by the progress made over the last half-century in identifying behavioral regularities that cognitive science can now explain.[37] But there is little doubt that he would have welcomed this work—for example, showing that biases such as loss aversion, availability, and anchoring are the result of deeply engrained heuristics and are regular rather than idiosyncratic.

Frank represented the "psychological" wing of American legal realism, which focused on how the psychology of legal decision-makers affected their determinations of fact and law. Most American legal realists, in contrast, fell into the "sociological" wing, which sought to find regularities of judicial behavior based on social factors such as class, legal education, and professional experience. But although they would likely have seen cognitive process as only one among many potential explanatory factors, they too would have sought to integrate developments in cognitive science into their explanations of legal behavior. In fact, the distinction between "psychological" and "sociological" arguably tracks divisions between modern cognitive and behavioral studies, which focus on individual psychology and shared assumptions within social groups, respectively.[38]

For legal realists both old and new, the cognitive turn does not represent a challenge. Instead, it is something that legal realism simply needs to assimilate—supplementing our knowledge in some cases, requiring correction of mistaken beliefs in others, and in general allowing us to better understand and predict legal behavior and its effects. In essence, the cognitive sciences have effectuated what American legal realists such as Frank aspired to, revealing how biases can shape the law in unintended and often undesired ways. They demonstrate how a metaphor or narrative can warp legal analyses in one direction or another, shifting the balance of equities in unexpected or harmful ways.[39] They help explain how racist or sexist views can creep into judicial decisions.[40] Studies have shown that US domestic judges are subject to implicit biases,[41] and there is considerable anecdotal

[36] ibid xxii.

[37] See, eg, Chris Guthrie, Jeffrey J Rachlinski, and Andrew J Wistrich, 'Inside the Judicial Mind' (2001) 86 Cornell L Rev 777; Susan D Franck and others, 'Inside the Arbitrator's Mind' (2017) 66 Emory LJ 1115.

[38] Van Aaken and Hirsch (n 21) 4, 5.

[39] Shiri Krebs, 'The Invisible Frames Affecting Wartime Investigations: Legal Epistemology, Metaphors, and Cognitive Biases' in Andrea Bianchi and Moshe Hirsch (eds), *International Law's Invisible Frames: Social Cognition and Knowledge Production in International Legal Processes* (OUP 2021) 124-40; Harlan Grant Cohen, 'Metaphors of International Law' in ibid 219–36; Moshe Hirsch, 'Regulators' Mindsets, Ingroup Favoritism, and the National Treatment Obligation in World Trade Organization Law' (2022) 23 German LJ 298.

[40] See, eg, Anna Spain Bradley, *Human Choice in International Law* (CUP 2021); Anna Spain Bradley, 'Advancing Neuroscience in International Law' in Harlan Grant Cohen and Timothy Meyer (eds), *International Law as Behavior* (CUP 2021) 191, 218–20 (describing studies); Anna Spain Bradley, 'The Disruptive Neuroscience of Judicial Choice' (2018) 9 UC Irvine L Rev 1.

[41] See, eg, Guthrie and others (n 37).

evidence of racial[42] and gender bias[43] at the international level. Many observers have noted the role of female judges in the identification of rape as an international crime,[44] and one study has suggested that "female judges are more favorably disposed towards discrimination cases filed by women."[45] More positively, as legal realists might have hoped, the cognitive sciences also suggest ways to debias the law, either by changing decision-making pathways to open space for other voices or to force reflection or by training decision-makers to see their biases.[46] Studies have, for example, suggested that even just revealing a particular bias can eliminate some of its influence,[47] as Frank believed. In these ways, cognitive sciences might provide a path to just the sort of self-aware, empirically minded social improvement that legal realists desired.

International legal realism thus embraces social and psychological data and influences in a way that other theories do not. Much of the work of legal realists gestured in the direction of cognitive science, asking similar questions about the unspoken, often invisible biases of legal actors, but without doing the hard, empirical work necessary to answer these questions. In many ways, developments in cognitive science, along with other social scientific studies of law, might be seen as bringing the legal realist approach to fruition. In fact, for modern self-described legal realists, legal realism, empirical analysis, and pragmatic adaptation are all aspects of the same approach.[48]

## 4. Common Challenges

In emphasizing the indeterminacy of rules, the discretion of those making legal decisions, and the need for judges to consider the social consequences of their decisions, both legal realist and cognitive scientific approaches have been accused of losing sight of the law itself. For many, law is defined by its autonomy (its ability to operate as something other than mere power) and by its normativity (its ability to provide its own reasons for action). In demystifying the law—in seeking to explain

[42] See, eg, Won L Kidane, *The Culture of International Arbitration* (OUP 2017) 5–6 (describing how African cultural differences can be interpreted by international arbitrators as incompetence).

[43] See, eg, Nienke Grossman, 'Sex on the Bench: Do Women Judges Matter to the Legitimacy of International Courts?' (2012) 12 Chi J Intl L 647, 654–64.

[44] See ibid.

[45] Erik Voeten, 'Gender and Judging: Evidence from the European Court of Human Rights' (2021) 28 J Eur Pub Policy 1453. See also Chapter 5 by Veronika Fikfak in this volume.

[46] See, eg, Moshe Hirsch, 'Cognitive Sociology, Social Cognition and Coping with Racial Discrimination in International Law' (2019) 30 Eur J Intl L 1319; Christine Jolls and Cass R Sunstein, 'Debiasing through Law' (2006) 35 JL Studies 199; Justin D Levinson, 'Forgotten Racial Equality: Implicit Bias, Decisionmaking, and Misremembering' (2007) 57 Duke LJ 345.

[47] See, eg, Douglas H Yarn, 'Heuristics and Biases', Ga ADR Prac & Proc § 5:8 (April 2023).

[48] Gregory Shaffer and Tom Ginsburg, 'The Empirical Turn in International Legal Scholarship' (2012) 106 Am J Intl L 1.

the "real" forces behind legal claims and interpretations—both legal realism and cognitive-behavioral studies risk robbing "law," as a concept, of all meaning. Sapped of its autonomy and normativity, the critics suggest, law becomes nothing more than an extension of the decision-maker's will or bias. And in doing so, both international legal realism and cognitive science risk undermining law's ability to constrain and to inspire.

### 4.1. Law as power

At the heart of the first critique is legal realism's intertwined commitments to rule skepticism and instrumentalism. The American legal realists' rule skepticism had a political goal. They wanted to demonstrate that conservative outcomes were not dictated by legal rules, in order to liberate the law to serve progressive purposes. New legal realists, too, see law as a purposive tool, a means to improve society and achieve social goods. They encourage empirical study to learn what works and what does not, lessons that can then be applied to improve the law.

Those embracing cognitive science often make similar appeals. If we can understand why people behave the way they do, we can learn how to "nudge" them toward better behaviors. As Doron Teichman and Eyal Zamir observe, "The use of nudges—'low-cost, choice-preserving, behaviorally informed approaches to regulatory problems'—has become quite popular at the national level in the past decade or so."[49] They see similar trends at the international level.[50] Notably, "[t]he UN Innovation Network has set up the UN Behavioural Science Group" to "help enable interventions to produce change to progress towards the Sustainable Development Goals."[51] Cognitive science becomes a means to achieving our ends.

Critics worry that these approaches undermine the ability of law to constrain the power of both states and lawyers. In piercing the veil of formalism and revealing the biases underlying legal decisions, there is a temptation to take the next step and view law as nothing more than power. If law is simply an argumentative practice rather than a body of rules, as Monica Hakimi argues;[52] if international actors simply invoke rules, instrumentally, to pursue their extra-legal goals; if the "law in action" (or the "operational code," as Michael Reisman put it[53]) is simply

[49] Doron Teichman and Eyal Zamir, 'Normative Aspects of Nudging in the International Sphere' (2021) 115 AJIL Unbound 263 (citing Cass R Sunstein, 'Nudges.Gov: Behaviorally Informed Regulation' in Eyal Zamir and Doron Teichman (eds), *The Oxford Handbook of Behavioral Economics and the Law* (OUP 2014) 719.

[50] ibid; see also Doron Teichman and Eyal Zamir, 'Nudge Goes International' (2019) 30 EJIL 1263.

[51] 'UN Behavioral Science Group' (UN Innovation Network) <www.uninnovation.network/behavioural-science> accessed August 4, 2023.

[52] Monica Hakimi, 'Why Should We Care about International Law?' (2020) 118 Michigan L Rev 1283.

[53] W Michael Reisman, *Folded Lies: Bribery, Crusades, and Reforms* (Free Press 1979) 15–36.

whatever states do, then law arguably becomes, in effect, an instrument of power rather than a constraint on it. It operates simply as apology.[54] The New Haven School's policy science approach represented an extreme version of this[55] and is often criticized as replacing international law with American foreign policy preferences.[56] But similar criticisms continue to echo regarding American approaches to international law more generally.

A more recent, subtler critique along similar lines is that international legal realism risks over-empowering the "invisible college of international lawyers." Martti Koskenniemi worries about "the kind of 'managerialism' that suggests that international problems—problems of 'globalization'—should be resolved by developing increasingly complicated technical vocabularies for institutional policy-making."[57] International lawyers predisposed to view legal outcomes as the results of bias could become "enchanted with the tools"[58] that cognitive science provides them. Rather than act as servants or protectors of the law, international lawyers could seek to become unelected managers who use their command of these tools to direct world policy. "At their worst," Koskenniemi argues, the tools of international law can "obscure the way power works and make particular intellectual or social hierarchies appear as natural aspects of our lives."[59] Along similar lines, Jan Klabbers underlines the unspoken agents in much of the new legal realist work. While scholars like Gregory Shaffer extol legal realist thinking for its "greater effectiveness" and its ability to "inform action" and facilitate "pragmatic, purposive interventions,"[60] Klabbers argues that Shaffer "leaves unsaid whose action and interventions he has in mind."[61] In new legal realist work, "the political question is systematically dodged."[62]

To critics, legal realist thinking encourages international lawyers to elevate functional concerns above all others.[63] In doing so, they remind some of "bureaucratic

[54] Martti Koskenniemi, *From Apology to Utopia: The Structure of International Legal Argument* (CUP 1989).

[55] For an extended discussion of McDougal and Lasswell's origins in and departures from American legal realism, see Neil Duxbury, *Patterns of American Jurisprudence* (Clarendon Press 1995) 161–203.

[56] Nigel Purvis, 'Critical Legal Studies in Public International Law' (1991) 32 Harvard Intl LJ 81.

[57] Martti Koskenniemi, 'The Politics of International Law—20 Years Later' (2009) 20 EJIL 7, 15.

[58] Martti Koskenniemi, 'Enchanted by the Tools? An Enlightenment Perspective' (2020) 35 Am U Intl L Rev 397, 406–11.

[59] Koskenniemi (n 57) 16.

[60] Shaffer (n 17).

[61] Jan Klabbers, 'Whatever Happened to Gramsci? Some Reflections on New Legal Realism' (2015) 28 Leiden J Intl L 469, 477. The piece by one of us in the same special issue, Daniel Bodansky, 'Legal Realism and Its Discontents' (2015) Leiden J Intl L 267, fares a bit better in Klabbers' account for at least identifying 'progressive politics' as a goal and making room for doctrine. And we should note that we think Klabbers' criticism of Shaffer's work is unfounded.

[62] ibid.

[63] See Adam N Steinman, 'A Constitution for Judicial Lawmaking' (2004) 65 U Pittsburgh L Rev 545, 559 ("Others, however, have read realism as embracing a normativity of 'functionalism,' by which judicial decisionmaking is evaluated in terms of the actual effects of such decisions on society"); Richard A Posner, 'Legal Formalism, Legal Realism, and the Interpretation of Statutes and the Constitution' (1987) 37 Case W Res L Rev 179, 181 (defining realism as "deciding a case so that its outcome best promotes public welfare in nonlegalistic terms; it is policy analysis").

authoritarianism"[64] and raise serious questions of legitimacy. From where do these international lawyers get their mandate? "[M]anagerialism has its concealed normativity that privileges values and actors occupying dominant positions in international institutions and who therefore have no reason to take a critical attitude to those institutions."[65] Behavioral nudges raise related concerns. As Teichman and Zamir explain, "critics of nudges have argued that such policies infringe on individual liberty. Specifically, nudges are manipulative, since they exploit people's cognitive limitations rather than engage them as deliberative rational agents."[66] When combined with legal realism's instrumentalism, lessons from behavioral science could encourage international lawyers to imagine themselves as noble world engineers, arranging and rearranging international rules for the good of everyone.[67]

## 4.2. Law as myth

Beyond elevating lawyers, the other intertwined criticism of both legal realism and cognitive science is that they can, taken to extremes, sap "law" of its distinctive character, namely its normativity.[68] The critique is more *apropos* of the naturalist philosophy of the Scandinavian legal realists than the American ones. Scandinavian legal realists such as Karl Hägerström and Alf Ross wanted to rid law of its metaphysical elements and replace them with a purely psychological understanding of law. As one commentator writes, "legal vocabulary," for Hägerström, was "not a matter of using concepts as reasons for human conduct but only a matter of using empty words or noises to cause the appropriate behavior."[69] Or,

[64] Martti Koskenniemi, 'Letter to the Editors of the Symposium' (1999) 93 Am J Intl L 351.

[65] Koskenniemi (n 57) 16.

[66] Teichman and Zamir (n 49) (citing Till Grüne-Yanoff, 'Old Wine in New Casks: Libertarian Paternalism Still Violates Liberal Principles' (2012) 38 Social Choice and Welfare 635, 636); Christopher McCrudden and Jeff King, 'The Dark Side of Nudging: The Ethics, Political Economy, and Law of Libertarian Paternalism' in Alexandra Kemmerer and others (eds), *Choice Architecture in Democracies* (Nomos/Hart 2016) 75, 104–10. For example, many multilateral environmental agreements change the default rule that states are bound by an agreement only if they affirmatively consent, by allowing treaty amendments to bind a state unless they specifically object and opt out. This behavioral nudge has become a common feature of treaty design—see Jean Galbraith, 'Treaty Options: Towards a Behavioral Understanding of Treaty Design' (2013) 53 Virginia J Intl L 309—but arguably infringes on the democratic authority of national legislatures to decide what treaty amendments to accept by allowing bureaucrats to bind a state by not exercising the state's right to opt out.

[67] As Teichman and Zamir note, influential international actors like the World Bank that act at some remove from politics already elicit concerns about accountability. "Since nudges offer a new and powerful tool to such unaccountable players in the international arena, they might be viewed as less legitimate." Teichman and Zamir (n 44) 267.

[68] cf Bodansky (n 56) 279–80 (discussing criticism that legal realism 'disenchants' the law); see also the dialogue between Joseph Weiler and Anne van Aaken, in which Weiler characterizes behavioralism as like a bun with the hamburger missing, and asks, "Where's the meat?": 'Questions for Anne van Aaken on Rationalist and Behavioralist Approaches to International Law' in Jeffrey L Dunoff and Mark A Pollack (eds), *International Legal Theory: Foundations and Frontiers* (CUP 2022) 409.

[69] Bjarap (n 15) 7.

in Hägerström's words, "The legal order is throughout nothing but a social machine, in which the cogs are men."[70] Similarly, Alf Ross argued that, in contrast to words like "table" and "chair," which refer to something that actually exists, words such as "right," "duty," "claim," and "ownership" are "without meaning, without any semantic reference." They could, in principle, be translated into non-normative language that talks only of causes and effects, and then eliminated altogether from our vocabulary.[71] The only reason to retain them is for convenience, because it is easier to use a simple word like "property" to denote a cluster of descriptive, non-normative propositions ("if one pays for a thing then one can exclude others from using it" and so forth). But we could achieve the same end if we used instead a word such as "tû-tû" that has no magical effect for us, which Ross seems to have viewed as preferable.[72]

Cognitive scientific approaches to international law have similarly been criticized for reducing law to mere behavioral regularities. Sungjoon Cho, for example, worries that reducing international law to behavioral norms and pathways robs the law of its normativity and devalues the norm-making processes of argumentation and deliberation.[73] In a sense, the concern regarding both is that, in explaining law as a function of social and psychological phenomena, it may become nothing more than a label for these phenomena. Skepticism becomes nihilism. Why should anyone care what the International Court of Justice says if they are simply "politicians in robes"—if their decisions are not determined by the law but simply reflect their policy preferences? In a world consisting solely of cause and effect, the only perspective possible seems to be that of Holmes' bad man, for whom the law had no normative force and who cared only about the consequences.

Scandinavian legal realists might respond that this is the reality of the matter and we shouldn't pretend otherwise. But, even if only a myth, the concept of law might still serve a useful function—it might help to inspire, to guide, and to constrain.[74] It might represent a "noble lie,"[75] which legal realism and cognitive-behavioral studies threaten to undermine. The placebo effect is real. And if belief in the rule of law is also real—and has real effects—then a true legal realist should take that into account too, as Alf Ross in his work apparently did.[76] Indeed, if the realists' objective is to use international law to make a better world, then robbing the law of its mythic force seems counter-productive.

[70] ibid 8 (quoting Axel Hägerström, *Inquiries into the Nature of Law and Morals* 354, Karl Olivecrona ed, CD Broad tr, Stockholm, Almquist and Wiskell 1953).

[71] Alf Ross, 'Tû-Tû' (1957) 70 Harvard L Rev 812, 822.

[72] ibid.

[73] Sungjoon Cho, 'A Social Critique of Behavioral Approaches to International Law' (2021) 115 AJIL Unbound 248.

[74] On the "rule of law" as an unqualified human good, see EP Thompson, *Whigs and Hunters: The Origin of the Black Act* (Breviary Stuff 1975) 208.

[75] Plato, *The Republic*, Book III, section 414(c).

[76] Jakob vH Holtermann, 'A Straw Man Revisited: Resettling the Score between H.L.A. Hart and Scandinavian Legal Realism' (2017) 57 Santa Clara L Rev 1.

In this connection, cognitive science could play an important role. It could not just reveal potential biases in the law but also investigate mechanisms that might help explain law's operation as an independent force *through* cognitive processes, separate from personal preferences. Moving past rational choice, it could discover mechanisms that help explain the power of oft-repeated legal catechisms, the value of legal scripts, and the weight of firmly established legal principles. Adopting language evocative of cognitive sciences, Dagan, Kreitner, and Kricheli-Katz describe legal doctrines as "schema"[77] "that routinely define the possibilities of lawmakers."[78] As they explain, "Law's normativity often constrains lawmakers' sense of choice by providing an internally consistent and reasoned schema for legal decision making that in some cases directs lawmakers to transcend their own interests."[79] Studying the ways international law doctrines can act as frames that change how international actors perceive a situation,[80] shift their interdependent views of acceptable action,[81] or provide the justificatory arguments expected by others can begin to explain law's special normativity and its autonomy from mere power or interest.[82] Some cognitive-behavioral experiments have begun to explore these questions, with intriguing results.[83]

### 4.3. Law as law

The fear that international legal realism and cognitive-behavioral studies will denude international law of its capacity to constrain and to inspire—and ultimately to effectuate change—is justified only if one takes international legal realism and cognitive-behavioral studies to their extreme: for example, by claiming that rules

[77] See Van Aaken and Hirsch (n 21) 4, 13 (describing the role of schema in cognitive and behavioral studies).

[78] Hanoch Dagan, Roy Kreitner, and Tamar Kricheli-Katz, 'Legal Theory for Legal Empiricists' (2018) 43 L and Social Inquiry 292, 297.

[79] ibid.

[80] See, eg, Christoph Engel and Michael Kurschilgen, 'The Coevolution of Behavior and Normative Expectations: An Experiment' (2013) 15 Am L and Econ Rev 578 (describing how the presence of norms or law can change behaviors within public goods games).

[81] See, eg, ibid (describing the coevolution of norms and behavior); Andrew M Bell, 'Leashing the "Dogs of War": Examining the Effects of LOAC Training at the U.S. Military Academy and in Army ROTC' (2014) 108 Proc ASIL 370 (describing how training in the law of war shifts assessment of proportionality and civilian harm).

[82] See Anne van Aaken and Jan-Philip Elm, 'Framing in and through Public International Law' in Andrea Bianchi and Moshe Hirsch (eds), *International Law's Invisible Frames: Social Cognition and Knowledge Production in International Legal Processes* (OUP 2022) 35.

[83] See, eg, Engel and Kurschilgen (n 80); Yahli Shereshevsky and Tom Noah, 'Does Exposure to Preparatory Work Affect Treaty Interpretation? An Experimental Study on International Law Students and Experts' (2018) 28 EJIL 1287, 1310 (finding that, depending on the shape of the rule, "rules can actually affect treaty interpretation"); Gentiana Imeri, 'The Expressive Function of Law Experimental Studies on the Behavioral Effect of Non-Coercive Law in Social Dilemma Settings', unpublished dissertation of the University of St Gallen (using experiments on focal point effects to explore the expressive function of law). See also Peat (n 23) (describing studies).

are radically indeterminate or that legal behavior can be fully explained and understood in cognitive and behavioral terms.

Some writers do, at times, suggest this kind of hegemonic, totalizing view. But most realists are realistic enough to recognize that there are more things in heaven and earth than are dreamt of in their philosophy. The original American legal realists, for example, did not, for the most part, seem to have believed in radical legal indeterminacy.[84] They thought that rules could constrain, even if not determine, decision—that law could operate as law rather than simply as prediction. Contemporary legal realists tend to agree. As one group explains, "[L]egal realism eschews analyzing law only in terms of parochial interests or power politics. It recognizes that modes of legal reasoning—substantive and technical, abstract and contextual—often constrain the sense of choice available to legal decision makers in directions that transcend their self- and group interest."[85] And cognitive scientists' efforts to *explain* behavior in terms of neuroscience, linguistics, psychology, and computer science does not exclude the possibility of *understanding* behavior in terms of reasons and rules—that is, in a normative manner. Indeed, if we accept Peter Winch's "rules thesis," then "understanding human action involves seeing the rules or proprieties in accordance with which it was produced, not just detecting regularities in the production."[86]

The answer to both sets of concerns about international legal realism and the cognitive sciences seems to lie in legal realism's original critical perspective. If "we are all legal realists now,"[87] then we must also all be active self-critics.[88] And there is some evidence that the original American legal realists saw things that way. Much as Martti Koskenniemi has suggested lawyers adopt a "culture of formalism" in response to their recognition of international law's indeterminacy,[89] Oliver Wendell Holmes adopted a more formalist approach when judging, criticizing other judges for their naked instrumentalism.[90] Purposivism in designing the law must be tempered by a recognition of one's role within it.

[84] See Leiter (n 9).

[85] Dagan, Kreitner, and Kricheli-Katz (n 78) 297.

[86] Philip Pettit, 'Winch's Double-Edged Idea of a Social Science' (2000) 13 History Human Sciences 63, 64.

[87] Cohen (n 5).

[88] See Natalie Davidson, 'Human Rights Realism' (2021) 54 Vanderbilt J Transnatl L 31 ("Their solution to these tensions is to conceive of normativity as an ongoing methodology: the constant critique and search for improvement of the law").

[89] Jan Klabbers, 'Towards a Culture of Formalism? Martti Koskenniemi and the Virtues' (2013) 27 Temple Intl and Comp LJ 417; Martti Koskenniemi, 'Between Commitment and Cynicism: Outline for a Theory of International Law as Practice' in *Collection of Essays by Legal Advisers of States, Legal Advisers of International Organizations and Practitioners in the Field of International Law* (United Nations 1999) 495.

[90] See, eg, *Lochner v New York* [1905] 198 US 45, 74–76 (Holmes J dissenting). See also Richard A Primus, 'Canon, Anti-Canon, and Judicial Dissent' (1998) 48 Duke LJ 243, 273–74 ("He was no classical formalist, but the greatest of his redeemed dissents—Lochner—presents itself as the very opposite of an opinion grounded in the practical consequences it would engender").

## 5. Conclusion

Legal realism and cognitive-behavioral studies share an interest in studying empirically how individuals think and behave. For both, focusing on the actual people who practice, argue about, interpret, and implement international law is essential to explaining how international law works. The two approaches can thus mutually enrich one another, albeit in different ways. For cognitive-behavioral studies, international law offers a rich vein of material to analyze; for international legal realism, cognitive-behavioral studies offer substantive insights that can help explain how international law develops, is interpreted, and affects behavior. Marrying legal realism's empiricism and pragmatism with cognitive-behavioral studies' rigor can thus be powerful and seductive.

Nevertheless, the two approaches remain distinct. On the one hand, cognitive-behavioral studies are interested in much more than legal behavior. On the other, international legal realism is open to many different modes and levels of analysis. In explaining the international legal process, cognitive-behavioral processes may in some cases be important factors; but in other cases, other causal factors may play a greater role, such as the structure of international society, the role of power and of doctrine, the social training of international lawyers, and so forth.

International legal realists must thus resist the enchantment of cognitive-behavioral studies' tools and empirical results, lest they surrender their characteristic pluralism, openness, and capacity for self-critique. Cognitive science can and should be an important part of international legal realism, but not the whole. It is when partnered rather than merged that the two can contribute most significantly and profoundly.

# 3

# Constructivism, Interpretation, and Cognitive Studies

*Ian Johnstone and Arun Mohan Sukumar**

## 1. Introduction

This chapter considers how cognitive studies can inform and augment constructivist approaches to international law. Our starting point is the constructivist insight that states (the principal creators and subjects of international law), like individuals, are social entities. Just as socio-cultural factors impact individual cognition,[1] the identity and behavior of states are determined in part by the social context (or structure) in which they are situated and by their interactions with other states. As the Introduction to this volume points out, cognitive processes can be explained at the individual level and at the social level. The first draws on psychology as well as neuroscience and focuses on a particular decision-maker's behavioral processes; the second draws on sociology and emphasizes the social cognition of individuals that is conditioned both by interpersonal and inter-group relations.[2] Although constructivist international relations theory is rooted in sociology, both perspectives are relevant to our analysis. Indeed, there is a complex relationship between psychological and sociological approaches to the understanding of how international law operates[3]—not least because how we think and act cannot be understood apart from the social interactions that have nurtured them.[4] In other words,

* We would like to thank Anne van Aaken and Moshe Hirsch for their thoughtful comments on a draft of this chapter, as well as Robert Howse who served as a discussant at the workshop where it was first presented. We would also like to thank the other participants in that workshop, whose comments and own presentations helped us to sharpen our thinking. We are grateful to Tommy van Steen for offering insights into cognitive science research. Finally, Fletcher School students Akshaya Mohan and Padmini Subhashree were instrumental in editing the final draft.

[1] Moshe Hirsch, 'Cognitive Sociology, Social Cognition and Coping with Racial Discrimination in International Law' (2019) 30 EJIL 1319–38.

[2] Van Aaken and Hirsch, Introduction to this volume, p 4.

[3] Anne van Aaken, 'Behavioral International Law and Economics' (2014) 55 HILJ 421; Tomer Broude, 'Behavioral International Law' (2015) 163 U Pa L Rev 1099; Moshe Hirsh, 'Social Cognitive Studies, Sociological Theory and International Law' in Andrea Bianchi and Moshe Hirsch (eds), *International Law's Invisible Frames: Social Cognition and Knowledge Production in International Legal Processes* (OUP 2021), 15–34.

[4] Robert Jervis, *Perception and Misperception in International Politics* (new edn, Princeton UP 2017) xxix.

Ian Johnstone and Arun Mohan Sukumar, *Constructivism, Interpretation, and Cognitive Studies* In: *International Legal Theory and the Cognitive Turn*. Edited by: Anne van Aaken and Moshe Hirsch, Oxford University Press.
 DOI: 10.1093/9780198909293.003.0004

how ideas, beliefs, and biases are formed is not a purely neurocognitive process but rather the result of interaction within and among social groups.

A central feature of that interaction is communication. Just as the relationship between individuals is impacted by communicative behavior, so is the relationship between states. States send signals to one another, they negotiate, they argue, and they engage in diplomatic conversation—sometimes hostile, sometimes friendly. Often that diplomatic conversation is about international law—how it is made, interpreted, and implemented. Occasionally it occurs in a courtroom. Often, it occurs in less formal settings. Accordingly, the central question this chapter seeks to answer is how cognitive studies can help to explain the argumentative and interpretive behavior of states and other international actors in a decentralized legal system.

Our central argument is that findings from research into the working of the human mind and inter-group relations help explain how the institutional environment in which rules are developed and interpreted shapes opinions and legal positions of states; and how practitioners who are part of this environment respond to certain stimuli. While we acknowledge the theoretical and practical obstacles to "getting inside the minds" of states, we identify avenues for improving the design of legal regimes and institutions to address biases and heuristics associated with individual and group decision-making. In particular, we focus on mechanisms that stimulate reasoned deliberation as opposed to purely intuitive and/or "automatic" cognition in global governance institutions.

The chapter is structured as follows. We begin in the next section by explaining how a key element of constructivist international relations theory—socialization—has impacted legal theory, highlighting the "logic of argumentation." In Section 3, we examine the practice of legal interpretation, which we conceive as an intersubjective enterprise situated within a particular type of "community of practice," namely interpretive communities. In Section 4, we highlight how key concepts from cognitive studies can help to illuminate that practice. In Section 5, we present a case study of cybersecurity regime-building. In Section 6, we briefly describe some of the limitations of the cognitive turn.

## 2. Social Constructivism and International Law

Because constructivist theory is built around how people construct their views of the world, insights from psychology and social cognition have much to offer. Social constructivism emerged as a response to the rational choice model embodied by structural realism and neo-liberal institutionalism.[5] These theorists do not reject

[5] John Ruggie, *Constructing the World Polity: Essays on International Institutionalization* (Routledge 1998).

"rationalism" but claim that it is incomplete. It does not explain how interests come to be defined or change, and it has little to say about the power of norms and ideas. Nor does it account for the importance of identity.[6]

Constructivists argue that the international system is shaped not only by material capabilities (military might, economic and natural resources) but also by social relationships between states and individuals. Because social relations and historical circumstances "construct" the international system, it is not immutable and can evolve over time.

Beyond that, three core insights are associated with social constructivist international relations (IR) theory. First, there is a mutually constitutive relationship between structure and agent: agents constitute the structure and the structure in turn constitutes the agent.[7] A simplistic application of this insight to international institutions is that states (as agents) create international organizations (the structure) and those institutions in turn impact not only how states calculate their interests but also how they define their interests and even identities. As collections of institutions and individuals, the "identity" of a state is a reflection of identities and interests of those institutions and individuals, and how they interact with each other.

Second, the nature of the relationship between states is constituted by shared knowledge, understandings, and expectations. Material resources have no *inherent* impact on international relations; they acquire meaning for action through the beliefs or understandings states hold about them. In Alexander Wendt's famous example, a state draws no particular conclusions about another state's behavior based *solely* on the number of nuclear weapons it has.[8] Five hundred British nuclear missiles are less threatening to the United States than ten North Korean ones. The relevance and impact of nuclear weapons depends on the structure of the relationship between the US and the UK, on the one hand, and the US and North Korea, on the other. In other words, states have certain perceptions and ideas about each other. The nature of the relationship between states, whether cooperative or hostile, is defined in part by those ideas.

Third, norms matter. Norms, in international relations theory, are defined as accepted standards of behavior for actors with a given identity.[9] They are intersubjective standards, accepted not by each actor individually (subjectively) or based on objective criteria or some ideal of appropriateness, but "intersubjectively" in the sense that they are shared and collectively understood by those who inhabit

[6] Martha Finnemore and Kathryn Sikkink, 'International Norm Dynamics and Political Change' (1998) 52 Intl Org 887, 902–05.

[7] Alexander Wendt, 'Anarchy Is What States Make of It: The Social Construction of Power Politics' (1992) 46 Intl Org 391, 399.

[8] Alexander Wendt, 'Constructing International Politics' (1995) 20 Intl Sec 71, 73.

[9] Peter Katzenstein, 'Introduction: Alternative Perspectives on National Security' in Peter Katzenstein (ed), *The Culture of National Security* (Columbia UP 1996), 1–32; Finnemore and Sikkink (n 6) 887.

the same social world.[10] Norms may be rooted in interests but take on a life of their own, impacting behavior independent from the exercise of material power or calculation of interests.

Those features of social constructivism resonate with multiple streams of international legal theory. Jutta Brunnée and Stephen Toope provide a good summary of the "state of the art" on constructivist international law (IL)/IR theory and apply some of the same insights.[11] These include the New Haven School,[12] transnational legal process,[13] acculturation,[14] practice theory,[15] and theories about legal discourse and argumentation.[16] More recent contributions focus on contestation in the development of norms[17] and pluralism in international law.[18] Moshe Hirsch, in collaboration with colleagues, has offered a comprehensive account of sociological approaches to international law.[19]

It is beyond the scope of this chapter to review all constructivist international legal theories. However, a thread that runs through them is socialization as an explanation for compliance. States comply with the law because, through interaction in the international legal system, they become socialized to and internalize its norms. By way of contrast, the enforcement model stipulates that "deep" compliance (behavior that would not happen but for the legal rule) depends heavily upon

[10] Here we are speaking about "norms" as a concept, not the extent to which a particular norm is actually shared or intersubjectively understood. Of course, if it is not shared at all, then, by definition, it would not be a norm as that term is used in IR theory (an "accepted standard or behavior").

[11] Jutta Brunnée and Stephen J Toope, 'Constructivism in International Law' in Jeffrey L Dunoff and Mark A Pollack (eds), *Interdisciplinary Perspectives on International Law and Relations: The State of the Art* (CUP 2012), 119–45.

[12] Myres S McDougal, Harold D Lasswell, and James C Miller, *The Interpretation of Agreements and World Public Order: Principles of Content and Procedure* (Yale UP 1967); W Michael Reisman and Andrew R Willard, *International Incidents: The Law That Counts in World Politics* (Princeton UP 1988).

[13] See Chapter 7 by Regina Jefferies in this volume. See also Harold Hongju Koh, 'Why Do Nations Obey International Law?', review of Abram Chayes and Antonia Handler Chayes, *The New Sovereignty: Compliance with International Regulatory Agreements* (Harvard UP 1995) and Thomas M Franck, *Fairness in International Law and Institutions* (Clarendon Press 1995).

[14] Ryan Goodman and Derek Jinks, 'How to Influence States: Socialization and International Human Rights Law' (2004) 54 Duke LJ 621.

[15] Jutta Brunnée and Stephen J Toope, *Legitimacy and Legality in International Law* (CUP 2013); Jens Meierheinrich, 'The Practice of International Law: A Theoretical Analysis' (2014) 76 LCP 1.

[16] Ian Johnstone, *The Power of Deliberation: International Law, Politics and Organizations* (OUP 2011); Ian Johnstone and Steven Ratner (eds), *Talking International Law* (OUP 2021); Abram Chayes and Antonia Handler Chayes, *The New Sovereignty: Compliance with International Regulatory Agreements* (Harvard UP 1998); Thomas M Franck, *Fairness in International Law and Institutions* (OUP 1998).

[17] Nicole Dietelhoff and Lisbeth Zimmermann, 'Things We Lost in the Fire: How Different Types of Contestation Affect the Robustness of International Norms' (2020) 22 Intl Stud Rev 51; Anette Stimmer, 'Beyond Internalization: Alternate Endings of the Norm Life Cycle' (2019) 63 Intl Stud Q 270.

[18] Anthea Roberts and others (eds), *Comparative International Law* (OUP 2018); Nico Krisch, 'Global Legal Pluralism' in Jeffrey L Dunoff and Mark A Pollack (eds), *International Legal Theory: Foundations and Frontiers* (CUP 2022), 240–58.

[19] Moshe Hirsch, 'Core Sociological Theories and International Law' in Moshe Hirsch and Andrew Lang (eds), *Research Handbook on the Sociology of International Law* (Elgar 2018) 389 and 403.

fear of sanctions.[20] Also by way of contrast, rational choice theory holds that compliance is the result of a cost–benefit analysis, in which states compare the benefits of reneging from a commitment with two kinds of cost: short-term loss as result of the other side reneging in response and longer-term reputational costs.

What does it mean to say states "internalize" the law? It may refer to what goes on in the minds of individual decision-makers. For example, having invested time and energy in the negotiation, adoption, and implementation of a treaty, government officials (leaders, diplomats, legislators, and bureaucrats) may genuinely come to believe in the value of the norms contained therein. Thomas Franck claimed that legitimate rules exert a "compliance pull" separate from any instrumental benefits that may accrue from playing by the rules.[21] He did not probe the precise causal mechanisms behind this compliance pull, but his use of the term "legitimacy" is revealing. In its sociological sense, a rule is legitimate if those subject to the rule believe it to be worthy of support. The compliance pull, therefore, is tied to an internalized belief in the merits of the rule rather than to the fear of punishment for breaking it.

Alternatively, socialization may result in the rules becoming internalized in domestic systems. Transnational legal process focuses not on what goes on in the heads of elites but rather on how the law becomes embedded in political, bureaucratic, and judicial routines.[22] This occurs through the adoption of implementing legislation and through more informal processes. Busy politicians and bureaucrats do not wake up each morning asking themselves whether or not it is in their country's interest to comply with a particular international legal obligation. Occasionally, high-level officials and decision-makers may ask themselves precisely that question, but those are unusual cases, not habitual. Compliance is the default position. Habits can be broken, but not easily.

"Acculturation" theory is a variation on the theme of internalization. It holds that, before decision-makers come to believe in the value of a norm (or even if they never do), they may "mimic" compliant behavior out of a desire to secure status among a valued reference group.[23] Ryan Goodman and Derek Jinks argue that states, as social organizations, have a tendency toward "isomorphism"; that is, they emulate standardized models of structural organization.[24] The authors claim the extent of isomorphism across states can only be explained by acculturation as opposed to coercion and persuasion. They do not specify exactly how acculturation functions, but suggest three possibilities: government leaders are directly

[20] George W Downs, David M Rocke and Peter N Barsoom, 'Is the Good News about Compliance Good News about Cooperation?' (1996) 50(3) Intl Org 379; Jack L Goldsmith and Eric A Posner, *The Limits of International Law* (OUP 2006).

[21] Thomas M Franck, *Fairness in International Law and Institutions* (OUP 1995).

[22] Koh (n 13) and Franck (n 13) 2599.

[23] Goodman and Jinks (n 14) 641.

[24] Goodman and Jinks (n 14) 648.

acculturated; members of special interest groups are acculturated (and they in turn persuade government leaders and domestic audiences); domestic audiences are acculturated (and they persuade or coerce government leaders).

Finally, a strand of the constructivist literature that has a direct bearing on the interpretation of international law concerns the "logic of arguing." Friedrich Kratochwil, Thomas Risse, Harald Müller, and other IR theorists draw on Habermas' theory of communicative action to posit a logic of arguing, separate from but related to the logics of consequences and appropriateness.[25] In rational choice theory (the logic of consequences), arguments are used strategically in order to win instrumental benefits, such as allied support for a given policy. In constructivist theory, argumentation is a device for arriving at intersubjective understandings about what constitutes appropriate behavior (the logic of appropriateness). The purpose of arguing is not only to win support but to try to persuade others of the merits of a particular course of action. In Habermas' ideal of communicative action, it also means being open to persuasion, to changing one's mind in response to "the force of the better argument."[26] From the perspective of international legal practice, legal discourse is a highly structured type of argumentation whose conventions are widely understood and accepted within the discipline.

## 3. Legal Interpretation and Interpretive Communities

Section 2 introduced three concepts: identity, socialization, and argumentation. All three are relevant to an essential feature of the practice of law at any level—interpretation—which itself is a cognitive process. In this section we explain what makes them especially relevant in the international legal system, focusing on the role of interpretive communities, a particular type of community of practice. We begin by explaining the centrality of interpretation to the functioning of the international legal system. We then describe the role of interpretive communities in that system. The section concludes by asking whether, globally, there is one interpretive community or many.

[25] Friedrich V Kratochwil, *Rules, Norms and Decisions: On the Conditions of Practical and Legal Reasoning in International Relations and Domestic Affairs* (CUP 1989); Thomas Risse, '"Let's Argue!": Communicative Action in World Politics' (2000) 54 Intl Org 1; Harald Müller, 'Arguing, Bargaining and All That: Communicative Action, Rationalist Theory and the Logic of Appropriateness in International Relations' (2004) 10 Eur J Int Relat 395. The logics of consequences and appropriateness were introduced by James G March and Johan Olsen, *Rediscovering Institutions: The Organizational Basis of Politics* (The Free Press 1989). For an explanation of the connection between the logic of arguing and international legal interpretation, see Johnstone (n 16) 20–27.

[26] Jürgen Habermas, *The Theory of Communicative Action* (Thomas McCarthy tr, vol 1 and 2, Beacon Press 1985).

## 3.1. Law as interpretation

Legal dispute settlement is fundamentally an exercise in interpretation. At the domestic level, interpretation typically occurs in courts. While some international legal disputes are settled through judicial or quasi-judicial means, many never find their way to a courtroom. In a decentralized legal system, the principal interpreters are government officials and lawyers who are institutionally and politically predisposed to interpretations that favor their government or state. As such, they are motivated by their positions to reach a particular conclusion.[27] How then is it even possible to speak of authoritative interpretation? Without an independent third-party arbiter, interpretation would seem to be an entirely subjective, self-interested enterprise and the quest for authoritative interpretation a fool's errand.

An alternative (constructivist) perspective is that interpretation of international law is intersubjective. It occurs through a process of discursive interaction that seeks to ascertain what the law means to the lawmakers (states) collectively rather than to any one of them individually or in the abstract. That is not to suggest legal discourse is simply the search for negotiated agreement on what the law means. Rather, it is a social-cognitive exercise that operates on the basis of a common frame of reference and accepted methodological approaches for uncovering the meaning of the disputed term.

Moreover, constructivist-inspired legal theorists see the lines between making, interpreting, and inducing compliance with the law as blurry.[28] Interpretation often involves refining, elaborating, or stretching the meaning of a term. Just as customary law develops through the practice of states and the reactions of other states to that practice, arguments about whether a particular incident or act complies with treaty law may constitute incremental expansion or modification of the law, even if framed as authoritative interpretation of a text (such as the United Nations (UN) Charter). In other words, new law is made through the process of (re-)interpreting and assessing compliance with existing law.

Where does this argumentation about interpretation occur? As noted above, it sometimes occurs in courtrooms, with lawyers on each side seeking to persuade judges of the merits of their interpretation, and with judges (on multi-judge panels) seeking to persuade each other. It also occurs in quasi-judicial settings (such as the UN Human Rights Committee), inter-governmental political bodies (such as the UN Security Council), negotiating forums, bilateral diplomatic exchanges (private and public), government policy documents and statements, domestic legislatures and bureaucracies, classrooms and academic journals, and the op-ed pages

[27] On "motivated reasoning," see Jervis (n 4) lxxiv.

[28] See, eg, Brunnée and Toope (n 15); Koh (n 13); Ian Johnstone, 'Law-Making by International Organizations: Perspectives from International Law/International Relations Theory' in Jeffrey Dunoff and Mark A Pollack (eds), *Interdisciplinary Perspectives on International Law and International Relations: The State of the Art* (CUP 2013), 266–92.

of newspapers.[29] It may occur among practitioners such as peacekeepers and humanitarian actors who, in the course of their operational work, engage in legal discourse. The key point is that all professional interpreters are situated. Texts do not have meanings before they are encountered in situations; the meanings they have are always a function of the circumstances in which they are encountered.[30]

## 3.2. The role of interpretive communities

How then are authoritative interpretations rendered? In this diffuse interpretive process, how are good legal claims distinguished from bad? The question is important because if there is no way of making that distinction, what would be the point of making a legal argument in a non-judicial setting? It is not required in the UN Security Council, for example. Yet, presumably some purpose is served or you would not hear such arguments. The purpose may be to win international support for a policy or action; it may be to neutralize domestic opposition against the action; it may serve to preserve a reputation for living up to one's commitments. None of those purposes would be served if every argument is as good as any other. Logic tells us there must be some mechanism for distinguishing good from bad legal claims. As one of us has argued elsewhere, that mechanism is the interpretive community.[31]

Framed that way, an interpretive community is an abstract concept whose existence can be inferred from the ubiquity of legal discourse outside of courtrooms. Who belongs to a particular interpretive community cannot be specified with precision. It is an amorphous constellation of actors that shares the assumptions, categories of understanding, and conventions that make reasoned argumentation about the meaning of a text possible.[32] The interpretive community sets the parameters for acceptable discourse and passes judgment on what constitutes the correct (or at least best) interpretation of the law. "Correctness" is not based on objective criteria but rather is the outcome of an intersubjective, discursive process.[33] If the

[29] Johnstone and Ratner (n 16).

[30] Stanley Fish, 'Fish v. Fiss' (1984) 36 Stan L Rev 1325. See also Andrea Bianchi, 'Reflexive Butterfly Catching: Insights from a Situated Catcher' in Joost Pauwelyn and others (eds), *Informal International Lawmaking* (OUP 2012) 200.

[31] Ian Johnstone, 'Treaty Interpretation: The Authority of Interpretive Communities' (1991) 12 Mich J Intl L 371; Johnstone (n 16) 20.

[32] Johnstone (n 16) 20, 7.

[33] Johnstone and Ratner (n 16) 7; Ingo Venzke, *How Interpretation Makes International Law: On Semantic Change and Normative Twists* (OUP 2012) 366. For an early exchange on the power of interpretive communities at the domestic level, see Owen Fiss, 'Objectivity and Interpretation' (1982) 34 Stan L Rev 739; Fish (n 30). For a recent comment on how cognitive biases and heuristics may affect treaty interpretation, see Anne van Aaken, 'The Cognitive Psychology of Rules of Interpretation on International Law' (2021) 115 AJIL 158 and see Jean d'Aspremont, 'The Multidimensional Process of Interpretation: Content-Determination and Law-Ascertainment Distinguished' in Andrea Bianchi, Daniel Peat, and Matthew Windsor (eds), *Interpretation in International Law* (OUP 2015) 111, 114.

interpretive community is able to pass a relatively cohesive judgment—in other words, if the weight of international legal opinion leans heavily in one direction—that can have an impact on future compliance (by impacting reputation) and may also contribute to the development of the law (by giving content to and extending the existing rules).

The idea of an interpretive community has taken hold in a modest body of legal literature.[34] Meanwhile, a larger parallel body of international relations literature on 'communities of practice' (CoPs) has emerged. CoPs are collectives of actors and institutions characterized by "mutual engagement, a joint enterprise, and a shared repertoire of words, gestures, tools, stories, symbols and ways of doing things."[35] This "shared repertoire" of practices—the most important and distinguishing aspect of CoPs—is what members use to communicate, bargain, or argue with each other. Unlike epistemic communities, CoPs do not have "shared causal beliefs";[36] that is, their participants do not necessarily agree on the goals of their joint enterprise. Instead, CoPs are simply characterized by "shared values and identities," "many-sided and direct relations," and "a degree of long-term interest" in pursuing said enterprise.[37]

The concept of community of practice draws heavily from a core tenet of "practice theory" advanced by sociologists such as Pierre Bourdieu and Anthony Giddens, namely that the practices of institutions reflect, organize, and tacitly reinforce the background beliefs and dispositions of its participants. Bourdieu labeled these background beliefs and dispositions the *habitus*, a cognitive structure.[38] The dispositions are so deeply ingrained that they operate largely below the conscious level.[39] They give participants in the community of practice a "sense of what is to be done in a given situation"—a "feel for the 'game.'"[40]

Bourdieu's *habitus* echoes Jürgen Habermas' common lifeworld: "a collective supply of interpretations [actors have] of the world and themselves, as provided by language, a common history or culture."[41] In similar terms, Ludwig Wittgenstein speaks of "know- how," a kind of knowledge that can only be acquired through

[34] For a review of literature on legal interpretive communities, see Johnstone (n 16) 33–41. For later writing on the concept, see the following chapters in Andrea Bianchi, Daniel Peat, and Matthew Windsor (eds), *Interpretation in International Law* (OUP 2015): d'Aspremont (n 33); Michael Waibel, 'Interpretive Communities in International Law'; and René Provost, 'Interpretation in International Law as a Transcultural Project'.

[35] Etienne Wenger, *Communities of Practice: Learning, Meaning, and Identity* (CUP 1999).

[36] Peter M Haas, 'Introduction: Epistemic Communities and International Policy Coordination' (1992) 46(1) Intl Org 1, 3.

[37] Emanuel Adler and Michael Barnett, 'A Framework for the Study of Security Communities' in Emanuel Adler and Michael Barnett (eds), *Security Communities* (CUP 1998) 29.

[38] See generally Anna Leander, 'Habitus and Field', *Oxford Research Encyclopedia of International Studies* (2010).

[39] Van Aaken and Hirsch, Introduction to this volume, p 4.

[40] Pierre Bourdieu, *Practical Reason: On the Theory of Action* (Stanford UP 1998) 25.

[41] Habermas (n 41) 209.

practice.[42] John Searle calls it "background knowledge."[43] Whatever the label, it connotes a socially acquired set of ingrained dispositions that guide how we think, speak, and act.

The idea of CoPs has begun receiving serious consideration by legal scholars who write about interpretation but do not necessarily use the term interpretive community.[44] Some have been studying the potential impact of legal practices[45] and institutional environments[46] on interpretations of the law. Jutta Brunnée and Stephen Toope have developed a full-blown "interactional theory of international law" that engages with the work of IR scholars on CoPs.[47] In developing the concept of "judicial habitus," Salvatore Caserta and Mikael Rask Madsen borrow another idea from Bourdieu, namely "capital." In simple terms, "capital" can be understood as competences.[48] Judges are seen to have the competence to interpret the law. That competence depends in part on the authority that comes with the office, but not entirely. They may also have what the authors call "legal academic capital, capitals derived from engagement in diplomacy and politics, and capitals derived from engagement in legal practice as attorneys."[49] Those "capitals" are not exclusive to judges. Other members of the interpretive community also possess them, to varying degrees.

## 3.3. One interpretive community or many?

Thus, a legal interpretive community is a community of practice forged around the enterprise of interpretation of the law. Above we spoke of a relatively cohesive

[42] Ludwig Wittgenstein, *Philosophical Investigations* (GEM Anscombe tr, Basil Blackwell 1968). See also Vincent Pouliot, 'The Logic of Practicality: A Theory of Practice of Security Communities' (2008) 62 Intl Org, 257, 255, 269.

[43] John Searle, *Expression and Meaning: Studies in the Theory of Speech Acts* (CUP 2011) 1, 4.

[44] See, eg, Jens Meierheinrich, 'The Practice of International Law: A Theoretical Analysis' (2014) 76 LCP 1; Jakob vH Holtermann, Mikael Madsen, and Nora Stappert, 'Legal Validity and the Importance of Epistemology for Research on Legal Norms' in Phil Orchard and Antje Wiener (eds), *Contesting the World: Norm Research in Theory and Practice* (forthcoming).

[45] Nikolas M Rajkovic, Tanja E Aalberts, and Thomas Gammeltoft-Hansen, 'Introduction: Legality, Interdisciplinarity and the Study of Practices' in Nikolas M Rajkovic, Tanja E Aalberts, and Thomas Gammeltoft-Hansen (eds), *The Power of Legality: Practices of International Law and Their Politics* (CUP 2016) 1.

[46] Karen J Alter, Laurence R Helfer and Mikael Rask Madsen, 'How Context Shapes the Authority of International Courts' (2015) 79 LCP 1; Jeffrey L Dunoff and Mark A Pollack, 'Practice Theory and International Law' in Moshe Hirsch and Andrew Lang (eds), *Research Handbook on the Sociology of International Law* (Elgar 2018) 252.

[47] Brunnée and Toope (n 15).

[48] Pierre Bourdieu and Loïc JD Wacquant, *An Invitation to Reflexive Sociology* (The University of Chicago Press 1992) 97. See also Chapter 10 by Mikael Rask Madsen and Salvatore Caserta in this volume.

[49] Scholars studying the professional traits of judges employ different categories. The three categories of capitals suggested are derived from a mapping of all international judges since the establishment of the Permanent Court of International Justice in 1922. See also Madsen and Caserta (n 48).

interpretive community that renders relatively coherent legal judgment on a particular act or incident, but what if the interpretive community is divided? What if there is not one interpretive community but many, each with their own background assumptions and cognitive frames?[50]

International legal scholars debate whether the "college of international lawyers" is *invisible* or *divisible*.[51] Oscar Schachter coined the term "invisible college" years ago to suggest that, regardless of where international lawyers are trained or work, they speak the same language—the language of law.[52] That gives international law its coherence and its constraining power. More recently, a group of self-described "comparative international law" scholars counter that there is no single "college" but many colleges characterized by fundamentally different approaches to international law.[53] Their claim is not simply that Chinese and Russian lawyers *interpret* the law differently from European, African, or American lawyers but that they have different and incompatible views on the sources of law and processes of interpretation.

A similar debate has been playing out over the fragmentation of international law into specialized areas: trade, environment, human rights, health, law of the sea, and so on. Moshe Hirsch in this volume argues that the "cultural cognitive" stream of sociology projects an image of international law as profoundly fragmented, with international legal decision-makers perceiving the legal order differently.[54] The concern is not about the existence of specialized areas of law *per se* but about the notion that there is no overarching mechanism or principle of international law to resolve conflicts among the fields.[55] If the divergences and conflicts between the discrete bodies become so great, one wonders, as Paul Stephan does, whether "the concept of international law retains any meaning" at all.[56]

Whether the question is about different parts of the world or different issue areas, delving into the cognitive sociology within and among communities of international lawyers can help to answer whether the "invisible college" metaphor still has traction.

[50] d'Aspremont (n 33).

[51] See Madsen and Caserta (n 48).

[52] Oscar Schachter, 'The Invisible College of International Lawyers' (1977–78) 72(2) NWULR 217; Johnstone (n 31).

[53] Harlan Grant Cohen, 'Finding International Law: Rethinking the Doctrine of Sources' (2007) 93 Iowa L Rev 65; Anthea Roberts and others (eds), *Comparative International Law* (OUP 2018).

[54] See Chapter 9 by Moshe Hirsch in this volume, Section 4.2.4.

[55] International Law Commission, 'Report of the Study Group on "Fragmentation of International Law: Difficulties Arising from the Diversification and Expansion of International Law"' (April 13, 2006), UNGA Doc A/CN.4/L.682, para 8.

[56] Paul B Stephan, 'Comparative International Law, Foreign Relations Law and Fragmentation: Can the Center Hold?' in Anthea Roberts and others (eds), *Comparative International Law* (OUP 2018) 63.

## 4. Interpretation: Insights from Psychology and Cognitive Sociology

In this section, we introduce a number of insights from cognitive studies that shed light on legal interpretation. The four clusters we consider are by no means exhaustive of the complex relationships between constructivist theory, interpretive processes, and cognition theories. Our purpose is simply to explore how several prominent ideas in cognitive studies can illuminate what is essentially a cognitive process: interpretation. The four clusters are dual-process cognition; groupthink; shared framing; and anchoring and adjustment. These insights from psychology and cognitive sociology not only explain the role of legal interpretation in global governance forums but also offer ways of thinking about regime design to overcome common problems of cooperation.

### 4.1. Dual-process cognition

Theorists of social cognition distinguish between "fast" and "slow" thinking.[57] The first involves the rapid, effortless, and largely unconscious processing of information; the second is slower, more deliberate, and self-conscious.[58] The distinction has implications for the cognitive functioning of CoPs, legal or otherwise. The dispositions and "know-how" of a legal interpretive community are what constrains idiosyncratic and unconventional interpretations, setting the boundaries of acceptable discourse. If those dispositions and habits of mind are deeply enough ingrained, certain modes of argument and substantive positions come to feel like common sense and trip off the tongue almost unthinkingly. Yet what seems like common sense within one interpretive community may not seem that way to another. In a pandemic, a health or human rights lawyer may view the scope of intellectual property rights very differently from that of a trade lawyer. An Indian lawyer may have a different view from an American one.

Participation in the decentralized international legal system, as noted above, is often discursive—a "diplomatic conversation" that includes explanation and justification, persuasion and dissuasion, approval and condemnation, on the basis of

[57] Daniel Kahneman and Amos Tversky, two economists who developed the model, call it System 1 and 2 thinking. Daniel Kahneman, *Thinking, Fast and Slow* (Farrar, Straus and Giroux 2013). Richard Thaler and Cass Sunstein call it automatic and reflexive thinking. Richard H Thaler and Cass R Sunstein, *Nudge: The Final Edition* (Penguin Books 2021) 47.

[58] On the two modes of cognition, see Vanina Leschziner, 'Dual-Process Models in Sociology' in Wayne H Brekhus and Gabe Ignatow (eds), *The Oxford Handbook of Cognitive Sociology* (OUP 2019), 169–91. On applications to international law, see Hirsh (n 3) 6; Benedikt Pirker and Jennifer Smolka, 'The Future of International Law Is Cognitive: International Law, Cognitive Sociology and Cognitive Pragmatics' (2019) 20 German LJ 430, 435.

law.[59] This discursive interaction can foster "System 2" (deliberate) thinking and perhaps even check the cognitive biases and heuristics associated with automatic cognition.[60] Indeed, a large body of literature on deliberative democracy is built on the basic proposition that the principled exchange of reasons (deliberation) is a way of ensuring all relevant considerations are taken into account, and irrelevant factors are seen for what they are.

Among the cognitive biases that deliberation (and deliberative thinking) can overcome is "fundamental attribution error."[61] People tend to over-attribute the actions of others to their personalities and identities than to situational factors.[62] This can be overcome by making people feel more accountable for their judgments. Drawing on the existing literature and an experiment he designed, Philip Tetlock found that if subjects know in advance that they will have to justify the judgments they make,

> [they] are more likely to rely on cognitively complex procedures in choosing among response alternatives, to display greater consistency and stability of judgment, to process persuasive messages in detail rather than to rely simply on their generalized evaluation of the source of the message, and to be more discriminating and responsive to evidence in evaluating others.[63]

This is consistent with the legal literature on "justificatory discourse."[64] The felt need to justify one's actions is an accountability mechanism in many international institutions (sometimes the only one). Understanding the cognitive processes at work and the socio-political roots of those processes can inform reform efforts. Opt-out clauses in law-making processes, for example, often include a requirement to explain why one is opting out. Similarly, the UN General Assembly (GA) recently approved, by a consensus, a requirement that a permanent member of the Security Council who exercises the veto power must immediately appear before the GA to explain why.[65] Whether this succeeds in inhibiting the use of the veto

[59] Abram Chayes and Antonia Handler Chayes, *The New Sovereignty: Compliance with International Regulatory Agreements* (Harvard UP 1995) 119.

[60] Moshe Hirsch, 'Cognitive Sociology, Social Cognition and Coping with Racial Discrimination in International Law' (2019) 30 EJIL 1319, 1327; see also Van Aaken and Hirsch, Introduction to this volume, p 8.

[61] Oxford Reference, 'Overview: Fundamental Attribution Error' (nd) <www.oxfordreference.com/display/10.1093/oi/authority.20110803095838476;jsessionid=D7DB9A088BA30DF38188 64BAC14BAEEA#:~:text=A%20pervasive%20tendency%20to%20underestimate,interpreting%20the%20behaviour%20of%20others>.

[62] Philip E Tetlock, 'Accountability: A Social Check on the Fundamental Attribution Error' (1985) 48(3) Soc Psychol Q 227.

[63] ibid 229.

[64] Chayes and Chayes (n 59); Johnstone (n 16).

[65] UNGA, 'Standing Mandate for a General Assembly Debate When a Veto Is Cast in the Security Council' (April 26, 2022) UN Doc A/77/L.52. Russia was required to do so twice.

remains to be seen, but at a minimum it shows respect to other member states by forcing the veto-wielding country to justify itself.[66]

Understanding dual-process thinking can also shed light on how participants in a community of practice change their minds. Given that practices tacitly (unreflexively) shape knowledge transmission and shared understandings, it is not clear when or how they ever get re-evaluated or rejected. One way to address this question is to examine the role of "feedback loops." Feedback loops provide real-time information to people that give them "an opportunity to change [their current course of] actions and push them towards better behavior."[67] If un-reflexive responses produce negative consequences, presumably that would provoke a rethinking of the response. Behavioral scientists note feedback loops are most effective when such information is presented in an intelligible manner, clearly conveying the options available to the individual in question.[68]

Moreover, one should not exaggerate the difference between System 1 and System 2 thinking. When faced with situations that look familiar and with which the practitioner has extensive expertise and accurate feedback, intuitive reactions may kick in. But in less familiar situations or when important new information comes to light, reflexive thinking in CoPs may be stimulated by feedback loops that allow states and non-state actors to deliberate and reassess the consequences of how a rule or norm was interpreted in the past. Such "loops" could take the form of review and monitoring mechanisms around the implementation of norms, or periodic meetings with NGOs and businesses, who are important actors within the CoP but may not be directly involved in the articulation or interpretation of rules. Feedback loops are understood in the behavioral science literature as conscious interventions to promote reflexive thinking, but reflexive thinking may also be the outcome of major exogenous shocks to interpretive or practice-oriented communities, prompting actors to re-evaluate closely held beliefs.[69]

## 4.2. Groupthink

"Groupthink," a term that found its way into international relations scholarship many years ago,[70] occurs when a group of people make bad decisions they would not otherwise make alone. It is spurred by a number of factors, including the urge

[66] John Rawls' publicity principle, cited by Richard H Thaler and Cass R Sunstein, *Nudge: The Final Edition* (Penguin Books 2021) 262.

[67] Thomas Goetz, 'Harnessing the Power of Feedback Loops', *WIRED* (June 19, 2011) <www.wired.com/2011/06/ff-feedbackloop>.

[68] ibid.

[69] See generally Giovanni Capoccia, 'Critical Junctures' in Orfeo Fioretos, Tulia G Falleti, and Adam Sheingate (eds), *The Oxford Handbook of Historical Institutionalism* (OUP 2016), 89–106.

[70] Irving L Janis, *Groupthink: Psychological Studies of Policy Decisions and Fiascoes* (2nd edn, Cengage Learning 1982); Jervis (n 4).

to conform, a desire for cohesiveness, an unwillingness to challenge the morality of members of the group, and the illusion of invulnerability.[71] It may create an echo chamber, having the effect of suppressing dissent and leading individuals to move toward more extreme versions of positions they held initially.[72] Groupthink is also associated with a suspicion of outsiders. Individuals want to be included in social groups and, once included, tend to trust those within the group more than others.[73] Richard Thaler and Cass Sunstein call this "identity-based cognition."[74] The underlying idea is that people are susceptible to social influence and have a desire to conform to the behavior of people with whom they identify.

Groupthink and some of the social cognition attributes associated with it are directly relevant to practice theorizing in international relations and international law. For example, social cognition theories can help explain why some words, actions, and gestures emerge as practices with intersubjective meaning. Insights from Communication Accommodation Theory (CAT)—which argues that individuals adapt their methods and manners of communication depending on the social setting or context they find themselves in—are particularly relevant in this regard.[75] CAT theorists have pointed out that the communicative practices of "low-power" individuals—that is, those with lower social, cultural, epistemic, or political status in a group setting—often tend to mimic those with higher status in order to obtain the latter's "social approval."[76] The motive for such linguistic accommodation, according to CAT, may be affective: "a desire for social approval from one's interlocutors, as a means to positively reinforce one's own personal and/or social identity."[77] Or it may be cognitive: "convergence to a common linguistic style often improves communicative effectiveness and has been associated with increased predictability of the other and, in turn ... increased mutual understanding."[78] For either or both reasons, the communicative interaction can smooth the way to shared meaning not

[71] Anne van Aaken and Tomer Broude, 'The Psychology of International Law: An Introduction' (2019) 30(4) EJIL 1225; see also Tomer Broude, 'Behavioral International Law' (2015) 163 U Pa L Rev 1099; Runar Hilleren Lie, 'The Influencers of International Investment Law: A Computational Study of ISDS Actors' Changing Behavior' (2022) 23 German LJ 350, 354; Veronika Fikfak, Daniel Peat, and Eva van der Zee, 'Bias in International Law' (2022) 23 German LJ 281, 285.

[72] Cass R Sunstein, 'The Law of Group Polarization' (1999) 91 Law and Economics Working Papers.

[73] Moshe Hirsch, 'Regulators' Mindsets, Ingroup Favoritism, and the National Treatment Obligation in World Trade Organization Law' (2022) 23(3) German LJ 298, 304, 309. There is evidence to suggest the psychological effect of exclusion is similar to physical pain; Kipling Williams, 'The Pain of Exclusion' (2011) 21 Sci Am Mind 30.

[74] Richard H Thaler and Cass R Sunstein, *Nudge: The Final Edition* (Penguin Books 2021) 75.

[75] Marko Dragojevic, Jessica Gasiorek, and Howard Giles, 'Accommodative Strategies as Core of the Theory' in Howard Giles (ed), *Communication Accommodation Theory: Negotiating Personal Relationships and Social Identities across Contexts* (CUP 2016) 36.

[76] Howard Giles, 'The Social Origins of CAT' in Howard Giles (ed), *Communication Accommodation Theory: Negotiating Personal Relationships and Social Identities across Contexts* (CUP 2016) 1.

[77] Marko Dragojevic, Jessica Gasiorek, and Howard Giles, 'Accommodative Strategies as Core of the Theory' in Howard Giles (ed), *Communication Accommodation Theory: Negotiating Personal Relationships and Social Identities across Contexts* (CUP 2016) 42.

[78] ibid 43.

only because of the quality of the information exchanged or persuasiveness of the arguments made but also because of the cognitive tendency toward convergence.

This idea of social approval gets to a deeper point about reputation, status, and how both relate to compliance with international law. This chapter has already alluded to the "acculturation" theory developed by Goodman and Jinks. Judith Kelly and Beth Simmons have done empirical work on performance indicators and rankings in international affairs, what they call "politics by numbers."[79] They conclude that states can be nudged in the direction of good behavior simply by being ranked on an index.[80] The reputational effects of social comparisons, it seems, apply to states as well as individuals. Teichman and Zamir add that the case for rankings and other forms of "nudging" is stronger at the international level than at the domestic level.[81] Because there is no global legislature or police force in the international sphere, techniques other than imposing binding, enforceable obligations are often needed to coax states into appropriate behavior. Of course, a reputation for "good behavior" is not the only kind of reputation a state cares about. A reputation for resolve may also be important, especially for states (and their leaders) that feel the need to preserve their credibility in the eyes of allies.[82] That will not always push in the direction of compliance. Either way, reputation is instrumental in the sense that what matters is the secondary benefits that go along with having a desirable reputation, whether it is future economic cooperation through treaties or the ability to maintain leadership of a defense alliance.

"Status" is related to but different from reputation as the latter term is used by rational choice theorists. For constructivist IL and IR theorists, status is tied to identity. Alistair Iain Johnston, in a seminal article, argues that "back-patting" can reinforce a state's identity and status, pushing it in the direction of pro-norm behavior.[83] Drawing on sociology and psychology, he describes the process as one of "pressure to conform."[84] From this perspective, status is not desired for instrumental reasons but as a good in itself—the psychological benefits to an actor that comes from a sense of self-worth.[85] Although the benefits are psychological, they depend on social affirmations of status, tied to association with a referent group

[79] Judith G Kelley and Beth A Simmons, 'Politics by Number: Indicators as Social Pressure in International Relations' (2014) 59 AJPS 55.

[80] See also Veronika Fikfak, Daniel Peat, and Eva van der Zee, 'Bias in International Law' (2022) 23 German LJ 281, 290.

[81] Doron Teichman and Eyal Zamir, 'Nudge Goes International' (2019) 30 EJIL 1263.

[82] Keren Yarhi-Milo, *Who Fights for Reputation: The Psychology of Leaders in International Conflict* (Princeton UP 2018); Joshua Kertzer, *Resolve in International Politics* (Princeton UP 2016). We'd like to thank Daniel Peat for drawing this literature to our attention.

[83] Alastair Iain Johnston, 'Treating International Institutions as Social Environments' (2001) 45 ISQ 487; see also Jeffrey T Checkel, 'Why Comply? Social Learning and European Identity Change' (2001) 55 Intl Org 553.

[84] Johnston (n 83).

[85] As Johnston explains, the strength of back-patting and praise depends on (a) one's self-categorization as a certain kind of actor and (b) which other actors, "by virtue of this self-identification, become important, legitimate observers of behavior" (ibid 501).

with whom one identifies or wishes to identify. This helps to explain the power of naming and shaming (or naming and praising), even when no material costs or benefits may follow.

### 4.3. Shared framing

The Introduction to this volume describes the importance of framing to the choices people make.[86] Defined as "generalized knowledge structures and abstract guidelines that assist people in understanding the world and forming expectations,"[87] frames exist in the minds of individuals, but socio-cultural factors explain how they come to be shared.[88] That sharing may come about through professionalization, for example indoctrination into the legal profession. It may also come about through shared experiences, for example participating in an international organization.

Framing matters to interpretation because it is a tool of persuasion. Whether a terrorist attack is framed in terms of the law on the use of force or as a criminal justice issue matters. Whether responding to an infectious outbreak is framed as global health law or human rights issue matters. Whether an innovative legal argument can be framed as a natural extension of existing law rather than an attempt to re-write the law matters.[89]

Moreover, how a legal issue is framed depends on the institutional context in which it is encountered. International organizations are the most concrete embodiment of that context. They are the "social environment" states inhabit.[90] From the perspective of practice theory, they are places where CoPs coalesce. From the perspective of legal theory, they are arenas for justificatory discourse—for legal claims to be made, defended, critiqued, and contested.

An important question is whether the discourse leads to socialization or whether it deepens polarization. As cognitive linguists Pirker and Smolka observe, using the language of law can have a socializing effect: "the existence of a limited number of ways of saying things—expressing rhetorical arguments and so on—is explained by the collective discursive socialization expressed by an individual."[91] Intensive interaction within institutions may even help to create Habermas'

[86] Van Aaken and Hirsch, Introduction to this volume, p 9.
[87] Andrea Bianchi and Moshe Hirsch (eds), *International Law's Invisible Frames: Social Cognition and Knowledge Production in International Legal Processes* (OUP 2021) 2.
[88] On the different meanings of framing, see Anne van Aaken and Jan-Philip Elm, 'Framing in and through International Law', in Bianchi and Hirsch (n 87), 35–54.
[89] Ian Johnstone, 'US-UN Relations after Iraq: The End of the World (Order) As We Know It?' (2004) 15 EJIL 813–38.
[90] Johnston (n 83) 502.
[91] Pirker and Smolska (n 58).

"common lifeworld."[92] A by-product of this socializing effect would be the intersubjective (shared) framing of legal disputes, reinforcing the cohesion of the interpretive community. According to this logic, participants in the discourse in and around the UN Security Council or the World Health Organization come to share an understanding of the legal issues that are at stake and a frame of reference for arguing about those issues. The background knowledge—the "know-how"—they share does not always produce agreement on a particular interpretation of the law, but it makes it possible for them to speak to one another rather than past one another.

This picture of convergence through discursive interaction is challenged by a stream of social cognition literature that highlights the role of power in struggles between rival social groups.[93] From this perspective, debates over the interpretation of legal terms are a quest for dominance. Any seemingly "authoritative interpretation" that comes out of the contestation is simply a semantic victory for one side over the other.[94] The victor, more often than not, will be the most materially powerful actor who can dictate how the debate is framed, whose voices will be heard, and the arguments that will be ruled as in or out of bounds. Or, if hegemony is understood in Gramscian terms, the semantic victory will go to the "technocrats," the legal and subject matter experts who dominate the debate. Expertise is important to many areas of law and policy, of course, but the cognitive tendency to defer to experts is misplaced if their decisions involve profound political and value choices dressed up as technocratic considerations.

## 4.4. Anchoring and adjustment

Insights from behavioral science and social cognition theories can help to explain how interaction between individuals (and states) generates intersubjective meanings. This is different from framing in that is it not about broad generalizations or mental constructs but specific meanings to be attributed to legal terms. Insights from cognitive science can help identify the micro-processes by which intersubjective legal formulations evolve, as well as offering scope for empirically analyzing such processes (eg through experimental testing).

The "anchoring and adjustment" bias, for example, may tell us a lot about how international law functions. Cognitively, people tend to anchor on what they know

[92] Corneliu Bjola, drawing on Habermas, speaks of an "institutional lifeworld." Corneliu Bjola, 'Legitimating the Use of Force in International Politics: A Communicative Action Perspective' (2005) 11(2) Eur J Int Relat 266.

[93] Moshe Hirsch and Andrew Lang, 'Introduction' in Moshe Hirsch and Andrew Lang (eds), *Research Handbook on the Sociology of International Law* (Elgar 2018) 5.

[94] Ingo Venzke, *How Interpretation Makes International Law: On Semantic Change and Normative Twists* (OUP 2012).

and then adjust from there. Ronald Dworkin's idea of "fit" illustrates the connection.[95] He described what common law judges do as akin to writing a chain novel, with each judge adding a chapter that extends beyond but fits with what has come before. Intersubjective legal interpretation is similar. When a new fact situation arises and government representatives engage in legal argumentation about whether existing law covers the situation, each will construct arguments that suit their government's interests but the more persuasive argument will be that which "fits" best with the law developed to that point. One "anchors" on existing interpretations and "adjusts" for new situations.

"Anchoring and adjustment" also helps to explain treaty-making processes. Governmental and inter-governmental officials often look to precedent when negotiating treaty terms. The negotiators of a treaty to end plastic pollution are looking to the Minamata Convention on Mercury, the Basel Convention on the Control of Transboundary Movements of Hazardous Wastes and their Disposal, and the Stockholm Convention on Persistent Organic Pollutants as models for implementation and financing mechanisms. There are good "rational design" explanations for this: if something has been tried in the past and we can learn from that experience, then why not? But there may also be cognitive reasons. The minds of negotiators naturally anchor on what they know in constructing new regimes rather than starting from scratch. Moreover, in trying to persuade others of the wisdom of an approach, it is useful to get them to focus on what is familiar rather than brand new. This may also have something to do with the status quo bias. People tend to attribute value to the status quo and default to it rather than expend energy to do something different.

## 5. Case Study: International Cybersecurity Governance

We offer the case study of the international cybersecurity regime as an example of how insights from psychology and social cognition theories could help explain the emergence of rules and intersubjective legal formulations in specialized domains of global governance. At the time of writing, there is no formal or authoritative mechanism at the UN or elsewhere to create rules for cyberspace. In its absence, a number of ad hoc inter-governmental[96] and

[95] Ronald Dworkin, *Law's Empire* (Harvard UP 1988).

[96] 'United Nations Group of Governmental Experts (UN GGE)', United Nations Office for Disarmament Affairs (nd) <https://disarmament.unoda.org/group-of-governmental-experts>; 'Developments in the Field of Information and Telecommunications in the Context of International Security', United Nations Office for Disarmament Affairs (nd) <https://disarmament.unoda.org/ict-security>; Open-Ended Working Group on Information and Communication Technologies, 'Open-Ended Working Group on Security of and in the use of Information and Communications Technologies', United Nations Office for Disarmament Affairs (2021) <http://meetings.unoda.org/open-ended-working-group-on-information-and-communication-technologies-2021>.

multistakeholder[97] entities have sought to fill the vacuum both by articulating voluntary norms of state behavior and offering their interpretations of how existing international law applies to cyberspace.[98]

The most prominent among these institutions is the UN Group of Governmental Experts (UN GGE) on cybersecurity, a small group of states that is composed of ten to twenty-five countries, including the five permanent members of the UN Security Council. The UN GGE, an ad hoc mechanism established in 2004, has been re-constituted six times over two decades, making it the longest-running institution of its kind since such expert groups were created by the UN in 1968.[99] With minimal guidance from the UNGA resolutions that established it, the UN GGE not only developed a set of stable practices around its deliberations and decision-making processes[100] but also developed a framework for "responsible state behavior in cyberspace" that comprised voluntary norms, application of existing rules to cyberspace, capacity-building efforts, and confidence-building measures (CBMs).[101] Indeed, the phrase "framework for responsible state behavior in cyberspace" has emerged as an intersubjective term-of-art within the cybersecurity norms processes.

It is worth highlighting the role of existing international law in the evolution of this framework of responsible behavior. Even though states, especially the great powers, differ in their views on how specific rules apply to their behavior in this domain, there is today a remarkable degree of overlap in the themes and arguments they address in various multilateral and multistakeholder forums pertaining to international cybersecurity governance. In other words, states and non-state actors know and recognize what they are talking about when they talk—and frequently disagree—about the application of international law to cyberspace. Legal concepts and interpretations on international cybersecurity issues carry

[97] 'Global Commission on the Stability of Cyberspace (GCSC)', The Hague Centre for Strategic Studies (nd) <https://hcss.nl/global-commission-on-the-stability-of-cyberspace-homepage>; The Paris Call for Trust and Security in Cyberspace (nd) <https://pariscall.international/en>; Let's Talk Cyber (nd) <https://letstalkcyber.org>; 'Community Talks on Cyber Diplomacy', Kaspersky (nd) <https://media.kaspersky.com/en/community-talks-on-cyber-diplomacy.pdf>.

[98] This section draws on findings from Arun Mohan Sukumar's dissertation, currently under contract to be published as a monograph. Michael N Schmitt (ed), *Tallinn Manual on the International Law Applicable to Cyber Warfare* (CUP Online 2013) <www.cambridge.org/core/books/tallinn-manual-on-the-international-law-applicable-to-cyber-warfare/50C5BFF166A7FED75B4EA643AC677DAE>; Michael N Schmitt (ed), *Tallinn Manual 2.0 on the International Law Applicable to Cyber Operations* (CUP Online 2017) <www.cambridge.org/core/books/tallinn-manual-20-on-the-international-law-applicable-to-cyber-operations/E4FFD83EA790D7C4C3C28FC9CA2FB6C9>; 'The Oxford Process on International Law Protections in Cyberspace', The Oxford Process (nd) <www.elac.ox.ac.uk/the-oxford-process>.

[99] VERTIC, 'Means to Reinforce Research on Nuclear Disarmament Verification: Report on a Series of Regional Conversations' 13 (2017) <www.vertic.org/media/assets/Publications/VM13.pdf>.

[100] Mark Raymond, 'Social Practices of Rule-Making for International Law in the Cyber Domain' (2021) 6(2) J Glob Secur Stud.

[101] UNGA, 'Group of Governmental Experts on Developments in the Field of Information and Telecommunications in the Context of International Security' (July 22, 2015) UN Doc A/70/174.

intersubjective meaning not only among Western or the so-called "like-minded" states comprising the United States, European Union, and some Asian states such as Japan and Singapore, but also among Chinese and Russian negotiators and lawyers.[102]

Following our elucidation of constructivist IL/IR theories in the first half of this chapter, we highlight below how the evolution of shared meanings of "international cyber law" could be analyzed through the lens of concepts used in cognitive science—especially community-centric concepts such as habitus and groupthink, as well as biases associated with anchoring and "mere exposure" effects. One way to explain this development is by thinking about legal discourse on international cybersecurity as being shaped and "regulated" by an interpretive community of international lawyers, private companies, diplomats, and NGOs, among others. Initiatives within the interpretive community that are designed explicitly to interpret international cyber law, such as the Tallinn Manuals and the Oxford Process, play a key role, of course. As Werner and Kessler have argued, the Tallinn Manuals "transform unstructured uncertainty into structured uncertainty"[103] and in the process become arbiters of the acceptability and merits of legal interpretation with respect to specific scenarios. But lawyers are not the only influential actors in determining parameters of acceptable legal discourse. The participation in various forms of non-legal stakeholders such as technology companies, NGOs, and activists, as well as military officials, all shape the application of existing rules to this domain.

Another way to analyze the evolution of "responsible state behavior" in tandem with the application of international law is to conceptualize the constellation of actors and groups who contribute to shaping international cybersecurity governance as a cyber CoP: they participate in multiple institutions with overlapping agendas and do not all have clearly defined goals or interests, but share the common purpose of developing rules for state activity in cyberspace. Routine practices of actors within the CoP acquire social significance over time and stabilize perceptions of what constitutes responsible behavior in cyberspace. In this case, perceptions of lawful conduct in cyberspace have been shaped, *inter alia*, by practices of articulating "voluntary" norms of state behavior. Despite characterizing these norms as non-binding guidelines, the UN GGE and several other institutions involved in international cybersecurity governance have frequently borrowed the vocabulary of existing international law, suggesting, in fact, that these norms are markers of lawful conduct in cyberspace. In other words, voluntary guidelines on,

[102] Anatoly A Streltsov, 'Application of International Humanitarian Law to Armed Conflicts in Cyberspace' (2012) <https://digital.report/wp-content/uploads/2016/04/169747-Streltsov-ENG.pdf>; 'Statement at Budapest Conference on Cyber Issues' (October 9, 2012) <http://vienna.china-mission.gov.cn/eng/zgbd/201210/t20121009_8848606.htm> accessed November 23, 2022.

[103] Oliver Kessler and Wouter Werner, 'Expertise, Uncertainty, and International Law: A Study of the Tallinn Manual on Cyberwarfare' (2013) 26 LJIL 793, 796.

say, the protection of critical infrastructure from cyber operations or monitoring malicious activity from one's territory have absorbed legal language, suggesting that they are adaptations of international law to cyberspace. The practices of these institutions have reflected and reinforced the perception that norm-articulation and law-interpretation are linked. Consequently, two essential pillars of the framework of responsible state behavior—that is, norms and international law—have evolved alongside and shaped intersubjective legal formulations.

What might such practices look like and why did the UN GGE conflate norms and international law in this manner in the first place? Cyber norms were always linked to international law because their articulation was itself the result of a compromise reached between the United States and Russia in the GGE: while the US wanted the norms to be "legal norms"—that is, reflective of existing law—Russia sought norms to lay the groundwork for a new cybersecurity treaty. Both states had their strategic reasons.[104] The result was that UN GGE norms slipped in and out of international law, at times drawing on and adapting existing legal principles, at other times reflecting wholly new obligations. Practices of the GGE reflected this blurring of political and legal commitments. The eleven norms articulated by the 2014–15 UN GGE are regularly described as the "*acquis*" of cybersecurity governance by many states, although they have no binding effect.[105] Since 2012, the UN GGE has had a section covering "norms, rules, and principles," offering little indication as to what is an interpretation of a binding rule and what is not. Meanwhile, in the broader community of practice, private and multistakeholder processes too began articulating cyber norms, and following the UN GGE, some of these "voluntary" norms were grounded in existing international law.[106] These institutions developed their own practices—for instance, recruiting international lawyers to develop the scope of non-binding norms—that reinforced the dominant thinking that norms and rules were essentially the same.

The social environment that facilitated the thinking that norms and law are intertwined can be conceptualized in many ways. Practice theorists, as we explained earlier in this chapter, would describe it as the *habitus* of the cyber CoP, referring to the dominant way of thinking among various practitioners as to how cybersecurity governance can be advanced. Practices of the UN GGE and other institutions reinforce the *habitus* of the CoP. While practice theorizing in IR and

[104] Eneken Tikk and Mika Kerttunen, *The Alleged Demise of the UN GGE: An Autopsy and Eulogy* (Cyber Policy Institute online 2017) <https://cpi.ee/wp-content/uploads/2017/12/2017-Tikk-Kerttunen-Demise-of-the-UN-GGE-2017-12-17-ET.pdf>.

[105] Heli Tiirmaa-Klaar, 'The Evolution of the UN Group of Governmental Experts on Cyber Issues: From a Marginal Group to a Major International Security Norm-Setting Body', The Hague Centre for Strategic Studies (December 9, 2021) <https://hcss.nl/wp-content/uploads/2021/12/Klaar.pdf>.

[106] See generally Global Commission on the Stability of Cyberspace, 'Norms: The Rules of the Road: GCSC Proposed Norms of Responsible Behaviour in Cyberspace' (2019) <https://hcss.nl/gcsc-norms>.

IL helpfully explains that certain practices can become "sticky" and, in turn, influence substantive legal formulations of the international cybersecurity regime, it does not satisfactorily answer why actors gravitate toward these practices. In other words, why do practitioners tacitly perceive certain practices to be reflective of the *habitus*?

This is one area where the "cognitive turn" could prove helpful. As Section 4 illustrated, insights from behavioral science and social cognition theories can explain both why certain beliefs shape the thinking of actors within an interpretive community and why words, gestures, and symbols emerging out of such beliefs—"practices"—become entrenched over time. In particular, group dynamics and various facets of "groupthink" that have been highlighted by cognitive studies could explain the evolution of practices, and through them, legal interpretation. In the case of international cybersecurity, CAT could explain why states and non-state actors came to speak of non-binding norms as functionally equivalent to binding international law in advancing responsible state behavior. With a landmark US–Russia compromise (high-power actors) setting the stage for the UN GGE's articulation of norms, while leaving their precise status ambiguous, private/multistakeholder groups (low-power actors) within the CoP may have sought to mimic the UN GGE's approach by similarly publishing "law-like" norms. The repeated reference by powerful states to the UN GGE's norms as the "*acquis*" of international cybersecurity rules may have similarly influenced other, less powerful actors to consider those norms as sacrosanct or concentrate their efforts toward implementing those norms rather than articulating new ones. Another relevant insight from cognitive science is the finding that learning in humans occurs through the use first of words that describe social relations over those that describe objects and persons.[107] It would be a fruitful agenda of research to study the emergence of "social relational" words and practices in the initial days of a global governance community to establish how actors should conduct their business before determining how specific rules or interpretations apply to state behavior in the domain. In international cybersecurity, as we have pointed out, the intersubjective formulation "framework of responsible state behavior" encompasses both voluntary norms and interpretations of existing law, tacitly communicating to actors that norms can shape markers of legality in this domain.

Other insights on group dynamics could also help explain the role and prominence of certain actors within the cyber CoP. Take, for instance, the "mere-exposure effect," which refers to the finding that the preferences of individuals toward objects and persons are shaped simply by their familiarity with them.[108] The familiarity

[107] Alison Gopnik, 'Three Types of Early Word: The Emergence of Social Words, Names and Cognitive-Relational Words in the One-Word Stage and Their Relation to Cognitive Development' (1988) 8(22) First Lang 49.

[108] Robert B Zajonc, 'Attitudinal Effects of Mere Exposure' (1968) 9(2) J Pers Soc Psychol 1.

of states—especially the US, Russia, and China—with GGE diplomacy arguably entrenched its practices over time and elevated the GGE into a semi-permanent forum for international cybersecurity governance. The creation of "like-minded" groups (Western states in the case of cybersecurity governance[109], developing countries with respect to climate change negotiations[110]) in various Conferences of State Parties illustrates the mere-exposure effect. Like-minded groups usually comprise those states who have already engaged with each other in the past on other issues, and not necessarily those whose substantive agendas perfectly align.

The mere-exposure effect could also explain why companies such as Microsoft have become increasingly important and well-regarded interlocutors in the cyber-norms processes. Even if states—including the United States, the country of its incorporation—do not all agree with Microsoft's positions on various aspects of international cybersecurity, there is no doubting the fact that the company is considered an important player in cyber diplomacy. In comparison to other companies such as Kaspersky or Siemens, which have also sought to orchestrate initiatives of their own in this domain, Microsoft may enjoy higher status and regard simply because it is familiar to other practitioners because of its longstanding engagement with the processes.[111]

Groupthink may also have had the effect of shaping substantive positions on international law among "like-minded" states. For example, there is a difference of opinion among individual states in the like-minded group on the applicability of the due diligence principle to cyberspace. France, Germany, and the Netherlands, in particular, champion a "cyber due diligence" rule, while the UK, US, and New Zealand are much more circumspect and do not recognize the rule's applicability to the domain.[112] Despite the US being in the camp of doubters, UN GGE reports since 2013 have called on states to not "knowingly allow" their territory to be used for wrongful cyber operations. Arguably, the need to keep the like-minded states together and advance responsible behavior in cyberspace suppressed dissenting views on due diligence—an attribute of groupthink in organizations and coalitions—of states like US or UK in the group. The point here is not that the compromise made by the latter states was the product of non-reflexive calculations but that the move to "join consensus" on the due diligence formulation in the UN

[109] 'Responding to Modern Cyber Threats with Diplomacy and Deterrence', US Department of State (October 19, 2020) <https://2017-2021.state.gov/responding-to-modern-cyber-threats-with-diplomacy-and-deterrence/index.html>.

[110] Carola Klöck, Paula Castro, and Florian Weiler, 'Coalitions in the Climate Change Negotiations' (2021) 55 LIEPP Policy Brief <https://sciencespo.hal.science/hal-03409340/file/LIEPP-PB-55-Klock.pdf>.

[111] Tobias Liebetrau and Linda Monsees, 'Assembling Publics: Microsoft, Cybersecurity, and Public-Private Relations' (forthcoming) Politics Gov 11(3).

[112] See 'Due Diligence', International Cyber Law in Practice: Interactive Toolkit (nd) <https://cyberlaw.ccdcoe.org/wiki/Due_diligence#:~:text=In%20the%20context%20of%20cyberspace,right%20of%20another%20state%3B%20and>.

GGE could be the result of pressures to "overvalue the approval" of other countries in this otherwise highly cohesive group.[113]

Anchoring and adjustment effects, explored in the previous section, can also help explain the dynamics of the cyber-norm negotiating processes.[114] The UN GGE was the center of a protracted debate over whether existing international law on the use of force applied to cyberspace. Arguably, the *jus ad bellum* and *jus in bello* were the starting point (the anchor) and discussions revolved around what adjustments, if any, were necessary to account for the particularities of cyberattacks. The US had little trouble seeing the "fit" between existing law and this new conflict domain. Others, including Russia, were reluctant to accept that interpretation and instead pushed for new law. In the end, the process has been largely about clarifying meanings, filling gaps, and making adjustments—rather than ignoring the existing legal edifice (the anchor) and starting from scratch.

Finally, cybersecurity regime-building has been a highly deliberative process involving a multiplicity of state and non-state actors in a variety of forums over an extended period. If cognitive biases (like the fundamental attribution error) threw off the search for consensus at various points along the way, it is possible that multistakeholder deliberation corrected for those errors. If, for example, the positions of Microsoft and other private actors was initially (and unconsciously) assumed to be a reflection of their narrow commercial interests, systematic engagement with them over the years might have induced a shift toward a more "deliberate" mode of thinking and greater openness to the substantive merits of what they had to say.

In summary, the cognitive turn can illuminate various aspects of the negotiations around rules of state behavior in cyberspace. Such insights could explain the working of CoPs, interpretive communities, and the institutions where they coalesce. Through this case study, we have sought to present insights from cognitive science that appear to be useful to understanding this exercise in regime-building, and these should be taken as "what-if" questions for future study rather than definitive propositions.

## 6. Limitations of Cognitive Approaches

Despite the considerable alignment between constructivist theses in IL/IR theory and insights from cognitive science that may help advance or modify them, it is also important to acknowledge key limitations in pursuing a research agenda that

113 Tomer Broude, 'Behavioural International Law' (2015) 163 U Pa L Rev 1128.

114 Tomer Broude and Yahli Shereshevsky, 'Explaining the Practical Purchase of Soft Law: Competing and Complementary Behavior Hypotheses' in Harlan Grant Cohen and Timothy Meyer (eds), *International Law as Behavior* (CUP 2021) 98.

synthesizes both. First are the well-known methodological challenges of translating individual mental processes to the level of the state. It is hard enough to get inside the heads of individuals. How does one get "inside the head" of a state? It is true that, by training its gaze on the psycho-social effects of communal interactions on individuals, cognitive science furthers the constructivist agenda of disaggregating and opening the "black box" of the state. But how? Just as it is hard to prove (or disprove) the core assumption of the realist variant of rational choice theory (that states are unitary, rational actors), it is not clear how the "cognitive turn" can help to prove (or disprove) that they are not.[115] Moreover, so many "cognitive biases" have been identified in the psychology literature and behavioral economics that it seems that these biases can be drawn on selectively to help explain virtually anything. As with the rational choice approach, there is a risk that cognitive factors will be used as possible explanations for everything, and therefore nothing.

Second, conceiving of states as "social" actors that have "relationships" raises a host of questions that are even more nettlesome than those raised by behavioral insights. In what ways, for example, are states susceptible to peer pressure? How do they become "socialized" or "acculturated" to a norm? In what ways are concerns about identity or status manifest? Social constructivism has struggled to answer these questions empirically because it is difficult to design research programs that can account for all the variables. While the sociological branch of cognitive studies reinforces the importance of asking these questions about state behavior, it does not provide a toolkit to answer them. Experimental studies, for example, may help to get inside the heads of decision-makers, but it is not possible to design experimental studies that tell us how states behave.

Third, because sociological/constructivist approaches are even harder to test empirically than behavioral insights, there is a risk that cognitive approaches may skew the scholarship toward reductive analyses driven exclusively by behavioral insights. Behavioral analyses often require rigorous and resource-intensive experiments: as legal researchers immerse themselves in an unfamiliar methodological terrain, they should be careful not to let the implementation and outcomes of experimental research eclipse the larger project of testing and refining theories of how and why rules are made, interpreted, and complied with.

## 7. Conclusion

A central premise of constructivist approaches to international law is that the lines between making, interpreting, and implementing the law are blurred. In this

[115] That being said, in this chapter we have shown how constructivist-cognitive analysis can shed light on some factors that increase or decrease the possibility of sharing certain cognitive features (eg what interpretation seems to 'fit' best with existing international law).

chapter, we have sought to identify how insights from psychology and cognitive sociology can illuminate the rule-making and interpretation process. Legal interpretation is essentially a cognitive process, and intersubjective interpretation has a social, communicative quality. Findings from research into the working of the human mind as well as the evolution of societal and inter-group relations are relevant to global governance, we argued, because those findings can help explain how the institutional environment in which rules are developed and interpreted shapes opinions and legal positions of states, and how practitioners who are part of this environment respond to certain stimuli individually and collectively.

Cognitive studies can not only shine light on international legal interpretation but in some cases can also improve institutional and regime design by helping policymakers understand and address biases and heuristics associated with individual and group decision-making. In particular, we pointed to the need for improved deliberation through the adoption of accountability mechanisms and feedback loops that allow for reasoned decisions as much as intuition and "automatic" cognition in global governance institutions. Constructivist scholarship has advanced a rich body of explanations for why states make and comply with rules. The cognitive turn in international law helpfully offers macro and micro elements that have the potential to strengthen or rebut those explanations. As several global governance regimes are fluid and informal—we presented in this chapter the case study of international cybersecurity governance—these insights will be especially relevant, given the uncertainty of outcomes and heightened cognitive load of individuals and groups in noisy environments. Just as importantly, cognitive science and research presents a methodological plank from which theoretically rich constructivist scholarship can be empirically tested.

These obvious advantages notwithstanding, constructivist scholars must approach such a synthesized research agenda with humility. This chapter has pointed out the obvious challenges of claiming to "get inside the mind" of states. Selective application of insights from cognitive science into existing theoretical strands does little to advance them, which is ultimately the goal of interdisciplinary research. Researchers who have engaged in rigorous empirical work using immersive ethnography and interviews are often best poised to assess the cognitive processes at play: experimental work - the mainstay of behavioral research – cannot simply be substituted for those methods. The "cognitive turn" in international law scholarship should be carefully navigated, even while acknowledging its prospects of advancing constructivist frontiers through insights into modern global governance.

# 4

# Critical Approaches to International Law and Cognitive-Behavioural Science

## Tensions and Contributions

*Shiri Krebs*

## 1. Introduction

Can cognitive and behavioural science provide meaningful insight to inform and advance critical approaches to international law? Can insights from critical international law studies contribute to cognitive-behavioural approaches to international law? Thus far, critical and cognitive-behavioural approaches to international law have developed mostly in scholarly silos, with little engagement between one another. This separation is perhaps not surprising, considering the different (if not opposing) sets of theoretical, methodological, and ideological commitments underlying each of these approaches.[1] At the same time, and despite their tensions and differences, critical and cognitive-behavioural approaches to international law also share a common interest in exposing systemic bias, power dynamics, and unchallenged assumptions ingrained in the study of international law. At their core, both approaches are committed to complexity: a reading of international law as a situated exercise, affected by geography, positioning, and motivations (at the social, institutional, and individual levels). Expounding upon these tensions and connections, in this chapter I argue that both critical and cognitive-behavioural approaches to international law can meaningfully engage with one another, creating an opportunity to develop a cognitive-behavioural critique of international law; a critique that is sensitive to the specific cognitive mechanisms that can explain bias in the international legal system, and that is geared towards various forms of transformation and change.

Is it theoretically consistent and practicably useful to integrate insights from both critical and cognitive-behavioural studies? As Foucault noted, 'criticism' is a matter of showing that 'things are not as self-evident as one believed, to see that

[1] Focusing on social science methods more broadly, Abere, Chilton, and Ginsburg argued that while social science 'is committed to a modernist view of knowledge', critical theory 'is committed to a critique of objectivity'. Daniel Abebe, Adam Chilton, and Tom Ginsburg, 'The Social Science Approach to International Law' (2021) 22 Chi J Intl L 1, 20.

Shiri Krebs, *Critical Approaches to International Law and Cognitive-Behavioural Science* In: *International Legal Theory and the Cognitive Turn*. Edited by: Anne van Aaken and Moshe Hirsch, Oxford University Press. 
DOI: 10.1093/9780198909293.003.0005

what is accepted as self-evident will no longer be accepted as such'.[2] Practising criticism, therefore, is 'a matter of making facile gestures difficult'.[3] According to Foucault, '[a] critique is not a matter of saying that things are not right as they are. It is a matter of pointing out on what kinds of assumptions, what kinds of familiar, unchallenged, unconsidered modes of thought the practices that we accept rest'.[4] Following Foucault, Butler concluded that 'the primary task of critique will not be to evaluate whether its objects —social conditions, practices, forms of knowledge, power, and discourse—are good or bad, valued highly or demeaned, but to bring into relief the very framework of evaluation itself'.[5] Critical theory, therefore, does not focus on (or is not necessarily committed to) offering concrete solutions or improvements to identified and contained problems within the existing system, but rather on the method of evaluation ('understanding understanding', as Mégret puts it).[6]

While sharing an interest in methods of evaluation, cognitive and behavioural approaches to international law are committed to empirical scientific inquiry. As Van van Aaken and Hirsch note in their Introduction to this book, the main thread tying the various strands within the vast cognitive-behavioural literature is the idea of bounded rationality, rejecting, at least to some extent, rational choice theory.[7] Bounded rationality refers to several types of biases and heuristics affecting decision-makers, such as prospect theory and framing effects.[8] The concept of bounded or imperfect rationality represents both the point of convergence with critical approaches to international law (rejection of the common representation of international law as 'objective' or 'neutral') and a point of tension (acceptance of 'universal' scientific methods and insights, as well as a commitment to empiricism and applied knowledge). While these tensions have largely kept scholarship from each of these camps apart, they are also at the heart of what I see as a potential for dialogue and collaboration, pushing the boundaries—and core assumptions—of both disciplines. To exemplify this potential for contribution and carve an intellectual space for engagement, this chapter proposes avenues for developing a cognitive-behavioural critique of international law, taking account of the roles of

[2] Michel Foucault, 'Practicing Criticism' (tr A Sheridan and others) in Lawrence D Kritzman (ed), *Politics, Philosophy, Culture: Interviews and Other Writings, 1977–1984* (Routledge 1988) 155.

[3] ibid.

[4] ibid 154.

[5] Judith Butler, 'What Is Critique? An Essay on Foucault's Virtue' in David Ingram (ed), *The Political: Readings in Continental Philosophy* (Basil Blackwell 2002) 220.

[6] Frédéric Mégret, 'International Criminal Justice: A Critical Agenda' in Christine Schwöbel (ed), *Critical Approaches to International Criminal Law: An Introduction* (Taylor & Francis Group 2014) 21. See also Frank Munger and Carroll Seron, 'Critical Legal Studies versus Critical Legal Theory: A Comment on Method' (1984) 6 Law and Pol 257, 274 (stating that 'Progressive critique, in the dialectical sense, includes a commitment to a historically situated analysis of social relations and struggle and, simultaneously, an examination of the ideological limits of one's own theory and method').

[7] Van Aaken and Hirsch, Introduction to this volume, pp 6–7.

[8] Daniel Kahneman, 'A Perspective on Judgment and Choice: Mapping Bounded Rationality' (2003) 58 Am Psychol 697.

both individual decision-makers and systemic elements in the perpetuation of bias and subjectivity in the operation of international law.

I proceed, in Section 2, by briefly introducing the core presuppositions of critical approaches to international law, focusing on critique as a method to question prevailing international law narratives, expose power dynamics and political interests embedded in international law, and identify systemic biases in both substantive international law norms and the structure of the international legal system. Section 3 then reviews in greater detail the concept of domination as an organising theme in international law. Next, Section 4 explores the existing tensions and potential connections between critical approaches to international law and recent advances in cognitive and behavioural studies. Using Van Aaken and Hirsch's introductory chapter as a baseline, this section briefly reviews the literature concerning the manifestation of cognitive bias and subjectivity in international law, identifying a shared theme or common ground with critical approaches to international law. The section then continues to identify three areas of tension between these approaches to international law: a universal versus localised approach to knowledge production, a commitment to empiricism versus epistemological deconstruction, and a research agenda that promotes pragmatic reform versus radical politics of resistance, contestation, and transformation. Following this theoretical and methodological exploration, Section 5 concludes, illustrating the benefits from a critical-behavioural engagement by integrating insights from both fields.

## 2. Critical Approaches to International Law

Critical approaches to international law draw on insights from both critical theory and its applications within the domestic legal context—the critical legal studies (CLS) movement. As opposed to classic approaches to international law, such as traditional positivism,[9] which invoke an assumption of legal objectivity or neutrality,[10] at the heart of critical approaches to international law is the nexus between law and politics. Critical approaches to international law expose the contingency of canonical legal narratives and the power dynamics, economic interests, and historical legacies shaping international law.[11] Some of the more established contemporary critiques of international law and institutions include (but are not limited to) feminist critiques of international law,[12] postcolonial perspectives and

[9] See Chapter 1 by Peat in this volume, p 21.

[10] See the detailed review of classical positivism in Chapter 1 by Peat in this volume, pp 23–28; See, also, Shirley V Scott, 'International Law as Ideology: Theorizing the Relationship between International Law and International Politics' (1994) 5 EJIL 313, 320.

[11] David Kennedy, *The Dark Sides of Virtue: Reassessing International Humanitarianism* (Princeton UP 2005) 21; David Kennedy, 'Theses about International Law Discourse' (1980) 23 German YB Intl L 353, 390–91; Marti Koskenniemi, 'The Politics of International Law' (1990) 1 EJIL 4, 25, 31.

[12] See, eg, Hilary Charlesworth, Christine Chinkin, and Shelley Wright, 'Feminist Approaches to International Law' (1991) 85 AJIL 613; Anne Orford, 'Feminism, Imperialism and the Mission

critiques,[13] Third World (and Fourth World) Approaches to International Law (TWAIL),[14] critical race theory, as applied in the context of the international legal system,[15] political economy and Marxism,[16] and localised knowledge studies, highlighting the operation of international law in different localities and domestic contexts.[17]

A pioneer of the critical analysis of international law, Martti Koskenniemi conceptualises international law as a language, portraying and historicising the political elements of this speech and the political actors speaking it.[18] Examining the development of international legal instruments through different periods in the history of modern international law, Koskenniemi demonstrates how powerful states, through their agents, created and interpreted international law as an instrument to further their geopolitical ambitions and colonial expansion.[19] Focusing on the compelling example of the international law norm permitting humanitarian interventions under some circumstances (mainly to stop severe human rights abuses), Anne Orford persuasively demonstrates how this international legal norm has been used to legitimise and rationalise postcolonial military interventions.[20] By tracing and historicising the colonial origins of this norm, Orford exposes the selectivity and double standards that often characterise states' decisions to intervene in some conflicts but not in others.[21] Addressing the social conflict approach to international law, Hirsch highlights the purported separation between international law and political interests, arguing that international legal scholarship must acknowledge the underlying political bias of international legal rules.[22]

of International Law' (2002) 71 Nord J Int Law 275. For additional literature on this interface, see Chapter 5 by Veronika Fikfak in this volume.

[13] See, eg, Anne Orford, *Reading Humanitarian Intervention: Human Rights and the Use of Force in International Law* (CUP 2003).

[14] See, eg, Bhupinder S Chimni, 'Third World Approaches to International Law: A Manifesto' (2006) 8 Intl Comm L Rev 3; Julia Dehm, 'Carbon Colonialism or Climate Justice: Interrogating the International Climate Regime from a TWAIL Perspective' (2016) 33 Windsor YB 129. TWAIL's literature will be further explored in Section 3.

[15] See, eg, Makau Mutua, 'Critical Race Theory and International Law: The View of an Insider-Outsider' (2000) 45 Vill L Rev 841. See also Tendayi E Achiume, 'Race, Refugees and International Law' in Cathryn Costello, Michelle Foster, and Jane McAdam (eds), *The Oxford Handbook of International Refugee Law* (OUP 2021), ch 2, 43–59.

[16] Ntina Tzouvala, *Capitalism as Civilisation: A History of International Law* (CUP 2020). See also Chapter 12 by Bagchi in this volume.

[17] See, eg, Luis Eslava, 'Istanbul Vignettes: Observing the Everyday Operation of International Law' (2014) 2 Lond Rev Int Law 3.

[18] Martti Koskenniemi, *From Apology to Utopia: The Structure of International Legal Argument* (CUP 2006).

[19] Martti Koskenniemi, *The Gentle Civilizer of Nations: The Rise and Fall of International Law 1870–1960* (CUP 2001); Martti Koskenniemi, *To the Uttermost Parts of the Earth: Legal Imagination and International Power 1300–1870* (CUP 2021).

[20] See, eg, Orford (n 13).

[21] ibid.

[22] Moshe Hirsch, 'The Sociology of International Law: Invitation to Study International Rules in Their Social Context' (2005) 55 U Tor LJ 891, 927.

The critiques of substantive international law norms are complemented by critiques of the structure and method of the international legal system. Existing critiques of international law have demonstrated how questions of jurisdiction, hierarchy, and specialisation have been answered to generate a particular scope of international legal order with specifically desired outcomes. For example, Koskenniemi argues that the fragmentation in international law's global governance (into 'areas of specialisation') has been designed to generate outcomes that are desired by the audience and participants of each area of specialisation or expertise.[23] Similarly, feminist critiques of international law argue that the core jurisdictional distinction in international law between 'public' and 'private' serves patriarchal interests and structures, shielding men and enabling crimes against women.[24]

In her book *Is International Law International?*, Roberts argues that the dominance of English in international legal discourse favours Anglo-American legal concepts and traditions, leading to the marginalisation of other legal traditions and perspectives.[25] Ammann continues this line of argument, adding that this language bias in international law perpetuates a structural bias that not only limits access to legal information but also hinders effective participation in international legal processes.[26] Ammann further argues that this structural language bias privileges perspectives and ways of thinking that are associated with international law's preferred languages, which can marginalise other viewpoints and contribute to a lack of diversity in international legal discourse.[27] In particular, she mentions the institutionalisation of language bias in international law through a narrow selection of working languages—mainly English and French—for prominent international institutions, such as the United Nations (UN) and the International Court of Justice (ICJ).[28]

Critiques of diversity—or rather the lack thereof—in the international legal system further explore various domestic, localised contexts within which international law is created and applied. Eslava, for example, criticises the lack of attention in international legal scholarship to the domestic everyday operation of international law, exposing how international law is exercised through 'national and local norms, administrative and spatial practices, ordinary artifacts, and our everyday lives'.[29]

[23] Martti Koskenniemi, 'The Politics of International Law: 20 Years Later' (2009) 20 EJIL 7, 9.

[24] See, eg, Christine Chinkin, 'A Critique of the Public/Private Dimension' (1999) 10 EJIL 38; Catharine A MacKinnon, 'Crimes of War, Crimes of Peace' (1993) 4 UCLA Women's LJ 59.

[25] Anthea Roberts, *Is International Law International?* (OUP 2017).

[26] Odile Ammann, 'Language Bias in International Legal Scholarship: Symptoms, Explanations, Implications and Remedies' (2022) 33 EJIL 821.

[27] ibid.

[28] ibid 832.

[29] See, eg, Eslava (n 17) 3.

While these contemporary critiques of international law and institutions rely on different methods and advance distinct arguments (similarly to the CLS movement), they share a commitment to progressive political ideologies, centring around the conceptualisation of domination (whether Western, colonial, patriarchal, capitalist, or white) and the imperative of its unmaking.[30]

## 3. Domination: A View from the South

To review and exemplify the central concept of *domination* in critical approaches to international law, this section highlights a particular faction within critical approaches to international law: TWAIL. Much like with critical approaches to international law generally, TWAIL also consists of diverse scholarship. Already in 1998 Karin Mickelson noted that there is 'no coherent and distinctive "Third World approach" to international law';[31] and in the two and a half decades since, the voices of TWAIL scholars have diversified even further. Moreover, it is not clear *what* a TWAIL 'approach' is, and whether it represents a theory, a methodology, an ideology, or a combination of elements from all three.

As a theory, TWAIL has been used to explain world politics and the behaviour of international institutions based on concepts such as orientalism, colonialism, and domination. TWAIL theories use issues of material distribution and imbalance of power to explain how international legal categories, norms, and doctrines are produced, and what political goals they serve.[32] While the issues they tackle are quite diverse—from environmental justice[33] to international criminal law,[34] gender,[35] and human rights[36]—they share a common basis for the explanation they provide for international phenomena, which is the domination of First World over Third World countries. For example, Chimni's analysis of customary international law identifies its roots in the Western economic, cultural, and political order, exposing the historic role of customary international law in furthering the interests of

[30] For a similar argument in the context of the CLS movement, see Mark Tushnet, 'Critical Legal Studies: A Political History' (1990) 100 Yale LJ 1515, 1516. See also Samuel Moyn, 'Reconstructing Critical Legal Studies' (4 August 2023) 134 Yale LJ; Nigel Purvis, 'Critical Legal Studies in Public International Law' (1991) 32 Harv Intl LJ 81, 89, 123.

[31] Karin Mickelson, 'Rhetoric and Rage: Third World Voices in International Legal Discourse' (1997) 16 Wis Intl LJ 353.

[32] Luis Eslava and Sundhya Pahuja, 'Between Resistance and Reform: TWAIL and the Universality of International Law' (2011) 3 Trade L and Dev 103.

[33] Usha Natarajan, 'TWAIL and the Environment: The State of Nature, the Nature of the State, and the Arab Spring' (2012) 14 Or Rev Intl L 177.

[34] Parvathi Menon, 'Self-Referring to the International Criminal Court: A Continuation of War by Other Means' (2015) 109 AJIL 260.

[35] Celestine I Nyamu, 'How Should Human Rights and Development Respond to Cultural Legitimization of Gender Hierarchy in Developing Countries' (2000) 41 Harv Intl LJ 381.

[36] Makau Mutua, 'Savages, Victims, and Saviors: The Metaphor of Human Rights' (2001) 42 Harv Intl LJ 201.

capitalist nations.[37] TWAIL theories are therefore fundamentally connected with other critical theories, such as critical race theory,[38] pointing to 'certain structural constraints that the world economy imposes on one set of countries as opposed to others'.[39]

TWAIL, however, is not merely a theory (or a set of theories). Some see TWAIL as a methodology, providing analytical tools to evaluate and critique international law.[40] While TWAIL is not a methodology in a scientific sense (it does not provide clear standards of measurement for an observed phenomenon), it offers a methodological approach for international legal analysis. From a methodological standpoint, TWAIL scholarship has been characterised as an epistemological deconstruction or inquiry,[41] reflecting 'on the etiology of the doctrines of international law and even the structure of the international law system itself'.[42] Using this methodological lens, TWAIL scholarship also reshapes existing methodologies, such as historicisation, by including global (as opposed to merely West-centric) historicisation.[43] Koskenniemi has criticised the Eurocentrism of traditional histories, emphasising that

> the problem with traditional histories is not only that the events and ideas—the substance of international legal history—tends to be Eurocentric. The very standards of historiography are European. To write a credible professional history of the field, one needs to adopt European notions of relevance so that even a critique of Eurocentrism may appear to arise from European preoccupations and political attachments.[44]

In this sense, TWAIL exposes—and aims to correct—accepted methodologies (including historicisation), highlighting how they *create*, instead of merely

[37] Bhupinder S Chimni, 'Customary International Law: A Third World Perspective' (2018) 112 AJIL 1, 6.

[38] Tendayi E Achiume and Devon W Carbado, 'Critical Race Theory Meets Third World Approaches to International Law' (2020) 67 UCLA L Rev 1462; James Thuo Gathii, 'Writing Race and Identity in a Global Context: What CRT and TWAIL Can Learn from Each Other' (2020) 67 UCLA L Rev 1610.

[39] Chimni (n 14). These connections also extend to Marxist approaches. Tzanakopoulos, for example, argues that law structures, justifies, and conserves 'the "values" of a ruling class projected upon an imagined "homogenous" society'. Antonios Tzanakopoulos, 'The Master's Tools and the Master's House: Marxist Insights for International Law' in Anne van Aaken and others (eds), *The Oxford Handbook of International Law in Europe* (OUP 2023), ch 17, 351–76.

[40] Anthony Anghie and Bhupinder S Chimni, 'Third World Approaches to International Law and Individual Responsibility in Internal Conflicts' (2003) 2 Chinese J Intl L 77.

[41] Mégret (n 6) 21. See also Vasuki Nesiah, 'Decolonial CIL: TWAIL, Feminism, and an Insurgent Jurisprudence' (2018) 112 AJIL 313, 315.

[42] Andrew F Sunter, 'TWAIL as Naturalized Epistemological Inquiry' (2007) 20 Can J L Juris 475, 490.

[43] Obiora Chinedu Okafor, 'Critical Third World Approaches to International Law (TWAIL): Theory, Methodology, or Both?' (2008) 10 Intl Comm L Rev 371.

[44] Martti Koskenniemi, 'Histories of International Law: Significance and Problems for a Critical View' (2013) 27 Temp Intl and Comp LJ 215, 222.

*represent*, the world.[45] TWAIL scholarship thus exposes the performative role of accepted standards of historiography, as well as questioning the separation between substantive norms and methods of international legal inquiry.[46]

Finally, in addition to its theoretical and methodological elements or contributions, TWAIL can also be seen as a political ideology, similarly to other political ideologies such as Marxism.[47] A significant aspect of the TWAIL community lies in its close connection to Third World activism and its decolonising agenda.[48] As an ideology, TWAIL aims to resist and reform international law, promoting democratisation of international law and the inclusion of Third World perspectives.[49]

Whether seen as a theoretical, methodological, or ideological contribution, TWAIL's critique centres around its commitment to exposing international legal norms and institutions as tools of domination and subordination.[50] The heart of TWAIL's critique lies in its scepticism towards hegemonic First World traditions and interpretations (such as legal positivism), revealing how legal systems are constructed to serve the interests of dominant or powerful countries. Beyond this direct self-interest, however, TWAIL critiques also demonstrate how existing legal systems may continue to perpetuate the domination of First World countries in the international legal system through stereotypes and bias against Third World countries. Can existing TWAIL-based critiques of international law (as well as other critical approaches to international law) benefit from insights gained from cognitive and behavioural studies? The following section considers such an engagement and its potential outcomes.

## 4. Cognitive Science and Critical Approaches to International Law: Tensions and Connections

### 4.1. A common ground: bias and subjectivity in international law

Cognitive-behavioural and critical approaches to international law both deny the portrayal of international law as a neutral system, external to the individuals and groups that operate and apply it, and devoid of bias and subjectivity. As Van Aaken and Hirsch note in their Introduction, the main thread tying the various strands

[45] Gavin Sullivan, 'Law, Technology, and Data-Driven Security: Infra-Legalities as Method Assemblage' (2022) 49 J Law Soc S31.

[46] Eg see Chimni's analysis concerning the distinction between formal and material sources of customary international law. Chimni (n 37).

[47] On Marxism and cognitive-behavioural studies, see Chapter 12 by Bagchi in this volume.

[48] James Thuo Gathii, 'The Agenda of Third World Approaches to International Law (TWAIL)' in Jeffrey L Dunoff and Mark A Pollack (eds), *International Legal Theory: Foundations and Frontiers* (CUP 2022), ch 7, 166, 170.

[49] Eslava and Pahuja (n 32).

[50] See, eg, ibid; Gathii (n 48).

within the vast cognitive-behavioural literature is the idea of bounded rationality, rejecting, at least to some extent, rational choice theory, and identifying subjectivity in group-based and individual-based decision-making processes.[51]

The term 'bias' refers to a 'systematic distortion of results or findings from the true state of affairs' and 'implies the presence of emotional and/or political prejudices that influence conclusions and decisions'.[52] Some biases—which are of particular interest to critical international law scholars—are systemic biases, ingrained in the design of a legal system, institution, or process. Critical analysis of treaty-making, for example, sheds light on the power imbalance among states during treaty negotiations, as well as the historical context of some treaty-making processes (for example, their colonial legacies), which lead to international treaties that are biased towards the interests of powerful countries. This is a structural bias in the sense that the outcomes of a legal mechanism are skewed towards an interested party (powerful countries) but also reflect a self-interest ('rational') approach on the part of that interested party. Martti Koskinniemi argues that the Nuclear Non-Proliferation Treaty (NPT) reflects such a systemic bias in international law, in favour of five countries who hold unique power within the international legal system: the five permanent members of the Security Council (China, France, the Russian Federation, the United Kingdom, and the United States). As Koskenniemi notes, this systemic bias goes against 'the deep-rooted popular sense that the existence of such weapons constitutes permanent hostage-taking by nuclear weapons States of most of the world's population'.[53] Another example of systemic bias in international law and institutions relates to the problem of selective (or biased) enforcement. In particular, the International Criminal Court has been criticised for its 'selective geographies of intervention', which 'appear to be driven by the Global North'.[54] This 'systematic distortion of results' may reflect both the interests of dominant countries in the international system and unconscious cognitive biases on the part of professional decision-makers (for example, on how they assess the gravity of crimes or the competence of national law enforcement systems).

While critical international law scholarship focuses on the structural element of bias in international law and institutions, cognitive and behavioural scholarship centres on individual decision-makers (and sometime on collective, or group-based, decision-making processes). This scholarship highlights the role of

[51] See Van Aaken and Hirsch's Introduction to this volume. Bounded rationality refers to several types of biases and heuristics—imperfect or irrational cognitive processes affecting decision-makers—such as prospect theory and framing effects. Kahneman (n 8).

[52] 'Bias', Oxford Reference <www.oxfordreference.com/view/10.1093/oi/authority.20110803095504939> accessed 1 March 2024.

[53] Martti Koskenniemi, 'What Is International Law For?' in Malcolm D Evans (ed), *International Law* (3rd edn, OUP 2006) 47.

[54] Sara Kendall, 'Critical Orientations: A Critique of International Criminal Court Practice' in Christine Schwöbel (ed), *Critical Approaches to International Criminal Law: An Introduction* (Routledge 2014) 57–58.

individuals (or groups) in decision-making processes, leading to biased decisions and outcomes.[55] The 'Global North' influences the design of international norms through recognised professionals and group dynamics (for example, within the ICJ, the International Law Commission, or UN committees). Colonial legacies, therefore, may influence the design and application of international law through people: lawyers, judges, diplomats, military commanders, immigration officers, and many more.

Decision-making biases refer to faulty mental processes that lead decision-makers to make sub-optimal decisions that deviate from normative principles.[56] These are a range of mental shortcuts, heuristics, and other cognitive processes that can lead to errors in judgement and decision-making (including in the context of international law).[57] In their influential studies of decision-making biases and heuristics, Kahneman, Slovic, and Tversky have grouped these biases under three broad categories: representativeness, availability, and anchoring.[58] Other relevant decision-making biases include confirmation bias, saliency bias, and automation bias, which will be further explored below.[59] These cognitive biases can be influenced by a variety of factors, including prior experiences, emotions, and social contexts. This leads to a focus on individual decision-makers as the main unit of analysis of the cognitive-behavioural approach, though Van Aaken expounds upon the possibility to apply behavioural insights to corporate actors such as states,[60] and Teichman and Zamir demonstrate how 'nudges' can be used to improve states' behaviour.[61]

Cognitive biases influence decision-makers' interpretation and application of international law in several ways. *First, decisions relating to matters of international law may be distorted or otherwise influenced by the design (or framing) of the legal norm.* For example, treaty design elements—such as an opt-in or opt-out preference—influence decision-makers' likelihood of joining an international regime. A decision to adopt an opt-in instead of an opt-out arrangement may trigger a risk aversion bias in favour of the existing status quo. Examining state behaviour patterns regarding treaty reservations, Galbraith utilises behavioural theories and methods to find evidence in support of status quo bias in international law

[55] See, eg, Anne van Aaken, 'The Individual in (International) Law' in Tom Sparks and Anne Peters (eds), *The Individual in International Law: History and Theory* (OUP 2024), ch 16, 354.

[56] Gilberto Montibeller and Detlof Von Winterfeldt, 'Cognitive and Motivational Biases in Decision and Risk Analysis' (2015) 35 Risk Anal 1230; David Arnott, 'Cognitive Biases and Decision Support Systems Development: A Design Science Approach' (2006) 16 Inf Syst J 55.

[57] Anne van Aaken, 'Behavioral International Law and Economics' (2014) 55 Harv Intl LJ 421.

[58] Daniel Kahneman, Paul Slovic, and Amos Tversky (eds), *Judgment under Uncertainty: Heuristics and Biases* (CUP 1982).

[59] Daniel Kahneman, Dan Lovallo, and Olivier Sibony, 'Before You Make That Big Decision' [2011] Harv Bus Rev 51.

[60] Van Aaken (n 57) 444.

[61] Doron Teichman and Eyal Zamir, 'Normative Aspects of Nudging in the International Sphere' (2021) 115 AJIL Unbound 263.

(explaining greater support for default rules).[62] Analysing a treaties dataset, she discovers that where treaties are designed using a default opt-out structure with regard to acceptance of ICJ jurisdiction, a significant majority of states (95 per cent) do not opt out and accepts the Court's jurisdiction. However, where treaties are designed based on an opt-in default structure, where states must actively accept the Court's jurisdiction, only a small fraction of states (5 per cent) go on to accept the Court's jurisdiction. A different example in this category relates to framing effects of the legal terminology. In previous studies I found that 'war crimes' framing adopted by international fact-finding missions (compared with a 'violation' framing) triggers in-group anger towards the mission and enhances denial of the factual findings.[63]

*Second, decisions relating to matters of international law may be influenced by decision-makers' biases that are external to the legal norm and its concrete terminology.* Such cognitive biases may be triggered by decision-makers' prior ideologies and beliefs (eg confirmation bias)[64] or by the circumstances of the legal assessment (eg outcome bias).[65] The cognitive-behavioural literature provides scientific methods to detect cognitive biases affecting decision-makers, as well as to measure the effects of concrete legal frames on decision-makers' performance (which may be moderated by decision-makers' characteristics and backgrounds or mediated by other factors). For example, Poulsen applies bounded rationality theories, including motivated cognition, to explain why decision-makers in developing countries tend to sign and ratify investment treaties against their interest.[66] In the context of military investigations and compliance with the rules of armed conflict, Broude and Levy find that outcome bias—exposure to ex post information about the outcomes of specific events—influences investigators' evaluations of ex ante decisions made by military commanders in real time. This is despite the fact that the law of armed conflict requires consideration only of the information that was available to decision-makers at the time the decision was made.[67]

[62] Jean Galbraith, 'Treaty Options: Towards a Behavioral Understanding of Treaty Design' (2013) 53 Va J Int L 309.

[63] Shiri Krebs, 'The Legalization of Truth in International Fact-Finding' (2017) 18 Chi J Intl L 83; Shiri Krebs, 'Law Wars: Experimental Data on the Impact of Legal Labels on Wartime Event Beliefs' (2020) 11 Harv Natl Sec J 106; Shiri Krebs, 'Experimental Data on the Efficacy of International Fact-Finding' in Rossana Deplano and Nicholas Tsagourias (eds), *Research Methods in International Law: A Handbook* (Elgar 2021), ch 15, 258–59.

[64] Shiri Krebs, 'The Invisible Frames Affecting Wartime Investigations: Legal Epistemology, Metaphors, and Cognitive Biases' in Andrea Bianchi and Moshe Hirsch (eds), *International Law's Invisible Frames* (OUP 2021), ch 7, 132–33.

[65] Tomer Broude, 'Behavioral International Law' (2014) 163 U Pa L Rev 1099.

[66] Lauge N Skovgaard Poulsen, *Bounded Rationality and Economic Diplomacy: The Politics of Investment Treaties in Developing Countries* (CUP 2015) 16–17.

[67] However, this observed outcome bias is somewhat modified by decision-makers' expertise. Tomer Broude and Inbar Levy, 'Outcome Bias and Expertise in Investigations under International Humanitarian Law' (2019) 30 EJIL 1303. For a detailed analysis of biases and heuristics affecting arbitrators, see Susan D Franck and others, 'Inside the Arbitrator's Mind' (2017) 66 Emory LJ 1115.

The different types and operation of the biases mentioned above are often interconnected, highlighting the connections and potential contributions of critical and cognitive-behavioural approaches to international law. For example, decision-making biases can contribute to the perpetuation of structural biases reflected in the design of legal tools, as some decision biases, such as confirmation bias, may lead to decisions that reinforce existing inequalities. At the same time, structural biases can also trigger cognitive biases by influencing the types of information and experiences to which decision-makers are exposed. Together, both critical and cognitive-behavioural approaches thus lay bare the power dynamics and bias in the structure and application of international law, elucidating the role of politics and ideologies in the design of international legal norms and in the outcomes of international legal processes. As Koskenniemi notes, 'A court's decision or a lawyer's opinion is always a genuinely political act, a choice between alternatives not fully dictated by external criteria. It is even a hegemonic act in the precise sense that though it is partial and subjective, it claims to be universal and objective.'[68]

## 4.2. Tensions: universalism/localisation, empiricism/deconstruction, pragmatism/resistance

Thus far, despite their common interest in exposing bias in the international legal system, critical and cognitive-behavioural approaches to international law have developed mostly in scholarly silos, with little engagement between one another. This separation is perhaps not surprising, considering the different (if not opposing) sets of assumptions and epistemological commitments underlying each of these approaches.[69] Three types of actual or perceived tensions—which are interconnected and intertwined—have thus far prevented a meaningful engagement between cognitive-behavioural and critical approaches to international law: the first tension lies between the universalist commitment of cognitive-behavioural sciences and the localised, situated approach to knowledge production advanced by critical theory. The second tension lies between the commitment of behavioural sciences to empirical inquiry and the general suspicion in which (some) critical approaches treat the 'neutrality' of facts and fact-finding (through a commitment to a critique of objectivity and a focus on the social construction of facts). The third tension relates to the ideological (or political) commitments of the research enterprise and its role in the world.

First, *universalism versus localisation*: the science of behaviour was developed as part of the empiricist era in Western philosophy. As such, it relies on the idea that the scientific method is universal and that problems or questions relating to

[68] Koskenniemi (n 53) 47.
[69] Abebe, Chilton, and Ginsburg (n 1) 20.

behaviour can be solved by applying universal scientific methods.[70] This idea of universalism of scientific methods is in constant tension with critical epistemologies, depicting the diverse social, cultural, and historical contexts that shape behaviour and exposing the contingencies of legal structures and their political functions.[71]

Second, *empiricism versus deconstruction*: while behavioural science is committed to empiricism, critical theory is not dependent upon—or fully committed to—an empirical inquiry. Some critical insights are not necessarily dependent upon empirical observations, cannot always be observed, or take issue with the act of observation itself (noting that facts are social constructs and thus are never 'found' or 'observed' but rather socially constructed).[72] Therefore, some critical scholars warned that adopting social science methods may undermine 'critiques of objectivity and neutrality' and may limit 'the theory's ability to combat structural forms of racial inequality'.[73] Against the cognitive-behavioural focus on a scientific process of empirical data collection and analysis, the methods of critique include 'epistemological deconstruction, historicization, law and literature and law and popular culture, interdisciplinarity, and field analysis'.[74] Through these methods and tools, critical approaches tend to highlight the contingency of both legal and factual frameworks, shedding light on counterfactuals and alternatives.[75]

Third, *pragmatism versus resistance*: at its core, the cognitive-behavioural project has a pragmatic agenda; it is designed to identify psychological mechanisms and to measure their effects on human behaviour. Similar to other policy-orientated approaches to legal studies (including empirical legal studies) that aspire to 'use law as an instrument of public policy',[76] behavioural studies typically aim to elicit recommendations that improve existing practices and decision-making processes in various contexts. Recent advances in cognitive-behavioural science focus on applied research questions, aiming to detect the effects of interventions on actual decision-makers (eg judges, military officers, humanitarian negotiators).[77] The insights drawn from such experiments are often tailored to the

[70] William M Baum, *Understanding Behaviorism: Behavior, Culture, and Evolution* (John Wiley & Sons 2017); Johannes Thome, 'The Problem of Universalism in Psychiatry' in Thomas Schramme and Johannes Thome (eds), *Philosophy and Psychiatry* (De Gruyter 2004) 140.

[71] (Cross-reference:) Note that some of this tension may partially be resolved by adopting non-universal conceptions of cognition (as discussed in Chapter 3 by Johnstone and Sukumar in this volume on the constructivist approach), as well as the cognitive-sociology approach (as presented by Chapter 9 by Hirsch in this volume).

[72] Ingo Venzke, 'Cognitive Biases and International Law: What's the Point of Critique?' in Andrea Bianchi and Moshe Hirsch (eds), *International Law's Invisible Frames* (OUP 2021) 56–57.

[73] Devon W Carbado and Daria Roithmayr, 'Critical Race Theory Meets Social Science' (2014) 10 Ann Rev L Soc Sci 149.

[74] Mégret (n 6) 21.

[75] Venzke (n 72) 70.

[76] Austin Sarat and Susan Silbey, 'The Pull of the Policy Audience' (1988) 10 Law and Pol 97.

[77] Broude and Levy (n 67); Ariella S Kristal and Ashley V Whillans, 'What We Can Learn from Five Naturalistic Field Experiments that Failed to Shift Commuter Behaviour' (2020) 4 Nat Hum Behav 169.

context and decision-makers involved in generating the findings. While valuable and influential, such recommendations typically focus on improving existing systems and frameworks and are constrained by what Sarat and Silbey called already in 1988 'The Pull of the Policy Audience'.[78]

In contrast, critical scholarship is often associated with a different type of scientific advancement and change. As noted above, critical theory does not aim to generate concrete recommendations or programmes for improving existing structures and processes. Instead, it provides ways to reevaluate and to question existing systems and processes. As such, critique is not—and should not be—constrained by what change or improvement is feasible within the constraints of existing systems. Instead, it invites scholars to question or resist the political imposition of power.[79] Moreover, some critiques—including those associated with the CLS movement and TWAIL—tend to view the role of legal scholarship as a mean to advance concrete social and political values, such as equality, diversity, and justice. This ideological commitment centres on resistance and contestation (rather than on practical or feasible improvements of existing systems), mapping, supporting, and participating in what Akbar, Ashar, and Simonson call 'Movement Law'.[80]

The tensions between these two approaches to the role of legal scholarship are twofold: first, there is a tension between pragmatism (a pragmatic approach to law reform that centres on feasible improvements to existing legal systems) and resistance (a commitment to continuously resist faulty legal systems in a variety of ways, including the development of radical alternatives to existing systems). Second, these is a tension between research that is ideologically motivated and the idea of perceived indifference towards the outcomes of the scientific inquiry.[81] In a recent article criticising TWAIL scholarship, Naz Modirzadeh characterises TWAIL's lack of concrete political outcomes as a 'failure', calling for a shift of TWAIL's critique from a focus on 'wellness' to concrete and feasible political action (within the pragmatic constraints of existing international law structures).[82] Modirzadeh's criticism of TWAIL scholarship reflects some of the abovementioned tensions, as what she sees as a failure (to mobilise law reform or improve existing policies) may also be interpreted as a successful act of resistance and contestation. The very definitions of 'failure' and 'success' may vary based on the theoretical, methodological, and ideological lenses through which an act (or a piece of scholarship) is judged.

Understanding these tensions is therefore a necessary first step in evaluating how critical and cognitive-behavioural approaches can meaningfully engage with

[78] Sarat and Silbey (n 76).

[79] Butler (n 5).

[80] Amna A Akbar, Sameer M Ashar, and Jocelyn Simonson, 'Movement Law' (2021) 73 Stan L Rev 821.

[81] 'once the method is deployed, the answers are to be pursued neutrally'. Abebe, Chilton, and Ginsburg (n 1) 20.

[82] Naz K Modirzadeh, '"[L]et Us All Agree to Die a Little": TWAIL's Unfulfilled Promise' (2023) 65 Harv Intl L J 79.

one another, enriching the discussion and pushing disciplinary boundaries. In fact, these tensions are at the heart of the contribution that such an engagement holds, as I further explore below.

### 4.3. Engagement and contribution

Building on the abovementioned point of conversion—while acknowledging the existing tensions—I identify three areas for possible interaction and engagement: the first is methodological, the second is theoretical, and the third proposes a disciplinary self-reflection.

First, behavioural sciences provide scientific standards and analytical approaches to test theoretical explanations and critiques. Therefore, this literature may contribute to critical scholarship through robust data collection methods, including tools to test theoretical arguments and competing explanations about systemic biases in international institutions. Indeed, already in 2011 Eslava and Pahuja called for a 'methodological turn' that will sharpen and advance TWAIL's contributions.[83] More recently, James Gathii, one of the leading TWAIL scholars, noted that social science methods can be 'fruitfully applied to answer questions that critical international law scholars are interested in'.[84] Critical legal scholars may choose to adopt and adapt experiments as a methodology to test arguments about bias in the international legal system (including comparing the outcomes or effects of concrete legal structures) and to use regression analysis to detect correlations and test hypotheses about the effects of diversity among international decision-makers and their propensity to support sanctions or interventions in Third World countries. For example, Gathii's study on the *American Journal of International Law*'s (AJIL's) racial bias utilised content analysis to measure the percentage of race-centred scholarship published in AJIL and AJIL Unbound throughout the years. He then continued to develop four hypotheses (or speculations) that may explain the findings. While some of these concrete hypotheses are impossible to test scientifically in their historical context, cognitive-behavioural methods can provide pathways to test the more general arguments concerning causes or sources of faulty decision-making processes in legal and academic institutions. For example, it is possible to design an experiment that measures the effects of various interventions (different topics, authors, citations) on editors' (or legal professionals') preferences. In parallel, critical scholarship may propose ways to improve or revise existing methods by critically examining the scope of data collection and sampling techniques by

[83] Eslava and Pahuja (n 32).

[84] James Thuo Gathii, 'Studying Race in International Law Scholarship Using a Social Science Approach' (2021) 22 Chi J Intl L 71, 105.

including relevant cultural elements as core variables, and by identifying omitted variables or deficiencies within core definitions.

Second, behavioural studies can provide critical scholars avenues to correct inequalities through the identification of the concrete mechanisms through which bias and discrimination operate (and are institutionalised). By identifying the concrete mechanisms through which bias and discrimination operate, behavioural studies are geared towards transformation and reform, with a potential to advance social change (at least to some degree, within an existing system or framework). For example, engaging with literature on hindsight bias may expand our understanding of the resilience of some international law narratives.[85] Hindsight theory, as well as anchoring bias, may support and strengthen critiques of international legal structure, as well as suggesting avenues for action and change. Acknowledging the psychological mechanisms that motivate decision-makers to prefer the status quo and devalue the benefits of change can provide the knowledge to create alternatives—for example, alternative treaty-design options—that are better aligned with, for example, the interests of Third World countries (in the context of a TWAIL critique). Moreover, cognitive-behavioural approaches provide a nuanced understanding of state 'interests' and their impact on state preferences and behaviour. While critical approaches focus mainly on material interests and power structures (somewhat similarly to realist theories),[86] cognitive-behavioural approaches expand the understanding of factors (including 'interests') that influence states' actions (through their decision-makers) to include identities, ideologies, and decision-making biases.[87] In parallel, critical theory can develop theoretical propositions that may push behavioural projects beyond their current pragmatic limitations.

Finally, engagement between critical and behavioural approaches to international law provides an opportunity for disciplinary self-reflection. Cognitive biases, such as confirmation bias and motivated cognition theories, are useful analytical tools to discern predispositions and ideological preferences affecting research projects; and systemic biases and power structures provide an opportunity to reflect upon a discipline's core assumptions and the limitations of accepted theories and methodologies.[88] An example of this reflective exercise concerns the role of individuals in both critical and cognitive-behavioural approaches. For some

[85] Venzke (n 72) 70.

[86] Daniel Peat, 'Perception and Process: Towards a Behavioural Theory of Compliance' (2022) 13 J Int Dispute Settl 179, 182.

[87] See Chapter 3 by Johnstone and Sukumar in this volume.

[88] For example, according to WEIRD psychology, 'Decades of psychological research designed to uncover truths about human psychology may have instead uncovered truths about a thin slice of our species—people who live in Western, educated, industrialized, rich, and democratic (WEIRD) nations.' Michael Muthukrishna and others, 'Beyond Western, Educated, Industrial, Rich, and Democratic (WEIRD) Psychology: Measuring and Mapping Scales of Cultural and Psychological Distance' (2020) 31 Psychol Sci 678.

cognitive-behavioural approaches (mainly cognitive psychology and behavioural economics), individuals represent a core actor, directly shaping international law and politics through their decisions and actions (which are influenced by cognitive biases). Behavioural studies demonstrate, for example, how existing beliefs and experiences distort state agents' decisions through the operation of decision-making biases (such as confirmation bias). In the past, critical approaches tended to downplay the dimension of individual agency and psychology, focusing instead on social, cultural, and legal structures.[89] In recent decades, however, decision-makers (and individuals' agency more generally) have taken greater prominence within critical theory.[90] Critical inquiry has thus offered insight concerning the role of individuals' autonomy and agency in both reproducing and changing existing social structures; shedding light on actors' definite freedom and situated knowledge, which is shaped by historically specific contexts and social structures.[91] Within this context, it seems that both critical and cognitive-behavioural approaches can reflect on and modify their insights based on the other discipline's contributions. Critical scholars can inform their critique based on the identification of concrete cognitive biases that shape state behaviour (through individual agents); behaviouralists can better contextualise their analysis, taking account of structural elements and historical contexts that shape and construct individuals' actions.

To demonstrate these general propositions, I offer three examples of concrete decision-making biases that can be utilised to support and advance critiques of international law and institutions: confirmation, saliency, and automation.

*Confirmation bias* generates 'unwitting selectivity in the acquisition and use of evidence'.[92] It refers to people's tendency to seek out and act upon information that confirms their existing beliefs, or to interpret information in a way that validates their prior knowledge. This makes confirmation bias—or cognitive consistency theory—a useful mechanism to explain systematic discrimination of—and even violence towards—minority groups.[93] For example, studies of implicit bias in the context of domestic law enforcement demonstrate that people of colour are more likely to be associated with violent intentions or possession of weapons, leading

[89] Douglas Kellner, 'Critical Theory and The Crisis of Social Theory' (1990) 33 Sociol Perspect 11, 15.

[90] ibid.

[91] James Bohman, 'Critical Theory' (2005) *Stanford Encyclopedia of Philosophy* <https://plato.stanford.edu/Entries/critical-theory> accessed 15 April 2024. See also Tamar Megiddo, 'The Missing Persons of International Law Scholarship: A Roadmap for Future Research' in Harlan G Cohen and Timothy Meyer (eds), *International Law as Behavior* (CUP 2021) 230–64, 231 ('We must recognize the central role of individuals in the everyday practice of international law: not only their impact their state's behaviour, but also their engagement with international law and their potential influence outside and irrespective of their state').

[92] Raymond S Nickerson, 'Confirmation Bias: A Ubiquitous Phenomenon in Many Guises' (1998) 2 Rev Gen Psych 175.

[93] Moshe Hirsch, 'Cognitive Sociology, Social Cognition and Coping with Racial Discrimination in International Law' (2019) 30 EJIL 1319.

to excessive and unjustified use of force.[94] Law enforcement officers are prone to evaluate a situation, including risk assessments and interpretation of behaviour, based on their expectations (which are shaped by social stereotypes). Indeed, critical race theory has thus benefitted from behavioural insights on the operation of confirmation (or cognitive consistency) bias. Critical approaches to international law (which are already connected with critical race theory) can similarly benefit from these insights, as applied to state violence in the international level. Decisions to resort to use of force in the international sphere are similarly affected by confirmation bias in the context of threat perception. In his seminal work on war and misperception, Robert Jervis utilised cognitive-behavioural insights, including confirmation bias, to explain how misperception (broadly conceived) of state actions and communications may lead to war (speculating that 'misperceptions might lead to World War III').[95] Returning to TWAIL critique, confirmation bias can explain legal decision-making processes leading to the perpetuation of systemic bias in international law. For example, it can explain inflictions of international sanctions against non-Western countries, as their actions and intentions are more likely to be perceived as threatening or violent, confirming prior beliefs linking Third World countries with violence and threat (and identifying some types of state-inflicted violence, typically linked with Third World countries, as justifying international intervention). Another example follows Anne Orford's critique of the selectivity characterising decisions to support humanitarian interventions in some conflicts but not in others.[96] One cognitive mechanism through which such selectivity may be exercised in legal decision-making processes is cognitive consistency and confirmation bias (leading decision-makers to interpret Third World countries' intentions and actions, as well as the gravity of these actions, more negatively than the way similar actions by Western countries are judged).

*Saliency* refers to features of stimuli that 'draw, grab, or hold attention relative to alternative features'.[97] When processing new information, salient features may capture decision-makers' attention, affecting their judgement.[98] The concept of salience can support critical theories, providing an explanation for structural biases in both domestic and international legal systems. Behavioural studies on implicit racial bias have demonstrated how race salience influences weapon identification in legal contexts, as well as how it may influence jurors' decision-making.[99]

[94] Gordon B Moskowitz and Devon Carter, 'Confirmation Bias and the Stereotype of the Black Athlete' (2018) 36 PS&E 139.

[95] Robert Jervis, 'War and Misperception' (1988) 18 J Interdiscip Hist 675, 690.

[96] Orford (n 13).

[97] E Tory Higgins, 'Knowledge Activation: Accessibility, Applicability, and Salience' in E Tory Higgins and Arie W Kruglanski (eds), *Social Psychology: Handbook of Basic Principles* (Guilford 1966) 135.

[98] Valerio Santangelo, 'Forced to Remember: When Memory Is Biased by Salient Information' (2015) 283 Behav Brain Res 1.

[99] Findings from six experiments conducted by Todd and others demonstrated that when race was salient, seeing Black (versus White) male faces led to an initial bias identifying a portrayed object as a

Within the counterterrorism literature, Landau and others utilised experiments to measure the effects of mortality salience on support for counterterrorism policies, finding that the salience of the 9/11 attacks on the Twin Towers increased support for President Bush and his counterterrorism policies.[100] In a similar way, the literature on saliency bias can be used to support TWAIL-based critiques of international law. For example, both race salience and mortality salience may explain why decision-makers within international criminal tribunals such as the International Criminal Court (ICC) have focused on African perpetrators, or why their complementarity assessments (in particular, evaluating the 'unable or unwilling' standard as reflected in article 17 of the Rome Statue)[101] may disadvantage African countries.

*Automation bias* refers to decision-makers' tendency to place an inappropriately high level of trust in technology-generated data.[102] As a result of this high level of trust, decision-makers may trust technology-generated outputs more than is rational. Skitka, Mosier, and Burdick found that decision-makers were more likely to make errors of omission and errors of commission when they were assisted by automated aids (such as a computer monitoring system).[103] Unpacking decision-makers' automation bias can provide evidence demonstrating how security preferences are generated and institutionalised, supporting critiques arguing that military technologies disproportionately target marginalised communities. For example, critiquing the prevalence and normalisation of surveillance technologies, Finn and Wright argue that drone technologies are used to normalise security preferences and present them as neutral and necessary.[104] Behavioural insights on automation bias can support this argument, identifying the cognitive dynamics—including automation bias—that motivate individuals to trust digital technologies and follow the outcomes of digital analysis.

A prevalent example in this context is the mounting reliance on digital technologies to assist legal decision-making processes during armed conflicts. Such technologies—including drone vision, collateral damage algorithms, and AI-based

'gun' (as opposed to 'tool'). Andrew R Todd and others, 'Category Salience and Racial Bias in Weapon Identification: A Diffusion Modeling Approach' (2021) 129 J Pers Soc Psychol 672; Samuel R Sommers and Phoebe C Ellsworth, '"Race Salience" in Juror Decision-Making: Misconceptions, Clarifications, and Unanswered Questions' (2009) 27 Behav Sci and L 599.

[100] Mark J Landau and others, 'Deliver Us from Evil: The Effects of Mortality Salience and Reminders of 9/11 on Support for President George W. Bush' (2004) 30 Pers Soc Psychol Bull 1136.

[101] Gregory S McNeal, 'ICC Inability Determinations in Light of the Dujail Case' (2006) 39 Case W Res J Intl L 325.

[102] Linda J Skitka, Kathleen L Mosier, and Mark Burdick, 'Does Automation Bias Decision-Making?' (1999) 51 Intl J Hum Comp Stud 991.

[103] ibid.

[104] Rachel L Finn and David Wright, 'Unmanned Aircraft Systems: Surveillance, Ethics and Privacy in Civil Applications' (2012) 28 CLSR 184.

targeting systems—are often perceived as 'precision technologies', supporting military decision-makers with accurate and timely information. At the same time, they distance human decision-makers from the outcomes of their decisions and legitimise military violence that follows algorithmic advice.[105] The literature in critical security studies, posthuman feminism, and TWAIL has critiqued the situated, limited view of the modern battlefield generated by military data practices.[106] Existing critiques shed light on the role of military technologies in threat and target generation, as well as on their effects on human agency (and the meaning of 'human' and 'humanism' more broadly). As Arvidsson observes, these military data practices are not separate from the humans they 'inform',[107] and as Gregory notes, different military participants (or viewers) see different things depending on their physical—but also cultural and political—positions.[108] These systemic critiques of military technologies can be supported and complemented by cognitive-behavioural studies identifying the effects of technology-related biases—including automation bias—on the application of core international law principles, such as distinction and proportionality.[109]

Information generated through military technologies (whether drone sensors or AI-powered algorithms) is mediated not only through systemic positioning, as identified by Gregory, Haraway, and others,[110] but also through human cognition.[111] Humans design military technologies (including the assumptions ingrained into their processes), apply the data these technologies generate to concrete circumstances, train algorithms with particular datasets, interpret their outputs, and communicate this interpretation to decision-makers up the chain of command. The tendency to trust technology-generated information more than one should (or more than is rational) thus means that other types of information may be unjustly disregarded, or that an AI-powered target identification, for example, may not have effective checks or control in place.

[105] Shiri Krebs, 'Above the Law: Drones, Aerial Vision, and the Law of Armed Conflict—A Socio-Technical Approach' (2023) 105 IRRC 1690.

[106] Donna Haraway, 'Situated Knowledges: The Science Question in Feminism and the Privilege of Partial Perspective' (1988) 14 Fem Stud 575, 582; Shiri Krebs, 'Drone-Cinema, Data Practices, and the Narrative of IHL' (2022) 82 HJIL 309.

[107] Matilda Arvidsson, 'Targeting, Gender, and International Posthumanitarian Law and Practice: Framing the Question of the Human in International Humanitarian Law' (2018) 44 Aust Fem LJ 9, 12

[108] Derek Gregory, 'From a View to a Kill: Drones and Late Modern War' (2011) 28 Theory Cult 188; Derek Gregory, 'Eyes in the Sky—Bodies on the Ground' (2018) 6 Crit Stud Secur 347.

[109] Krebs (n 105).

[110] Gregory (n 108); Haraway (n 106).

[111] Krebs (n 105).

As a result, the cognitive assemblages linking humans and machines must be studied holistically. In her defining work on cognitive assemblages, Kathryn Hayles observes that 'international treatises delineating so-called laws of war ... assume that agency and consequently decisional power lie entirely with humans without considering the effects of technical mediations'.[112] She therefore expands the human-centric cognitive process of data interpretation to include 'processes occurring at multiple levels and sites within biological life forms and technical systems',[113] focusing on the interconnectedness of humans and technical systems. This interconnectedness captures the heart of what I see as the mutual benefits of scholarly engagement between critical and cognitive-behavioural approaches to international law. It invites us to consider findings from different fields of study as a necessary exercise to understand legal decision-making processes and their weaknesses. In the context of military data practices, this process allows us to evaluate how vision sensors and AI-powered algorithms affect human consciousness, unconscious, and nonconsciousness, and at the same time, how human cognition feeds back into technical systems.[114]

## 5. Conclusion

Despite their differences—methodologically, theoretically, and ideologically—both critical and cognitive-behavioural approaches to international law share a commitment to complexity: a reading of knowledge production as a situated exercise, affected by geography, positioning, and motivations. Bringing together critical and cognitive-behavioural approaches to international law has many benefits, methodologically and theoretically. On the one hand, critical approaches to international law can find support—and a potential for greater impact—through interacting with cognitive-behavioural theories and methods. On the other hand, behavioural scholarship can benefit from a critical exploration of some of the discipline's underlying assumptions, including core measurements and definitions. Adopting a critical lens to expand our understanding of the international legal system can also provide cognitive-behavioural approaches with tools to reflect on the politics of measurement and to consider creative alternatives and more meaningful changes. This type of engagement can also provide each discipline with useful tools for self-reflection, improvement, and growth, through continuously challenging and rethinking existing baselines and boundaries, as well as the

[112] N Katherine Hayles, 'Cognitive Assemblages: Technical Agency and Human Interactions' (2016) 43 Crit Inq 32, 35.
[113] ibid 32.
[114] ibid 33.

role of scholarship more broadly. The main benefit, though, is not disciplinary; it is humanistic: openness to alternative approaches and a genuine consideration of scholarly tensions and the type of change scholarship can and should make in the world can foster fruitful collaborations that advance international law scholarship, offering both pragmatic improvements and long-term resistance to—or reimagination of—existing tools.

# 5

# A Cognitive-Behavioural Approach to Feminist Studies

*Veronika Fikfak*

## 1. Introduction

Feminist studies have sought to provide us with a critical analysis of international law. In particular, they have aimed to show how existing structures, processes, and methodologies of international law marginalise women by failing to take into account their lives and experiences. In many respects, this literature has argued for a need for women to be represented in the international legal community, including on judicial and arbitration panels, and for their different voices to be heard as an essential part of international law. In their writings, feminist scholars have eschewed doctrinal analysis of the law and rejected quantitative methodologies used in political sciences and law and economics literature. Instead, through a powerful critical and constructivist approach, they have questioned the underrepresentation of women in positions of power and influence and imagined what law would look like—what its focus and approach would be—if more women and other minority groups were involved and included in the making and the application of international law and legal rules. Today, the Third World Approaches to International Law (TWAIL) and feminist as well as other critical approaches have proliferated and become mainstream in international law, a testament to what powerful and well-evidenced critique of scholars can achieve.

In this chapter, I want to show how even without referring to cognitive studies, feminist theory has used many cognitive concepts to support its major claims about the lack of women and the male-dominated international law. In fact, there are several areas of overlap between feminist studies and cognitive approaches. Specifically, both disciplines depart from rational choice assumptions and highlight various cognitive biases. I specifically show how both feminist theory and cognitive studies seek to uncover stereotyping, salience, and status quo biases, as well as intergroup bias. Both are able to reveal structural inequality and systemic problems of subordination. Yet, they achieve this through different approaches: whilst feminist studies adopt a critical and constructivist approach, cognitive studies employ a range of in-person experiments, quantitative empirical studies, and computer modelling. Some of these methods have been shunned or rejected by feminist scholars, since in the past they had been used to perpetuate inequalities

Veronika Fikfak, *A Cognitive-Behavioural Approach to Feminist Studies* In: *International Legal Theory and the Cognitive Turn*. Edited by: Anne van Aaken and Moshe Hirsch, Oxford University Press. 
DOI: 10.1093/9780198909293.003.0006

and the status quo—a male-dominated world and neoliberal reliance on markets, deregulation, and away from redistribution, with little attention paid to the vulnerable. But methods have evolved during the last thirty years and multiple disciplines are increasingly adopting a more data-informed approach. In this context, this chapter engages in an experiment, an 'as if' exercise, in which I explore what we could understand and explain about the causes of neglect and oppression of women in traditional international law if we adopted the cognitive approach and its methods. In doing this, I do not wish to argue that feminist studies lack a methodology or that they require one. I merely wish to show how cognitive science can contribute to feminist studies specifically through structured empirical quantitative studies, controlled experiments, and computer modelling.

The chapter focuses on the idea which gave birth to feminist studies, namely that women are largely absent at international level, be it at the international judiciary, international organisations and diplomacy, or governmental decision-making level; and that this carries serious implications for the focus and approach of traditional international law. First, I show how cognitive modelling can allow us to understand *why* there is a lack of women at the international level and show how persistent this lack is. To understand the structures within the international college, I consider the role of individuals as structure makers and structure takers and aim to shed light on how our embeddedness in society and culture shapes our perceptions of reality and of each other. In this regard, behavioural and physiological sciences can illuminate why and how discrimination arises, to what extent the biases that drive it are unconscious, and how insidious they are.

Second, I examine the argument often made to support greater representation of women in international legal bodies, namely that women think differently than men (giving rise to the assumption that women bring a different voice to adjudication), and that therefore more women in positions of power would lead to different international decisions and in turn international law. This argument is examined through the results of large n-scale studies, which seem to suggest only limited differences between men and women and argue against ascribing cognitive differences to individuals based on gender. Bringing both parts together, the implication is that national societies and the culture of international community seem to matter more than differences in cognition between genders.[1]

My chapter therefore seeks to take an experimental look at feminist studies through the lens of cognitive studies. The chapter underlines the benefits of methodologies used by cognitive-behavioural studies for feminist theory, both in assessing the status quo and in testing out the solutions to it. Insights from these sciences can help us understand better why discrimination and structural inequality towards marginalised groups arises and endures. They can also help us illuminate

[1] See Chapter 10 by Mikael Rask Madsen and Salvatore Caserta in this volume.

the presumed and often hidden assumptions about gender in international law. By debunking some of these myths, we can then focus on the underlying problem and put forward better arguments to ensure equal representation of women on international (legal/judicial) bodies.

The chapter proceeds as follows: Section 2 introduces the intersection between feminist and cognitive studies, Section 3 shows how methods used in cognitive science can uncover the creation of a glass ceiling and show how insidious bias is, Section 4 uses cognitive science to debunk the myth of a different voice, and Section 5 concludes.

## 2. The Intersection between Feminist and Cognitive Studies

There are several areas of overlap between feminist studies and cognitive approaches. Specifically, both areas depart from rational choice assumptions and highlight various cognitive biases. In this section, I specifically show how both feminist theory and cognitive studies seek to uncover different biases, such as stereotyping, salience, status quo bias, and intergroup bias. In particular, I want to show how even without explicitly referring to cognitive studies, feminist theory has used many cognitive concepts to support its major claims about the lack of women and the male-dominated international law.

### 2.1. Feminist approaches to international law

Feminist studies of international law use critical analysis to show how the 'structures, processes, and methodologies of international law marginalize women by failing to take account of their lives or experiences'.[2] The approach takes as its central concern the position of women, placing them at the core of inquiry with a specific aim to redress their structural inequality and oppression in political, social, and economic systems. In this regard, feminist studies seek to do several things: first, uncover and highlight the lack of women (or their very low participation) in senior positions in international institutions (from international judiciaries to international organisations, such as the fact the there has never been a woman United Nations (UN) secretary general, and the underrepresentation of women in other international law-making bodies like the International Law Commission); second, understand how the social constructs of male and female roles lead to different experiences for men and women and then consider how

[2] Christine Chinkin, 'Feminism, Approach to International Law' (October 2010) in Rudiger Wolfrum (ed), *Max Planck Encyclopedia of Public International Law* <https://opil.ouplaw.com/display/10.1093/law:epil/9780199231690/law-9780199231690-e701> accessed 7 August 2023.

international law should reflect and address these in substances and process of the law. In this regard, feminist studies emphasise that traditional international law may appear gender neutral, but in fact its content reflects (and regulates) a male-dominated world of geo-politics, with a particular focus on sovereignty, war and peace, trade, human rights, and international organisations. It fails to take into account specific concerns of women, such as slavery, human trafficking, gender-based crimes, and so on. In addition to uncovering the invisibility of women and the biases and silences of international law and international legal order, feminist legal theory openly seeks to put forward an agenda for the advancement and empowerment of women.

Of course, these are only three main branches of feminist scholarship. Many other scholars have applied the feminist approach to a broad array of topics outside of representation and women's lived experiences. Ratna Kapur and Vasuki Nesiah have analysed postcolonial feminist approaches,[3] Anne Orford studied gendered narratives of humanitarian intervention,[4] Gina Heathcote has looked at the law of force and structural bias feminism,[5] Yoriko Otomo examined state sovereignty from a feminist psychoanalytical perspective,[6] Emily Jones has looked at environmental law and military technologies, and many others.[7] In all of these, feminist studies have been used to critique normative and institutional structures of international law, finding them deeply unequal and committed to masculine (and imperial) power and thus 'in need of significant reconstruction'.[8] More recently, the debate has also tackled the issue of 'the received male/female duality', examining potential possibilities 'that more fluid conceptions of gender and sexuality open for analyzing the law's enduring exclusionary effects'.[9]

## 2.2. Cognitive studies and human biases

Traditional approaches to law, so-called rational choice theory, assume that people are rational and know what they want and are thus able to rank different choices according to the utility they derive from them.[10] But as early as in the mid-1950s,

[3] Ratna Kapur, *Gender, Alterity and Human Rights: Freedom in a Fishbowl* (Elgar 2018).

[4] Anne Orford, *Reading Humanitarian Intervention: Human Rights and the Use of Force in International Law* (CUP 2003).

[5] Gina Heathcote, *The Law on the Use of Force: A Feminist Analysis* (Routledge 2011).

[6] Yoriko Otomo, 'Her Proper Name: A Revisionist Account of International Law' (2014) 2 London Review of International Law 149.

[7] Hilary Charlesworth, Gina Heathcote, and Emily Jones, 'Feminist Scholarship on International Law in the 1990s and Today: An Inter-Generational Conversation' (2019) 27 Feminist Legal Studies 79.

[8] Diane Otto, 'Feminist Approaches to International Law' (*Obo*) <www.oxfordbibliographies.com/display/document/obo-9780199796953/obo-9780199796953-0055.xml> accessed 7 August 2023.

[9] ibid.

[10] Eyal Zamir and Doron Teichman, *Behavioral Law and Economics* (OUP 2018) 7. For a summary and defence of rational choice theory, see the founding father of law and economics, Richard Posner, 'Rational Choice, Behavioral Economics, and the Law' (1997) 50 Stanford Law Review 1551.

Herbert Simon introduced the concept of bounded rationality. Bounded rationality recognises that we have limited cognitive capacities. As such, we do not always behave in a fully rational manner.[11] According to Simon, our bounded rationality shows through when a problem is sufficiently difficult,[12] leading us to choose solutions that are merely satisfying as opposed to optimal.[13] It was in the early 1970s that Kahneman and Tversky pushed the boundaries of bounded rationality further by showing that even simple problems can induce suboptimal choices.[14] They argued that in addition to making 'good enough' decisions, people predominantly rely on simple, intuitive, rule-of-thumb decision-making. When making decisions, Kahneman and Tversky showed that people rely on a limited number of mental shortcuts (ie heuristics) which reduce the complex tasks of assessing probabilities and predicting values to simpler judgemental operations.[15] In general, these shortcuts are quite useful: since they come about automatically, they allow people to allocate their mental energy elsewhere. However, Kahneman and Tversky showed that the use of heuristics may also lead to severe and systematic errors, known as cognitive biases.[16]

Cognitive studies focus on exposing these biases and how they affect our decision-making. According to Hastie and Rasinski, cognitive biases can be categorised into three broad classes of systematic errors in judgement: sins of imprecision, sins of commission, and sins of omission.[17] The first group relates to the discrepancy between criteria we are supposed to apply and the reality of human judgement. Studies have shown that as individuals we rarely alter our own subjective probability judgements in response to new, diagnostic information. Instead, we remain (over)confident in the accuracy of our own assessment, making shortcuts that overestimate the likelihood of an event or its frequency not by investigating statistics but based on how many similar instances are brought to mind (availability heuristic),[18] or focusing on items that are more prominent or emotionally striking and ignoring those that are unremarkable (salience bias) and believing that multiple events can co-occur at the same time (conjunction fallacy). Similarly, we adjust out decisions depending on how outcomes are framed.

[11] Herbert Simon, 'A Behavioral Model of Rational Choice' (1955) 69 The Quarterly Journal of Economics 99.

[12] Herbert Simon, *The Sciences of the Artificial* (3rd edn, vol 1, The MIT Press 1996).

[13] Simon (n 11).

[14] Amos Tversky and Daniel Kahneman, 'Judgment under Uncertainty: Heuristics and Biases' (1974) 185 Science 1124.

[15] ibid.

[16] ibid. Note that in the literature the terms 'bias' and 'errors' in cognitive processing are used interchangeably; however, certain scholars dispute that bias is necessarily an error to rational/normal/valid behaviour. They specifically question whether valid behaviour/normal/rational behaviour exists and therefore reject the terminology of 'error'. Arie W Kruglanski and Icek Ajzen, 'Bias and Error in Human Judgment' (1983) 13 European Journal of Social Psychology 1.

[17] Reid Hastie and Kenneth A Rasinski, 'The Concept of Accuracy in Social Judgment' in Daniel Bar-Tal and Arie W Kruglanski (eds), *The Social Psychology of Knowledge* (CUP 1988) 193.

[18] Tversky and Kahneman (n 14).

Kahneman and Tversky have shown that we have a clear preference for uncertain loss (compared to certain loss) but also a preference for certain gain (compared to uncertain gain). How things are framed or 'labelled' therefore shapes our perception of them and how we react to them. In the context of prospect theory, we are risk-seeking when outcomes are framed as losses but risk-averse when outcomes are framed as gains.[19]

The second group of biases—the 'sins of commission'—note that although we are required to treat certain information as irrelevant for judgement (such as the race of a victim or the attractiveness of a defendant), we nevertheless take it into account and use it to affect our assessment of guilt or innocence or other decision-making processes. Similarly, we remain over-reliant on information that is or ought to be irrelevant to our judgements, including, for example, the belief that past investments justify further expenditures (sunk cost fallacy), or we rely on reference points as 'anchors' (anchoring effect). We also tend to interpret, favour, or recall information in a manner that confirms our beliefs or values and thus expresses preference when none should be had (confirmation bias).[20]

The third group—the 'sins of omission'—reveals that biases can also have the opposite effect. In certain situations, we fail to use information that is relevant to inform our judgements, for example by sticking to the status quo and perceiving any change from this baseline as a loss (status quo bias) or we underemphasise situational and environmental explanations for an individual's observed behaviour whilst over-emphasising personality-based explanations (correspondence bias).

These shortcuts that we make in our decision-making most typically involve stereotyping, drawing distinctions between groups on the basis of their group membership. Once we belong to a social group, we tend to differentiate ourselves by group membership and use our biases to help us maintain a favourable image of ourselves and attribute positive traits to our friends and our reference group. It is the formation of such an 'ingroup' that leads to discrimination. Once we identify as part of an ingroup, we see other members of the ingroup as 'trustworthy, cooperative, peaceful, and honest' and we provide each other with preferential treatment. In contrast, members of the 'outgroup' are believed to be 'untrustworthy, competitive, quarrelsome, and dishonest'.[21] In this context, although intended to merely provide positive favouritism towards ingroup members, our behaviour is

[19] Jack S Levy, 'Prospect Theory and International Relations: Theoretical Applications and Analytical Problems' (1992) 13 Political Psychology 283; James Davis (ed), *Psychology, Strategy and Conflict* (Routledge 2013) 5.

[20] See Anne van Aaken and Moshe Hirsch's Introduction to this volume; Raymond S Nickerson, 'Confirmation Bias: A Ubiquitous Phenomenon in Many Guises' (1998) 2 Review of General Psychology 175.

[21] Marilynn Brewer, *Intergroup Relations* (2nd edn, Open UP 2003, repr 2009) 51; Susan T Fiske, *Intergroup Biases: A Focus on Stereotype Content* (2015) 3 Current Opinion in Behavioural Sciences 45, 54.

accompanied by a number of biases that sustain and reinforce discriminatory behaviour and potentially lead to 'outgroup' negativity.[22]

## 2.3. A cognitive lens on feminist studies

First, like cognitive studies, feminist scholars seek to expose the silences and biases of international law. In *The Boundaries of International Law*, Chinkin and Charlesworth speak of the biased 'vocabulary of international law'.[23] Although the terminology may appear neutral, they note the gendered nature of the basic concepts of international law; for example, the paired dichotomies of intervention–non-intervention; sovereign–domestic jurisdiction; protector–protected; objective–subjective; action–passivity; public–private; and combatant–non-combatant. This 'gendered coding of binary oppositions' suggests that *stereotyping* is in operation, namely that dichotomies are used to assign traits to different categories (eg women and men). In particular, as feminists show, the respective first term is associated with 'more highly valued male characteristics or identity' and dictates the 'law's priorities and values to be protected'.[24] In contrast, the second term is assigned to women, who are seen as passive, weak, domestic, private, non-powerful, protected, non-combatant, and so on.

But these dichotomies are not merely about stereotyping inherent in international law and the manner in which international legal scholarship constructs gender. As Chinkin shows, they are also about keeping the status quo intact. On the distinction between the public and private, she notes that the 'public realm of the workplace, the law, economics, politics, and intellectual life are regarded as the natural and proper province of men and the private world of the home as that of women'.[25] This division is not coincidental or merely descriptive: instead, the distinction has a 'normative' dimension as well—'greater legal and social significance is accorded to the public world than to the private ... The distinction drawn between the public and the private vindicates and makes natural the division of labour and the allocation of rewards between the sexes'.[26] Chinkin's argument effectively underlines what cognitive studies would consider the *status quo bias*: that international legal rules through their content, processes, and silences seek to maintain a specific visual distinction between sexes, a hierarchical picture that plays a performative role, including by keeping women in their traditional

[22] Brewer (n 21) 65–68, 21. See also John F Dovidio and Samuel L Gaertner, 'Stereotypes and Evaluative Intergroup Bias' in Diane M Mackie and David L Hamilton (eds), *Affect, Cognition and Stereotyping: Interactive Processes in Group Perception* (Elsevier Science 1993) 167, 175.
[23] Hilary Charlesworth and Christine Chinkin, *The Boundaries of International Law: A Feminist Analysis* (Manchester UP 2000) xvii, 337.
[24] Chinkin (n 2).
[25] ibid.
[26] ibid.

roles—for example, maintaining the division of labour, areas, and knowledge in a manner that favour the male and support the dominance of men; and *salience bias*: presenting international law as a legal system that privileges certain issues as more worthy of attention and neglects and ignores others considered of little importance. In addition to uncovering *stereotyping*, feminist studies therefore also criticise the male *default* and *status quo*.

Third, like cognitive studies, feminist theory emphasises the structural nature of bias against women and, in particular, the perpetual absence and exclusion of women from international legal institutions, the sidelining of women's experiences in shaping and applying international law rules, and the lack of (any) engagement with feminist scholarship from traditional international legal scholars.[27] This ignorance and blindness stems from what cognitive sciences label as *intergroup bias*; that is, bias in favour of ingroups at the expense of outgroups. Intergroup relations literature reveals the significant effects of social identity on individuals' cognitive processes and behaviour. Since as humans we seek to belong to social groups, we tend to distinguish ourselves through group membership[28] and tend to 'evaluate one's own membership group more favourably than a nonmembership group'.[29] Empirical studies have persuasively demonstrated that once people identify with a particular social group, they are likely to provide ingroup members preferable treatment.[30] Intergroup bias can therefore include discriminatory behaviour, prejudicial attitude, or stereotyping through cognition.[31] This bias can explain several aspects that feminist theories seeks to uncover: the absence of women in international institutions (eg if women are considered and excluded as the outgroup, they will not be heard, and it is unlikely or less likely that men as the ingroup would promote them or accepted into their group); the stereotyping of specific issues as 'female' issues (eg sexual violence, trafficking, home and family life, and the silence of the discipline in this context); the ignorance of feminist studies by

27 Emily Jones, *Feminist Theory and International Law* (1st edn, Routledge 2023); Emily Jones, 'Posthuman Feminism and Global Constitutionalism: Environmental Reflections' [2022] Global Constitutionalism 1; Hilary Charlesworth, 'Talking to Ourselves? Feminist Scholarship in International Law' in Sari Kuovo and Zoe Pearson (eds), *Feminist Perspectives on Contemporary International Law: Between Resistance and Compliance?* (Oxford 2014) 17; Charlesworth, Heathcote, and Jones (n 7) 29–93; Hilary Charlesworth, 'Feminist Critiques of International Law and Their Critics' (1995) 13 Third World Legal Studies 1.

28 Brewer (n 21) 20. See also Jan Stets and others, 'Getting Identity Right' (2020) 37 Advances in Group Processes 191.

29 Miles Hewstone, Mark Rubin, and Hazel Willis, 'Intergroup Bias' (2002) 53 Annual Review of Psychology 575.

30 Walter Stephan and Cookie W Stephan, *Intergroup Relations* (Routledge 1996) 92–93; Brewer (n 21) 43 et seq.

31 David Wilder and Andrew F Simon, 'Affect as a Cause of Intergroup Bias' in Rupert Brown and Samuel L Gaertner (eds), *Blackwell Handbook of Social Psychology: Intergroup Processes* (Blackwell 2003) 153; Diane M Mackie and Eliot R Smith, 'Intergroup Relations: Insights from a Theoretically Integrative Approach' (1998) 105 Psychological Review 499.

mainstream scholarship (eg if traditional international law scholarship is viewed as the ingroup, then scholars criticising their approach as biased or discriminatory would automatically be treated as the outgroup), and so on.

Although this section suggests there are important links between feminist scholarship and cognitive studies, feminist scholars have been reluctant to engage with cognitive approaches. In addition, rather than questioning structural inequalities, cognitive studies usually tend to be limited to uncovering weaker forms of bias and mild prejudice (such as cognitive shortcuts and errors). Whilst cognitive-psychological studies may seek to understand the causes of these heuristics, they usually stop short of seeking out solutions or question the structure as such.[32] In this regard, feminist scholarship is much more ambitious, refusing to accept the status quo or the intergroup bias as a given and challenging the current gaps and silences in international law as well as reshaping the structures of international legal order. As other chapters have noted, this results in tensions between cognitive science and feminist and other critical approaches (such as TWAIL).[33]

## 3. Using Cognitive Science to Show the Pervasiveness of Bias

Feminist studies, especially those tracking the underrepresentation of women on judicial benches and arbitration panels, note the consistent lack of women in these fora over time. In spite of the great need to ensure diversity, these studies note that time and time again women lose out in elections to men; and that efforts to increase the percentage of females on the bench are often only temporarily reflected in the judicial panels. Psychological and behavioural studies can help us explain why this is the case and uncover how effective measures like quotas can promote female representation in international law. These are especially interesting since certain courts—like the European Court of Human Rights—require state parties to nominate at least one female out of three proposed candidates to the Council of Europe.[34] By looking at studies that have explored such solutions, we can see how effective such measures are likely to be in redressing gender bias inherent in the international legal sphere.

[32] There are some exceptions to this. Patricia G Devine and others, 'A Gender Bias Habit-Breaking Intervention Led to Increased Hiring of Female Faculty in STEMM Departments' (2017) 73 Journal of Experimental Social Psychology 211; Molly Carnes and others, 'The Effect of an Intervention to Break the Gender Bias Habit for Faculty at One Institution: A Cluster Randomized, Controlled Trial' (2015) 90 Academic Medicine 221.

[33] See Chapter 4 by Shiri Krebs in this volume.

[34] Parliamentary Assembly of the Council of Europe, 'Committee on the Election of Judges' <https://pace.coe.int/en/pages/committee-30/AS-CDH> accessed 9 April 2024.

### 3.1. Modelling bias and the glass ceiling

Recently, studies in psychology have shown that even small preferences for men (rather than women) in an organisational setting can create and maintain gender disparities and lead to the creation of a glass ceiling. Through a computer simulation Du, Nordell, and Joseph explored how interpersonal discrimination affects the dynamics within the organisation and how from the bottom up such small gender biases (either expressed by providing women fewer opportunities for being involved on projects or by assessing their work slightly less generously than men's) can lead to great gender disparities in the corporate hierarchy and block women and other marginalised groups from achieving top positions within the organisation.[35] The study looked at situations where women's successes are valued at 2 per cent less than men's in a single situation,[36] or women are provided with 2 per cent less credit than men,[37] or are penalised for exhibiting non-feminine behaviour such as self-promotion;[38] similarly if they receive 2 per cent fewer opportunities for work or growth than men. In these cases, even the small effect of the bias translated into a considerably lower rate of promotability for women. Even more importantly, when these interpersonal discrimination biases were repeated over and over again and reinforced at every level of the organisational hierarchy (ie every time that men were being given a preference for opportunities or promotion over women), the effect of the bias was amplified and with repeat iterations created a glass ceiling, where at higher levels of the hierarchy women were no longer visible. For example, being given an opportunity to work on a project meant that the individuals had the opportunity to succeed and show their skills, which in turn led to more opportunities for work and for promotion. If, at each turn, women were disadvantaged by only 2 per cent, over time this meant that it was not the depth of bias that worked to their detriment but rather its repeat iteration and the frequency with which that preference was given to men through the hierarchical

[35] Richard F Martell, David M Lane, and Cynthia Emrich, 'Male-Female Differences: A Computer Simulation' (1996) 51 American Psychologist 157.

[36] Corinne A Moss-Racusin and others, 'Science Faculty's Subtle Gender Biases Favor Male Students' (2012) 109 Proceedings of the National Academy of Sciences 16474; Emilio J Castilla, 'Gender, Race, and Meritocracy in Organizational Careers' (2008) 113 American Journal of Sociology 1479; Chieh-Chen Bowen, Janet K Swim and Rick R Jacobs, 'Evaluating Gender Biases on Actual Job Performance of Real People: A Meta-Analysis 1' (2000) 30 Journal of Applied Social Psychology 2194; Janet Swim and others, 'Joan McKay versus John McKay: Do Gender Stereotypes Bias Evaluations?' (1989) 105 Psychological Bulletin 409; Janet K Swim and Lawrence J Sanna, 'He's Skilled, She's Lucky: A Meta-Analysis of Observers' Attributions for Women's and Men's Successes and Failures' (1996) 22 Personality and Social Psychology Bulletin 507; Alice H Eagly, Mona G Makhijani, and Bruce G Klonsky, 'Gender and the Evaluation of Leaders: A Meta-Analysis' (1992) 111 Psychological Bulletin 3.

[37] Heather Sarsons and others, 'Gender Differences in Recognition for Group Work' (2021) 129 Journal of Political Economy 101.

[38] Richard F Martell, Cynthia G Emrich, and James Robison-Cox, 'From Bias to Exclusion: A Multilevel Emergent Theory of Gender Segregation in Organizations' (2012) 32 Research in Organizational Behavior 137.

structure within the organisation that led to the creation of pervasive disparities in the corporate hierarchy. Differences in promotion opportunities significantly altered career trajectories but only for a small number of individuals who benefitted immensely, whilst others—mostly women—were losing out consistently. The more levels of hierarchy existed within the organisation, the greater the resulting bias at the end. Those women who were found at the top level of the hierarchy had a greater track record of successes than their male counterparts, showing that women had to work much harder and show more successes than men to achieve the same level in the hierarchy.

From international legal perspective, this study is especially important because it suggests that even in hierarchies and societies where discrimination is not visible, several forces—such as more opportunities for growth or success—could be leading to underrepresentation of women in international judicial and quasi-judicial panels, international organisations, and international legal college more generally. First, the study shows how even a small preference for men tends to have a great impact on the composition of bodies, panels, and organisations. In international law, this preference can be seen frequently: when states nominate candidates to judicial positions, they often propose men or when required to nominate multiple candidates, they often put men at the top of their lists. In the European Court of Human Rights (ECtHR), where states send a list of three candidates, one of which needs to be a woman, states only rarely put women at the top of the list or propose an all-women list. When the voting takes place afterwards, the Council of Europe members give precedence to those candidates that are ranked first.[39] As a consequence, only 30–35 per cent of judges at the ECtHR are women and there are still cases that are adjudicated in men-only panels.[40] Unless gender is made a priority, the salience bias will push towards male appointments.

The problem is even more visible before a more traditional international law body, like the International Court of Justice, where judges' tenure lasts longer than at the ECtHR. There, the number of women has only recently raised to four out of fifteen judges and whilst these appointments have been celebrated, they are still very few and far between. In addition, counsel appearing before the Court are mainly men. Recently, legal teams have started including female members, but these are usually at the junior end.[41] Although certain changes can be noticed, the lack of opportunities for women mean that there are fewer chances to show one's skills and fewer opportunities for success, which in turn reduces the potential

[39] This was the case until the Council of Europe started to be more heavily involved in the judicial selection process. Now, the ordering is alphabetical, though preferences of states may trickle through in other ways.

[40] Stéphanie Hennette Vauchez, 'More Women—But Which Women? The Rule and the Politics of Gender Balance at the European Court of Human Rights' (2015) 26 EJIL 195.

[41] Iben Vagle, 'The (Un)Changing Face of ICJ Advocacy' (5 December 2023) *EJIL:Talk!* <www.ejiltalk.org/the-unchanging-face-of-icj-advocacy> accessed 1 February 2024.

to be appointed to a panel next time around. The PITAD Investment Law and Arbitration Database shows this more clearly, with the majority of the investment arbitrators being male.[42] Only two female arbitrators stand out—consistently appearing in arbitration panels and in terms of numbers outperforming all their male colleagues in frequency of appointments.[43] Beyond these two exceptional females, a small group of white men are consistently claiming appointments, blocking any chances of diverse appointments. Of course, the vicious circle is determined by states and investors who choose arbitrators. In this regard, social networks are important, but the salience bias pushes states to opt for those arbitrators that have served before and/or for those that tend to favour one or the other party, and so on. It is this group that benefits most from the opportunities and is able to achieve more success, thus guaranteeing future appointments. A close group of arbitrators therefore controls this area and has created a glass ceiling that seems almost impossible to break.

## 3.2. The complex dynamics of societal norms and the culture of the international legal community

The second aspect in which Du, Nordell, and Joseph's study can help illuminate the underrepresentation of women in the international legal college is that it reveals how biases develop through interaction of community culture and wider societal norms. As another chapter in this volume explains, socio-cultural factors affect how humans acquire and process information.[44] In particular, cognitive sociologists show that individuals in different cultures have different attention patterns and perceive reality in different ways.[45] Socio-cultural structures thus often underlie individuals' cognitive processes, though they vary and different social groups are likely to show different cognitive-cultural patterns.[46]

[42] Malcolm Langford, Daniel Behn, and Runar Hilleren Lie, 'The Revolving Door in International Investment Arbitration' (2017) 20 Journal of International Economic Law 301.

[43] Susan Franck, 'The Diversity Challenge: Exploring the "Invisible College" of International Arbitration' (2015) 53 Columbia Journal of Transnational Law 429; Sergio Puig, 'Social Capital in the Arbitration Market' (2014) 25 EJIL 387; Shashank P Kumar and Cecily Rose, 'A Study of Lawyers Appearing before the International Court of Justice, 1999–2012' (2014) 25 EJIL 893.

[44] See Chapter 9 by Moshe Hirsch in this volume, citing Karen Cerulo, 'Representation and Integration: An Introduction' in Karen Cerulo (ed), *Culture in Mind: Toward A Sociology of Culture and Cognition* (Routledge 2002) 113; Eviatar Zerubavel, 'Cognitive Sociology: Between the Personal and the Universal Mind' in Wayne H Brekhus and Gabe Ignatow (eds), *The Oxford Handbook of Cognitive Sociology* (OUP 2019) 31, 37–38.

[45] Karen A Cerulo, Vanina Leschziner, and Hana Shepherd, 'Rethinking Culture and Cognition' (2021) 47 Annual Review of Sociology 63, 64.

[46] Hirsch (n 44). For a criticism of the reductionist view assuming that law is only a mirror of society, see, eg, David Nelken, 'Towards a Sociology of Legal Adaptation' in David Nelken and Johannes Feest (eds), *Adapting Legal Cultures* (Hart 2001) 12, 15.

In their model, Du, Nordell, and Joseph focus not only on personal preferences but also note that corporations—like societies—are complex social systems, where social norms and stereotypes diffuse over time through individuals and levels within the organisation, and back and forth between organisation and broader society.[47] For example, they note that individuals tend to be harsher on women who do not display the culturally prescribed behaviour stereotypical of their perceived gender, or they tend to see them as less risk-taking.[48] In addition, family leave and flexible working time play significant roles in limiting the upward mobility of women in the workplace.[49] These stereotypical views are pervasive and place emphasis on innate or learned differences between men and women, implying immutability and permanence, although in fact there is often very little basis for them.

However, the interactions between these perceptions and different structures and hierarchical levels create feedback processes. These are difficult to explain through simple empirical analysis and so instead we need complex social system approaches to understand how individual-level differences or biases are influenced by overarching cultural norms, and how these propagate from lower levels to the top levels of an organisational structure.[50] By modelling separately and together the operation of organisational and societal norms at meso and macro level, how they interact and create feedback loops, and how they reproduce gender disparities in the long term, Du, Nordell, and Joseph show how prevalent bias is within society at large.

In this regard, the study is also better able to explain previous studies, which showed that intergroup bias is insidious in this context. For example, studies of the Israeli army, law students, and blue-collar work groups showed that a greater proportion of men results in more bias against women.[51] As more men appear in organisations or communities, especially if in higher positions, gender disparities increase. Scholars have shown that this only works one way: in the few settings

[47] Yuhao Du, Jessica Nordell, and Kenneth Joseph, 'Insidious Nonetheless: How Small Effects and Hierarchical Norms Create and Maintain Gender Disparities in Organizations' (2022) 8 Socius 23780231221117888.

[48] Renate Schubert and others, 'Gender Specific Attitudes towards Risk and Ambiguity: An Experimental Investigation', Technical Report [2000] Economics Working Paper Series; Ernesto Reuben, Paola Sapienza, and Luigi Zingales, 'Taste for Competition and the Gender Gap among Young Business Professionals', Technical Report [2015], National Bureau of Economic Research; Linda Babcock and Sara Laschever, *Women Don't Ask: Negotiation and the Gender Divide* (Princeton UP 2004).

[49] Joan Williams and Nancy Segal, 'Beyond the Maternal Wall: Relief for Family Caregivers Who Are Discriminated against on the Job' (2003) 26 Harvard Women's Law Journal 77; Becky Pettit and Jennifer Hook, 'The Structure of Women's Employment in Comparative Perspective' (2005) 84 Social Forces 779; Claudia Goldin and Lawrence F Katz, 'A Most Egalitarian Profession: Pharmacy and the Evolution of a Family-Friendly Occupation' (2016) 34 Journal of Labor Economics 705; Julia B Bear, 'Forget the "Mommy Track": Temporal Flexibility Increases Promotion Aspirations for Women and Reduces Gender Gaps' (2021) 45 Psychology of Women Quarterly 294.

[50] Benjamin Ewert, Kathrin Loer, and Eva Thomann, 'Beyond Nudge: Advancing the State-of-the-Art of Behavioural Public Policy and Administration' (2021) 49 Policy and Politics 3.

[51] Asya Pazy and Israela Oron, 'Sex Proportion and Performance Evaluation among High-Ranking Military Officers' (2001) 22 Journal of Organizational Behavior 689.

where women dominated higher levels of the corporate hierarchy, there was little evidence that men were disadvantaged in promotion. Whilst women's lack of representation in certain occupations exacerbates disadvantage, men—especially heterosexual white men, when in short supply—enjoy a 'glass escalator, where they are put on a fast track to advanced positions'[52] and 'their evaluation is not affected by their proportion'.[53]

These descriptions speak of overrepresentation of men in different settings and are similar to what one notices in the international legal college.[54] Du and others' study can thus help us understand that the absence of women in the international legal community is, on one hand, a result of intergroup bias, where men as the ingroup favour other men. On the other hand, however, the glass ceiling is also a result of a complex dynamic social system, where personal biases stemming from wider societal stereotypes (or how we think women should behave) influence how women are perceived. These wider cultural and societal norms directly influence the power dynamics in international law—including international law appointments and promotions—and in turn who gets to sit on international courts and tribunals. When states propose candidates, stereotypes of what role women should play may direct nominations to international fora. Even if today's international law community seeks to establish a more diverse and inclusive culture, the fact that individual member states have not espoused the same values and that national societies remain gender-biased will continue to push the feedback loops towards gender disparities. When thinking about *why* women are underrepresented and have been silenced in international law, we cannot disregard the pervasiveness of the influence of the surrounding society and culture. Specifically, we cannot look for causes of discrimination only at the international level (eg as intergroup bias), but also have to turn our attention to domestic level, from where proposals for nominations come (and also from where stereotypes are likely to stem).

### 3.3. Effectiveness of quotas

Du and others' study shows the insidiousness of bias and raises the question of a glass ceiling and specifically how difficult it is to redress inequalities and discrimination within a closed group, where broader societal values (and biases) may be pushing towards a small preference for one gender. One of the 'fixes' that the study tests are gender quotas; that is, the requirement to achieve a specific number or representation of women in an organisation. The arguments for a quota of women

[52] Michelle J Budig, 'Male Advantage and the Gender Composition of Jobs: Who Rides the Glass Escalator?' (2002) 49 Social Problems 258; Adia Harvey Wingfield. 'Racializing the Glass Escalator: Reconsidering Men's Experiences with Women's Work' (2009) 23 Gender and Society 5.

[53] Pazy and Oron (n 51).

[54] Puig (n 43).

have also been debated in international law.[55] As mentioned earlier, the ECtHR has a requirement that one of the three candidates proposed to the Court from each member state has to be a woman. Similar requirements for the presence of women can be implied or are increasingly expected elsewhere.[56] The question Du and others' study explores is whether these quotas work and whether they redress the gender bias and prevent the development of a glass ceiling.

The study tested whether the requirement to promote women until 70 per cent representation is achieved inside the organisation would redress the gender bias. The results of the model show that regardless of the time period the quota measure was introduced for, once the quotas were no longer applied, the dynamics returned to normal and gender disparities arose again. This was due to the operation of the same dynamics—the personal/societal bias based on stereotypes, which gave men more opportunities for growth and promotion, and over time completely nullified any progress made by the quota measure. The study shows that the impact of a quota requirement is only temporary and that gender disparities will return to normal over time unless the societal and cultural norms within the community also change. The conclusion therefore is that in addition to adopting specific measures to increase the number of women in international legal college, the culture of the local community has to be strong enough to overpower macro-level gender norms (societal norms about whether women fit within certain roles, whether they should be in those roles, etc—ie societal norms which affect and create interpersonal bias). Until then, the glass ceiling in international law will continue to exist.

Du and others' model extends our understanding of how the glass ceiling arises and why it can be resistant to change. By synthesising existing psychological and structural theories of discrimination into a mathematical model, the study has quantified how complex systems can produce and maintain inequality. The modelling shows how pervasive bias is—how it trickles from lower (domestic) levels to higher (international) levels, and how a specific community—international legal college—is not immune to the prevailing cultural and societal stereotypes. In many ways, the model shows how minimal preferences at the level of an individual can have an impact at the systemic level and can effectively exclude one group (women) from decision-making processes and thus create long-term structural inequality. The terms used by feminist studies such as 'oppression' and 'discrimination' seem more than apt. Cognitive studies help to (1) pinpoint the variables that lead to discrimination—individual preferences (which can lead to conscious or unconscious bias), societal influence (eg stereotyping and expectations of women); (2) understand the processes and feedback loops that arise from these, such as the bottom-up influence of domestic on international levels

[55] Jessica Kim and Kathleen M Fallon, 'Making Women Visible: How Gender Quotas Shape Global Attitudes toward Women in Politics' (2023) 19 Politics and Gender 981.

[56] Vagle (n 41).

and then the intergroup relationships that give preference to ingroup members, leading to structural inequality; and (3) understand the resistance of these existing structures to any temporary interventions, such as quotas. In the end, the model reveals that the solution to status quo are *permanent* quotas in favour of the discriminated group.

## 4. Using Cognitive Science to Debunk the Myth of a Different Voice

There are two arguments made for a higher representation of women on international judicial benches. First, the equal representation argument, which essentially posits that women and men should be equally represented on international bodies. Under this argument, it is clear that states are under an obligation to ensure that both men and women are given equal opportunities to participate. It also claims that the legitimacy of international courts and tribunals can be adversely affected by sex-underrepresentative benches. As many have claimed, the 'time is ripe to achieve sex-representative international court benches'.[57]

The second argument is more outcome motivated. Many argue that women bring a different experience and a different voice to a judicial panel, and that this has implications for the content and focus of international law. This argument is made across different areas of scholarship: by some feminist scholars, in general international literature, as well as in other law scholarship.[58] In the next sections, I explain how the argument about women's 'different voice' is really an argument about cognition—the assumption that women and men think differently and therefore approach adjudication (and or treaty making) differently. I then query whether the evidence supports such a view and conclude by arguing that the 'different voice' argument is a damaging myth that imposes too many requirements on women as 'women' on judicial panels and perpetuates stereotypes. Bringing together both cognitive insights and feminist studies, I conclude that the second argument about a 'different voice' should be abandoned, but that the first argument for equal representation remains valid and should stand on its own.

[57] Nienke Grossman, 'Achieving Sex-Representative International Court Benches' (2016) 110 AJIL 82.

[58] Nienke Grossman, 'Sex on the Bench: Do Women Judges Matter to the Legitimacy of International Courts?' (2011) 12 Chicago Journal of International Law 647; Patricia Wald, 'Women on International Courts: Some Lessons Learned' (2011) 11 International Criminal Law Review 401, 403; Josephine Jarpa Dawuni, 'African Women Judges on International Courts: Symbolic or Substantive Gains' (2018) 47 University of Baltimore Law Review 199, 232–34, 243–44; Fionnuala Ní Aoláin, 'More Women—But Which Women? A Reply to Stéphanie Hennette Vauchez' (2015) 26 EJIL 229.

### 4.1. Stereotypical views of women's cognition and contribution

The scholarly literature suggests that women judges bring a different perspective to the law than their male counterparts.[59] Carol Gilligan argues that women and men resolve moral problems differently. She says that women define themselves through their connections with others and perceive morality in terms of these interconnections, whilst men tend to define themselves in terms of individual achievement and autonomy and stratify morality based on a hierarchy.[60] Specifically, she argues that women are more likely to view the resolution of conflicts as a problem of care and responsibility, leading to the creation of a care-based feminine jurisprudence, as opposed to the more rights-centred approach characteristic of men that leads to clear winners and losers.[61] Some authors speak of 'emotional differences' and underline the previously mentioned stereotypes of risk-taking; others underline that the male perspective tends to emphasise separation, individual rights, and abstract rules, whilst women's experience affects perspectives on the law itself and legal processes.[62] Other scholars argue that women seek different outcomes from legal processes than their male colleagues and that they attach different weights to the factual aspects of identical situations.[63] In this regard, women due to their differing socialisation and life experiences are said to gather information, seek interpretations, uphold values, and determine case outcomes in a different way than men.[64] Thus gender influences should be found in all legal contexts and areas of law.[65]

Additionally, Gilligan argues that women are outsiders in male-dominated professions, causing women to have greater empathy for individuals and groups outside the mainstream.[66] It is argued that this is especially the case in the context of cases directly involving women-related policy issues: sexual harassment, sexual violence, and discrimination claims. In essence, the message is that female judges are prone to protect other women as representatives of their class, though some of

[59] Susan L Miller and Shana L Maier, 'Moving beyond Numbers: What Female Judges Say about Different Judicial Voices' (2008) 29 Journal of Women, Politics and Policy 527, 529.

[60] Carol Gilligan, *In a Different Voice: Psychological Theory and Women's Development* (reprint edn, Harvard UP 2016). However, note that this may be culturally dependent: Geert Hofstede, 'Dimensionalizing Cultures: The Hofstede Model in Context' (2011) 2 Online Readings in Psychology and Culture <https://scholarworks.gvsu.edu/orpc/vol2/iss1/8> accessed 10 April 2024.

[61] Fiona Kay and Elizabeth Gorman, 'Women in the Legal Profession' (2008) 4 Annual Review of Law and Social Science 299, 321; Ann C Scales, 'The Emergence of Feminist Jurisprudence: An Essay' (1986) 95 Yale Law Journal 1373.

[62] Gilligan (n 60).

[63] Phyllis Coontz, 'Gender and Judicial Decisions: Do Female Judges Decide Cases Differently Than Male Judges?' (2000) 18 Gender Issues 59, 71.

[64] Suzanna Sherry, 'Civic Virtue and the Feminine Voice in Constitutional Adjudication' (1986) 72 Virginia Law Review 543, 583.

[65] Christina L Boyd, Lee Epstein, and Andrew D Martin, 'Untangling the Causal Effects of Sex on Judging' (2010) 54 American Journal of Political Science 389, 390.

[66] Gilligan (n 60).

the accounts add that in these cases women bring a different understanding and experience to the issue of differential treatment and minority protection.[67]

These accounts do foreground several things: first, they put forward the stereotypical view of women and the different voice that they are supposed to bring to the discussion. They speak of a different cognitive process that women undergo—their caring and cooperative role, the empathy and other emotions that are seen as 'feminine'—and underline their impact for the areas of law specific to the female experience, such as discrimination and sexual harassment. It is important to underline that there is little empirical proof that women's cognitive processes differ from men's—whether rational or unconscious errors in decision-making are concerned.[68] In fact, medical scholars have found 'that most gender differences are not large enough to support the assumption of sexual dimorphism in terms of brain anatomy, brain function, cognition, and behaviour'. Instead, 'brain and cognitive features are modulated by environment, culture, and practice' and in addition to hormone levels and so on interact with 'current gender stereotypes'.[69]

In addition to reinforcing the stereotypes about women, these narratives therefore also create unrealistic (and baseless) expectations about what role women decision-makers should play once in their position.[70] In this regard, the description puts forward an almost instrumental view of women, as being there to represent other women, help explain experiences of other women, and make decisions in favour of other women. When women find themselves in those positions, they are therefore seen 'as representative of their gender, rather than as expert lawyers'.[71] Of course, the question arises to what extent women justices can really be said to be characteristic of the 'general' female group from which they are drawn. The higher you go in your career, the more likely you are to break new legal ground, but the less characteristic you are of the general group of women. Prior empirical studies have found that women who are the most outspoken advocates for women's issues are likely to occupy positions at the extreme liberal or conservative ends and thus

[67] Charles M Cameron and Craig P Cummings, *Diversity and Judicial Decision-Making on the U.S. Courts of Appeals* (30 March 2003) (unpublished manuscript, on file with author); Gerard S Gryski, Eleanor C Main, and William J Dixon, 'Models of State High Court Decision Making in Sex Discrimination Cases' (1986) 48 Journal of Politics 143; Jennifer L Peresie, 'Female Judges Matter: Gender and Collegial Decisionmaking in the Federal Appellate Courts' (2005) 114 Yale Law Journal 1759.

[68] Lutz Jäncke, 'Sex/Gender Differences in Cognition, Neurophysiology, and Neuroanatomy' (2018) F1000Research, 7, F1000 Faculty Rev-805. https://doi.org/10.12688/f1000research.13917.1; Namrata Upadhayay and Sanjeev Guragain, 'Comparison of Cognitive Functions between Male and Female Medical Students: A Pilot Study' (2014) 8 Journal of Clinical and Diagnostic Research BC12.

[69] Jäncke (n 68).

[70] Juliana Santos de Carvalho and Justina Uriburu, 'Problematising Diversity: The Change That International Lawyers (Do Not) Want for International Courts' (2022) 10 London Review of International Law 391, 409, who speak of this as a 'burden of the minority'.

[71] Liesbeth Lijnzaad, 'The Smurfette Principle: Reflections about Gender and the Nomination of Women to the International Bench' in Freya Baetens (ed), *Identity and Diversity on the International Bench: Who Is the Judge?* (OUP 2020) 29.

voice extreme dissenting views in criminal and economic cases.[72] It was not their gender that was key to their outspokenness but rather their political positions. Even in narratives that do not speak of representation, the expectation is that the minority candidate will show affinity or adjudicate with more sensitivity towards their own community.[73]

The instrumental and reductionist view of what role women (should) play in decision-making roles is reinforced by the *Smurfette* principle, namely the fact that when women sit on decision-making bodies, they will still generally constitute a minority. As Liesbeth Lijnzaad, judge at the International Tribunal for the Law of the Sea, argues, the image of one woman in a group of all men reinforces the image from popular visual culture about the role of *Smurfette*, 'the one woman' singled out as 'the only woman' in the room of men.[74] Whilst 'her presence suggests progress', it has little true impact.[75] Namely, when members of minority are treated as mere 'tokens', perceived to be there for no other reason than because of their group membership and identity, studies have shown that their behaviour mirrors the behaviour of the majority.[76] Effectively, individual minority members tend to adapt to the majority members in the group. In this regard, even if a 'different voice' exists, it is lost. The mere presence of women may therefore not 'be enough to have a discernable effect on the output of that environment'.[77] Instead, studies have shown that a critical mass is needed for minority members to exhibit different behaviour.[78] Once this critical mass is reached, the impact of a different voice from these minorities can be visible, as 'group interactions will change and substantive differences in the behaviour of the involved groups will begin to emerge'.[79]

### 4.2. Inconclusive evidence of a different voice

The expectations are reinforced by some domestic studies, which find that women at the US state Supreme Court level were more likely to produce pro-female decisions.[80] Similarly, a study of the Michigan State Supreme Court, examining a

[72] David W Allen and Diane E Wall, 'Role Orientations and Women State Supreme Court Justices' (1993) 77 Judicature 156.
[73] De Carvalho and Uriburu (n 70).
[74] ibid.
[75] ibid.
[76] Paul M Collins Jr, Kenneth L Manning, and Robert A Carp, 'Gender, Critical Mass, and Judicial Decision Making' (2010) 32 Law and Policy 260.
[77] ibid.
[78] ibid.
[79] ibid.
[80] Susan W Johnson and Donald R Songer, 'Judge Gender and the Voting Behavior of Justices on Two North American Supreme Courts' (2009) 30 Justice System Journal 265; Phyllis Coontz, 'Gender and Judicial Decisions: Do Female Judges Decide Cases Differently than Male Judges?' (2000) 18 Gender Issues 59.

period of over thirteen years, found that 59 per cent of the time white Republican female judges abandoned their party to vote to support female litigants in divorce cases.[81] Others have found that in sex discrimination cases women judges were 10 per cent more likely to find for the party alleging discrimination.[82] Similarly, a study of state supreme courts noted that female justices had a higher likelihood of supporting the woman's side in cases related to property settlement on divorce, birth control, child support, sex discrimination, and sexual assault.[83] At the federal court of appeals level, female judges were more likely than their male counterparts to side with female plaintiffs in cases of employment discrimination.[84] A study of the Ontario Court of Appeal showed that women judges had a higher likelihood of ruling against male litigants in family law cases and defendants in criminal sexual assault cases.[85]

Yet, for every study that has shown that female judges vote differently than their male counterparts or side more often with female plaintiffs, there are studies that have found no evidence of the different voice. Kritzer and Uhlman and separately Gruhl find that in criminal cases there were no significant differences between women and men judges, but rather that male judges were more likely to give lesser sentences to female defendants.[86] In the only study in the European Union, Garoupa and others showed that the gender of the chamber (according to percentage of male judges) was not a driver of empirical results, though they note that the gender of the rapporteur may have been important.[87]

In the international legal context, in particular, only a few studies have looked at the impact of women judges on outcomes. The results of these studies have not been necessarily consistent. First, Erik Voeten studied the judgments of the ECtHR and found that consistent with the above literature, female judges were much

[81] Ewert, Loer, and Thomann (n 50). Elaine Martin and Barry Pyle, 'Gender, Race, and Partisanship on the Michigan Supreme Court' (2000) 63 Alabama Law Review 1205, 1225. Also Allen and Wall (n 72) 156 (finding in a sample of state supreme court women justices that they function as representatives of their gender in the pro-women decisions they make compared to men, as outsiders, and provide a different voice). Similar results were reported in Wisconsin and Minnesota. Elaine Martin and Barry Pyle, 'Gender and Racial Diversification of State Supreme Courts' (2002) 24 Women and Politics 35.

[82] Boyd and others (n 65) 390.

[83] Allen and Wall (n 72) 165.

[84] Sean Farhang and Gregory Wawro, 'Institutional Dynamics on the U.S. Court of Appeals: Minority Representation under Panel Decision Making' (2004) 20 Journal of Law, Economics, and Organization 299; Donald R Songer, Sue Davis, and Susan Haire, 'A Reappraisal of Diversification in the Federal Courts: Gender Effects in the Courts of Appeals' (1994) 56 Journal of Politics 425, 436.

[85] James Stribopoulos and Moin A Yahya, 'Does a Judge's Party of Appointment or Gender Matter to Case Outcomes? An Empirical Study of the Court of Appeal for Ontario' (2007) 45 Osgood Hall Law Journal 315, 319.

[86] Herbert M Kritzer and Thomas M Uhlman, 'Sisterhood in the Courtroom: Sex of Judge and Defendant as Factors in Criminal Case Disposition' (1977) 14 Social Science Journal 77; John Gruhl, Susan Welch, and Cassia Spohn, 'Women as Criminal Defendants: A Test for Paternalism' (1984) 37 Western Political Quarterly 456.

[87] Angela Huyue Zhang, Jingchen Liu, and Nuno Garoupa, 'Judging in Europe: Do Legal Traditions Matter?' (2018) 14 Journal of Competition Law and Economics 144.

more likely than their male counterparts to find in favour of a violation in discrimination cases filed by women but not on other issues.[88] However, female judges were on average more likely to find violations regardless of applicant gender, especially in physical integrity rights cases. This finding was also consistent with the literature on gender and international relations, which suggested that female decision-makers may be less willing to trade off physical integrity rights over security concerns. Beyond this, however, the results did not suggest a considerable difference in how men or women approached decision-making, or that they were more favourably disposed towards applicants. The proportion of female judges does not correlate significantly with a greater probability of a violation finding by the Court.[89]

My own research on damages has also found conflicting results. In general, the ECtHR tends to disregard victim characteristics in determining non-pecuniary damage and instead looks at the respondent state and the frequency with which it violates a given article of the Convention. Yet, taking into account the composition of the adjudication panel, the empirical analysis shows that female-majority panels disregard the violating state and instead focus on the victim and her characteristics. Specifically, they look at who the victim is, what their age may be and whether they are vulnerable, and how they may have contributed to the violation (or were blameless). These awards are generally higher than awards by male-majority panels.[90] Women-majority panels therefore appear to take a different approach to the assessment of pain and suffering in the context of damage setting, but the impact of this can be confusing and inconsistent. In certain cases, women judges were found to be harsher on women victims, whilst in others they were more generous towards them.

In sum, there is very little that can be conclusively discerned from these various empirical cognitive studies. The conclusions of the different studies are inconsistent and occasionally contradictory, and the effect of gender is difficult to isolate. Scholars have noted that education and training that judges of both genders undergo and the processes by which they obtain their jobs could potentially erase any pre-existing gender differences.[91] Often—especially on positions at the extreme liberal or conservative ends—it is easier to point to political leanings rather than gender as determinative of women's positions.

[88] Erik Voeten, 'Gender and Judging: Evidence from the European Court of Human Rights' (2021) 28 Journal of European Public Policy 1453.

[89] Beyond the composition of judicial panels, Voeten also found that women filed fewer applications before the Court than men and that they were disproportionately likely to file property rights cases, addressing longstanding inequities concerning pensions, divorce, inheritance, and housing.

[90] Veronika Fikfak, 'Bias on the Bench' (working paper).

[91] Lani Guinier, Michelle Fine, and Jane Balin, *Becoming Gentlemen: Women, Law School, and Institutional Change* (Beacon Press 1997); John Gruhl, Cassia Spohn, and Susan Welch, 'Women as Policymakers: The Case of Trial Judges' (1981) 25 American Journal of Political Science 308; Barbara Palmer, 'Women in the American Judiciary' (2001) 23 Women and Politics 91.

## 5. Conclusion: Debunking the Myth

Since the distinct voice argument therefore appears elusive, perhaps it is time to move away from the myth of a 'different voice' as the argument *for* female presence in decision-making roles. As cognitive studies have shown, there are few biological differences between the two genders, and it is mostly stereotypes constructed by society and culture that direct our 'different' behaviour. Even then, the results are inconclusive and outcomes in individual cases are difficult to predict. Yet, if we continue to expect of women to think, behave, and decide differently, we reinforce and perpetuate a myth of a 'different voice', a stereotype that singles out women as different from men; essentialises, categorises them into one category, rather than allowing them to exist on multiple axes (seeing identity as monolithic and static); strips them of agency by requiring them to show affinity and act as representatives of their gender; and imposes on them the burden of expectations about changing the system from within and for the better of other women.[92] As Judith Butler argues, representation requires 'a stable category' to make groups visible.[93] Underlying women's '"shared experiences" to increase their visibility and legitimate them as political subjects worthy of representation may reinstate essentialising structures of power, the very structures from which feminist emancipation is sought'.[94] By focusing on how women are different from men and how they are similar to each other, we run the risk of perpetuating stereotypes about groups and subsequent ingroup–outgroup bias. By reducing women to one single label, we reinforce and perpetuate a myth.

This applies a fortiori also to feminist studies. As put by those whose self-confessed confrontational reading of traditional and feminist scholarship emphasised their strong 'walling practices' (ie practices that divide and categorise), reinforcing 'a liberal, elitist, and gender essentialist status quo of international law and its institutions',[95] perhaps what is needed now is a radical reimagining of a future where more 'diverse voices can engage with (or against) the international legal order'.[96] We should rather argue in favour of diversity along multiple axes and multiple categories of views and experiences. In this context, the fluidity and complexity of identities has to be recognised and taken into account, as well as reconciled with representational politics.[97] Cognitive studies—especially experimental and modelling practices—that can debunk certain myths as stereotypes appear crucial in this process of 'taking down walls' between groups as well as areas of international law.

92 De Carvalho and Uriburu (n 70).

93 Judith Butler, *Gender Trouble: Feminism and the Subversion of Identity* (1st edn, Routledge 2006) 6–7.

94 De Carvalho and Uriburu (n 70) 415.

95 ibid.

96 ibid.

97 Judith Baxter, 'Positioning Language and Identity: Poststructuralist Perspectives' in Sian Preece (ed), *The Routledge Handbook of Language and Identity* (Routledge 2016) 34; Jasbir K Puar, '"I Would Rather Be a Cyborg Than a Goddess": Intersectionality, Assemblage, and Affective Politics' (2012) 2 philoSOPHIA 49.

# 6

# Liberal Normative Theories of International Law and the Cognitive Turn

*Robert Howse*

## 1. Introduction

Liberalism is a political and legal theory that posits the role of government, and perhaps all forms of governance, as securing the rights and interests (or "preferences") of individuals, (ideally) resolving conflicts between interests through representative institutions and the rule of law such that, to use Kant's formulation, the freedom of each can co-exist with the freedom of all.

Liberal theorists differ on the meaning of normativity in liberalism: some see liberalism as positing an abstract ideal of freedom (and perhaps equality) against which to assess the legitimacy of existing institutions. Others view liberalism as a program for transforming the real world in accord with liberal ideals. Some kinds of liberals view the individual self as an ideal rational actor whose preferences are formed autonomously from sub-rational commitments such as to family or nation. Others see the individual self as essentially embedded in culture and community. These differences of approach extend to liberal normative theories of international law.

Where liberal theorists are of the kind that seek to transform the real world and to understand the freedom of individual selves as itself embedded in community and culture—that is, in real-world particulars—there is the possibility of a fruitful engagement with behavioral and cognitive studies.

The way in which human beings perceive and understand the world has been explored by researchers in a range of disciplines, including psychology, neuroscience, economics, sociology, anthropology, and philosophy. Studies in social cognition look at the way that social constraints and biases affect people's perceptions of their environment, and their own choices for action within it. Since to be meaningful in understanding the world and useful in acting within it, information must be selected and processed, the tools people use to achieve that selection and processing are crucial to cognition. Behavioral studies relate these heuristics to the way in which individuals make decisions.[1]

[1] See on cognitive-behavioral studies, Anne van Aaken and Moshe Hirsch's Introduction to this volume.

Robert Howse, *Liberal Normative Theories of International Law and the Cognitive Turn* In: *International Legal Theory and the Cognitive Turn*. Edited by: Anne van Aaken and Moshe Hirsch, Oxford University Press. 
DOI: 10.1093/9780198909293.003.0007

A fundamental aspect of the liberal normative theory of international law is the "bottom-up" approach, which roots governance and obligation in the interests and rights of individuals as reflected through representative democratic institutions. In focusing on individuals, in relationship to social and political institutions, there is a common ground concerning the relevant unit of analysis between normative liberal theory and cognitive science and social science.

In this chapter, I seek to explore, in a preliminary fashion, some areas where there could be fruitful encounter between liberal normative theories of international law and behavioral and cognitive studies. I examine below, for instance, the relevance of altruism in human behavior to the possibilities of liberal global justice with a redistributive element, the relationship of perceptions of shared values to the possibility of international legal cooperation among liberal states, and the influence of group affiliation and bias on how states and societies are viewed as "liberal" or not, and in the case of commercial liberalism (free trade) how "friend-shoring" as opposed to non-discriminatory multilateralism is supported by studies on whom individuals trust as trading partners and why.

There is a range of issues in liberal normative theory where cognitive science and social science have something to say, but how much will depend on the extent to which liberal theory promises or is committed to the realization of international law in the world or whether it is understood merely as an ideal theory that allows us to characterize international norms as liberal in some abstract sense. If one were to try to articulate a fruitful encounter of cognitive and behavioral studies from these perspectives on the different strands of liberal normative theory, a good beginning would be Machiavelli's notion that one should take human beings as they are to achieve normative goals in politics, rather than as they ought to be. In the mission to use cognitive and behavioral studies to find ways to identify and correct individuals' choices, where biases or other informational constraints cause those choices to deviate from what a fully rational agent would decide, one can detect something of the hubris of the radical Enlightenment project: the idea that as far as possible individuals should make choices on the basis of reason alone.

As far as the variant of normative liberal theory that is committed to trade liberalization and even deeper economic integration goes, these various insights suggest that pushback against new "big" trade deals or negotiations in the World Trade Organization (WTO) may not have a lot to do with resistance to the liberal theory itself, but much more with a lack of trust or identification in the context of multilateralism that includes a very large range of countries, including perceived adversaries.

This chapter starts with an overview on liberalism as a normative theory (Section 2) and then turns to liberalism in international law with a special focus on the "bottom-up" approach to justifying international legal norms as well as potential frictions with cosmopolitanism (Section 3). The chapter then discusses different views about human agency in international liberalism, both from the perspective of free human agency in cosmopolitan liberalism and the abstract moral agent in Rawls to cultural embeddedness as a context for free agency (Section 4). The next section connects cognitive-behavioral science to normative liberalism in international law. Although a purely deontological ideal of freedom is central to liberalism, once liberals become concerned about how freedom can be an effective principle in the world, the ways individuals think and decide matter. The discussion here focuses on two specific examples: distributive justice and international trade (Section 5). The last section discusses the potential and limitations of behavioral approaches to normative liberal theory in international law and points to Jon Elster's scholarship as a way forward—combining normative political theory with insights about human knowledge, inter alia from cognitive-behavioral sciences (Section 6).

## 2. Liberalism and Normative Theory

Liberalism is a political and legal theory that posits the role of government, and perhaps all forms of governance, as securing the rights and interests (or "preferences") of individuals, resolving conflicts between interests through representative democratic institutions and the rule of law such that, to use Kant's formulation, the freedom of each can co-exist with the freedom of all.

"Political liberalism" in the form articulated by the pre-eminent Anglo-American liberal political philosopher John Rawls seeks to articulate principles of justice that would underpin the design of institutions in a liberal society and provide some background rules for their operation.[2] Perfectionist liberalism aims to institute the liberal ideal of free self-development of the individual as a moral ideal that corresponds to the demand for a liberal political society. For liberal perfectionists, liberal political institutions should be designed not only for the maximization of individual choice consistent with the freedom of all but also to encourage or privilege a way of life that favors self-making over tradition, and supports individuals in breaking from their roots, experimenting with different life choices, and conducting their lives as "choosers." Political liberalism is tolerant of different comprehensive doctrines of the good, including traditional and religious conceptions, as long as collective decisions are premised upon, or can be defended, based on principles of justice that individuals would choose through a veil of ignorance, unaware of their particular social position, ethnicity, religion, and so on.

In Michael Doyle's words,

[2] John Rawls, *A Theory of Justice* (Harvard UP 1971). He bases his theory on the assumption of rational, self-interested, and risk-averse individuals.

> Liberalism has been identified with an essential principle—the importance of the freedom of the individual. Above all, this is a belief in the importance of moral freedom, of the right to be treated and a duty to treat others as ethical subject, and not as objects or means only. This principle has generated rights and institutions.[3]

The Kantian strand in liberal theory, of which Rawls is arguably the leading contemporary heir, is influenced by Kant's account of moral freedom as divorced from sense perception and the understanding of objects in the world. The former is the realm of practical, the latter of pure reason. Moral freedom is an idea or ideal and is autonomous from the actual forces that cause most people to behave in the real world most of the time. In Kant's short writings on history such as *Perpetual Peace* (which has had a significant influence on international legal theory),[4] he made a variety of conjectural attempts to reconcile the ideal of moral freedom with historical action in the world.

Montesquieu represents a strand of classical or Enlightenment liberalism very different than that of Kant, as is illustrated well by Montesquieu's definition of freedom as "the opinion of each concerning their own security." For Montesquieu, each individual's freedom of action depends on how they perceive others around them, whether the state as well as non-state sources of insecurity (such as religious authorities). How far can they go without having to fear punishment or constraint that threatens their security?[5] In more recent times, Judith Shklar's "liberalism of fear" presents itself very much as in Montesquieu's vein. Shklar does not propose an abstract model of moral freedom or posit the kinds of political and social institutions that are rationally implied by it. Instead, for Shklar, freedom begins with the kinds of real-world social and political hedges against despotic cruelty that appear to function most of the time in actual liberal democracies—the rule of law, representative democracy, and market freedoms albeit with limits.[6] These societies are far from exemplifying any ideal of liberal justice—they are full of racism and gender and class inequality. But they are still the best hope for freedom when one considers the (all too real) dangers of authoritarianism and totalitarianism. Shklar notably turned to literature—Shakespeare, Moliere, Hawthorne, and others—to understand the forces of social behavior and the entanglement of individuals with societal arrangements. In her studies on cruelty and snobbery in *Ordinary Vices*,

[3] Michael Doyle, 'Kant, Liberal Legacies, and Foreign Affairs' (1983) 12 Philosophy and Public Affairs 205.

[4] Immanuel Kant, *Toward Perpetual Peace and Other Writings* (Pauline Kleingeld ed, David Colclasure tr) (Yale UP 2006).

[5] I develop elsewhere Montesquieu's liberalism in relation to international law and politics. See Robert Howse, 'Montesquieu on Commerce, Conquest, War and Peace' (2006) 31 Brooklyn Journal of International Law 693.

[6] Judith Shklar, 'The Liberalism of Fear' in Nancy L Rosenblum (ed), *Liberalism and the Moral Life* (Harvard UP 1989) 5.

she is particularly attentive to how class and power positions can structure or bias individuals' perceptions of social reality.

Shklar developed her theory in opposition to what she regarded as the discredited social utopian liberalism of the radical Enlightenment, the target of her first book, *After Utopia*. Enlightenment liberalism seeks to free individuals from prejudices and from institutions of coercion built upon prejudices, above all official religion and absolute monarchy. The radical Enlightenment's most extreme hopes imply that human beings might be totally freed of prejudice and organize a society entirely on the basis of reason.

## 3. Liberalism and International Law

Since for liberal theory the source of rights and obligations is fundamentally the moral freedom of the individual—a free, equal, and (on many liberal accounts) rational agent—liberal theory is bound to have a "bottom-up" focus.[7] The justice and legitimacy of international—that is, *inter*-state—law is not derivative from any autonomous understanding of right or justice *between states*, but rather the ability of international law to enable or facilitate states to create and maintain those institutions that fulfill liberal justice *within* the boundaries of each state. State representatives who enter into international legal arrangements (such as treaties) do so as agents of the individuals within their borders, in order to serve the interests (or "preferences"), and fulfill the rights, of those individuals.

As Anne-Marie Slaughter puts it, the challenge for traditional or classical international law is that

> we must learn to reframe every international issue, which we are accustomed to thinking about in terms of 'state to state' interaction, in terms of the interaction between individuals and specific government institutions. Rethinking international politics in this way has broad implications for how we think about the creation and maintenance of international order.[8]

As Slaughter argues: "A Liberal theory of international law would privilege [those] issue areas, doctrines, and developments ... *most likely to achieve its substantive goals*."[9]

[7] Andrew Moravcsik, 'Liberal Theories of International Law' in Jeffrey L Dunoff and Mark A Pollack (eds), *Interdisciplinary Perspectives on International Law and International Relations* (CUP 2013) 83.
[8] Anne-Marie Slaughter, 'A Liberal Theory of International Law' (2000) 94 Proceedings of the ASIL Annual Meeting 240.
[9] ibid 246.

Slaughter mentions human rights as an obvious example here, but she also alludes to commerce, environment, and peace as concerns of liberal citizens and societies. In "The Law of Peoples," John Rawls proposes principles "identified … by rational agents fairly or reasonably"[10] that would underpin international legal obligations. These rational agents are not individuals, however, as in Rawls' original position that determines the principles of justice for domestic institutions, but rather representatives of existing liberal states.

The principles that should underpin international law according to Rawls are:

> "1. Peoples (as organized by their governments) are free and independent, and their freedom and independence is to be respected by other peoples.
> 2. Peoples are equal and parties to their own agreements.
> 3. Peoples have the right of self-defense but no right to war.
> 4. Peoples are to observe a duty of nonintervention.
> 5. Peoples are to observe treaties and undertakings.
> 6. Peoples are to observe certain specified restrictions on the conduct of war (assumed to be in self-defense).
> 7. Peoples are to honor human rights."[11]

Rawls observes that there is a certain "fit" between such principles and the way in which international law has been transformed in the post-World War II period, "which tends to restrict a state's right to wage war to cases of self-defense (this allows collective security), and … also tends to limit its right of internal sovereignty."[12]

## 3.1. The "bottom-up" approach to justifying international legal norms

Ronald Dworkin's effort late in life to formulate a liberal theory of international law echoes in many ways the "bottom-up" approach of Slaughter and Rawls. Dworkin's theory derives the normative content and justification of international law from the internal political morality of the democratic constitutional state. With respect to human rights, for example, "Any state, even one that has so far been just and benign … improves its legitimacy when it promotes an effective international order that would prevent its own possible future degradation into tyranny."[13] Likewise, with respect to international law constraints on the use of force: these are justified by the state's duty to provide for the security of its citizens, which can be threatened from outside as well as from within the state.

[10] John Rawls, 'Law of Peoples' (1993) 20 Critical Inquiry 36, 40.
[11] ibid 46.
[12] ibid 42.
[13] Ronald Dworkin, 'A New Philosophy for International Law' (2013) 41 Philosophy and Public Affairs 2, 27.

The reality of international law as positive law is of course that it binds in most cases both liberal and non-liberal states. A fundamental difficulty for "bottom-up" liberal theories of international law just discussed is the apparent lack of justification for non-liberal states accepting an international legal order formed to fulfill or advance the rights and interests of the citizens of existing liberal states. This has led John Tasioulas to make a sharp criticism: "Dworkin's theory of international law ... effaces dramatic contrasts between conditions in liberal democracies and those that obtain globally, oversteps the parameters within which a normative theory of international law can be usefully elaborated."[14] (For Tasioulas, at least Rawls, in introducing the concept of "well-ordered" though not liberal states, is more in touch than Dworkin with the reality of conditions "that obtain globally.")

In "The Law of Peoples," Rawls attempts to address this difficulty by introducing the category of states that are not liberal in the strong sense of possessing those institutions that would characteristically be generated through adhesion to liberal principles of justice but nevertheless sufficiently "well-ordered" to participate in the creation and maintenance of international legal order based on Rawls' principles. A "well-ordered" non-liberal society is "peaceful and not expansionist; its legal system satisfies certain requisite conditions of legitimacy in the eyes of its own people; and, as a consequence of this, it honors basic human rights."[15] By contrast with "well-ordered" non-liberal societies, tyrannical and dictatorial societies cannot be accepted as members in good standing of a reasonable society of peoples.[16]

Clearly, on Rawls' liberal theory, the sort of international law that matters is that which has its content determined by the representatives of liberal and "well-ordered" societies. Even if "tyrannical and dictatorial" states are still bound by, for example, the rules on the use of force in the United Nations (UN) Charter, or the provisions of the UN Covenant on Civil and Political Rights, one cannot expect such states to view such norms as legitimate and, implicitly, to accept them as a basis for interaction with liberal and "well-ordered" societies. By contrast, according to Ronald Dworkin,

> if a significant number of states, encompassing a significant population, has developed an agreed code of practice, either by treaty or by other form of coordination, then other states have at least a prima facie duty to subscribe to that practice as well, with the important proviso that this duty holds only if a more general practice to that effect, expanded in that way, would improve the legitimacy of the subscribing state and the international order as a whole.[17]

[14] John Tasioulas, '"Fantasy upon Fantasy": Some Reflections on Dworkin's Philosophy of International Law' (2021) 3 Jus Cogens 33, 47.
[15] Rawls (n 10) 37.
[16] ibid.
[17] Dworkin (n 13) 19.

Dworkin appears to consider the possibility that even states that are dictatorships or tyrannies might still improve their legitimacy by adhering to international norms that are primarily justified based on principles common to liberal states or to serve or complete the aims of liberal democratic constitutional order.

Slaughter and Rawls tend to operate from an optimism that "a growing part of the world *is* composed of Liberal states."[18] As Rawls puts it, "[a] long run aim, as specified by the law of peoples is to bring all societies to honor eventually that law, to be full and-self standing members of the society of well-ordered peoples, and so to secure human rights everywhere."[19] In any event, "well-ordered" and liberal peoples ought to use existing (the UN) or new international institutions to "expose to public view the unjust and cruel institutions of oppressive and expansionist regimes and their violation of human rights." In the case of *non*-"well-ordered societies, economic sanctions or military pressure ... to change their ways" may be acceptable.

## 3.2. "Bottom-up" political liberalism versus cosmopolitanism

The versions of "bottom-up" liberal international law described above all emphasize the central concern that international law support and aid liberal states in performing their constitutional functions. This view has been vigorously challenged by cosmopolitan liberals, who see rights bearing individuals as "citizens of the world" and challenge the division of the world into sovereign states as a barrier to the fulfillment of individual freedom. Cosmopolitan international law therefore seeks to construct a conception of the function and substantive content of international law that aims to weaken the significance of state borders, a state of affairs where international law protects entitlements than individuals have as a consequence of their humanity itself, regardless of whether these are protected by state institutions in any given case. Thinkers like Thomas Scanlon, Charles Beitz, and Thomas Pogge have suggested that, to be consistent with the commitment to liberal individualism, Rawls should apply the original position to a society of free, equal, and rational individuals encompassing the whole world.[20] This would have very significant implications for distributive justice, as it would entail applying the difference principle, that inequalities be justified as making the least advantaged better off, to schemes of international cooperation, like global trade, finance, and investment (an exercise that Pogge would attempt to complete).[21]

[18] Anne-Marie Slaughter, 'International Law in a World of Liberal States' [1995] EJIL 503, 514.

[19] Rawls (n 10) 61.

[20] See, for an extended analytical and historical account of these responses to Rawls, Katrina Forrester, *In the Shadow of Justice: Postwar Liberalism and the Remaking of Political Philosophy* (Princeton UP 2019) chapter 5.

[21] See Thomas Pogge, 'The Role of International Law in Reproducing Massive Poverty' in Samantha Besson and John Tasioulas (eds), *The Philosophy of International Law* (OUP 2010), and for a critique,

In "The Law of Peoples" Rawls explicitly responds to this line of critique (or reconstruction) of his theory. According to Rawls,

> While I think the difference principle is reasonable for domestic justice in a democratic society, it is not feasible, I believe, as the way to deal with the general problem of unfavorable conditions among societies ... there are various kinds of societies in the societies of peoples and not all of them can reasonably be expected to accept any particular liberal principle of distributive justice; and even different liberal societies adopt different principles for their domestic institutions.[22]

This last comment seems to put in question whether the difference principle is even essential to the functioning of the original position at all; that is, in the domestic context.

My colleague Thomas Nagel has backed Rawls' view on this in his now classic article "Global Justice." Nagel emphasizes that requirements for egalitarian (re-) distribution "depend on a strong condition of associative responsibility ... such responsibility is created by specific and contingent relations such as fellow citizenship."[23]

While, for example, Pogge's cosmopolitan liberal theory of international law emphasizes redistribution of resources, there are also ordo-liberal or libertarian versions such as that of Ernst-Ulrich Petersmann that espouse the imperative to remove state-created obstacles to economic activity across national boundaries, advancing the right to trade of "citizens of the world."[24] As Ileana Porras has observed, the concept of freedom of commerce, at least tolerance of foreign traders, goes back to the roots of the idea of cosmopolitan right in Immanuel Kant, for whom the fundamental norm to be honored by all states (and perhaps peoples) was that of hospitality: "the nonhostile reception of a foreigner arriving in native shores" for peaceful purposes, above all commerce.[25] Petersmann's ordo-liberalism, which seeks to constitutionalize economic freedom (indicated by its very language of constitutionalism), runs into the problem of determining at a global level the proper justified limits to freedom of contract and property rights, indeed the meaning of rights, which goes to just social relations. A global

Robert Howse and Ruti Teitel, 'Global Justice, Poverty and the International Economic Order' in the same volume.

22 Rawls (n 10) 63.

23 Thomas Nagel, 'The Problem of Social Justice' (2005) 33 Philosophy and Public Affairs 113, 125.

24 Ernst-Ulrich Petersmann, 'German and European Ordo-Liberalism and Constitutionalism in the Post-War Development of International Economic Law' (2020) EUI Department of Law Research Paper No 2020/01 <https://ssrn.com/abstract=3584153>.

25 Ileana M Porras, 'Liberal Cosmopolitanism or Cosmopolitan Liberalism?' in Mortimer NS Sellers (ed), *Parochialism, Cosmopolitanism, and the Foundations of International Law*, ASIL Studies in International Legal Theory (CUP 2012).

ordo-liberal constitution would not be a true constitution constructed by a political community through an inclusive and representative process.[26]

Normative liberal theories that stress freedom of commerce often (beginning at least with Montesquieu) stress the advantage of commerce as a means of overcoming prejudices about other peoples and societies that may lead to more peaceful and stable international relations. Commercial agreements entail a benign form of interdependence: "The natural effect of commerce is to bring peace. Two nations that negotiate between themselves become reciprocally dependent, if one has an interest in buying and the other in selling."[27] Efforts to test empirically the hypothesis that commerce serves peace raise doubts about normative liberal theory's argument for commerce on these grounds.[28]

## 4. Liberalism and the Self: Divergent Views with Implications for International Law

Clearly connected to the debate about political versus cosmopolitan justice in normative liberal theory is the question of how liberal theory understands human agency. Rawls' conception of deciding on just institutions behind a veil of ignorance depends on a conception of the "unencumbered self," famously criticized by Michael Sandel: "the self, shorn of all contingency-given attributes, assumes a kind of supra-empirical status, essentially unencumbered and given prior to its ends."[29] While Sandel would argue for a communitarian or "situated" self as the subject of democratic justice, Rawls' unencumbered self has led to doubts among liberals as well as other scholars committed to individualism. Amartya Sen wonders:

> if the justice of what happens in a society depends on a combination of institutional features and actual behavioural characteristics, along with other influences that determine the social realization, then is it possible to identify 'just' institutions for a society without making them contingent on actual behavior (not the same as 'just' or 'reasonable' behavior)?[30]

For Will Kymlicka, it is the context of culture—"the existence of a viable community of individuals with a shared heritage, language, history, etc."—that individuals are able to develop their capacities to make free choices. Thus, liberalism

[26] See Robert Howse, 'Human Rights in the WTO: Whose Rights, What Humanity? Comment on Petersmann' (2002) 13 EJIL 651.

[27] Montesquieu, De l'esprit des lois, XX:2. How these effects might have been understood by Montesquieu as operating in reality raises many complexities. See Howse (n 5).

[28] See, for instance, Katherine Barbieri, *The Liberal Illusion: Does Trade Promote Peace?* (University of Michigan Press 2002); Katherine Barbieri and Gerald Schneider, 'Globalization and Peace: Assessing New Directions in the Study of Trade and Conflict' (1999) 36 Journal of Peace Research 387.

[29] Michael J Sandel, *Liberalism and the Limits of Justice* (CUP xxxx) 94.

[30] Amartya Sen, *The Idea of Justice* (Belknap 2009) 68.

requires "that we can identify, protect, and promote cultural membership, as a primary good."[31]

In contrast to the view of free human agency in cosmopolitan liberalism, and the abstract moral agent in Rawls, Kymlicka's insistence on culture as a context for free agency points to an emphasis on, for example, minority and other collective rights in international law and gives considerable importance to the right of peoples both to internal and external self-determination.

Judith Shklar is another liberal theorist who departs substantially from Rawls' conception of the unencumbered self or abstract individual moral agency, as a foundation for liberal institutions of justice. For Shklar, this conception of the self already supposes latent liberal values in assuming that agents can and should choose in isolation from their actual beliefs and commitments, religious and secular. In a letter to Rawls, Shklar pointedly asks: "You cannot evade the demand for demonstrably accurate historical evidence to show that these are indeed the latent values. 'How latent? How latent? How widely shared? How deeply held and by whom at what times? In peace and in war, in secure and insecure times?'"[32] For Shklar, liberal politics is a hedge of reason against cruelty and injustice, which, she argues, history has amply shown are the normal ways in which humans have treated each other since time immemorial. Shklar sharply criticizes ideals such as peace through world law that have attracted some liberals: "Law does not by itself generate institutions, cause wars to end, or states to behave as they should. It does not create a community."[33] At the same time, Shklar sees merit in the kind of international legal rules that allow for practical, mutually self-interested cooperation between states: she gives the example of the regulation of postal communications. Finally, Shklar praises the Nuremberg trials not as an exercise of international legal justice but rather as political pedagogy.

## 5. Cognitive Approaches, Normative Liberal Theory, and International Law

The way in which human beings perceive and understand the world has been explored by researchers in a range of disciplines, including psychology, neuroscience, economics, sociology, anthropology, and philosophy. Studies in social cognition look at the way that social constraints and biases affect people's perceptions of their environment, and their own choices for action within it. Since to be meaningful in understanding the world and useful in acting within it, information

[31] Will Kymlicka, *Liberalism, Community and Culture* (Clarendon 1989) 168–69.

[32] Letter from Judith Shklar to John Rawls, November 10, 1986. I am grateful to Alexandre Lefebvre for drawing my attention to this letter (Harvard Archives).

[33] Judith Shklar, *Legalism: Law, Morals and Political Trials* (Harvard UP 1964) 131.

must be selected and processed, the tools people use to achieve that selection and processing are crucial to cognition. Behavioral studies relate these heuristics to the way in which individuals make decisions. Examples include information economics, which is concerned with how information costs (including problems such as asymmetric information) affect the operation of markets (microeconomics, including public choice theory examining "political markets"), and behavioral law and economics (examining how cognition and informational challenges impact the (economic) consequences of legal rules). Behavioral studies generally suggest that the ability to make decisions based on reason alone is constrained by the ways in which people select and process information,[34] for instance the perception of risk is not simply a matter of calculating the probability that a given harmful event will occur and the extent of the harm if it does occur. If it is rather the perception of security (including miscalculations) that matters, this has implications for how a liberal state can fulfill its promise of security. Cognitive and behavioral studies, and their approaches to human cognition and agency, have different implications or offer different challenges for different version of normative liberal theory.

The Kantian strand in liberal theory is heavily influenced by Kant's account of moral freedom as divorced from sense perception and the understanding of objects in the world. The former is the realm of practical, the latter of pure reason. Moral freedom is an idea or ideal and is autonomous from the actual forces that cause most people to behave in the real world most of the time. In Kant's short writings on history such as *Perpetual Peace* (which has had a significant influence on international legal theory), he made a variety of conjectural attempts to reconcile the ideal of moral freedom with historical action in the world.

Cognitive and behavioral studies have little to say to a purely deontological ideal of freedom as central to liberalism. Where liberals are concerned about how freedom can be an effective principle in the world, such studies can be highly relevant. Montesquieu represents a strand of liberalism very different than that of Kant, as is illustrated well by Montesquieu's definition of freedom as "the opinion of each concerning their own security." For Montesquieu, each individual's freedom of action depends on how they perceive others around them, whether the state as well as non-state sources of insecurity (such as religious authorities). As noted at the outset, a fundamental aspect of the liberal normative theory of international law is the "bottom-up" approach, which roots governance and obligation in the interests and rights of individuals as reflected through representative democratic institutions. In focusing on individuals, in relationship to social and political institutions, there is a common ground between liberal theory and cognitive science and social science. Anne van Aaken notes: "liberal international relations scholarship frequently seeks to unpack the 'black box' that represents the

34 See Van Aaken and Hirsch (n 1).

State ... Individuals can be and are [scrutinized] as actors, rights holders or as part of international organisations."[35]

Cohen and Meyer observe: "Even where our primary concern is the action of the state, those actions may be the product themselves of different actors, whether collective bodies of elected officials, military leaders, trade negotiators, or judges, each with different motivations and decision-making processes."[36] But as Cohen and Meyer also emphasize, the concern with behavior implies the importance of understanding the effects of international law in the real world. One could understand liberal normative theory merely as aimed at generating the implications for engagement with international law that come from the foundational (domestic) normative commitments of a liberal society. This is the character of Dworkin's (albeit not fully developed or completed) liberal theory as discussed above. Rawls also, in "The Law of Peoples," as we have seen, is focused on generating the kind of international law content that could be generated by liberal societies in interaction with others, including other liberal as well as non-liberal societies. While, as noted above, he expresses some hope that human rights will spread globally, he is not fundamentally concerned with international law as an agent of change.

Rawls' theory depends heavily on a deontological conception of the unencumbered self. This ideal or idealized conception has an uneasy relationship to the behavior of actual human beings in a real social context—a difficulty as we saw that Amartya Sen raised with Rawls' theory to the extent that it promises to provide a basis for social and political institutions that are durable and capable of rallying allegiance from citizens over time, as well as ab initio just. There is a range of issues in liberal normative theory where cognitive science and social science have something to say, but how much will depend on the extent to which liberal theory promises or is committed to the realization of international law in the world or whether it is understood merely as an ideal theory that allows us to characterize international norms as liberal in some abstract sense.

If one were to try to articulate a fruitful encounter of cognitive and behavioral studies from these perspectives on the different strands of liberal normative theory, a good beginning would be Machiavelli's question in the *Prince* as to whether normative theory should take human beings as they really are or imagine them as they ought to be. Machiavelli himself is concerned with "effective truth"—knowledge that can change the world. Thus, his own teaching is that one should take human beings as they really are because only by doing so can one build a sound society; for example, turning class tensions and resentments into a dynamic force for ensuring that politics is not simply dominated by one group that oppresses others (checks

[35] Anne van Aaken, 'The Individual in (International) Law and Economics' in Tom Sparks and Anne Peters (eds), *The Individual in International Law* (OUP 2024) 354.

[36] Harlan Grant Cohen and Timothy Meyer, 'International Law as Behavior: An Agenda' in Harlan Grant Cohen and Timothy Meyer (eds), *International Law as Behavior*, ASIL Studies in International Legal Theory (CUP 2021) 7.

and balances, taken up by Montesquieu as well). Kantian/Rawlsian liberalism is concerned above all with moral freedom as a normative ideal. Not being particularly concerned with bringing about such an ideal in the real world, it can afford to leave questions of actual human cognition and behavior largely to other kinds of scientific studies. For Montesquieu (very influenced by Machiavelli) and Shklar (in turn influenced by Montesquieu), accepting how human beings actually are is critical in crafting political and social institutions that hedge against the worst sides of human character. *Within* behavioral law and economics itself, at least to the extent to which it is policy-oriented, there is a question that cross-cuts with Machiavelli's, as it were: is it justified under liberal principles to guide or correct *individual* choices where those choices are made in ways that reflect the kinds of "bounded rationality" identified in cognitive psychology and behavioral law and economics?[37] In the mission to use cognitive and behavioral studies to find ways to identify and correct individuals' choices, where biases or other informational constraints cause those choices to deviate from what a fully rational agent would decide, one can detect something of the hubris of the radical Enlightenment project: the idea that as far as possible individuals *should* make choices on the basis of reason alone.

## 5.1. Distributive justice

In the case of the controversy between political liberals and cosmopolitans on global (distributive) justice, political liberals like Rawls and Nagel, in responding to cosmopolitans, cannot but resort to empirical judgments about the plausibility of generating a conception of global redistribution based on liberal principles, including the kind of social solidarity that may be needed to support it. Here cognitive studies might have something important to say about the plausibility of such judgments. For example, Alesina and Glaeser attribute differences in the commitment to a redistributive welfare state in Europe and the United States not to differences in liberal principles as such but rather to perceptions as to whether poverty is a consequence of misfortunate or reflects a lack of individual effort at economic security by the poor.[38] On the other hand, in a survey of all the empirical evidence available pertinent to the question, Miller and Sundas found that social solidarity at least understood as national identity was not a strong element in redistributive or social justice commitments.[39] It would seem that differences in perceptions of

[37] See Sanjit Dhami and Cass Sunstein, *Bounded Rationality: Heuristics, Judgment, and Public Policy* (MIT Press 2022) chapter 9.

[38] Alberto Alesina and Edward L Glaeser, *Fighting Poverty in the US and Europe* (OUP 2004). See also Dhami and Sunstein (n 37) 162.

[39] David Miller and Ali Sundas, 'Testing the National Identity Argument' (2014) 6 European Political Science Review 237.

individual desert as between different societies are a stronger obstacle to global or cosmopolitan social justice than the kind of solidarity that exists among those who recognize each other as fellow citizens in a nation-state.[40]

Cognitive and behavioral studies have explored patterns of altruistic conduct among human beings.[41] Game-theoretical experiments generally reveal that agents have certain other-regarding preferences, even where the others are strangers; people desire outcomes that are not inequitable and show concern for the situation of the worst-off.[42] Nevertheless, how other-regarding agents are likely to be depends upon their assumptions about the conduct of others. People are altruistic but do not want to be deceived. Thus, trust may be critical to acceptance of redistributive justice, and trust is arguably a bigger problem between different societies. The difficulty may not be so much as Nagel suggests people's unwillingness to *assume responsibility* toward others who are not their "own" but to *trust* those others not to take advantage. A range of social psychology literature anchors trust not in observed behavior of others over time (reputation) but in emotions of affinity or identity.[43] The project of global (distributive) justice falters then not on the failure to imagine or accept duties toward others, or care for their wellbeing, but on trust that others, those with whom we do not share a particular social identity or emotive connect, will reciprocate such duties.

As a general matter, cognitive scholarship is much more supportive of the kind of understanding of the (liberal) self-espoused by, for example, Kymlicka and Shklar, where preferences and choices are deeply embedded in specific communities and contexts—"our" social group in the relevant sense,[44] as opposed to the cosmopolitan liberal self, as sketched, for example, by my colleague Jeremy Waldron:

> The cosmopolitan may live all his life in one city and maintain the same citizenship throughout. But he refuses to think of himself as *defined* by his location or his

[40] On the possibilities and determinants of inter-group cooperation, see Carsten KW De Dreu, Jorg Gross, and Angelo Romano, 'Group Formation and the Evolution of Human Social Organization' [2023] Perspectives on Psychological Science.

[41] See, generally, Serge-Kristoff Kolm and Jean-Mercior Ythier (eds), *Handbook of the Economics of Giving, Altruism, and Reciprocity* (North-Holland 2006).

[42] Yet, there is the problem of abstraction: Paul Slovic, '"If I Look at the Mass I Will Never Act": Psychic Numbing and Genocide' (2007) 2 Judgment and Decision Making 79.

[43] See Jonathan Mercer, 'Rationality and Psychology in International Politics' (2005) 59 International Organization 75, 95–99.

[44] See Moshe Hirsch, 'Social Cognitive Studies, Sociological Theory, and International Law', Andrea Bianchi and Moshe Hirsch (eds), *International Law's Invisible Frames – Social Cognition and Knowledge Production in International Legal Processes* (OUP 2021), 15, 16 "While social-psychological literature traditionally highlights individuals as the basic unit of analysis [footnote omitted], recent publication in the sphere of social cognition (a branch of social psychology) acknowledge that individuals' mental processes are also influenced by cultural features [footnote omitted]. Thus, for example, Fiske and Taylor explain in their influential book on social cognition that 'many of the central assumptions about how people think about other people turn out to be culturally bound.'"

> ancestry or his citizenship or his language. Though he may live in San Francisco and be of Irish ancestry, he does not take his identity to be compromised when he learns Spanish, eats Chinese, wears clothes made in Korea, listens to arias by Verdi sung by a Maori princess on Japanese equipment, follows Ukrainian politics, and practices Buddhist meditation techniques. He is a creature of modernity, conscious of living in a mixed-up world and having a mixed-up self.[45]

Of course, a perfectionist version of liberal theory might seek *to turn individuals into cosmopolitans*, despite their initial embeddedness in a particular culture. And as discussed in the Introduction to this book, cultural features influence perception and additional cognitive processes. Kymlicka wants to nourish particularistic cultures as contexts of liberal choice, thus emphasizing the importance of minority rights and self-determination in international law; Shklar, on the other hand, also cares about minorities but her concern is different, namely that it is in majoritarian form that particularism is likely to turn into chauvinistic xenophobic oppression—she is less idealistic in general than Kymlicka about the impact of cultural embeddedness on freedom.

In theories such as those of Rawls and Slaughter, the distinction between liberal and non-liberal states (with Rawls introducing a third category of "well-ordered" societies) is intended to do significant work in determining the scope and ambition of international legal commitments, and the extent to which liberal societies manage international conflict and cooperation through thick legal norms as opposed to traditional power-political diplomacy. However, as Kahl points out, in such theories it is not clear "why the majority of public and elite opinion within liberal democracies should be expected" to adopt liberal norms. Further, "the source and mechanism for the shared perceptions between liberal democracies is left almost completely unexplained. This is especially problematic given that these shared perceptions and understanding are the most important components in an explanation seeking to demonstrate how ideational factors generate the special quality of democratic relationships."[46]

As Kahl's analysis suggests, liberal intersubjectivity as presented in liberal theory as a basis for thick international legal relations between liberal states *supposes* that the *substance* of shared liberal norms, such as a commitment to solving conflict through peaceable means, law rather than violence, is what underpins greater comprehension and trust between liberal societies in international legal relations. However, as discussed above in relation to the notion of global (distributive) justice, such comprehension and trust may instead reflect the preference, well

[45] Jeremy Waldron, 'Minority Cultures and the Cosmopolitan Alternative' (1992) 25 University of Michigan Journal of Law Reform 751, 754. In later writing, Waldron has significantly qualified or nuanced the position implied in this passage.

[46] Colin H Kahl, 'Constructing a Separate Peace: Constructivism, Collective Liberal Identity, and Democratic Peace' in Glenn R Chafetz (ed), *The Origins of National Interests* (Routledge 1999) 100.

documented in the cognitive studies literature, of social groups to interact with other groups they perceive as like themselves.[47] As Koschut observes, perceptions of other groups as like ourselves may be influenced, sometimes strongly, by emotional affinity or sympathy, as opposed to awareness of specific shared (eg liberal) values and institutions.[48]

In the case of the liberal democracies that thinkers like Rawls and Slaughter seem to have in mind, Kahl suggests that considerable path dependency may be at work, the original affinity between liberal democracies in the old and new world being forged through bonding in reaction to a perceived common enemy, Soviet Communism: "this sense of common identity survived the collapse of the Soviet Union." It is not clear whether this common identity is cemented more through affinities and mutual cultural exposure in (films, music, literature, etc) as opposed to perceptions of shared liberal values.

Once perceiving a society as "like ourselves" creates emotional bonds, "amity," it is quite difficult to alter this felt affinity. This may have important implications for how liberal societies perceive democratic backsliding and its reflection in altered attitudes toward compliance with international human rights law, for example. Alarm has been raised much more quickly and broadly about such backsliding in countries like Poland, Hungary, and Turkey, whereas it has been late in the case of Israel, where especially in the case of Americans, there has been a strong traditional feeling of amity. If emotionally backed amity is more fundamental to affiliative bonds than the perception of shared values or norms at least alone, then this has implications for strategies to legitimize or rally public support for transnational projects of "thick" legal integration; in the case of the European Union, too much emphasis may have been put on values and norms, *Verfassungspatriotism* for example, in attempting to produce the requisite transnational social solidarity. The reluctance to explore an emotional basis for the requisite solidarity may in part be due to liberals' discomfort with emotions in politics, often associated with the evils of "populism." As Chantal Mouffe has pointed out, "today right-wing movements are much more successful than left-wing ones. I am very concerned that the left is much too rationalistic, and believes that 'we should only use arguments, mobilizing affects and passions, that's what the fascists do.'"[49]

In "Authoritarian International Law," Thomas Ginsburg argues that "rising authoritarianism will produce shifts within existing international law structures,

[47] See John C Turner, *Rediscovering the Social Group* (Basil Blackwell 1987). See also Dhami and Sunstein (n 37) on in-group trust: 163.

[48] Simon Koschut, 'No Sympathy for the Devil: Emotions and the Social Construction of the Democratic Peace' (2018) 53 Cooperation and Conflict 320.

[49] David Klemperer, 'Interview: Chantal Mouffe on Democracy, Populism and Why the Left Needs to Read Spinoza', Tocqueville21, August 19, 2021 <https://tocqueville21.com/interviews/interview-chantal-mouffe-on-democracy-populism-and-why-the-left-needs-to-read-spinoza> accessed August 8, 2024. See also Robert Howse, 'Epilogue: In Defense of Disruptive Democracy—A Critique of Anti-Populism' (2019) 17 ICON 641.

including the continued decline of human rights enforcement, although perhaps with more innovation in and commitment to international economic law."[50] In contrast to Slaughter's thickly integrating law among liberal nations, where authoritarian states influence lawmaking (especially in regional institutions), we see, according to Ginsburg, "thinner models of cooperation that demand little of members and can be discarded once their political purpose has been achieved."[51]

At the same time, the liberal/non-liberal division of the world, especially where non-liberal is indicated by what Rawls calls "outlaw" states, may reinforce distrust against states or societies perceived as unlike us, and the tendency to view those unlike as real or potential enemies.[52] The tendency of individuals in liberal democracies to overestimate the obstacles to international legal relations with states felt to be non-liberal enemies is reflected in the demise of the Iran nuclear Joint Comprehensive Plan of Action (JCPOA) agreement, negotiated during the Obama Administration. It was relatively easy for Donald Trump and Benjamin Netanyahu to create a perception among a large group of citizens and legislators that Iran was cheating on the agreement, despite the lack of objective un-doctored evidence that serious cheating was taking place.

The division between liberal and non-liberal states in normative liberal theories sustains the perception that some kinds of international legal relations are appropriate to relationships among liberal states but that others are designed specifically to manage issues between liberal and non-liberal states. In most liberal democracies there initially was little public debate about the consequences for domestic public policy of international investment agreements (IIAs) with investor-state dispute settlement (ISDS) arbitrators, especially bilateral investment treaties (BITs). It was assumed that in imposing international norms, such a "fair and equitable" treatment and limits on the expropriation of property rights were directed to non-liberal (mostly developing) states as a remedy to protect outward capital investment from the liberal democracies where the rule of law was underdeveloped or largely (in liberal terms) non-existent, and where policy-making was presumed to be often arbitrary and discriminatory because of a lack of liberalism and/or democratic institutions.[53] This stylized or stereotyped division of liberal capital exporting versus non-liberal capital importing states had significant consequences. As often interpreted by ISDS arbitrators, these treaties provided for regulatory stabilization (through "fair and equitable" treatment and "regulatory takings" doctrines) that created state liability for regulatory changes even when made through representative democratic procedures in accord with the liberal rule of law. Moreover, it turned out that despite well-established liberal democratic

[50] Thomas Ginzburg, 'Authoritarian International Law?' (2020) 114 AJIL 221, 225.
[51] ibid 257.
[52] See Koschut (n 48) 332, 'the liberal emotion norm of enmity'.
[53] See Rudolf Dolzer 'The Impact of International Investment Treaties on Domestic Administrative Law' (2004–05) 37 New York University Journal of International Law and Politics 953.

institutions, developed states' officials sometimes engaged in arbitrary or discriminatory conduct toward foreign investors of the kind assumed only to occur in non-liberal states, this especially being the case where there were strong local political pressures to do so, and were often uncorrected by domestic courts (North American Free Trade Agreement (NAFTA) claims against Canada).[54]

To return to the relationship of liberalism and peace, some recent scholarship challenges the notion that the likelihood of individuals preferring peace to war depends on perceived shared liberal values. Examining the existence of liberal and other norms through a survey of students and others in the United States, China, and Russia, Bakker found that only in the case of Americans did the regime type significantly influence the willingness to engage in armed conflict, as opposed to perception of the specific threat, an attitude Bakker describes as "hawkishness."[55] Interestingly, hawkishness is no less likely to be present in people who adhere to liberal norms and in all cases seems to be a more important in willingness to back going to war than considerations as to whether other values are shared or divergent.[56] Moreover, Bakker found that in both Russia and China there was a significant identification with liberal norms by the populations surveyed, despite the current regime type. This raises further complexities for any liberal theory of international law that depends on the classification of other societies as liberal or something else.

## 5.2. Commercial liberalism and cognitive and behavioral studies

As already noted, normative liberal theory often includes a commitment to free or at least liberalized trade—and this goes considerably beyond the case of libertarian, or ordo-liberal variants such as the libertarian global constitutionalism of Petersmann. For, as already observed, other kinds of normative liberal theorists see free or freer trade as an agent or accessory of core liberal concerns such as achieving or stabilizing peaceful relations between states, or reducing destructive national prejudices through communication and interaction at the people-to-people level between different nations.

Yet there is strong evidence that people prefer to trade with those whom they *already* perceive as like themselves,[57] raising doubts about the robustness of this

[54] See Robert Howse and Gunes Ünüvar, 'Sowing the Seeds of an ISDS Legitimacy Crisis? The Notorious First Wave of NAFTA Chapter 11 Awards' in Helene Ruiz Fabri and Edoardo Stoppioni (eds), *International Investment Law: An Analysis of the Major Decisions* (Hart 2022).

[55] On hawkishness, see generally Daniel Kahneman and Jonathan Renshon. 'Why Hawks Win' (2007) 158 Foreign Policy 34. See also James Davis, *Psychology, Strategy and Conflict: Perceptions of Insecurity in International Relations* (Routledge 2012).

[56] Femke E Bakker, 'The Microfoundations of Normative Peace Theory: Experiments in the US, Russia and China' (2020) 2 Political Research Exchange 1, 20–22.

[57] See the discussion of inter-group relations and social identity in Hirsch (n 44): 'Empirical studies have persuasively demonstrated that once people identify with a particular social group, they are

latter proposition about the benefits of trade. Carnegie and Gaikwad find, conducting a survey experiment in both the US and India:

> When a trading partner is an adversary, a minority (only 39 percent) of respondents prefer increased trading relations; by contrast, a majority—a full 58 percent—prefer to trade when the partner is an ally. As expected by the security externalities theory, the effect of switching from an ally to an adversary on support for trade is negative and significant, but this gap grows when trade is expected to increase the partner's military capability. In that scenario, only 30 percent of citizens express support for trade with an adversary."[58]

At the same time, as Carnegie and Gaikwad note, some of their results provide albeit limited and qualified support for the trade serves peace dimension of liberal normative theory:

> Although baseline support for free trade is lower for adversaries than for allies, respondents upgrade their evaluation of free trade agreements when informed that trade will help foster peace not only for allies, but also for adversaries. Evidently, when trade reduces the possibility of conflict, many voters who would be averse to trade with adversaries prefer increased economic integration. It is noteworthy that information about the peace-inducing aspects of trade attenuates aversion toward trade with adversaries."[59]

Still, in the end, Carnegie and Gaikwad observe: "Even when we consider the best-case scenario discussed above (that is, when trade does not increase the size of the partner's military and reduces the chance of a conflict), more respondents prefer trading with allies (74 percent) than with adversaries."[60]

The findings here about preferences for trading with allies are complemented but also challenged in some ways by other recent research. For example, Spilker, Bernauer, and Umana found, based on evidence from Costa Rica, Nicaragua, and

likely to view in-group members more positively, and grant them favourable treatment compared that that granted to out-group members', citing Walter Stephan and Cookie Stephan, *Intergroup Relations* (Westview Press 1996). For trade, so-called gravity models, predicting trade flows, are based on two components: the gross domestic product (GDP) and the distance between countries. To this, non-geographical distance has been added using proxies for cultural proximity as language, religion, origins of the legal system, colonial ties, etc. Luigi Capoani, 'Review of the Gravity Model: Origins and Critical Analysis of Its Theoretical Development' (2023) 3 SN Business and Economics 95 <https://doi.org/10.1007/s43546-023-00461-0>.

[58] Allison Carnegie and Nikhar Gaikwad, 'Public Opinion on Geopolitics and Trade: Theory and Evidence' (2022) 74 World Politics 167, 186.

[59] ibid 185.

[60] ibid.

Vietnam, that not only cultural similarities were a significant factor in preferences for trading partners but also the political system; this goes back to the questions of what in fact leads to people's perceptions of a state as an "ally"—how much do emotive or cultural affinities play a role and to what extent is it a matter of judgments about specific features of the political system (like the other state also being a democracy)?[61] Chen, Pevehouse, and Powers focus specifically on the important of democracy in preferences for trading partners among the American public and legislators, arguing that democracy—even apart from its connection to alliance perceptions and cultural affinities—is significant because it is assumed that democratic states are less likely to renege on obligations in trade agreements, and when they do to suffer greater punishment at least in the form of reputation effects, as was the case with the US in the wake of the Trump Administration's trade policies.[62]

Overall, these studies would strongly underpin the strategy of "friend-shoring" that has found favor in some trade policy circles—focusing new efforts at thicker international economic cooperation or deeper integration on agreements among like-minded states, where (as former Canadian trade and foreign minister Chrystia Freeland puts it)

> trade deals are one way to define who our friends are ... Replicated across the world's democracies, friendshoring is an historic opportunity for our workers and our communities. It can make our economies more resilient, our supply chains true to our most deeply held principles, and protect our workers and the social safety net they depend on from unfair competition created by coercive societies and race-to-the-bottom business practices.[63]

This friend/adversary dichotomy in the new trade policy is arguably connected to what Kurtz and Van Aaken observe as the reframing of trade as a security issue, with greater emphasis on conflict with adversaries.[64]

The proliferation of preferential trade agreements has often been used as supposed evidence that the WTO is dysfunctional or ineffective in moving forward at least a neoliberal or ordo-liberal agenda of deeper integration. But if citizens strongly prefer to engage in such exercises in the future with fellow democratic states or ones perceived as friends, allies, or culturally similar, then the pursuit of

[61] Gabriele Spilker, Thomas Bernauer, and Victor Umaña, 'Selecting Partner Countries for Preferential Trade Agreements: Experimental Evidence from Costa Rica, Nicaragua, and Vietnam' (2016) 60 International Studies Quarterly 706.

[62] Frederick R Chen and others, 'Great Expectations: The Democratic Advantage in Trade Attitudes' (2023) 75(2) World Politics 316–52.

[63] Remarks at Brookings Institution, October 11, 2022 <https://deputypm.canada.ca/en/news/speeches/2022/10/11/remarks-deputy-prime-minister-brookings-institution-washington-dc> accessed April 8, 2024.

[64] Anne van Aaken and Jürgen Kurtz, 'Beyond Rational Choice: International Trade Law and the Behavioral Political Economy of Protectionism' (2019) 22 Journal of International Economic Law 601.

such agreements would really say nothing about any institutional failure of the WTO except the failure to transform all WTO Members into liberal democracies. The case of China illustrates how fundamentally delusional was the notion that the road from tyranny to liberal democracy would pass through the WTO system.

As far as the variant of normative liberal theory that is committed to trade liberalization and even deeper economic integration goes, these various insights suggest that pushback against new "big" trade deals or negotiations in the WTO may not have a lot to do with resistance to the liberal theory itself, but much more with a lack of trust or social identity in the context of multilateralism that includes a very large range of countries, including perceived adversaries. Or perhaps, to put it a little differently, the implications are for the second-order theory of the institutions appropriate to realizing commercial liberalism. The philosopher and General Agreement on Tariffs and Trade and European Union architect Alexandre Kojeve, who combined a commitment to commercial liberalism with a demand for transnational social equity, saw these goals as most achievable through building up regional blocs that would then more fully integrate among themselves; that is, beginning not from cosmopolitanism in seeking what Kojeve called the universal and homogenous state but from thicker and more particularistic forms of solidarity and identity.[65]

## 6. Conclusion: A Critical Assessment of the Potential and Limits of Cognitive and Behavioral Studies for Understanding Liberal International Law

It is useful to recall that cognitive and behavioral studies became prominent in the legal academy as a challenge to the stylized rational actor model of law and economics; that is, as a corrective rather than a novel way of theorizing international law. By this time, ironically, the triumph of Stiglitzian information economics had long made the stylized rational actor model quaint in the economics discipline itself, even if it continued to enjoy favor among policy economists in institutions like the International Monetary Fund and World Bank, or neoliberal think tanks. Since conventional Chicago School law and economics had a relatively minimal impact on international legal theory in the first place, it would be surprising if this corrective lens were to be at all transformational. Yet as I have endeavored to show in this chapter, there are many controversies and questions about the aspirations of international law, the entanglement of liberalism with different views of human behavior, its sources in reason, perception, and emotion, and its changeability. Here some of the preoccupations of cognitive and behavioral studies—how individuals

[65] See Robert Howse, 'Kojeve's Latin Empire', originally published in Policy Review (2004) <www.hoover.org/research/kojeves-latin-empire> accessed April 8, 2024.

perceive others, the influence of identity and emotional affinity and trust, and so on—cross-cut those of liberal normative theories of international law. Yet in illuminating such questions and controversies, cognitive and behavioral studies will never have a monopoly, certainly not methodologically. Liberal normative theory including of international law will doubtless continue to draw on sources such as literature, political history, and the history and tradition of political philosophy in understanding human knowledge and character as they relate to liberal ideals and their realization. As such, the way that, for example, Jon Elster, in works like *The Cement of Society* and *Political Psychology*, brings together insights about human knowledge, character, and behavior from all these sources in an ecumenical and eclectic fashion, to inform a range of choices for institutional design for liberal democracies. This is not a bad model for a fruitful engagement of liberal international legal theory and cognitive and behavioral studies.

# 7

# Transational Legal Process, Cognition, and Context

*Regina Jefferies*

## 1. Introduction

Harold Koh's transnational legal process (TLP) theory emerged during a time in which 'international legal compliance' scholarship produced a wide range of theoretical approaches interrogating whether, why, and how states comply with international law.[1] As a norm-based theory, TLP provides a conceptual framework for understanding how a variety of state and non-state actors interact in diverse domestic and international fora to 'make, interpret, enforce, and ultimately, internalize rules of transnational law'.[2] Since introducing the theory in 1994, Koh has continued to refine TLP with reference to international legal theory, interdisciplinary international law scholarship, and contexts beyond its original legal compliance orientation. These developments have also coincided with the interdisciplinary, 'empirical turn' in international law[3] and the more recent emergence of a strain of literature which de-centres compliance to focus more broadly on how international law functions.[4]

This chapter addresses the question of how cognitive-behavioural science might provide a means for bringing additional clarity to under-described aspects of TLP, including the process of 'internalization' and the concept of 'transnational legal substance'. In particular, the chapter explores how empirical inquiry can contribute to the type of mid-range theorizing generally missing from TLP's theoretical assumptions but which is necessary to fully engage with it. The 'interaction-interpretation-internalization' process which lies at the heart of the TLP approach is elusive and lacks clarity about when, why, and how the process works (or fails). This chapter argues that cognitive studies may clarify when, why,

[1] Harold Hongju Koh, 'Transnational Legal Process' (1996) 75 Neb L Rev 181; Regina Jefferies, 'Transnational Legal Process: An Evolving Theory and Methodology' (2021) 46 Brooklyn J Intl L 311, 312.

[2] Harold Hongju Koh, 'The 1998 Frankel Lecture: Bringing International Law Home' (1998) 35 Hous L R 623, 635–36.

[3] Gregory Shaffer and Tom Ginsburg, 'The Empirical Turn in International Legal Scholarship' (2012) 106 AJIL 1.

[4] See David Hughes, 'How States Persuade: An Account of International Legal Argument upon the Use of Force' (2019) 50 Georgetown J Intl L 839.

Regina Jefferies, *Transnational Legal Process, Cognition, and Context* In: *International Legal Theory and the Cognitive Turn*. Edited by: Anne van Aaken and Moshe Hirsch, Oxford University Press. © Regina Jefferies 2025.
DOI: 10.1093/9780198909293.003.0008

and how interactions are more likely to result in the adoption of rules or interpretations which reinforce an underlying norm. For example, differences in the cognitive styles of border enforcement officials can impact risk perception and the degree to which affective states and emotional perceptions influence how people perceive, interpret, and act. That, in turn, can influence how officials may privilege certain rules over international human rights obligations. The concept of 'social proof' might also be useful in explaining when and why certain actors are more likely to adopt a practice or apply a rule when they observe others, and particularly 'similar others', behaving in a certain manner.[5]

The concept of 'transnational legal substance' similarly evades a clear description. However, cognitive-behavioural studies could clarify when, how, and why new norms, interpretations, or international rules emerge out of a transnational legal process. As the discussion regarding the cognitive styles of border enforcement officials illustrates, recurring interpretations that challenge the application or understanding of a particular norm on a broad scale and over time could influence how norms are understood, or even raise questions about the development of international law. The concept of 'social proof' may provide similar insight into the emergence of 'transnational legal substance', for example where a cascade of non-compliant states adopt behaviours that challenge rather than reinforce an underlying norm.

The chapter begins by outlining the central aspects of TLP theory, focusing on norm 'internalization' and 'transnational legal substance',[6] as well as the human connection inherent in TLP's theoretical approach. While states may represent the primary actors of importance in international law, TLP explicitly recognizes the role of individuals in the international law-making process and state practice and (non)compliance with regard to international law, an insight often shared by interdisciplinary, empirical scholarship. Locating individuals within relational spaces of transnational legal processes thus allows us to understand the role of individuals as both constitutive of, and shaped by, the state, as well as international law. Furthermore, such an approach allows us to interrogate and make visible how the interpretation, application, and evolution of international law are influenced by individuals and the cognitive processes informing, influencing, and driving their behaviour.

The chapter then turns to cognitive sociology and cognitive psychology as a means for confronting the absence of detail regarding the *who*, *how*, and *why* of

[5] Robert B Cialdini and others, 'Compliance with a Request in Two Cultures: The Differential Influence of Social Proof and Commitment/Consistency on Collectivists and Individualists' (2016) 25 Pers Soc Psychol Bull 1242, 1243; Shubhangi Roy, 'Theory of Social Proof and Legal Compliance: A Socio-Cognitive Explanation for Regulatory (Non) Compliance' (2020) 22 German LJ 238, 239.

[6] Harold Hongju Koh, 'Transnational Legal Process and the "New" New Haven School of International Law' in Jeffrey Dunoff and Mark Pollack (eds), *International Legal Theory: Foundations and Frontiers* (CUP 2022) 113–14.

'internalization', and the production of 'transnational legal substance'. Each of the three case studies discussed below draw upon international refugee law to explore how cognitive-behavioural studies might enrich understandings of individual actors, institutions, states' understanding and adoption of norms, and the development of international law. The first example explores how the perception of risk can drive agency behaviour at both the institutional and individual actor level, and sheds light not only on questions of state internalization and compliance but also on how competing legal norms are interpreted and reconciled (or not). The second case study examines how cognitive psychological concepts of social identity (including self-categorization) might provide a foundation for understanding why people perceive and act according to a sense of obligation in international law. The final example interrogates the impact of norm non-compliance on the interpretation and understanding of legal norms, with potential implications for TLP's conceptions of norm internalization and the production of transnational legal substance.

## 2. The Human Connection in Transnational Legal Process Theory

Koh presents TLP as a normative theory of 'how public and private actors ... interact in a variety of public and private, domestic and international fora to make, interpret, enforce, and ultimately internalize rules of transnational law'.[7] Koh labels the theory as 'normative' in that international legal norms structure and drive actor behaviour within a transnational legal process.[8] At the same time, the interactivity of actor behaviour may also contribute to the development of new norms.[9] The jurisprudential roots of TLP intertwine with the New Haven School of International Law, 'a policy-oriented jurisprudence' that conceives international law as an interdisciplinary, transnational, authoritative decision-making process rather than a static set of rules.[10] Despite the New Haven School's policy-orientation, it was similarly presented as a normative theory whereby law and legal decisions should be evaluated by 'their degree of contribution to the achievement of a public order of human dignity'.[11] Ultimately, the orientation towards policy and action in furtherance of a future public order (which often tracked the policy priorities of the United States) ran in tension with the theory's normative claims.[12] Still, the New

[7] Koh (n 1) 183–84.

[8] Harold Hongju Koh, 'Keynote Address: Emerging Law of 21st Century War' (2016) 66 Emory LJ 487, 487–88.

[9] ibid.

[10] Eisuke Suzuki, 'The New Haven School of International Law: An Invitation to a Policy-Oriented Jurisprudence' (1974) 1 Yale J World Pub Ord 1.

[11] W Michael Reisman, 'Theory about Law: Jurisprudence for a Free Society' (1999) 108 Yale LJ 935, 939.

[12] Burns H Weston, 'McDougal's Jurisprudence: Utility, Influence, Controversy' (1985) Proceedings ASIL 266, 272–73.

Haven School has had a significant influence on international legal theory, particularly in the US, with the later emergence of a 'new' New Haven School within which TLP theory falls.[13]

TLP theory also counts amongst its forebears a number of normative legal theoretical approaches, such as the international human rights movement, law and society, and critical legal studies (CLS).[14] This normative component of TLP theory also includes some features associated with constructivism in international relations theory, in that TLP posits that international norms traverse a transnational legal process which ultimately reconfigures state interests and identities.[15] That reconfiguration of interest and identity, occurring within a state's domestic structure and inviting a deeper examination into the inner workings and components of the state, ultimately influences state action and compliance with international law. This constructivist orientation encourages researchers to delve into the people, institutions, and rules constructing state interest on the international plane—an area ripe for interdisciplinary exploration.

TLP theorizes that 'obedience'—or internalized compliance—can be achieved through 'repeated interaction with other governmental and nongovernmental actors in the international system'.[16] Transnational legal process can drive state compliance in four steps: interaction, interpretation, internalization, and obedience.[17] The internalization step is further divided into three categories, encompassing social, political, and legal internalization, despite the clear conceptual difficulties in disentangling these categories from one another.[18] Koh also identifies numerous 'agents of internalization' helping to bring about norm internalization. Those agents include *transnational norm entrepreneurs* and *governmental norm sponsors*, outlined in Section 3, as well as *transnational issue networks*, *interpretive communities and law-declaring fora*, *bureaucratic compliance procedures*, and *issue linkages*. Still, the concept of norm internalization is not well described in the literature[19] and often appears to simply occur through the adoption of rules or legal interpretations within a transnational legal context which align with relevant norms. While scholars have critiqued the absence of detail around internalization, as well as the mystery of *why* states internalize norms, few have engaged in the type of mid-range theorizing necessary to test TLP's theoretical assumptions.[20]

[13] Harold Hongju Koh, 'Is There a "New" New Haven School of International Law?' (2007) 32 Yale J Intl L 559.

[14] Koh (n 1) 187–89. See also Chapter 4 by Shiri Krebs in this volume.

[15] Koh (n 12) 570; and see also Chapter 3 by Ian Johnstone and Arun Mohan Sukumar in this volume.

[16] Koh (n 1) 203.

[17] Koh (n 2) 644.

[18] ibid 646.

[19] See Jefferies (n 1) 313, (n 4) 314, and (nn 5–6) (citing scholars who have advanced these critiques).

[20] See eg, Jutta Brunée and Stephen J Toope, *Legitimacy and Legality in International Law: An Interactional Account* (OUP 2010) 118–19; Ryan Goodman and Derek Jinks, 'How to Influence States: Socialization and International Human Rights Law' (2004) 54 Duke LJ 621, 626, n 8; Andrew K Woods, 'A Behavioral Approach to Human Rights' (2010) 51 Harvard Intl LJ 51, 75.

Scholars have also noted TLP's limited descriptive and explanatory impact, particularly in terms of understanding precisely *how* state behaviour contributes to the creation of 'transnational legal substance' and how norms come to be internalized within a multi-faceted state where countless organizations and individuals repeatedly interact over time to interpret and enact understandings of legal obligation in various relational contexts.[21] Without illuminating the specific mechanisms and actors which enliven the relational spaces through which state behaviour is enacted, the possibility that TLP might describe the 'complex process of interaction, interpretation, and norm-internalization by which transnational law is made in the twenty-first century' remains inchoate.

Goodman and Jinks characterize Koh's version of internalization as an approach through which 'actors are consciously convinced of the truth, validity, or appropriateness of a norm, belief, or practice'—in other words, actors are persuaded to comply.[22] Goodman and Jinks also point to the concepts of acculturation and socialization, which function differently than persuasion and add to the concept of internalization. Within acculturation, they identify not only the social pressures to conform but also the cognitive pressures which are mutually reinforcing.[23] 'Cognitive pressure' refers to both extrinsic pressures impacting cognition, such as distractions, fatigue, or temporal pressure, and intrinsic pressures, such as the pressures associated with internalized social roles and expectations.[24] Cognitive pressures not only form part of the environment in which organizations act but also 'suggest that states may be more inclined to conform their behaviour to community expectations—and that they are unlikely to sustain, over the long term, an idiosyncratic interpretation of any norm that the international community considers central'.[25] Conforming behaviour to community expectations reduces cognitive pressures in several respects, including reducing pressures associated with the social-psychological costs of non-conformity, and reaping the social-psychological benefits of conformity.[26]

The concept of 'transnational legal substance' also lacks detail, despite the significant legal theoretical implications it carries for how international law is created, the sources of international law, and how norms gain their normativity. In describing the types of norms characterizing TLP, Koh points to the ideals of a

[21] See n 18.

[22] Goodman and Jinks (n 19) 635; Harold Hongju Koh, 'Internalization through Socialization' (2005) 54 Duke LJ 975.

[23] Goodman and Jinks (n 19) 639.

[24] ibid at 639–40; Alison Wray, 'Formulaic Sequences as a Regulatory Mechanism for Cognitive Perturbations during the Achievement of Social Goals' (2017) 9 Top Cogn Sci 569, 584. Cognitive pressures contribute to 'cognitive load', which occurs when the cognitive demands of a task deplete a person's available cognitive resources, such as attention and memory. See Moshe Hirsch, 'Cognitive Sociology, Social Cognition and Coping with Racial Discrimination in International Law' (2020) 30 EJIL 1319, 1328.

[25] Goodman and Jinks (n 19) 684.

[26] ibid 640.

Kantian system of global governance where states respect values such as 'democracy, the rule of law, individual freedom, and the mutual advantages derived from peaceful intercourse'.[27] Koh argues that these norms constitute 'transnational public law concepts', 'rooted in shared national norms and emerging international norms that have similar or identical meaning in every national system'.[28] Examples include the concept of 'cruel, inhuman or degrading treatment' and 'transborder trafficking' in international criminal law.[29] He places significant emphasis on the role of the courts in safeguarding these ideals and 'correcting' interpretations and practices that diverge from underlying norms.

The normative orientation of TLP suggests that only rules which align with shared norms can be 'uploaded', 'downloaded', or 'horizontally transplanted' and emerge as transnational legal substance. Therefore, an action that does not align with an underlying norm, no matter how pervasive or widespread, cannot transmute into transnational legal substance. This would have implications for international legal theories about state practice, norm conflict, and treaty interpretation, in addition to complicating ideas such as state consent and sovereignty. Indeed, TLP theory acknowledges the complexity of sources of international law, new fora for interpreting international law, and the variety of forms of dispute resolution that now exist. The theory also provides space for people—particularly bureaucrats, but also private actors—to influence both transnational law and process. This provenance places the broad contours of TLP theory in context and sets the stage for understanding how TLP has continued to develop as a theoretical framework for thinking about international law and the influence of people in a transnational process.

## 3. Cognitive-Behavioural Science: Filling the Law–Action Gap

Cognitive studies provide a set of methodological tools and concepts that have the potential to reveal the actors and processes of norm internalization, *why* certain norms are internalized, and the effect of human behaviour on norm interpretation and contestation. Cognitive science involves the 'interdisciplinary study of mental processes involved in the acquisition, classification and interpretation of knowledge in human environment as well as the decision on the appropriate action based upon it'.[30] Although empirical and theoretical international legal scholarship has looked to individual behaviour as a means for understanding state

[27] Harold Hongju Koh, 'The Trump Administration and International Law' (2017) 56 Washburn LJ 413, 466.

[28] Koh (n 6) 114. On the 'universality' of international law, see Luis Eslava and Sundhya Pahuja, 'Beyond the (Post)Colonial: TWAIL and the Everyday Life of International Law' (2012) 45 VRU 195.

[29] Koh (n 6) 114.

[30] Hirsch (n 23) 1320.

interests and action, other scholars have pointed to the importance of recognizing the 'central role of individuals in the everyday practice of international law' and 'their engagement with international law and their potential influence outside and irrespective of their state'.[31] Indeed, some streams in cognitive science, such as cognitive sociology and constructivism, emphasize the influence of social groups on individuals' cognitive processes.

Theorizing the role of *individuals* both within and outside the organization of a state aligns with TLP's analytical framework, which envisions individual actors such as *governmental norm sponsors*. The category of governmental norm sponsors includes governmental officials who act within state structures as 'allies and sponsors' for the norms promoted by nongovernmental actors.[32] However, this seemingly straightforward category obscures a more complex range of state actors responsible for interpreting and implementing norms in various contexts, and a much more complex process of interaction, than is currently described by Koh.

Still, TLP provides a useful baseline framework and methodology for engaging in mid-range theorizing and testing some of the behavioural assumptions linked to the processes of internalization and the production of transnational legal substance. The theory itself provides a context for the enquiry into those behavioural assumptions and processes, as well as a methodology through which to draw insights and methods from the cognitive sciences to understand the research questions.[33] Legal implementation may be viewed as a behavioural manifestation of how people interpret and make judgements about the application and salience of law and norms. Analysing implementation also provides a window into whether and how individual actors are consciously convinced of the 'truth, validity, or appropriateness of a norm',[34] as well as the influence of acculturation, socialization, and cognition.

Yet, the individual does not act in isolation. In this chapter, cognitive sociology is understood as the study of 'the mechanisms by which cultural processes enter into individual minds and shape the micro foundations of social action',[35] and provides an empirical basis for linking externally observable cognitive processes and sociocultural context. This approach to cognitive sociology draws interdisciplinary connections to cognitive psychology, which concerns the cognitive processes—such as attention, perception, learning, memory, language, problem solving, reasoning,

[31] Tamar Meggido, 'The Missing Persons of International Law Scholarship: A Roadmap for Future Research' in Harlan Grant Cohen and Timothy Meyer (eds), *International Law as Behavior* (CUP 2021) 230, 231.

[32] Koh (n 2) 648.

[33] Rossana Deplano and Nikolaos Tsagourias, 'Introduction' in Rossana Deplano and Nikolaos Tsagourias (eds), *Research Methods in International Law: A Handbook* (Elgar 2021) 1–7.

[34] Goodman and Jinks (n 19) 635.

[35] Wayne H Brekhus and Gabe Ignatow, 'Cognitive Sociology and the Cultural Mind: Debates, Directions, and Challenges' in Wayne H Brekhus and Gabe Ignatow (eds), *The Oxford Handbook of Cognitive Sociology* (OUP 2019) 2.

and thinking—and the aspects of the brain involved in making sense of our surroundings and taking action.[36]

The following three examples, drawn from international refugee law, demonstrate how considering insights from the cognitive-behavioural sciences can provide a sort of 'corrective lens' for addressing the shortcomings of TLP theory outlined above and help researchers to make sense of how people—embedded within a particular social, legal, and organizational context—perceive, interpret, and implement international legal obligations.

### 3.1. International refugee law and the actors and processes of norm 'internalization'

One of Koh's paradigmatic examples of a transnational field of law is that of international refugee law, which he frequently draws upon to illustrate aspects of TLP theory. Various norms underpin this legal framework, including the prohibition on 'cruel, inhuman or degrading treatment', which is inextricably linked to the prohibition on *refoulement* and non-penalization of refugees outlined in the *Convention against Torture*, the *1951 Refugee Convention*, and the subsequent *1967 Protocol*.[37] This section explores how recent research from the field of cognitive sociology can be employed to tease out—and test—the concept and process of norm internalization. In particular, it shows how differences in people's cognitive styles can impact their risk perceptions and the degree to which affective states and emotional perceptions outweigh assessments of probability in the application of law.[38] This section underscores how the individual behaviour of border enforcement officials can provide evidence of understanding and salience of norms, while also implicating questions of state responsibility and the hierarchy of norms in international law.

Within the European Union, a variety of supranational, national, and subnational actors engage in bureaucratic practices of identifying, sorting, and returning asylum seekers that influence how (or whether) international refugee law is applied to people seeking protection. Among those actors, both European Union (EU) Member State border enforcement officials and the European Border and Coast Guard Agency (EBCG, or FRONTEX) play a key role in interacting

[36] Michael W Eysenck and Mark T Keane, *Cognitive Psychology: A Student's Handbook* (Taylor & Francis 2015) 1.

[37] *Convention Relating to the Status of Refugees*, 189 UNTS 150, 28 July 1951 (entered into force 22 April 1954) (*1951 Convention*); *Protocol relating to the Status of Refugees*, 606 UNTS 267 (entered into force 4 October 1967) (*1967 Protocol*). See also *Convention against Torture and Other Cruel, Inhuman or Degrading Treatment or Punishment*, opened for signature 10 December 1984, 1465 UNTS 85 (entered into force 26 June 1987) ('*CAT*') art 3. There exist numerous other international instruments containing a prohibition on *refoulement*.

[38] Mauro Martinelli and Giuseppe Alessandro Veltri, 'Do Cognitive Styles Affect Vaccine Hesitancy? A Dual-Process Cognitive Framework for Vaccine Hesitancy and the Role of Risk Perceptions' (2021) 289 Soc Sci Med 114403.

with asylum seekers at the external borders of the EU in this transnational legal structure.[39] A critical part of that role requires identifying and determining how to process people seeking international protection, particularly those who arrive irregularly. Yet, these tasks of perception, categorization, and sorting people involve more than mechanically applying the law in discrete cases and implicate the types of microprocesses through which actors are 'exposed to, receive, process, and then act upon the normative arguments that predominate in particular social environments'.[40]

The 'dual-process model of cognition' framework within the cognitive sociology literature draws heavily from cognitive psychology, as well as other fields of cognitive science.[41] The dual-process model conceptualizes how cognition can inform behaviour[42] at both the System 1 (*automatic* cognition) level and the System 2 (*analytic* cognition) level as outlined in the Introduction to this volume.[43] Automatic cognition is often characterized by reliance on heuristics, 'which reduce the complex task of assessing probabilities and predicting values' but which can 'lead to severe and systematic errors'.[44] System 1 cognition is intuitive and is 'based on associations acquired through experience and calculates information quickly and automatically'.[45] While people possess the capacity for both automatic and analytic cognition, a person's 'cognitive style', or propensity for automatic or analytic cognition, can arise through 'systematic exposure to socially patterned experiences'.[46]

The concept of risk is used here as a means for understanding 'the specific ways in which people perceive and respond to a host of hazards and conditions of

[39] European Parliament and Council Regulation (EU) 2016/1624 of 14 September 2016 on the European Border and Coast Guard and amending Regulation (EU) 2016/399 of the European Parliament and of the Council and repealing Regulation (EC) No 863/2007 of the European Parliament and of the Council, Council Regulation (EC) No 2007/2004 and Council Decision 2005/267/EC [2016] OJ L251/1; European Parliament and Council Regulation (EU) 2019/1896 of 13 November 2019 on the European Border and Coast Guard and Repealing Regulations (EU) 1052/2013 and (EU) 2016/1624 [2019] OJ L295/1.

[40] Alastair Iain Johnston, 'Treating International Institutions as Social Environments' (2001) 45 ISQ 487, 488.

[41] Andrew Miles, Raphaël Charron-Chénier, and Cyrus Schleifer, 'Measuring Automatic Cognition: Advancing Dual-Process Research in Sociology' (2019) 84(2) American Sociological Rev 308, 308.

[42] Jonathan St BT Evans, 'In Two Minds: Dual Process Accounts of Reasoning' (2003) 7 Trends Cogn Sci 454; Jonathan St BT Evans, 'Dual-Processing Accounts of Reasoning, Judgment and Social Cognition' (2008) 59 Annual Rev of Psychology 255; Daniel Kahneman, *Thinking, Fast and Slow* (Penguin 2011); KE Stanovich and RF West, 'Individual Differences in Reasoning: Implications for the Rationality Debate?' (2000) 23 BBS 645; Martinelli and Veltri (n 37) 2.

[43] Introduction to this volume, Section 4.

[44] Martinelli and Veltri (n 37) 2; Hirsch (n 23).

[45] Giuseppe A Veltri, 'The Challenges of Cultural Segmentation: New Approaches from Computational Social Science' in S Salvatore and others (eds), *Methods and Instruments in the Study of Meaning-Making* (Springer 2023) 31, 33.

[46] Gordon Brett and Andrew Miles, 'Who Thinks How? Social Patterns in Reliance on Automatic and Deliberate Cognition' (2021) 8 Sociol Sci 96, 97; Gordon Brett and Soli Dubash, 'The Sociocognitive Origins of Personal Mastery' (2023) J Health Soc Behav 1, 2.

threatening uncertainty'.[47] People's perceptions of risk are not straightforward, and risk is itself socially constructed and produced.[48] Risk is not sensed but perceived by individuals in a particular social and cultural context.[49] Thus, rather than being driven by objective calculations of risk, individual risk perception has an affective element, involves people's cognitive systems,[50] and is influenced by '*socio*mental lenses grounded in particular social environments'.[51] These socio-cognitive lenses impact how people process information and shape understandings of the existence of risk and appetite for risk level. The intuitive and automatic nature of System 1 cognition particularly lends itself to the influence of socio-cognitive biases, which function as 'shortcuts made by humans in judgment and decision-making that lead to suboptimal decisions'[52] and influence decision-making.

Empirical studies using the dual-process framework suggest that both cognitive style (System 1 vs. System 2) and affective risk perception may play a critical role in individual decision-making at multiple levels within transnational legal frameworks.[53] This research provides an example of how a cognitive approach to international law might provide empirical insight into whether, or how, a border enforcement official's style of thinking and perception of risk influence how and why they resort to the application of certain legal rules when encountering people seeking protection, particularly when legal frameworks may overlap.[54]

Perception of risk depends upon *whose* risk is perceived,[55] can occur with or without an individual's conscious awareness,[56] and is linked with the cognitive processes of 'categorization' and 'interpretation'. Therefore, a border enforcement official belonging to a police or military unit who has been socialized to a security-defensive culture may perceive as a risk a person of unknown identity approaching the European coast in a fishing boat. While an individual crossing the Mediterranean seeking protection may perceive a range of risks influenced by their own sociocultural experience, from the seaworthiness of their form of transport, to

47 Iain Wilkinson, *Risk, Vulnerability and Everyday Life* (Routledge 2010) 8.

48 Daina Cheyenne Harvey, 'Risk, Culture, and Cognition' in Wayne H Brekhus and Gabe Ignatow (eds), *The Oxford Handbook of Cognitive Sociology* (OUP 2019) 449, 451.

49 Baruch Fischhoff, Paul Slovic, and Sarah Lichtenstein, '"The Public" vs. "The Experts": Perceived vs. Actual Disagreements about Risks of Nuclear Power' in Vincent T Covello and others (eds), *The Analysis of Actual Versus Perceived Risks* (Springer 1983) 235.

50 Harvey (n 47) 450.

51 Hirsch (n 23), citing Eviatar Zerubavel, *Social Mindscapes: An Invitation to Cognitive Sociology* (Harvard UP 1997) 31 (emphasis in original).

52 Veronica Fikfak, Daniel Peat, and Eva van der Zee, 'Bias in International Law' (2022) 23 German LJ 281, 282; Hirsch (n 23).

53 Evans (n 41); Martinelli and Veltri (n 37); Justin T Pickett and Shawn D Bushway, 'Dispositional Sources of Sanction Perceptions: Emotionality, Cognitive Style, Intolerance of Ambiguity, and Self-Efficacy' (2015) 39 Law Hum Behav 624.

54 Regine Paul, 'Harmonisation by Risk Analysis? Frontex and the Risk-Based Governance of European Border Control' (2017) 39 J European Integration 689; Fikfak and others (n 51).

55 Lennart Sjöberg, 'Emotions and Risk Perception' (2007) 9 Risk Manag 223.

56 Philip M Merikle and others, 'Perception without Awareness: Perspectives from Cognitive Psychology (2001) 79 Cognition 115.

the consequences of being forced to return to the place they fled, or the treatment they might receive from border enforcement officials upon arrival. In this example, a border enforcement official with a propensity for automatic cognition may be more influenced by cognitive biases, such as where 'threat assessments are associated with recent negative experiences or events producing the risk'[57] ('availability heuristic'), to make decisions about how or whether to refer an asylum seeker to a refugee status determination (RSD) process. These decisions can have a profound impact on a person's ability to access international protection. Is it more likely, then, that this official, who perceives a person arriving at a border as a security risk, will act in a manner that privileges the criminalization of attempted entry over the norm of non-penalization? Or that policies of deterrence might take precedence over respect for fundamental rights and the principle of *non-refoulement*, where joint FRONTEX and Member State border operations result in the pushback of asylum seekers?[58]

This case study, in which state actors reflexively apply different normative frameworks underpinned by different sources of international law, reflects how differences in people's cognitive styles, risk perception, affective states, and emotional perceptions may influence how people understand legal obligations or rights. Bordering practices frequently prioritize distinct conceptions of security, sovereignty, and policy goals over robust RSD procedures. These practices emerge through transnational political and legal discourses,[59] as well as administrative practices,[60] and the actions of organizational leadership.[61] Yet rather than suggesting a threat to the authority of international law, disagreements over legal obligations and rights perhaps marks a critical waypoint in thinking about how the communicative practice of international law might ultimately reorient thinking around the relationship amongst competing norms. This example underscores the importance of enquiring into how cognition, perception, and risk tie into individual decision-making that may have an aggregate impact on how norms are understood,[62] what type of action constitutes state practice, the hierarchy of norms,

[57] Andrew Denovan and others, 'Perception of Risk and Terrorism-Related Behavior Change: Dual Influences of Probabilistic Reasoning and Reality Testing' (2017) 8 Front Psychol 1, 8. The 'availability heuristic' is a form of cognitive bias where people focus 'on items that are more prominent or emotionally striking and ignore[e] those that are unremarkable'. Fikfak and others (n 51).

[58] European Parliament, Committee on Civil Liberties, Justice and Home Affairs, *Report on the Fact-Finding Investigation on Frontex Concerning Alleged Fundamental Rights Violations* (Working Document, 14 July 2021) <www.europarl.europa.eu/cmsdata/238156/14072021%20Final%20Report%20FSWG_en.pdf> accessed 21 October 2023.

[59] Sarah Léonard and Christian Kaunert, 'The Securitisation of Migration in the European Union: Frontex and Its Evolving Security Practices' (2020) 48 J Ethnic and Migration Studies 1417; Alexander Betts, 'The Refugee Regime Complex' (2010) 29 RSQ 12.

[60] Léonard and Kaunert (n 59).

[61] Jan Beyers, 'Policy Issues, Organisational Format and the Political Strategies of Interest Organisations' (2008) 31 WEP 1188; Nina Græger, 'European Security as Practice: EU-NATO Communities of Practice in the Making?' (2016) 25 Eur Secur 478.

[62] Ingo Venzke, *How Interpretation Makes International Law: On Semantic Change and Normative Twists* (OUP 2012) 63–64, 67.

and the applicability of potentially overlapping legal frameworks. Examining the cognitive styles and risk perceptions of individual officials who routinely engage in communicative practices and processes of interpretation and decision-making thus presents one mechanism through which to test and further hypothesize the contours of the process of internalization and raises important questions related to the production of transnational legal substance, discussed in Section 4.

## 3.2. The role of US Customs and Border Protection (CBP) officials in processing asylum seekers and *why* states 'internalize' norms

The migration 'crisis' at the US–Mexico international border has reached seemingly new crescendos throughout successive Republican and Democratic presidential administrations, despite the decades-long existence of federal policies of deterrence aimed at preventing the entry of people into the US.[63] Following his election in 2020, then-President Elect Joe Biden committed to reversing many of the immigration policies of the Trump Administration to the relief of many US legal scholars who had consistently and convincingly highlighted the ways in which US practice diverged from its international legal obligations.[64] This section looks to scholarship from the field of cognitive psychology and cognitive sociology to examine an approach through which to develop more credible explanations of *why* actors comply with international law, using the example of 'metering' in the United States. 'Metering' refers to the process of turning back asylum seekers at land ports of entry in order to limit the number of applicants that CBP receives, and constitutes one example of a controversial policy aimed at preventing and regulating the entry of asylum seekers.[65]

Koh frequently looks to US immigration law for examples of how various actors within a transnational legal process engage in a strategy of 'interaction-interpretation-internalization' to challenge the implementation of policies that violate international refugee law.[66] In Koh's retelling of this strategy in the context of then-President Trump's 'Muslim ban', he identifies and describes a range of public and private actors and actions aimed at resisting and preventing the implementation of the policy in light of US international legal obligations.[67] Those

[63] Gabriella Soto and Daniel E Martinez, 'The Geography of Migrant Death: Implications for Policy and Forensic Science' in Krista E Latham and Alyson J O'Daniel (eds), *Sociopolitics of Migrant Death and Repatriation* (Springer 2018) 67.

[64] See Philip G Schrag, Andrew I Schoenholtz, and Jaya Ramji-Nogales, *The End of Asylum* (GUP 2021); Harold Hongju Koh, *The Trump Administration and International Law* (OUP 2019); Ruth Ellen Wasem, 'More Than a Wall: The Rise and Fall of US Asylum and Refugee Policy' (2020) 8(3) J Migration and Human Security 246.

[65] Joint Statement of Undisputed Facts Concerning the Parties' Cross-Motions for Summary Judgment, *Al Otro Lado v. Nielson*, 327 F.Supp.3d 1284 (2018) (No 619), filed as *Al Otro Lado, Inc., et al. v. Kelly, et al.*, 17-cv-05111 (CDC, 12 July 2017) 7.

[66] Koh (n 26) 441.

[67] ibid 422–30.

largely structural and process-orientated descriptions, however, do not delve into *why* various actors either acted in support of or opposition to the Muslim ban. Similarly, examinations of metering by CBP officials do not interrogate why officials at different levels of the agency either supported or opposed the policy in the face of clear transnational legal obligations.

The practice of metering was first instituted informally during the Obama Administration. However, CBP officials later successfully advocated for the adoption of metering at ports of entry throughout the southern border, as well as the eventual codification of metering as a federal policy.[68] On 1 November 2021, roughly eleven months after taking office, the Biden Administration issued a policy memorandum purporting to rescind several CBP memoranda codifying the metering policy.[69] However, rather than overturning the policy, the Administration's approach further codified a central component of the metering policy—the characterization of asylum seekers as a subset of international travellers requiring CBP's attention and resources, much like travellers for pleasure and commercial travellers. This reframing of asylum seekers as a category of travellers that can be deprioritized in favour of 'other vital priorities'[70]—irrespective of the non-derogable obligation of *non-refoulement*—marks a significant change not only in how asylum seekers are processed at land borders but also in how the US understands the principle of *non-refoulement*. This reframing has continued with the introduction of the CBP One mobile application and the recent adoption of a requirement that asylum seekers use CBP One to schedule an appointment to seek asylum at the southern land border, or face ineligibility for asylum under US domestic law (in violation of US international legal obligations).[71]

### 3.2.1. Social identity theory, self-categorization theory, and *why* US officials prioritize military and security considerations over humanitarian and refugee protection obligations

How can we then understand the behaviour of border officials in this context? Social identity theory and self-categorization theory are corresponding and related concepts relating to the connection between a person's self-concept and group behaviour.[72] A social identity is a person's understanding that they belong to a group,

[68] ibid.

[69] Troy A Miller, 'Guidance for Management and Processing of Undocumented Noncitizens at Southwest Border Land Ports of Entry' (CBP Memorandum, 1 November 2021), purporting to rescind and supersede Kirstjen Nielsen, 'Prioritization-Based Queue Management' (CBP Memorandum, 5 June 2018), CBP Commissioner, 'Prioritization-Based Queue Management' (CBP Memorandum, 27 November 2019), CBP Office of Field Operations, 'Metering Guidance' (CBP Memorandum, 27 April 2018), and CBP Office of Field Operations, 'Metering Guidance' (CBP Memorandum, 30 April 2020).

[70] Miller (n 69) 1.

[71] Circumvention of Lawful Pathways, 88 Fed Reg 31314 (May 16, 2023) (to be codified at 8 CFR pt 208) <www.govinfo.gov/content/pkg/FR-2023-05-16/pdf/2023-10146.pdf> accessed 21 October 2023.

[72] Michael A Hogg, 'Subjective Uncertainty Reduction through Self-Categorization: A Motivational Theory of Social Identity Processes' (2011) 11 European Rev Social Psychology 223, 224–25.

or social category,[73] while the practice of defining and evaluating the self in terms of inter-group social comparisons forms a central aspect of social identity theory. Self-categorization theory derives from social identity theory and 'examines how individuals' self-definition varies as a function of perceived difference from others within a given social setting'.[74] The theory centres the cognitive process of *categorization*, or 'understanding what something is by knowing what other things it is equivalent to, and what other things it is different from'.[75] These categorizations are both socially and cognitively influenced and can shape attitudes and behaviour;[76] an insight relevant to questions about why people, particularly in an institutional or group context, internalize norms.

Recent work on the psychology of legal obligation in international politics uses social identity theory to confront approaches to understanding legal obligation which assume that 'structural features of the compliance environment shape preferences'.[77] Defining legal obligation as a subjective belief in the legitimacy of international law, Bayram argues that obligation towards international law has psychological foundations that are influenced by a person's cosmopolitan social identity, which opens the door to an empirical examination of variations in *individual* decision-makers' behaviour and beliefs.[78] Thus, rather than settling for general descriptions of actor behaviour largely bounded by structure or process, this study examines the heterogeneity in actors' sense of legal obligation.

The idea of 'cosmopolitan social identity' is 'characterized by attachment to the world community' and reflective of 'the part of an individual's self that transcends national boundaries and is tied to the international community as a whole'.[79] The study found, after a survey of German parliamentarians, that parliamentarians with a cosmopolitan social identity demonstrated a higher degree of normative respect for international law, motivated by a sense of legal obligation, than parliamentarians with low levels of cosmopolitan social identity.[80] This study makes visible a cognitive psychological foundation for obligation in international law—social identity—that might be used to attain a deeper understanding of state action in relation to asylum seeker reception and processing.[81] CBP officials whose

[73] Jan E Stets and Peter J Burke, 'Identity Theory and Social Identity Theory' (2000) 63 Social Psychology Q 224, 225.

[74] Sarah V Bentley, Katharine H Greenaway, and S Alexander Haslam, 'Cognition in Context: Social Inclusion Attenuates the Psychological Boundary Between Self and Other' (2017) 73 J Experimental Social Psychology 42.

[75] Geoffrey J Leonardelli and Soo Min Toh, 'Social Categorization in Intergroup Contexts: Three Kinds of Self-Categorization' (2015) 9 Soc Personal Psychol Compass 69, 69–70.

[76] Michael A Hogg and Scott A Reid, 'Social Identity, Self-Categorization, and the Communication of Group Norms' (2006) 16 Commun Theory 7, 7–8.

[77] A Burcu Bayram, 'Due Deference: Cosmopolitan Social Identity and the Psychology of Legal Obligation in International Politics' (2017) 71 Intl Org S137, S137.

[78] ibid.

[79] ibid S138.

[80] Burcu Bayram (n 77).

[81] Dia Anagnostou and Alina Mungiu-Pippidi, 'Domestic Implementation of Human Rights Judgments in Europe: Legal Infrastructure and Government Effectiveness Matter' (2014) 25 EJIL 205.

self-identity is defined in terms of comparisons with other nation-state military and law enforcement officials, could provide a theoretical and methodological path into examining *why* officials prioritize or enact certain legal obligations, such as laws penalizing irregular movement or trafficking, over frameworks that emphasize humanitarian search and rescue, or international refugee protection obligations.[82]

### 3.2.2. Using 'issue framing' to understand *why* officials perceive asylum seekers as 'irregular entrants' rather than as people seeking international protection

The concepts of social identity theory (including self-categorization) also interact with the cognitive sociological concept of 'issue-framing', which posits that people's 'interpretive schemata' influence our perceptions and preferences.[83] Frames help us to make sense of the world by allowing us 'to locate, perceive, identify, and label'.[84] Scholarship on 'framing effects' draws from cognitive psychology to examine the effects of exposure to different frames on individuals.[85] Issue-framing occurs when the description of a problem influences the 'decision maker's—mostly unconscious—choice of how to address a broader problem' 'by making certain aspects of an information set more salient to the detriment of others'.[86] Issue-framing interacts with the concept of categorization in that frames function as a sort of lens which affects the categorization of a problem and influences people's reaction to that problem.[87]

In an ethnography of the asylum screening process in Brazil, Jensen found that asylum officials use frames to 'make asylum seekers legible and evaluate their claims'.[88] Frames are not uniform and are 'influenced by social identities and personal biography',[89] which highlights the importance of an individual's position within a social context and the reflexivity of individual experience. Applying this approach to the behaviour of CBP officials at the US–Mexico border could provide

[82] This understanding of social identity raises the prospect that there may also be a degree of self-selection into the job of border official, where a person's self-identity is so aligned. That may, in turn, suggest a further connection with the principle of 'social proof', explored in Section 3.3, for those officials who do not self-select.

[83] Frank Mols, 'What Makes a Frame Persuasive? Lessons from Social Identity Theory' (2012) 8(3) Evid Policy 329, citing Erving Goffman, *Frame Analysis: An Essay on the Organization of Experience* (Harvard UP 1974).

[84] ibid 329.

[85] ibid; Goffman (n 83) 21.

[86] Anne van Aaken and Jan Philip-Elm, 'Framing in and through Public International Law' in Andrea Bianchi and Moshe Hirsch (eds), *International Law's Invisible Frames: Social Cognition and Knowledge Production in International Legal Processes* (OUP 2021) 33–54.

[87] Jeffrey T Polzer, Katherine J Stewart, and Jessica L Simmons, 'A Social Categorization Explanation for Framing Effects in Nested Social Dilemmas' (1999) 79 Organ Behav Hum Decis Process 154.

[88] Katherine Jensen, 'From the Asylum Official's Point of View: Frames of Perception and Evaluation in Refugee Status Determination' (2023) 49 J Ethnic and Migration Studies 3455, 3461.

[89] ibid 3468. See also Manuela Romano, '"Refugees are Streaming into Europe": An Image-Schema Analysis of the Syrian Refugee Crisis in the Spanish and British Press' (2019) 27 CJES 39.

insight into why officials might default to prioritizing a view of individuals encountered at the border as 'irregular entrants' rather than as people seeking international protection. That distinction—irregular entrant versus asylum seeker—is precisely the framing that forms the basis for the metering policy, which, at its core, transforms asylum seekers into a subset of international travellers that may be prioritized (or deprioritized) according to agency policy. This allows CBP officials to deprioritize their mandatory refugee claims referral function, under domestic and international law, and instead apply laws penalizing irregular travellers.

### 3.3. Offshore refugee processing, or contestation and normative change

The practice of transferring people seeking international protection to third countries for 'offshore processing' of their refugee claims as part of a strategy of deterrence and responsibility shifting implicates a range of norms in international refugee and human rights law.[90] While general state practice reflects the principle that asylum seekers and refugees be processed in the territory of the state of arrival, or the state which otherwise exercises jurisdiction or control, offshore processing arrangements raise fundamental questions about the compatibility of those practices with the principle of *non-refoulement*, the right to seek and enjoy asylum, and the prohibition on torture, and cruel, inhuman, or degrading treatment, amongst other human rights.[91]

In April 2022, the United Kingdom enacted the Nationality and Borders Act and entered into an agreement with Rwanda to establish an 'Australian-style' offshore processing system for some asylum seekers.[92] The spread of Australian offshore processing, a system widely condemned under international human rights law,[93] occurred amongst the UK's increasingly militarized response to migrant sea crossings, a broader 'hostile environment' approach towards migrants, and the active promotion of the policy by the Australian government.[94] Yet, the practice of

[90] See UN High Commissioner for Refugees, 'Serious Allegations of Abuse, Self-Harm and Neglect of Asylum Seekers in Relation to the Nauru Regional Processing Centre, and Any Like Allegations in Relation to the Manus Regional Processing Center' (Submission to the Australian Senate Legal and Constitutional Affairs Committee, 12 November 2016).

[91] UN High Commissioner for Refugees, 'Guidance Note on Bilateral and/or Multilateral Transfer Arrangements of Asylum-Seekers' (May 2013).

[92] Nationality and Borders Act 2022; Melanie Gower, Patrick Butchard, and CJ McKinney, 'The UK-Rwanda Migration and Economic Development Partnership' (Research Briefing, House of Commons Library, 20 December 2022).

[93] Kaldor Centre for International Refugee Law, 'Submission on the Nationality and Borders Bill 2021' (UK House of Commons, Public Bill Committee, 15 October 2021).

[94] Honourable George Brandis QC, High Commissioner for Australia to the United Kingdom, at the Public Bill Committee's third sitting on Thursday 23 September 2021, UK House of Commons; Ian Paterson, 'Contesting Security: Multiple Modalities, NGOs, and the Security-Migration Nexus in Scotland' (2023) 8 EJIS 172.

offshore processing did not begin in Australia. It began in the US with the interdiction and transfer of Haitian and other asylum seekers to Guantanamo Bay, Cuba for processing protection claims.[95] Interestingly, Koh was part of the team from Yale Law School that litigated (and lost) the challenge to that practice before the US Supreme Court in 1993.[96]

In what scholars have described as a form of policy transfer, Australia subsequently adopted the US practice which has formed part of the policies of successive Australian governments of different parties (despite significant domestic and international challenges by civil society and other actors).[97] But what insights might the cognitive sciences hold for thinking about the spread of offshore processing and related policies (such as pushbacks) beyond an original, outlier state? The concept of 'social proof', or the idea that one way people 'determine appropriate behaviour for themselves in a situation is to examine the behaviour of others', and particularly similar others,[98] could be useful in illuminating the contours of the process of internalization and the production of transnational legal substance.[99]

The tension between TLP's suggestion that the interaction amongst actors in a transnational legal process is juris generative, while also contending that the same processes drive compliance with an underlying norm through the process of internalization, characterizes one of the theory's principal weaknesses.[100] The paucity of detail leaves the impression that the processes tend to unify towards ultimately homogenous state action. While the principle of social proof originates in social psychology, it has cognitive aspects that tie into its character as a form of informational social influence.[101] It is the initial comparison with the behaviour of others in the search for social proof that involves cognitive functions such as error and reward processing, mismatch detection, and increased allocation of attention, and ultimately sets the stage for the person's own action.[102]

Numerous studies have demonstrated the interaction of cognitive processes with the principle of social proof. For example, Schnuerch and Gibbons found

[95] Daniel Ghezelbash, *Refuge Lost: Asylum Law in an Interdependent World* (CUP 2018); Azadeh Dastyari, *United States Migrant Interdiction and the Detention of Refugees in Guantánamo Bay* (CUP 2015).

[96] *Sale v. Haitian Centers Council, Inc.*, 509 US 155 (1993).

[97] Ghezelbash (n 95); Dastyari (n 95).

[98] Robert B Cialdini and others, 'Compliance with a Request in Two Cultures: The Differential Influence of Social Proof and Commitment/Consistency on Collectivists and Individualists' (2016) 25 Pers Soc Psychol Bull 1242, 1243; Shubhangi Roy, 'Theory of Social Proof and Legal Compliance: A Socio-Cognitive Explanation for Regulatory (Non) Compliance' (2020) 22 German LJ 238, 239.

[99] Research on norm diffusion might also provide interesting insights. See, eg, Beth A Simmons, Paulette Lloyd, and Brandon M Stewart, 'The Global Diffusion of Law: Transnational Crime and the Case of Human Trafficking' (2018) 72 Intl Org 249.

[100] Venzke (n 62) 34.

[101] Roy (n 98) 239.

[102] Robert Schnuerch and others, 'Multiple Neural Signatures of Social Proof and Deviance During the Observation of Other People's Preferences' (2016) 53 Psychophysiol 823; Robert Schnuerch and Henning Gibbons, 'Social Proof in the Human Brain: Electrophysiological Signatures of Agreement and Disagreement with the Majority' (2015) 52 Psychophysiol 1328.

that neural processes consistently differentiate between conformity and non-conformity with group behaviour, and that conformity carries particular motivational significance relating to reward processing and attentional prioritization.[103] The idea that people tend to look to the actions of others, whether consciously or unconsciously, for evidence about appropriate behaviour encompasses more than a social component, which has not yet been fully explored in international law and compliance scholarship. Woods has similarly examined how social proof might either enhance respect for human rights regimes, or contribute to conditions ripe for rights violations.[104] Shubhangi recently used the concept of social proof to argue that legal compliance or non-compliance 'cascades across different rules and can create a perception about legal compliance at large, which in turn guides initial expectations with respect to new laws'.[105] Shubhangi argues that 'the cognitive tendency of our brain to use behaviours of others as a proxy for any missing information when required to make a decision' impacts our understanding of the law and legal compliance and can, over time, create path dependencies towards compliance or non-compliance.[106]

Considering the principle of social proof in relation to the proliferating practice of offshore processing amongst states belonging to the same identity group suggests the existence of cognitive-behavioural processes underlying broader phenomena such as policy transfer and the limits of transnational legal substance. Does the adoption of offshore processing in one outlier state—here the US—influence whether individuals in other states, such as Australia and the United Kingdom, perceive that behaviour as appropriate or worth emulating? In an in-depth empirical case study of Australia and the US, Ghezelbash documents how policymakers in Australia followed legal and policy developments in the US relating to the interdiction and transfer of asylum seekers to Guantanamo Bay, upon which they ultimately modelled Australia's Pacific Solution in 2001.[107] Similarly, the UK has monitored, consulted, and relied upon Australia's experience with offshore processing to create its own 'Australian-style' regime.[108] Various high-level representatives of the Australian government advocated for the adoption of offshore processing in the UK and the debate surrounding the Nationality and Borders Act clearly indicates the Australian influence.

103 Schnuerch and others (n 102) 1340.
104 Woods (n 20) 53.
105 Roy (n 98).
106 ibid 239, 241.
107 Ghezelbash (n 95) 100.
108 Home Office, *Memorandum of Understanding between the Government of the United Kingdom of Great Britain and Northern Ireland and the Government of the Republic of Rwanda for the Provision of an Asylum Partnership Arrangement* (MoU, 2022) <www.gov.uk/government/publications/memorandum-of-understanding-mou-between-the-uk-and-rwanda> accessed 21 October 2023; Margherita Matera, Tamara Tubakovic, and Philomena Murray, 'Is Australia a Model for the UK? A Critical Assessment of Parallels of Cruelty in Refugee Externalization Policies' (2023) 36 J Refug Stud 271.

In 2019, the United States further expanded its reliance on 'offshore processing'-type policies and practices, concluding three 'Asylum Cooperative Agreements' with the governments of Guatemala, El Salvador, and Honduras, in order to transfer asylum seekers from the United States to Northern Triangle countries for 'offshore' processing.[109] These agreements preceded the 2021 Nationality and Borders Bill in the UK. Although the Biden Administration moved to suspend the agreements and initiate the legal process to terminate them in February 2021 (for policy reasons), in favour of a 'comprehensive regional framework',[110] the Administration did not rescind the regulations that enabled their implementation. Therefore, the United States' willingness to invoke a provision of domestic law to justify the agreements established a precedent for the use of this same legal mechanism by a future US administration, while providing a blueprint to other states.[111]

The principle of social proof suggests that the behaviour of policymakers in Australia, and subsequently the UK, may have been influenced by the US adoption of offshore processing and non-compliance with the obligation of *non-refoulement*. Indeed, the principle suggests that the behaviour of the US may have been further reinforced by Australia and the UK's adoption and expansion of its initial offshore processing model. Officials within Australia, the UK, and the US were clearly aware of law and policy developments elsewhere, which has motivational significance for reward processing and attention prioritization,[112] even where those developments ultimately challenged the underlying normative framework. Looking to the UK's behaviour, for example, in relation to referent actors like Australia and the US raises significant questions about whether cognitive-social processes might be involved in the process TLP labels as internalization, involving the actions of a variety of individuals within a particular organizational context. Can a cascade of non-compliance aided by cognitive-social processes have a corrosive effect on the interpretation and understanding of legal norms? Testing that relationship might also help to resolve a central weakness in TLP theory regarding the tendency of interaction in a transnational legal process to both generate transnational legal substance and drive compliance through the process of internalization.

[109] US Department of State, *Agreement Between the Government of the United States of America and the Government of the Republic of Guatemala on Cooperation Regarding the Examination of Protection Claims* (26 July 2019); US Department of State, *Agreement Between the Government of the United States of America and the Government of the Republic of El Salvador for Cooperation in the Examination of Protection Claims* (20 September 2019); US Department of State, *Agreement Between the Government of the United States of America and the Government of the Republic of Honduras for Cooperation in the Examination of Protection Claims* (25 September 2019).

[110] President Joseph Biden, *Creating a Comprehensive Regional Framework To Address the Causes of Migration, To Manage Migration Throughout North and Central America, and To Provide Safe and Orderly Processing of Asylum Seekers at the United States Border* (Executive Order 14010, 2 February 2021).

[111] 8 USC § 1158(a)(2)(A); 8 CFR § 208.30(e)(7) (2023); *Implementing Bilateral and Multilateral Asylum Cooperative Agreements Under the Immigration and Nationality Act*, 84 FR 63994 (19 November 2019).

[112] Schnuerch and others (n 102) 1340.

## 4. The Implications and Limitations of the Cognitive Turn

The three examples outlined above each highlight potential contributions of cognitive-behavioural studies to the development of the concepts of norm internalization and transnational legal substance—developments that might be achieved by undertaking a cognitive-scientific approach to the people involved in a transnational legal process. TLP's claim that a variety of actors initiate and engage in processes of interaction and norm interpretation emphasizes the importance of individuals, and individual state actors, in international law. At the same time, drawing lessons from cognitive-behavioural science to fill the rather significant theoretical gaps regarding the process of internalization and the concept of transnational legal substance holds potential lessons for broader conversations about international legal theory. This section explores that potential before concluding with insights into the possible limitations of a cognitive turn.

### 4.1. Implications of linking TLP theory and the cognitive sciences

Empirical observations of behaviour can be analysed within the framework of TLP theory to illuminate actors and processes of norm internalization, why certain norms are internalized (or not), and the effect of law on norm interpretation and contestation, as well as the production of transnational legal substance. TLP as a theory and methodology provides a means through which to connect those individual-level empirical insights to the development of law and norms in juris generative fora. This section identifies ways in which cognitive-behavioural science might bring additional clarity to under-described aspects of TLP and offers additional contributions to important legal and theoretical debates in international legal scholarship, including how international law and norms develop and change, the hierarchy of norms, and whether a process of norm internalization may result in compliance with international law.

First, while the approach outlined above supports the theoretical insight that international law is a form of communicative practice and process,[113] it also highlights the need to explore how law—and norms—develop and change over time. That exploration requires further, systematic inquiry into the reflexive relationship between legal doctrine and practice, as outlined in the above examples investigating the concepts of social proof, cognitive style, and risk perception. A focus on practice tends to overemphasize how actors empowered to make authoritative interpretations of legal rules shape the behaviour of people (and organizations) engaging in legal implementation. For example, liberal assumptions

[113] Venzke (n 62) 33.

regarding the primary role of courts as protectors of norms, and the tendency that authoritative interpretations will ultimately march forward with time, reflect that focus.[114] However, unwavering attention to authoritative interpreters and juris generative fora misses potentially critical ways in which the conduct of state officials, for whom states bear responsibility under international law, often render normative and legal obligations operational, influencing how legal issues are framed before courts, parliaments, and even international organizations and the types of cases and issues that ultimately arise in those spaces. A closer look at these individuals through an empirical, cognitive-behavioural lens makes clear the need to understand whether, or how those interpretations might influence our understandings of norms in the face of continuing norm-application.[115] Concepts such as social proof provide a means through which to test our understandings of the micro- and macroprocesses involved in how norms gain (or lose) their normativity and the scope of individual behaviour within that process.

Second, an empirical, cognitive behavioural science-informed approach to international legal theory may have implications for our understandings of hierarchies of norms. Affect framing, categorization, risk perception, and cognitive style influence the ways in which individuals perceive, interpret, and act in situations involving competing or overlapping legal frameworks. Cognitive processes influence how, why, and whether people behave in certain ways in concrete social contests. While the primary starting point for resolving questions about the rights and obligations of states in international law generally begins with the sources outlined in Article 38(1) of the Statute of the International Court of Justice (ICJ), those sources are not hierarchically arranged.[116] Instead, questions regarding normative hierarchy tend to arise in practice, with actors resorting to a range of interpretive practices aimed at resolving potential and actual conflict with reference to underlying sources.[117] How individuals act in specific circumstances where compliance with one legal obligation or right may lead to the violation of another, or where compliance with one may result in a limitation or potential violation of other rights or obligations, may reveal a great deal about the salience of norms.[118]

Finally, the methodological approach outlined in this chapter could assist scholars in testing whether and how a theoretical process such as norm internalization might lead to international legal compliance. The approach could also inform an enquiry into the contours of such a process. Examining the cognitive and social aspects of individual behaviour could contribute to a better understanding

114 Koh (n 27) 417.
115 Venzke (n 62).
116 Erika de Wet, 'Sources and Hierarchy of International Law: The Place of Peremptory Norms and Article 103 of the UN Charter within the Sources of International Law' in Samantha Besson and Jean d'Aspremont (eds), *The Oxford Handbook of the Sources of International Law* (OUP 2017) 627.
117 ibid.
118 ibid 628.

of how domestic, or even hyper-local, social contexts may be highly relevant to legal compliance and emerging understandings of international law within a transnational legal process. Furthermore, whether or how a particular norm influences state behaviour necessarily involves an enquiry into the behaviour of individual state actors and provides one approach for addressing the question of how to link empirical research with a fundamentally individual orientation to the behaviour of states.[119]

## 4.2. Limitations of a cognitive science-informed theoretical approach

Notwithstanding the promise of cognitive science to enrich international legal theory, several cautionary points deserve further mention. The turn to cognitive science for the understanding of *individual* decision-making, judgement, and behaviour in a transnational legal process must acknowledge people's embeddedness in particular social contexts and the social embeddedness of experience.[120] Indeed, work in critical neuroscience has highlighted that cognitive processes themselves are influenced by their social environment and that human behaviour must be understood in social context.[121] State officials do not always uniformly implement the law, even where discretion is highly circumscribed or the statutory language is clear. Rather than describing a means for coercing, cajoling, preventing, punishing, or rewarding individual behaviour that achieves or hinders the objectives of a particular legal regime, the empirical approach outlined in this chapter seeks to contribute to an endeavour to reveal and advance our understanding of the theoretical connections between individual behaviour, normativity, and the interpretive practice of international law.

Another potential limitation lies in the perception that individual behaviour might be perfectly (or near-perfectly) controlled by empirically identifying and regulating variables that influence cognitive processes. A transnational legal process is a complex system in which a variety of actors and legal frameworks interact to produce interpretations and actions in a myriad of contexts. This type of system is characterized by many interacting components 'showing emerging properties that cannot be understood in terms of the properties of the individual isolated components'.[122] Individual behaviour is fundamentally relational and occurs within 'networks of interactions from which new patterns of behavior may emerge'.[123]

[119] Tomer Broude, 'Behavioral International Law' (2015) 163 U Pa L Rev 1099, 1121–22.

[120] Brendan Gough, Majella McFadden, and Matthew McDonald, *Critical Social Psychology: An Introduction* (Red Globe Press 2012).

[121] Suparna Choudhury, Saskia Kathi Nagel, and Jan Slaby, 'Critical Neuroscience: Linking Neuroscience and Society through Critical Practice' (2009) 4 BioSocieties 61.

[122] Maxi San Miguel, 'Frontiers in Complex Systems' (2023) 1 Front Complex Syst 1.

[123] Fabio Bento, Marco Tagliabue, and Ingunn Sandaker, 'Complex Systems and Social Behavior: Bridging Social Networks and Behavior Analysis' in TM Cihon and MA Mattaini (eds),

This suggests that the legal decision-making and interpretative practice of individuals are mediated and influenced by top-down legal structures and by the context and circumstances of the relational interactions themselves. An approach focusing on empirics as a means for influencing behaviour assumes a level of mastery over a complex system characterized by a large number of elements and feedback loops that may defy our assumptions about those influences. If anything, the cognitive turn might reveal the futility of attempts to enact external controls to tightly restrict or manipulate individual behaviour.[124]

## 5. Conclusion

Despite the ongoing relevance of TLP to debates within international legal theory and compliance, the absence of systematic, empirical examinations of central concepts like the process of internalization and transnational legal substance has left a gap in understanding how those ideas interface with individual (and group level) behaviour, as well as the legal and normative effects within international law. The methodological approach outlined here, combined with insights from the cognitive sciences, provides a sort of 'corrective lens' for addressing these issues. Although Koh pays particular attention to individuals in international law, cognitive sciences contain a multitude of approaches for disentangling the complex relationship between individuals within or outside of a state and the social, political, and legal forms of internalization that influence observance and development of legal norms and international law.[125]

Rather than representing a move towards managerialism, the cognitive science-informed approach outlined here invites a critical examination of how otherwise less visible actors, spaces, and even assumptions underlying transnational decision-making influence formal legal processes and the development of international law. The approach also highlights the discursive nature of law in social context, and that cognitive processes are embedded within, and influenced by, that context. The three case studies demonstrate how cognitive processes may influence individual or group understandings of legal obligation, framing of legal problems, or even what behaviour is acceptable within a socio-legal context. The process-orientated framework of TLP provides one avenue for undertaking additional research into understanding not only why or how cognitive influences occur but also the potential implications of that behaviour for international legal theory.

*Behavior Science Perspectives on Culture and Community* (Association for Behavior Analysis International 2020) 67–89.

[124] See, generally, Sungjoon Cho, 'A Social Critique of Behavioral Approaches to International Law' (2021) 115 AJIL 248.

[125] Koh (n 2) 633–35, 642–43.

# 8

# From Economic to Behavioural Analysis of International Law

## What Have We Learned So Far?

*Anne van Aaken and Tomer Broude*

### 1. Introduction

Economic analysis of *international* law was a late-comer to the economic analysis of law, yet the rational choice approach to international law has a long history. Economic analysis of law started in the 1970s at the Law Schools of Chicago and Yale and has since not only conquered US Law Schools but has also gained prominence in other countries of the world and respective academic programmes. Yet, although international law actually should have been of primary research interest (since economics is profoundly interested in self-governance, cooperation and exchange mechanisms), given that it has no centralized enforcement and thus cannot rely on the background assumption that law is enforced as in most national law and economic models, it started only in the late 1990s.[1] Here, theory is even more needed to understand under what conditions actors cooperate and comply with self-set norms. The economic analysis of international law came in two main variants—realism[2] and institutionalism.[3] Both relied on states as rational and unitary actors, echoing earlier international relations (IR) theory.[4]

More generally, there has been an empirical[5] and experimental[6] turn in international legal scholarship using social sciences as an external view to understand international law.[7] This external view is shared by both rationalist and behavioural

[1] Jeffrey L Dunoff and Joel P Trachtman, 'Economic Analysis of International Law' (1999) 24 Yale Journal of International Law 1.

[2] Jack L Goldsmith and Eric A Posner, *The Limits of International Law* (OUP 2005).

[3] Andrew Guzman, *How International Law Works: A Rational Choice Theory* (OUP 2008); Andrew Guzman, 'A Compliance-Based Theory of International Law' (2002) 90 California Law Review 1823.

[4] Anne van Aaken, 'Rationalist and Behavioralist Approaches to International Law' in Jeff Dunoff and Mark Pollack (eds), *International Legal Theory* (CUP 2022) 261.

[5] Greg Shaffer and Tom Ginsburg, 'The Empirical Turn in International Legal Scholarship' (2012) 106 American Journal of International Law 1.

[6] Jeffrey L Dunoff and Mark A Pollack, 'Experimenting with International Law: A Reader's Guide' (2017) 28 European Journal of International Law 1317.

[7] Daniel Abebe, Adam Chilton, and Tom Ginsburg, 'The Social Science Approach to International Law' (2021) 22 Chicago Journal of International Law 1.

Anne van Aaken and Tomer Broude, *From Economic to Behavioural Analysis of International Law* In: *International Legal Theory and the Cognitive Turn*. Edited by: Anne van Aaken and Moshe Hirsch, Oxford University Press.
 DOI: 10.1093/9780198909293.003.0009

approaches. Moreover, the behavioural approach is largely situated in empirical work, often based on experiments and other empirical social science approaches. In that, it is a theory which is inductively constructed. Experimental studies, field studies, behavioural game theory, and other empirical approaches shed light on cognitive and motivational deviations from the rational choice model. Economic analysis used to rely heavily on the rational choice assumption to explain international negotiations, treaty design, and compliance with international law.[8] The actions of international courts and tribunals, and their interactions with other international actors, were also explained within the rational choice paradigm.[9] The new behavioural literature sheds light on boundedly rational decisions and exposes numerous cognitive biases that can affect international legal decision-making processes, be it in international negotiations, rational design literature and economic contract theory as applied to international law, international adjudication (and interpretation), substantive and procedural law, or compliance theory.[10] The behavioural approach does not negate the strategic interests of international legal actors but rather highlights deviations from the rational pursuit of these interests and takes into account framing of interests. This chapter aims to consider numerous insights gained from the behavioural approach. It also discusses its limitations, especially with respect to the unit of analysis (individuals, elite decision-makers, states, and other collective decision-making entities, such as non-state actors, including militant groups and multinational corporations) in international

[8] Instead of many articles, see Goldsmith and Posner (n 2); Eric A Posner and Alan O Sykes, *Economic Foundations of International Law* (Harvard UP 2013); Robert E Scott and Paul B Stephan, *The Limits of Leviathan: Contract Theory and the Enforcement of International Law* (CUP 2006); Joel P Trachtman, *The Economic Structure of International Law* (Harvard UP 2008).

[9] Anne van Aaken and Tomer Broude, 'Arbitration from a Law and Economics Perspective' in Thomas Schultz and Federico Ortino (eds), *The Oxford Handbook of International Arbitration* (OUP 2017) 874; Karen J Alter, 'The Multiple Roles of International Courts and Tribunals' in Jeffrey L Dunoff and Mark A Pollack (eds), *Interdisciplinary Perspectives on International Law and International Relations The State of the Art* (CUP 2013) 345; Karen J Alter, 'Agents or Trustees? International Courts in their Political Context' (2008) 14 European Journal of International Relations 33; Anne van Aaken and Tomer Broude, 'Economic Analysis of International Adjudication' [2020] Max Planck Encylopedia of International Procedural Law; Anne van Aaken, 'Interests, Strategies and Veto Players: The Political Economy of Interpreting Customary International Law' (2022) 11 ESIL Reflections <https://esil-sedi.eu/esil-reflection-interests-strategies-and-veto-players-the-political-economy-of-interpreting-customary-international-law> accessed 3 May 2024.

[10] Anne van Aaken, 'Behavioral International Law and Economics' (2014) 55 Harvard International Law Journal 421; Tomer Broude, 'Behavioral International Law' (2015) 163 University of Pennsylvania Law Review 1099; Daniel Peat, Veronika Fikfak, and Eva van der Zee, 'Behavioural Compliance Theory' (2021) 13 Journal of International Dispute Settlement 167; Jean Galbraith, 'Treaty Options: Towards a Behavioral Understanding of Treaty Design' (2013) 53 Virginia Journal of International Law 309; Jean Galbraith, 'Deadlines as Behavior in Diplomacy and International Law' in Harlan Grant Cohen and Timothy Meyer (eds), *International Law as Behavior* (ASIL Studies in International Legal Theory, CUP 2021) 19; Harlan Grant Cohen and Timothy Meyer (eds), *International Law as Behavior* (CUP 2021); Anne van Aaken and Tomer Broude, 'The Psychology of International Law: An Introduction' (2020) 30 European Journal of International Law 1225.

law and theory. The chapter argues that the latter calls for an accurate denomination of actors involved in decisions as well as an examination of the validity of behavioural insights in all circumstances.

Almost all international legal theory approaches are based on (explicit or more implicit) assumptions about human behaviour, which should be validated empirically. In our view, having a realistic picture about human and/or state behaviour should also be the basis for any (international) legal theory; it does not exclude normative, analytical, or doctrinal reasoning (eg in effect utile reasoning); that is, the internal point of view, in the words of HLA Hart.[11] Empirically grounded knowledge of human behaviour and cognition as a micro-foundation for theories can also be a bridge between different international legal theories,[12] at least when they *also* want to explain and not only argue normatively. The behavioural turn in the economic analysis of international law can highlight potential links and overlaps with behavioural assumptions included in other major international legal theories, such as constructivism and critical legal studies, including Third World Approaches to International Law (TWAIL) and feminist theory. Behavioural approaches are stronger in that respect than rational choice in that they also test the underlying behavioural assumptions of rational choice (or other approaches to international legal theory, including constructivist theories) and thus lay the empirical groundwork for other theories about the smallest unit of analysis—the individual actor and decision-maker. The renunciation from the state or international organizations as the sole relevant unit of analysis in international law has gathered pace and thus encourages the focus on individual behaviour.[13]

We do not wish to address the use of behavioural insights by governments and international organizations targeting individual behaviour or citizens or consumers,[14] as, for example, in tobacco control, working to achieve the Sustainable Development Goals;[15] but at least wish to flag that international organizations

[11] Herbert LA Hart, *The Concept of Law* (OUP 1961).

[12] See Anne van Aaken and Moshe Hirsch's Introduction to this volume. See also Janice Gross Stein, 'The Micro-Foundations of International Relations Theory: Psychology and Behavioral Economics' (2017) 71 International Organization S249.

[13] Tom Sparks and Anne Peters (eds), *The Individual in International Law* (OUP 2024); for economic analysis specifically, see Anne van Aaken, 'The Individual in (International) Law and Economics' in Tom Sparks and Anne Peters (eds), *The Individual in International Law* (OUP 2024) 341; Tamar Megiddo, 'The Missing Persons of International Law Scholarship: A Roadmap for Future Research' in Harlan Grant Cohen and Timothy Meyer (eds), *International Law as Behavior* (ASIL Studies in International Legal Theory, CUP 2021) 230; Tamar Megiddo, 'Methodological Individualism' (2019) 60 Harvard International Law Journal 219.

[14] United Nations, Behavioural Science Report (2021) <https://digitallibrary.un.org/record/3929741?v=pdf> accessed 3 May 2024. See also Lauren Manning and others, 'Behavioral Science around the World Vol II: Profiles of 17 International Organizations' (eMBeD Report, World Bank Group, 2020) <https://documents1.worldbank.org/curated/en/453911601273837739/pdf/Behavioral-Science-Around-the-World-Volume-Two-Profiles-of-17-International-Organizations.pdf> accessed 3 May 2024.

[15] See, for more details, Anne van Aaken, 'Behavioural Sciences Used by the United Nations to Achieve the Sustainable Development Goals: A Roadmap and Some Stop Signs' (2024) 4 Journal of Environmental Law and Policy 1.

have become highly active in that matter which raises its own questions for international law. In addition, in this contribution we address the role of individual decision-making in international law, but nevertheless focus on the state, given that individual behaviour can often be attributed to the state under international law.[16] Here, we are mainly interested in the contribution of behavioural insights to international governance questions, including compliance.

The chapter proceeds as follows. After briefly highlighting the defining features of economic analysis of international law, since it is still the benchmark of behaviourally orientated approaches (Section 2), we turn to behavioural insights as they are mainly used in behavioural analysis of international law. We highlight the different ways in which behavioural insights can be and are used in practice and connect them to other theories of international law. When behavioural science is applied within the state-to-state context, both law-making and compliance as governance mechanisms need to be re-theorized (Section 3). The next section turns to limitations of the approach: empirical and theoretical (Section 4). The last section concludes and formulates research desiderata (Section 5).

## 2. Rationalist Approaches to International Legal Theory

Explaining how international cooperation can be sustained is at the heart of rational choice theories of international law. The rationality assumption has long been the basis of positive as well as normative economics. Positive (neo)classical economics, followed by IR scholars, assumed rational actors, although never denying that there might—occasionally—be lapses from rationality. However, these were deemed not to matter much: economics is concerned with the average behaviour of actors. The central tenets of the rationalist paradigm are utility maximization, stable preferences, rational expectations, and optimal processing of information.[17] A change in behaviour is attributed to a change in constraints or incentives (eg a budget constraint due to a change in prices or legal constraints), not to a change in preferences. Preferences are assumed to be fixed for analytical reasons: only if preferences are assumed to be fixed can a change in behaviour be attributed to a change in circumstances (including law). The latter is the main difference vis-à-vis constructivist theories that ask how preferences come about and change.[18] Note that the analysis focuses on actors, not structures or systems, as in sociology;[19] those come into play only as (positive or negative) restraints.

[16] Such as military commanders; see, eg, Tomer Broude and Inbar Levy, 'Outcome Bias and Expertise in Investigations under International Humanitarian Law' (2019) 30 EJIL 1303.

[17] Gary S Becker, *The Economic Approach to Human Behavior* (University of Chicago Press 1976) 14.

[18] See Chapter 3 by Ian Johnstone and Arun Mohan Sukumar in this volume.

[19] See Chapter 9 by Moshe Hirsch in this volume.

Note also that the rationalist assumption is firmly committed to methodological individualism (who or whatever the relevant unit of analysis is—persons or legal persons, such as states).[20] This also leads to the neglect of interactive influence of preferences, as explored by cognitive sociology.[21] The standard models of rationalist theory, seen as a model of instrumental rationality, have minimal assumptions about human cognition, such as completeness, transitivity, and independence of irrelevant alternatives.[22] When dealing with choices under uncertainty, as is the case in international law, this 'expected utility' concept[23] assumes that preferences are independent from the circumstances in which they are revealed, which implies that the description and format of alternative decisions have no influence over the decision itself (an axiom known as 'descriptive invariance').[24] These assumptions do not reveal anything about the content of preferences but rather form the basis for a formal concept of (thin) rationality.

These assumptions of thin rationality are sometimes transferred to collective or corporate actors such as states or international organizations. It is thus either assumed that potential biases cancel each other out on the aggregate level or do not even occur within corporate actors. It is routine to assume that states strategically pursue their own individual self-interests. All thus depends on how state preferences are defined (if the state is indeed the unit of analysis). Assumed preferences differ between realism (power and relative gains) and institutionalism (most often absolute gains), though;[25] and those differences are also reflected in the economic analysis of international law (more realist[26] or more institutionalist[27] variants).

Rational choice analysis has been used to conceptualize or reframe international law generally, including its sources. It has been employed to explain the structure or function of particular international legal rules or institutions, diagnose substantive problems, and suggest better legal solutions. It has also been prominent

[20] This doctrine demands that social phenomena must be explained by showing how they result from individual actions. It was elaborated more theoretically first in Max Weber, Guenther Roth, and Claus Wittich, *Economy and Society* (Bedminster Press 1922/1968) 13 et seq.

[21] Van Aaken and Hirsch (n 12).

[22] For a comprehensive treatment, see Shaun H Heap and others, *The Theory of Choice: A Critical Guide* (3rd Aufl edn, Blackwell 1997). Independence of irrelevant alternatives means that the relative attractiveness of two choices does not depend upon the other choices available to the actor.

[23] See Gary S Becker, *Accounting for Tastes* (Harvard UP 1996) 5–7. In expected utility theory, expected utility of an option X is composed of the sum of all outcomes x weighted by their probability p. The expected utility hypothesis is first and foremost a normative model—how should people decide if their decision is to be rational (normative decision theory)? However, rationalists often use it as an assumption in descriptive models.

[24] Richard Cookson, 'Framing Effects in Public Goods Experiments' (2000) 3 Experimental Economics 55; Amos Tversky and Daniel Kahneman, 'The Framing of Decisions and the Psychology of Choice' (1981) 211 Science 453.

[25] Robert Powell, 'Absolute and Relative Gains in International Relations Theory' (1991) 85 American Political Science Review 1303.

[26] Goldsmith and Posner (n 2).

[27] Guzman (n 3); Trachtman (n 8).

in explaining (non)compliance with international law[28] and enforcement problems.[29] The main tools used by rationalist approaches are game theory (modelling strategic interactions), economic contract theory, agency problems (for international courts and organizations), and public choice theory, in case the unitary state assumption is relaxed.[30]

In order to understand the creation and operation of treaties and custom, many different games have been developed in order to depict the respective problem structure (eg cooperative and non-cooperative games, symmetric and asymmetric games, zero-sum and non-zero-sum games, simultaneous and sequential games, and games with perfect or imperfect information),[31] depending on the underlying assumptions of the situation and the actors. Customary international law has been analysed by rationalist scholars, including using game theory, explaining custom in various problem structures.[32] The use of soft law has been explained as well by drawing on focal points, reputation and transaction costs.[33] Because treaties are ostensibly the most important source of international law, economic contract theory lends itself easily as a tool for analysis of treaty making. Contract theory analyses, generally in the presence of asymmetric information (which may lead to moral hazard and adverse selection), why and how actors construct contractual arrangements.[34] It is based on information economics and the distribution of risks in a contract. Enforceable contracts represent a mechanism for achieving compliance with cooperative goals that are supposed to benefit the collective interest (maximizing the joint surplus) of parties whose particular interests may diverge at a given time. Because contracts or treaties are necessarily incomplete, contract theory deals with the question of how to deal with opportunistic behaviour, unforeseen circumstances or informational asymmetries between parties.[35]

[28] Benedict Kingsbury, 'The Concept of Compliance as a Function of Competing Conceptions of International Law' (1998) 19 Michigan Journal of International Law 345.

[29] See n 8.

[30] For details, see van Aaken (n 4).

[31] Mostly, games applied in international law are pure coordination games (as in civil aviation), the prisoners' dilemma game (as in security issues), the stag hunt game (a trust game), and the battle of the sexes game (as the US and Europe in the postwar era over the shape of the international economic order where both saw the absolute need to coordinate, but differed on what the order should look like).

[32] Edward T Swaine, 'Rational Custom' (2002) 52 Duke Law Journal 559; George Norman and Joel P Trachtman, 'The Customary International Law Game' (2005) 99 American Journal of International Law 541.

[33] Andrew T Guzman and Timothy Meyer, 'International Soft Law' (2010) 2 Journal of Legal Analysis 171; Gregory C Shaffer and Mark A Pollack, 'Hard Law and Soft Law' in Jeffrey L Dunoff and Mark A Pollack (eds), *Interdisciplinary Perspectives on International Law and International Relations: The State of the Art* (CUP 2013) 197.

[34] Patrick Bolton and Mathias Dewatripont, *Contract Theory* (MIT Press 2005).

[35] Scott and Stephan (n 8). For further insights derived from contract theory for trade law and investment law, see Simon Schropp, *Trade Policy Flexibility and Enforcement in the WTO: A Law and Economics Analysis* (CUP 2009); Anne van Aaken, 'International Investment Law Between Commitment and Flexibility: A Contract Theory Analysis' (2009) 12 Journal of International Economic Law 507.

A great challenge is to understand why states comply with international law[36]—and the idea of what compliance means is itself contested as being too static a concept and neglecting interpretation.[37] Because there is no central international enforcement mechanism, as in national legal orders, the puzzle has always been why and under which conditions states change their behaviour because of international law. The key insight is that, in repeated interactions, several mechanisms can create incentives for states to comply. Much of the scholarly debate has been dominated by rival advocates of managerial[38] as opposed to (realist) enforcement-orientated approaches,[39] and the competing school of transnational legal process.[40] From a rationalist, game-theoretical perspective, there are occasions where effectiveness is difficult to explain (eg in one-shot prisoners' dilemma games and especially in global public goods or commons constellations).[41] Indeed, enforcement, if costly to the punisher, is seen as a second-order prisoners' dilemma (sanctioners' dilemma) since all actors prefer to free-ride on the enforcement measures by other players,[42] especially in multilateral treaties where reciprocity is not direct. Realist theorists have used basic game-theoretical concepts to explain international behavioural regularities (including compliance) as a function of national self-interest, deeming international law epiphenomenal. Nevertheless, more differentiated explanations for compliance with international law have been offered, drawing on retaliation, reciprocity, reputation,[43] and outcasting.[44] Whereas weak reciprocity (*do ut des* or *quid pro quo*) has been acknowledged as maybe one of

[36] Compliance is different from effectiveness: the latter asks about causality between law and states behavior, whereas the former just descriptively states that states' behaviour is in conformity with the law, for whatever reason. For a rationalist treatment in the field of international relations, see George W Downs, David M Rocke, and Peter N Barsoom, 'Is the Good News about Compliance Good News about Cooperation?' (1996) 50 International Organization 379.

[37] Robert Howse and Ruti G Teitel, 'Beyond Compliance: Rethinking Why International Law Really Matters' (2010) 1 Global Policy 127.

[38] Abram Chayes and Antonia Handler Chayes, *The New Sovereignty: Compliance with International Regulatory Agreements* (Harvard UP 1998).

[39] For an excellent discussion, see Ingrid Wuerth, 'Compliance' in Jean d'Aspremont and Sahib Singh (eds), *Concepts of International Law: Contributions to Disciplinary Thought* (Elgar 2018) 117.

[40] As explored by Harold Hongju Koh, 'Transnational Legal Process and the "New" New Haven School of International Law' in Jeffrey L Dunoff and Mark A Pollack (eds), *International Legal Theory: Foundations and Frontiers* (CUP 2022) 101. See, for that theory and how cognitive-behavioural studies can further the insights, Chapter 7 by Jefferies in this volume.

[41] Samuel Barkin and Yuliya Rashchupkina, 'Public Goods, Common Pool Resources, and International Law' (2017) 111 Amercian Journal of International Law 376.

[42] See Richard Cornes and Todd Sandler, *The Theory of Externalities, Public Goods, and Club Goods* (CUP 1986). For global public goods, see Scott Barrett, *Why Cooperate? The Incentive to Supply Public Goods* (OUP 2007); Scott Barrett, 'International Cooperation and the International Commons' (1999) 10 Duke Environmental Law and Policy Forum 131; and Duncan Snidal, 'The Game Theory of International Politics' (1985) 38 World Politics 25, 27, 28.

[43] Guzman (n 3).

[44] Oana A Hathaway and Scott Shapiro, 'Outcasting: Enforcement in Domestic and International Law' (2011) 212 Yale Law Journal 252.

the most important pillars of human cooperation, well proven by manifold experiments[45] as well as a pillar of international law,[46] the concept of reputation has in turn also been critically discussed.[47] Some delve into the details of treaty design in order to explain compliance;[48] some look at the choices states have regarding entering a treaty, having reservations, and exiting a treaty.[49] Overall, rationalist approaches in international legal theory remain rather pessimistic on international cooperation, especially in global commons and global public good constellations.

## 3. Behavioural Approaches to International Legal Theory

Behavioural approaches usually still have as a benchmark the rational choice model and also retain their focus on strategic interests and interactions. Yet, there are important differences in assumptions which allow the bridging with other theories of international law: people do not conform to the rational choice assumption on cognitive and motivational grounds. They have other-regarding preferences, can be spiteful, have a notion of strong reciprocity,[50] and care for fairness and equity,[51] in addition to their limited cognitive abilities.

Behavioural science, as a compound of cognitive psychology and behavioural economics, has revolutionized many fields of traditional law and economics as well as theories and means of regulation and public policy.[52] Behavioural sciences are

[45] Samuel Bowles and Herbert Gintis, *A Cooperative Species: Human Reciprocity and Its Evolution* (Princeton UP 2011); Ernst Fehr and Simon Gächter, 'Fairness and Retaliation: The Economics of Reciprocity' (2000) 14 Journal of Economic Perspectives 159.

[46] Bruno Simma, *Das Reziprozitätselement im Zustandekommen völkerrechtlicher Verträge. Gedanken zu einem Bauprinzip der internationalen Rechtsbeziehungen* (Duncker & Humblot 1972); Robert O Keohane, 'Reciprocity in International Relations' (1986) 40 International Organization 1.

[47] George W Downs and Michael A Jones, 'Reputation, Compliance, and International Law' (2002) 31 Journal of Legal Studies 95; Rachel Brewster, 'Reputation in International Relations and International Law' in Jeffrey L Dunoff and Mark Pollack (eds), *Interdisciplinary Perspectives on International Law and International Relations: The State of the Art* (CUP 2013) 524.

[48] Brett M Frischmann and James C Hartigan, 'Compliance Institutions in Treaties' (2011) 7 Review of Law and Economics 89. A survey on empirical work on compliance finds that the effectiveness of law depends on the issue-area (economic treaties being the most effective) and the institutional design (adjudicatory bodies lead to more effectiveness): Steven J. Hoffman et al., 'International treaties have mostly failed to produce their intended effects' (2022) 119 Proceedings of the National Academy of Sciences of the United States of America (PNAS) 1.

[49] Laurence R Helfer, 'Exiting Treaties' (2005) 91 Virginia Law Review 1579; Laurence R Helfer, 'Not Fully Committed? Reservations, Risk and Treaty Design' (2006) 31 Yale Journal of International Law 367.

[50] Herbert Gintis, 'Strong Reciprocity and Human Sociality' (2000) 206 Journal of Theoretical Biology 169.

[51] This has also been found in primates and it is highly unlikely that primates show this behaviour but humans do not (yet we assume so in rationalist theories): Frans de Waal, *The Age of Empathy: Nature's Lessons for a Kinder Society* (Harmony Books 2009); see also n 45.

[52] Instead of many, see Eyal Zamir and Doron Teichman (eds), *The Oxford Handbook of Behavioral Economics and the Law* (OUP 2014) and Eyal Zamir and Doron Teichman, *Behavioral Law and Economics* (OUP 2018).

also beginning to be used by international organizations with the behavioural turn of the United Nations and its agencies as well as the World Bank, the European Union, and the Organisation for Economic Co-operation and Development (OECD).[53] Yet, those usually use behavioural sciences for regulation of citizens/consumers in order to induce behavioural change, but not yet, at least officially, for dealing with inter-state relations or governance. Furthermore, this turn of international organizations to behavioural science happens largely below the radar of international lawyers—an omission, given that it matters how international organizations work nowadays. This is especially so given that also United Nations (UN) agencies need to act on the basis of law and are limited by law.

Behavioural sciences have also long been used in IR scholarship, primarily in security studies,[54] and the 'behavioural revolution' has spread more recently to other areas of IR scholarship, including the study of international political economy and international organizations.[55] Insights from these approaches are starting to be used to analyse international law as well,[56] influencing a growing body of international legal theory addressing issues of treaty design, global public goods, and commons,[57] as well as compliance.[58]

Several biases and heuristics—that is, systematic deviations from the rationalist assumptions discovered through behavioural research, both cognitive and motivational—are increasingly integrated into international legal scholarship.[59] For example, while rational choice theory assumes that people perceive outcomes in absolute terms (expected utility), the well-established prospect theory which has been used for a long period of time in IR to explain states' behaviour[60] posits that individuals assess their loss and gain perspectives in an asymmetric manner. People ordinarily perceive outcomes as either gains or losses, rather than as final states, and feel losses more strongly than that of equivalent gains. Losses and gains are defined in relation to some reference point—usually (but not invariably) the status quo or an (perceived) entitlement. A loss counts more than a gain (loss aversion) and actors are risk seeking in the domain of losses. Loss aversion also adds to

[53] World Bank, World Development Report 2015 (World Bank Group, 2015) <www.worldbank.org/content/dam/Worldbank/Publications/WDR/WDR%202015/WDR-2015-Full-Report.pdf> accessed 3 May 2024.

[54] Rose McDermott, *Political Psychology in International Relations* (Michigan UP 2004); James Davis (ed), *Psychology, Strategy and Conflict* (Routledge 2013).

[55] Emilie M Hafner-Burton and others, 'The Behavioral Revolution and International Relations' (2017) 71, Supplement 2017 International Organization S1.

[56] See n 10.

[57] Anne van Aaken, 'Behavioral Aspects of the International Law of Global Public Goods and Common Pool Resources' (2018) 112 Amercian Journal of International Law 67; Arden Rowell and Josephine van Zeben, 'A New Status Quo? The Psychological Impact of the Paris Agreement on Climate Change' (2016) 7 European Journal of Risk Regulation 49.

[58] See Peat and others (n 10).

[59] For an overview, see Zamir and Teichman (n 52) chapter 2.

[60] Jack S Levy, 'Prospect Theory and International Relations: Theoretical Applications and Analytical Problems' (1992) 13 Political Psychology 283.

the importance of default rules, prevalent in international law (including the analysis of sources).[61] Default rules, like opt-in or opt-out rules, change the behaviour of actors, including states, although they should not exhibit such a strong influence on decisions according to rationalist assumptions. The endowment effect, namely the tendency to place a higher value on objects and entitlements people already have compared with objects and entitlements they do not, may inhibit efficient transactions and negotiations to move forward and thus also hinder international cooperation.[62] Over-confidence—that is, the tendency for actors' subjective confidence in their judgements—is reliably greater than the objective accuracy of those judgements, and the fundamental attribution error[63] tends to produce more hawkish decisions in international conflict situations.[64]

Framing effects similarly violate the rationalist axiom of 'descriptive invariance'. A framing effect exists 'when different ways of describing the same choice problem change the choices that people make, even though the underlying information and choice options remain essentially the same'.[65] Many experiments explore those effects,[66] including in public goods games. The mechanism at work is that frames influence beliefs, and beliefs in turn influence behaviour.[67] Specific examples abound: framing ultimatum games[68] as a product of resource scarcity generates higher offers and fewer rejections;[69] framing negotiations as taking place in an international rather than a business context triggers more cooperative behaviour;[70] and supposedly framing a prisoners' dilemma as an assurance game can increase cooperation.[71] Framing thus seems to be highly important in order to understand what games states play.[72] Do they think they are situated in a prisoners'

[61] Tomer Broude and Caroline Henckels, 'Not All Rights Are Created Equal: A Loss–Gain Frame of Investor Rights and Human Rights' (2021) 34 Leiden Journal of International Law 93.

[62] Daniel Kahneman, Jack L Knetsch, and Richard H Thaler, 'Experimental Tests of the Endowment Effect and the Coase Theorem' (1990) 98 Journal of Political Economy 1325.

[63] The fundamental attribution error denotes the tendency to attribute other people's behaviour to their personal attitudes and motivations rather than to environmental influences and constraints; see, for details, Zamir and Teichman (n 52) chapter 2.

[64] Daniel Kahneman and Jonathan Renshon, 'Hawkish Biases' in Trevor Thrall and Jane K Cramer (eds), *American Foreign Policy and the Threat of Fear: Threat Inflation since 9/11* (Routledge 2009) 79.

[65] Cookson (n 24) 55; and see Tore Ellingsen and others, 'Social Framing Effects: Preferences or Beliefs?' (2012) 76 Games and Economic Behavior 117, 118 for different theories about framing.

[66] ibid.

[67] Martin Dufwenberg, Simon Gächter, and Heike Hennig-Schmidt, 'The Framing of Games and the Psychology of Play' (2011) 73 Games and Economic Behavior 459.

[68] In this experiment, the proposer makes an offer of how to share a fixed amount, which the recipient can accept or reject. If the recipient rejects, both get nothing. In a *homo economicus* model, a proposer would offer the smallest monetary unit, and the recipient would accept it. Yet experiments do not obtain this result.

[69] Colin F Camerer, *Behavioral Game Theory: Experiments in Strategic Interaction* (Princeton UP 2003) 75.

[70] Richard J Eiser and Kum Kum Bhavnani, 'The Effect of Situational Meaning on the Behaviour of Subjects in the Prisoner's Dilemma Game' (1974) 4 European Journal of Social Psychology 93.

[71] Brian Skyrms, *The Stag Hunt and the Evolution of Social Structure* (CUP 2004).

[72] For details, see Anne van Aaken and Jan-Philip Elm, 'Framing in and through International Law' in Andrea Bianchi and Moshe Hirsch (eds), *International Law's Invisible Frames: Social Cognition and Knowledge Production in International Legal Processes* (OUP 2022) 35.

dilemma when working on climate change treaties or rather in a stag hunt game that is an assurance game? They would need respectively different approaches to negotiations as well as different institutions. Framing is one important connecting point to constructivist theories, where states have certain perceptions and ideas about each other.[73] Equally, the behavioural approach would focus on beliefs as well as the framing of interests of states.

Behavioural game theory has focused on the motivational aspect of behaviour and social preferences, especially in public goods games which are, if one regards the international order as a public good, especially pertinent since they explain factors upholding social order in a non-centralized setting. Repeated findings that individuals systematically engage in collective action to provide public goods without an external authority enforcer[74] have led some to label such outcomes as 'better than rational'.[75] Such outcomes occur where reciprocity, reputation, and trust can help to overcome the strong temptations of short-run self-interest.[76] These experiments suggest that rationalist theories may be faulted for neglecting: (1) reciprocity *strictu sensu*, (2) the distinction between (perceived) fair and unfair sanctions, (3) altruism, spitefulness, and preferences for equality, (4) the role of trust and communication, (5) the intentions of the other players, and (6) the 'type' of actor. Further, it has been suggested that these factors are 'probably relevant in all domains in which voluntary compliance matters'[77]—as in international law.

The implications for international law and theory are relatively clear. Behavioural analysis can work on several 'flight heights'. It can contribute to the understanding of issue-areas of law, such as human rights or environmental law (compliance), where rationalists tend to be more pessimistic than reality; it is better suited to understand what international courts 'do in fact', since experiments have been conducted with national judges[78] and international arbitrators[79] which have shown their deviations from the rationalist assumptions.

Behavioural sciences can also help to construct a theory of cooperation in international affairs. Or they can use behavioural insights for the design of the law itself. The 12th Ministerial Conference (MC12) of the World Trade Organization (WTO) gives two examples of how behavioural insights can be used on the

[73] See Chapter 3 by Johnstone and Sukumar in this volume.

[74] Elinor Ostrom, 'A Behavioral Approach to the Rational Choice Theory of Collective Action' (1998) 92 American Political Science Review 1, 2. For an application to international public goods and commons, see Anne van Aaken, 'Behavioral Aspects of the International Law of Global Public Goods and Common Pool Resources' (2018) 112 AJIL 67.

[75] Leda Cosmides and John Tooby, 'Better Than Rational: Evolutionary Psychology and the Invisible Hand' (1994) 84 American Economic Review 327.

[76] Ostrom (n 74) 3.

[77] Ernst Fehr and Bettina Rockenbach, 'Detrimental Effects of Sanctions on Human Altruism' (2003) 422 Nature 137.

[78] Chris Guthrie, Jeffrey J Rachlinski, and Andrew J Wistrich, 'Blinking on the Bench: How Judges Decide Cases' (2007) 93 Cornell Law Review 1.

[79] Susan Franck and others, 'Inside the Arbitrator's Mind' (2017) 66 Emory Law Journal 1115.

inter-state level for treaty design; those cannot only be used on the WTO level, but also for regional or bilateral trade treaties to enhance sustainability.

First, attention can be paid to the 'ground rules' for negotiation of particular disciplines, such as opt-ins/-outs (positive or negative listing in trade speak[80]) as has been done with respect to acceptance of international jurisdiction more generally.[81] Research demonstrates that states will opt in significantly less frequently than opting out;[82] the default thus influences the willingness to commit. Default rules in trade treaties, based on insights concerning the status quo bias, matter. At MC12, opt-out was used for the Ministerial Decision on the Agreement on Trade-Related Aspects of Intellectual Property Rights (the Covid Waiver)[83] which states in para 1, fn 1: 'Developing country Members with existing capacity to manufacture COVID-19 vaccines are encouraged to make a binding commitment not to avail themselves of this Decision.' This represents the use of an enhanced opt-out mechanism for developing countries with manufacturing capacity, such as India and China. This enhanced opt-out was especially important for reluctant (developed) countries to commit.

Similarly, psychological mechanisms were presumably employed for the Agreement on Fisheries Subsidies. Deadlines have generally been identified as a nudge since they can counteract procrastination and forgetfulness.[84] Specifically, a last-minute consensus has been proposed as a possible nudge in negotiations.[85] But deadlines can also be applied to treaty design.[86] The Agreement on Fisheries Subsidies states in Article 12: 'If comprehensive disciplines are not adopted within four years of the entry into force of this Agreement, and unless otherwise decided by the General Council, this Agreement shall stand immediately terminated.' Missing the deadlines means missing the opportunity to capture the gains from the agreement and is likely perceived as a loss. This looming termination thus induces loss aversion about losing the Agreement, building up pressure to adopt measures within four years. This psychological mechanism of loss aversion can also be used for other sustainability concerns in treaty design. Note that the new reference point from which a loss is perceived is a sustainability goal in the Fisheries Agreement. It is thus a public good whose non-provision is a perceived loss, turning away from

[80] Tomer Broude and Shai Moses, 'The Behavioral Dynamics of Positive and Negative Listing in Services Trade Liberalization: A Look at the Trade in Services Agreement (TiSA) Negotiations' in Martin Roy and Pierre Sauvé (eds), *Research Handbook on Trade in Services* (Elgar 2015) 385.

[81] Galbraith (n 10).

[82] ibid.

[83] Ministerial Decision on the TRIPS Agreement, adopted 17 June 2022, WT/MIN(22)/30.

[84] Eyal Zamir, Daphna Lewinsohn-Zamir, and Ilana Ritov, 'It's Now or Never! Using Deadlines as Nudges' (2017) 42 Law and Social Inquiry 769.

[85] Doron Teichman and Eyal Zamir, 'Nudge Goes International' (2020) 30 European Journal of International Law 1263.

[86] And are used in treaty design: ibid.

the market paradigm of reciprocity as a sole motivator for cooperation in international trade.[87]

Behavioural insights can thus be used to move forward treaty negotiations concerning collective action problems. Furthermore, treaty amendments or authoritative interpretations could move from opt-in (by some majority rule) to an opt-out mechanism (potentially with a requirement to explain the opt-out) in matters covering global commons or public goods.

Compliance theories in international law rely on a variety of mechanisms, including norm spirals,[88] focal points, expressive law theories,[89] and international courts.[90] They either assume a unitary state or break up the black box of the state to explain compliance—for example, through national political processes[91] or national courts.[92] From a rationalist perspective, other mechanisms have been identified, namely retaliation, reciprocity, reputation,[93] and outcasting.[94] Furthermore, rewarding can be considered under certain conditions.[95] Behavioural research can also illuminate the puzzle of compliance in collective action constellations and not only bilaterally where it is considered more likely by rationalist scholars, by drawing attention to the above-mentioned factors which are important to uphold cooperation.[96] Factors such as (1) internalized norms of cooperation, sustained by emotions such as guilt and shame and underlying moral norms such as fairness concerns; (2) concern for the specific behaviour of others, such as reciprocity as well as diffused reciprocity;[97] (3) communication and trust-building; and (4) sanctions imposed on non-cooperators while taking into account the many ways of sanctioning that are possible in international law lead to a more optimistic and also more nuanced picture of international law. Those factors help to construct a theory of the international order as well.[98]

[87] For details, see Anne van Aaken, 'Making Trade Agreements Contribute to Sustainability: The Potential of Behavioural Science' in Geraldo Vigidal and Kathleen Claussen (eds), *The Sustainability Revolution in International Trade Agreements* (OUP 2024) 23.

[88] Martha Finnemore and Kathryn Sikkink, 'International Norm Dynamics and Political Change' (1998) 52 International Organization 887.

[89] Alex Geisinger and Michael Ashley Stein, 'A Theory of Expressive International Law' (2007) 60 Vanderbilt Law Review 77; Tom Ginsburg and Richard H McAdams, 'Adjudicating in Anarchy: An Expressive Theory of International Dispute Resolution' (2004) 45 William and Mary Law Review 1229.

[90] Karen J Alter, 'Do International Courts Enhance Compliance with International Law?' (2003) 25 Review of Asian and Pacific Studies 51.

[91] Harold Hongju Koh, 'Why Do Nations Obey International Law?' (1997) 106 Yale Law Journal 2599 and Chapter 7 by Jefferies in this volume.

[92] Anthea Roberts, 'Comparative International Law? The Role of National Courts in Creating and Enforcing International Law' (2011) 60 International and Comparative Law Quarterly 57.

[93] Guzman (n 3).

[94] Hathaway and Shapiro (n 44).

[95] Anne van Aaken and Betül Simsek, 'Rewarding in International Law' (2021) 115 American Journal of International Law 195.

[96] Peat, Fikfak, and van der Zee (n 10).

[97] Keohane (n 46) and references in n 45.

[98] For an elaboration, see Anne van Aaken, 'Experimental Insights for International Legal Theory' (2020) 30 European Journal of International Law 1237.

A behavioural perspective further allows for a more differentiated view on the mechanisms as discussed by the rational choice approaches. First, retaliations, such as sanctions or the use of military force is costly for the sanctioning state(s). Thus, a so-called second-order prisoners' dilemma would ensue where states free-ride on sanctioning efforts or others. It has been well researched that individuals punish non-cooperative behaviour, even if it is costly to themselves. On the state level, the latest example is the far-reaching and costly sanctions against Russia by Western countries. From a behavioural perspective, spite and fairness considerations mitigate the sanctioner's dilemma, but much depends on the perceived type of the non-cooperative state. Thus, states not complying due to incapacity do not draw spite. Treaty regimes therefore need to have sorting mechanisms in place—to sort incapacity from other reasons of non-compliance, stressing the importance of monitoring and fact-finding, including by international courts. Sorting devices are crucial for the international system to work and they are indeed included in treaties. This also draws attention to the role of (reliable) information in international law. Again here, if the behavioural approach is correct, the advancement of technology as an information-revealing device, would enhance international cooperation considerably by providing reliable sorting of state conduct.

Direct reciprocity, although an important building block of IR, is undesirable in many particularly difficult constellations, especially global public goods and commons, since reacting with non-compliance as an answer to initial non-compliance can unravel the whole cooperative effort. Thus, non-violent outcasting as a device is more promising for global public goods constellations defined as the use of techniques to deny non-compliant states the benefits of social cooperation and membership or use of markets.[99] Outcasting penalizes by shutting the violating state or its economic operators out of the 'club' or suspending them temporarily, depriving them of the benefits of cooperation with damaging consequences. Enforcement can also be carried out by non-state actors, such as private banks in the Financial Action Task Force (FATF) mechanism. Outcasting is not a particular form of retaliation since it occurs solely *within* the treaty framework and is not costly for the states who outcast[100]—complying members collectively withdraw their promises to the violating member. Outcasting as a penalty is practically pervasive and is used effectively via treaty law (eg Article 4 of the Montreal Protocol banning the import of the substances listed in the Annexes from non-parties,[101] the Convention

[99] For details, see Anne van Aaken, 'Trust, Verify or Incentivize? Effectuating Public International Law Regulating Public Goods through Market Mechanisms' (2010) 104 Proceedings of the ASIL Annual Meeting 153; Anne van Asken, 'Effectuating Public International Law through Market Mechanisms?' (2009) 165 Journal of Institutional and Theoretical Economics 33.

[100] Outcasting is costly for the enforcing countries only if the outcast country is so important that cooperation (and its benefits) break down completely.

[101] Montreal Protocol on Substances That Deplete the Ozone Layer, Sept 16, 1987, S Treaty Doc No 100-10, 1522 UNTS 29. The Montreal Protocol is a protocol to the Vienna Convention for the Protection of the Ozone Layer, March 22, 1985, TIAS No 11,097,1513 UNTS 324.

on International Trade in Endangered Species of Wild Fauna and Flora,[102] or the Basel Convention[103]). Many regional organizations like the African Union, the Organization of American States, the Council of Europe, and the European Union have some sort of outcasting device for members breaking their rules or principles (eg by revoking voting rights or via expulsion). The mechanism of outcasting can well be explained by a rationalist approach. Yet, all treaty regimes allow for (re-) admission which is crucial from a behavioural perspective.[104] Outcasting, also in sport events, for example, not only provokes material costs for the violating state but also immaterial costs via impacting its status and reputation and even identity. This is only insufficiently analysed by the rational choice approach, while the behavioural approach is able to illuminate those mechanisms.

## 4. Limitations

There are two main limitations coming into play when using behavioural insights for international legal theory. One concerns the inductive approach based on experimental evidence conducted with individuals which is then applied to states—the unit of analysis problem. The other concerns the inherent methodological individualism of the traditional behavioural approach, following the rational choice approach.

### 4.1. Unit of analysis

Crucial for the use of behavioural approaches is the careful choice of the unit of analysis. Which is the relevant unit of analysis for international legal theory? Whose behaviour is at issue? Is it the state as a unitary actor/'black box'/'billiard ball' or is it individual actors, such as judges, political leaders, military commanders, trade negotiators, or other individuals, whose actions and decisions are attributable to the state under international law? Are we concerned with 'elite' decision-makers, experts, or the general public or both? Or is it small decision-making groups, acknowledging that many decisions regarding international law-related conduct are made by such groups, and that group psychology is often different from individual decision-making?[105] We believe that all units of analysis are relevant to

[102] Convention on International Trade in Endangered Species of Wild Fauna and Flora (CITES), March 3, 1973, 993 UNTS 243, Arts III, IV, and V.

[103] Basel Convention on the Control of Transboundary Movements of Hazardous Wastes and Their Disposal, March 22, 1989, 1673 UNTS 126, reprinted in 28 LM 657 (1989).

[104] Van Aaken and Simsek (n 95).

[105] Norbert L Kerr, Robert J MacCoun, and Geoffrey P Kramer, 'Bias in Judgment: Comparing Individuals and Groups' (1996) 103 Psychological Review 687; and with respect to international judicial decision-making, focusing on 'conformity effects', see Broude (n 10) 1143–49; and also van Aaken (n 10) 445–49.

behavioural international legal theory. Much of international law decision-making is in essence made by individuals or small decision-making groups; while the very term 'state conduct' implies that states are regularly assimilated to individual actors, and importantly—states are held internationally responsible for individual acts and decisions. Whereas rational choice and public choice have long explored domestic political processes and interactions between national and international politics (the 'two-level game'),[106] behavioural international political economy is still in its earliest stages—even 'embryonic'[107]—though potentially of great importance for international law. The two-level-game framework can thus be used with rationalist assumptions (as it has been hitherto) or behavioural assumptions[108] and it can be connected to international legal process theories.

The second challenge derives from the *experimental basis* of the core of behavioural research. As demonstrated by some of the studies in this book, as well as others, applying experimental psychology and its methods to international law, international legal theory, and IR is not beyond reach.[109] Some of the experimental results have intuitive appeal and have also been confirmed by field studies (eg in the realm of commons).[110] Through analysis of decision-making in controlled conditions, experiments can have high internal validity and the potential to uncover causal effects; but they may suffer from external validity problems due to several reasons, as discussed below. Still, in combination with other research methods, experiments are a very useful complementary tool for informing about decision-making under controlled conditions, focusing on the smallest or otherwise applicable unit of decision-making.

Applying experimental insights to individual decision-makers whose acts are in turn attributed to the state (eg treaty negotiators, diplomats, or state officials such as military commanders) or to international judges is no major problem[111]—the

[106] Robert D Putnam, 'Diplomacy and Domestic Politics: The Logic of Two-Level Games' (1988) 42 International Organization 427. This is a fundamental paradigm explaining international trade treaties; Gene M Grossman and Elhanan Helpman, 'Protection for Sale' (1994) 84 American Economic Review 833; Gene M Grossman and Elhanan Helpman, 'Trade Wars and Trade Talks' (1995) 103 Journal of Political Economy 675. For an international law analysis, see Anne van Aaken and Joel P Trachtman, 'Political Economy of International Law: Towards a Holistic Model of State Behavior' in Alberta Fabricotti (ed), *Political Economy of International Law: A European Perspective* (Elgar 2016) 9.

[107] Jan Schnellenbach and Christian Schubert, 'Behavioral Political Economy: A Survey' (2015) 40 European Journal of Political Economy 395.

[108] For trade law, see behavioural political economy explanation of protectionist trade policies; see Anne van Aaken and Jürgen Kurtz, 'Beyond Rational Choice: International Trade Law and the Behavioral Political Economy of Protectionism' (2019) 22 Journal of International Economic Law 601. See also Gene M Grossman and Elhanan Helpman, 'Identity Politics and Trade Policy' (2020) 88 The Review of Economic Studies 1101, who used to base their theory on rational choice political economy.

[109] For discussions in international law, see Broude (n 10) 1133–34; Dunoff and Pollack (n 6). For a discussion in IR, see Robert Powell, 'Research Bets and Behavioral IR' (2017) 71 International Organization S265.

[110] Elinor Ostrom, *Governing the Commons: The Evolution of Institutions for Collective Action* (CUP 1990).

[111] Franck and others (n 79); Tomer Broude and Inbar Levy, 'Outcome Bias and Expertise in Investigations under International Humanitarian Law' (2020) 30 European Journal of International Law 1303.

unit of analysis is the individual (as in most experiments). Applying experimental insights to the state is more problematic since aggregation problems arise and face the same criticism as rational choice theory when applied to the state as such—reverting to the unit of analysis problem. Generally, there are two ways of dealing with this issue: either to simply attribute nonstandard preferences, beliefs, and decision-making directly to states; or to leave the analysis at the individual level and face the problem of aggregation from individual to collective decision-making.[112] At least for default rules, empirical work shows that the behaviour of individuals and states is similar.[113]

Breaking up the 'black box' state and applying experimental insights to national political processes is still in its infancy and surely confronts significant obstacles.[114] Insights from experimental economics have been applied to law concerning corporate actors, showing that experimental insights can fruitfully be applied to organizations.[115] Furthermore, purely rationalist theories of state action reflect the outdated assumptions of the pre-behavioural revolution era.[116] Rather than insisting that behavioural researchers justify extrapolating from experimental insights regarding individuals to states or other collectives, it is precisely this disconnect—of presumed state rationality—that needs justification. Nevertheless, other means of inquiry must surely complement experimental research, such as field studies and other empirical research, for example agent-based modelling which is able to capture the complexities of processes and multiplicity of actors.

The third significant challenge or constraint is that of *external validity*. To what extent can conclusions from experimental research and other behavioural empirical studies with clearly circumscribed research questions, circumstances and subjects, be generalized and carried over to other contexts and to the real world? This is an overarching problem in psychological experimental and otherwise empirical research, far from unique to international law. We therefore submit that the usual disclaimers apply regarding methodology, research design, and the implications of results (such as their predictive value, which should be carefully circumscribed). The external validity issue should not be a barrier to behavioural research, merely a permanent speed-bump on the way to enhanced knowledge.[117]

[112] Edmund Chattoe-Brown, 'Is Agent-Based Modelling the Future of Prediction?' (2023) 26 International Journal of Social Research Methodology 143; Katharina Luckner and Veronika Fikfak, 'Not All Nations at All Times: How States Imitate Each Other's Behavior towards Non-Compliance with International Law Norms—An ABM Proposal' (2023) 3420 CEUR Workshop Proceedings <https://ssrn.com/abstract=4361321>.

[113] Galbraith (n 10).

[114] Schnellenbach and Schubert (n 107); Zamir and Teichman (n 52).

[115] Decision-making in groups and thus organizations can cut both ways—alleviate biases and heuristics or strengthen them. cf Colin F Camerer and Ulrike Malmendier, 'Behavioral Economics of Organizations' in Peter Diamond and Hannu Vartiainen (eds), *Behavioral Economics and Its Applications* (Princeton UP 2007) 235.

[116] Hafner-Burton and others (n 55).

[117] For a more critical discussion of the external validity problem, see Jeff Dunoff and Mark Pollack, 'Experimenting with International Law: A Reader's Guide' (2017) 28 EJIL 1317.

Nevertheless, we would like to point out that subjects with a professional background may, when deciding in their professional context, not exhibit the classical biases and heuristics as the subjects on which many of the experiments on behavioural insights are based, namely students or laypeople. And even if experiments are done with professionals in a certain issue-area, it remains unclear how far those can be transposed from one issue-area to another—or one community of practice to another.[118]

Fourth, an issue arising throughout the chapters in this book is the question of how international law, in comparison with social norms, practices, beliefs, or other authority (such as political figures) *affects behaviour* relevant to international law. Does the 'choice architecture' of international law and its 'nudges' influence behaviour of the relevant actors, and if so, how? What is the relevance of culture, communities of practice and background for behaviour connected to law? There is certainly progress in research, yet evidence is still scarce.

Fifth, and not unconnectedly, how does international law interact with *the domestic sphere* in a behavioural sense? Given that much of the impulses for law-making and effectuation of international law takes place nationally, how does it influence decision-makers? And how and who would be affected?

## 4.2. Methodological individualism

The second limitation of the behavioural approach as it currently stands is that it focusses too much on the individual, isolated decision-maker as a micro-foundation. A purely individualistic approach can lead to neglect of the social and political conditions, networks, and implications of individual actions on yet other individuals.[119] Even if 'political phenomena result from underlying individual attitudes and behavior, individual-level descriptions do not always capture all explanatorily salient properties"[120] Behaviour, including that of states, is relational.[121] Experimental research by behavioural economists has already hinted that information about the behaviour of others' may influence individual decisions whether to engage in certain behaviour or not; or more generally: 'the average subjects steal the more, the more others steal'.[122] Behaviour is also influenced by

[118] Anne van Aaken, Tomer Broude, Christoph Engel, and Katharina Luckner, 'Identifying Communities of Practice in International Law: An Experimental Study with Frontline Humanitarian Negotiators' (on file with the authors).

[119] Benjamin Ewert, Kathrin Loer, and Eva Thomann, 'Beyond Nudge: Advancing the State-of-the-Art of Behavioural Public Policy and Administration' (2021) 49 Policy and Politics 3.

[120] Christian List and Kai Spieckermann, 'Methodological Individualism and Holism in Political Science: A Reconciliation' (2013) 107 American Political Science Review 629.

[121] See Luckner and Fikfak (n 112).

[122] Armin Falk and Urs Fischbacher, '"Crime" in the Lab-Detecting Social Interaction' (2002) 46 European Economic Review 859.

social interaction phenomena, such as 'peer pressure' or 'neighbourhood effects'.[123] Social norms are also said to play a huge role.[124] They can be defined as 'a rule of behaviour such that individuals prefer to conform to it on condition that they believe that (a) most people in their reference network conform to it (empirical expectation), and (b) that most people in their reference network believe they ought to conform to it (normative expectation)'.[125] Those expectations also contain consequences for cooperation.[126] Although it is difficult to speak of classical social norms in the international sphere, surely there are networks of states which are bound by not only empirical, but by normative expectations and imitation effects as well.[127] Indeed, the very definition of social norms is similar to intersubjective understandings of international custom. Here, a bridge to sociological theories could and should be built. Practice theory is one such theory which can be easily combined with cognitive insights. Practice originates in the decisions of agents, navigating a social environment shaped by normative convictions, as recognized by cognitive sociologist Pierre Bourdieu.[128] To leverage its full potential, practice theory needs to understand cognition and motivation of the individuals constituting the respective community of practice, including their learning processes. Also for constructivists, understanding how and why norms and beliefs diffuse and motivate means reverting to the smallest building block—the individual. Embedding a realistic picture of the individual in international legal theories is thus needed—but the individual needs in turn to be embedded in its environment.

## 5. Conclusion

If international legal theory is to be evidence-based, then behavioural insights can and do provide a promising basis on which to build new, unified and behaviourally informed theories of international law. Even normative theories, such as international liberalism, can question the normative assumptions of the 'models of

[123] ibid.

[124] See also Cristina Bicchieri and Deshani Ganegonda, 'Determinants of Corruption: A Socio-Psychological Analysis', in Philip M Nichols and Diana C Robertson (eds), *Thinking about Bribery: Neuroscience, Moral Cognition and the Psychology of Bribery* (CUP 2016) 177.

[125] Cristina Bicchieri, *Norms in the Wild: How to Diagnose, Measure, and Change Social Norms* (OUP 2017) 35.

[126] Felix Kölle and Simone Quercia, 'The Influence of Empirical and Normative Expectations on Cooperation' (2021) 190 Journal of Economic Behavior and Organization 691. For a more relational approach concerning the international law against corruption, see Anne van Aaken, 'Effectuating International Law against Corruption: Behavioral Insights' (2024) 22 International Journal of Constitutional Law 562.

[127] See Luckner and Fikfak (n 112).

[128] Omar Lizardo, 'Pierre Bourdieu as Cognitive Sociologist' in Wayne H Brekhus and Gabe Ignatow (eds), *The Oxford Handbook of Cognitive Sociology* (OUP 2019) 65; Pierre Bourdieu, *Practical Reason: On the Theory of Action* (Polity Press 1998); see also Chapter 10 by Madsen and Caserta in this volume.

man' they use.[129] Yet, a behavioural basis for international legal theory still needs to be better developed on several accounts; thus plenty of research desiderata remain which reflect the current limitations. First, it would be desirable to mitigate the external validity problem of the experiments. For that, it would be necessary to conduct experiments with elite decision-makers, including in international negotiations. The latter is most probably not possible, thus other empirical proxies would need to be used for international negotiations. Second, more research and adapted theories for the interaction between the international and national level need to be developed based on behavioural insights. This could bridge the gap, for example to transnational legal process theories.[130] Third, behavioural science needs to open further to cognitive sociology and social cognition and research normative and empirical network effects. Behavioural economics thus needs to broaden its horizon and can learn from other theories and vice versa. Furthermore, given the better social science methods towards understanding complexity, triangulation of social science methods should be used, including agent-based modelling. Silos should be broken up between the theories; putting the pieces of the puzzle of how international law works together may one day lead to 'unity of knowledge'.[131]

[129] See Chapter 6 by Howse in this volume.
[130] See Chapter 7 by Jefferies in this volume.
[131] Edward O Wilson, *Consilience: The Unity of Knowledge* (Alfred A Knopf 1998).

# 9

# Sociological Analysis of International Law and the Cognitive Turn

*Moshe Hirsch**

## 1. Introduction

Systematic research at the intersection of sociology and cognition began in the late 1990s,[1] with international law scholars increasingly turning their attention to the socio-cognitive dimension of international law. The bourgeoning scholarship at this interdisciplinary juncture integrates some well-known sociological concepts (such as socialization) with insights gained from new cognitive and behavioural studies (such as cognitive biases). While the conventional sociological approach to international law principally explores society's influence on decision-makers' behaviour and vice versa (eg via social norms), the recent cognitive-sociological analysis of international law largely highlights the influence of society on legal decision-makers' *perceptions of reality* (via cognitive processes like attention or memory).[2]

This chapter aims to explore some major implications of cognitive-behavioural studies for the sociological analysis of international law. To cope with this task, we will discuss the two major streams in cognitive-sociological literature: the embodied-cognitive approach (prominently inspired by Bourdieu) and the cultural-cognitive perspective (notably developed by Zerubavel and his followers). Embodied-cognitive scholars view cognitive structures (particularly the 'habitus') as unconsciously grounded in various features of the human body and material environment. Cultural-cognitive scholars underscore that distinct cognitive patterns (such as norms of attention) prevail in different social groups, occasionally leading people from different societies to view the same reality in divergent manners. Each of the above streams in cognitive sociology casts a different

* I am very grateful to Anne van Aaken and Mikael Madsen for their insightful comments on earlier drafts of this chapter. Thanks also to Noga Weiss for excellent research assistance.

[1] See, eg, Tuukka Kaidesoja, Mikko Hyyryläinen, and Ronny Puustinen, 'Two Traditions of Cognitive Sociology: An Analysis and Assessment of Their Cognitive and Methodological Assumptions' (2022) 52 Journal for the Theory of Social Behaviour 528, 529.

[2] The term 'perception' refers in this chapter to various cognitive processes (eg attention, categorization, interpretation, and memory) through which people acquire and process information. On the main principles of cognitive studies, see Section 3.

Moshe Hirsch, *Sociological Analysis of International Law and the Cognitive Turn* In: *International Legal Theory and the Cognitive Turn*. Edited by: Anne van Aaken and Moshe Hirsch, Oxford University Press. 
DOI: 10.1093/9780198909293.003.0010

light on international law and influences the ways we conceive the international legal system and its institutions.

Cognitive-behavioural studies influence the sociological approach to international law in many ways. This chapter highlights four major implications of these studies. The first implication is that cognitive literature confirms and reinforces the central assumption of the sociological perspective regarding the influence of socio-cultural factors on individual legal decision-makers. Cognitive studies show that social groups guide not only individuals' behaviour but also their mental process through which they perceive and comprehend their environment. Thus, understanding the normative behaviour of international law decision-makers (including adjudicators or national policy-makers) often necessitates an examination of cognitive patterns predominating in their particular communities (such as norms of categorization).

The second implication turns the spotlight to the deeper unconscious layer of social influence. Cognitive-behavioural studies reveal that cognitive processes often occur below the level of consciousness; with individuals frequently unaware of the impact of socio-cultural factors on the way they process information. As elaborated below, once habituated by society to perceive and think in a distinct manner, the particular socio-cognitive pattern often becomes a blind spot, causing legal decision-makers to not pay attention to alternative cognitive options.

The third and fourth major implications of cognitive-behavioural studies for the sociological perspective on international law signal two theoretical shifts in the recent cognitive-sociological approach to international law. The third consequence is primarily sparked by the Bourdieu's influential embodied cognition scholarship, which is significantly associated with critical international legal theory (emphasizing intimate links between law, power, and politics). In light of this combination in Bourdieu's writings, the new cognitive-sociological analysis of international law gravitates towards a critical analysis of international law. This theoretical inclination exposes links between cognitive hegemony and international law; suggesting a distrustful attitude regarding the pretentious neutrality of international tribunals.

The fourth implication is related to the important role played by cultural-cognitive scholarship in the development of cognitive sociology; the recent cognitive-sociological approach to international law gravitates towards legal pluralism in international legal theory. Cultural-cognitive writings project an image of the international community as profoundly fragmented along cognitive lines, indicating that legal decision-makers—socialized into different cultures—often use different lenses to perceive normative situations. These writings suggest that international adjudicators drawn from different societies are susceptible to cultural-cognitive misunderstandings and biases, with this vulnerability threatening the legitimacy of international tribunals. As elaborated below, the above implications of cognitive-behavioural studies for the sociological approach to international law highlight certain challenges to the international legal system, offering some legal strategies to address these challenges.

The chapter is structured as follows: Section 2 will provide a bird's-eye view of the core assumptions underlying the conventional sociological perspective on international law, followed by Section 3 which will succinctly expose some key principles arising from cognitive sociology and social cognition studies pertaining to international law. Section 4.1 will present the two main approaches in cognitive sociology (the embodied-cognitive and cultural-cognitive perspectives) and Section 4.2 will analyse four major implications of cognitive-behavioural studies for the new cognitive-sociological approach to international law. Section 5 will recap some of the key conclusions and briefly discuss some limits of current socio-cognitive analysis of international law.

## 2. The Sociological Perspective on International Law

Before analysing the implications of new cognitive studies for the sociological approach to international law, this section succinctly exposes the core tenets of the conventional sociological perspective on international law. Sociologists of law have long emphasized that law is rooted in communities, with laws being expressive types of those communities.[3] Since law emerges from and operates within social groups, Emile Durkheim's famous statement is thus significant for legal researchers as well: society is more than the individuals who compose it; society has a life of its own that stretches beyond our personal experience.[4] Consequently, the fundamental idea that reverberates in numerous sociological studies is that the social whole of a group is greater than the sum of the individuals comprising the group; and knowledge about social relations cannot be derived solely from knowledge about the individuals who belong to the group.

Sociology explores social groups and interactions between individuals and social groups and one of the fundamental assumptions is that individuals' behaviour and their normative choices are significantly affected by socio-cultural factors and processes (such as socialization).[5] A central debate in sociological literature (which has a significant bearing on socio-legal analysis) revolves around the effect of social patterns (such as norms or identity) on individuals; that is, to what extent and how does the social structure constrain people in society? While

[3] Roger Cotterrell, *Law, Culture and Society: Legal Ideas in the Mirror of Social Theory* (Ashgate 2006) 161; see also Mathieu Deflem, *Sociology of Law: Visions of a Scholarly Tradition* (CUP 2008) 7–8.

[4] Emile Durkheim, *Sociology and Philosophy* (Free Press 1953) 54–55.

[5] See, eg, Richard T Schaefer, *Sociology Matters* (5th edn, McGraw-Hill 2011) 2–3; George Ritzer and Wendy W Murphy, *Introduction to Sociology* (5th edn, SAGE 2020) 2–3; Anthony Giddens and Philip Sutton, *Sociology* (9th edn, Polity 2021) 8–9; Reza Banakar and Max Travers, 'Introduction' in Reza Banakar and Max Travers (eds), *An Introduction to Law and Social Theory* (Hart 2002) 1, 3.

agency-orientated approaches emphasize the active and creative aspects of human behaviour, structure-orientated approaches underline the constraining nature of uniform social structures (eg norms) on individuals, prominently through social control and socialization processes.[6] It is worth emphasizing that individuals also influence their social structure. Socio-cultural factors do not only constrain individuals but also equip them with a 'toolkit' of resources, enabling them to construct certain strategies of action.[7]

Sociological analysis of *international law* begins from the premise that international legal rules and institutions are embedded in the socio-cultural features of communities. Thus, the particular socio-cultural features (including values) prevailing in a group affect the formation, interpretation, and implementation of international legal rules in the specific community. For example, social norms prevailing in a particular region (such as Latin America or South-East Asia) are likely to affect the particular international legal rules and institutions developed in this regional context. International legal decision-makers (including adjudicators or military commanders) are socialized into a particular culture and their decisions in a range of legal issues are influenced by some elements of this culture. International law does not only *reflect* societal factors but often also *affects* socio-cultural processes, such as processes of socialization or social control that are occasionally influenced by international tribunals and other legal institutions.[8]

Sociological inquiries into national and international laws share some similarities (eg some overlap between legal rules and social norms) but also present some distinctive features. In many cases, the international dimension displays some characteristics that, although present to some degree in national legal systems, are more intensified in international law. For example, many national legal systems operate in multi-cultural societies; but the international legal system is characterized by intensified multi-cultural settings. As discussed below, this feature presents some challenges to international tribunals.[9]

While international law cannot be fully disentangled from socio-cultural processes undertaken in various communities, it is clear that it does not fully mirror the culture of those communities.[10] For example, certain international norms

[6] On the structure–agency debate, see George Ritzer and Jeffrey Stepnisky, *Sociological Theory* (9th edn, McGraw-Hill 2013) 510; Ritzer and Murphy (n 5) 19–20; Giddens and Sutton (n 5) 95–99; James Fulcher and John Scott, *Sociology* (4th edn, OUP 2011) 53; Banakar and Travers (n 5) 4–5; Sharon Hays, 'Structure and Agency and the Sticky Problem of Culture' (1994) 12 Social Theory 57.

[7] See, eg, Ann Swidler, *Talk of Love: How Culture Matters* (University of Chicago Press 2001) 104–05, 82–83, 104–17. See also Giddens and Sutton (n 5) 9.

[8] See, eg, Moshe Hirsch, 'The Sociological Perspective on International Law' in Jeffrey L Dunoff and Mark A Pollack (eds), *International Legal Theory: Foundations and Frontiers* (CUP 2022) 282, 282–83.

[9] See Section 4.2.2.

[10] For a criticism of the reductionist view assuming that law is only a mirror of society, see, eg, David Nelken, 'Towards a Sociology of Legal Adaptation' in David Nelken and Johannes Feest (eds), *Adapting Legal Cultures* (Hart 2001) 12, 15.

or identities are often *partially* institutionalized in international legal rules. Employing sociological tools can not only explain why some international legal rules have evolved in a particular social context but may also constitute an interpretative tool to clarify the content of international legal provisions. A sociological examination may also suggest some better legal mechanisms for coping with challenges faced by international law, such as enhancing compliance with international law.[11] Sociological analysis also furthers our understanding of the social limits of international law. Thus, for example, it would be naïve to assume that the mere establishment of legally binding rules in a treaty is sufficient to engender a dramatic and meaningful normative change in a certain community (eg eliminating racial or gender discrimination). In certain cases, socio-cultural factors inspire a cultural resistance inhibiting the formation or internalization of international legal rules (eg with regard to resistance to rules relating to international trade in certain products or services).[12]

Sociological studies of international law commonly explore a variety of interactions between socio-cultural factors and the *behaviour or beliefs* of individual decision-makers, for example the influence of particular norms or identity on adjudicators. Cognitive-sociological analysis of international law is primarily concerned with the ways social groups affect *cognitive processes* through which legal decision-makers acquire and process incoming information. This recent cognitive stream in the sociological analysis of international law draws on empirical knowledge and insights gained from several adjacent cognitive sciences, principally social cognition and cognitive-sociological studies.

## 3. Social Cognition and Cognitive Sociology: Some Core Principles

This section briefly introduces some key principles arising from studies in social cognition (a branch of social psychology) and cognitive sociology pertaining to international law. Although there are some significant differences between the methodologies and theories employed by researchers from the two disciplines, there are also substantial similarities and overlap. Many cognitive sociologists are notably informed by social cognition studies, and recent social cognition literature increasingly acknowledges that individuals' mental processes are also influenced

[11] See, eg, Moshe Hirsch, *Invitation to the Sociology of International Law* (OUP 2015) 168 et seq. On employing a sociological analysis for enhancing the application of human rights in investment tribunals' jurisprudence, see Moshe Hirsch, 'Social Movements, Reframing Investment Relations, and Enhancing the Application of Human Rights Norms in International Investment Law' (2020) 37 LJIL 127, 144–48.

[12] Eg Joel Richard Paul, 'Cultural Resistance to Global Governance' (2001) 22 Michigan Journal of International Law (2001) 1, 30 et seq.

by cultural features.[13] These two disciplinary streams in cognitive science complement each other and are valuable for cognitive-sociological analysis of international law.

### 3.1. Mental representations and selective processes

The point of departure of social-cognitive studies is that people do not directly sense their physical environment but rather cognitive processes *mediate* between sensory input from the environment and behaviour.[14] Cognitive processes (such as attention, categorization, and memory) filter in/out, interpret, and store incoming information. Such processes construct in the mind mental representations that organize our knowledge and expectations about various social objects in our environment.[15] Thus, what we perceive in our mind is constructed not solely from observed data but also from the context and meaning attributed to the data (including our already existing mental representations).[16] As Friedman aptly states: '[s]trictly speaking, what human beings see, feel, taste, touch, and smell is not the world per se but a version of the world their minds have created'.[17]

Humans are frequently exposed to ample information; but due to their limited cognitive capacity, cognitive processes (such as attention) are commonly selective and inherently imply the exclusion of some information.[18] To cope with the large amounts of information from different channels and make decisions under uncertain circumstances, people also resort to heuristics ('rules of thumb') to reduce complex situations into simpler and manageable ones.[19] These mental shortcuts provide quick guidelines but may also lead to systemic errors.[20]

[13] See, eg, Susan Fiske and Shelley Taylor, *Social Cognition: From Brain to Culture* (4th edn, SAGE 2021) 17, 28–29.

[14] Fiske and Taylor (n 13) 12, 17; Martha Augoustinos, Iain Walker, and Ngaire Donaghue, *Social Cognition* (3rd edn, SAGE 2015) 20; Joel M Charon, *Symbolic Interactionism* (10th edn, Pearson 2009) 28, 43.

[15] Augoustinos and others (n 14) 20–21; Karen Cerulo (ed), *Culture in Mind: Toward A Sociology of Culture and Cognition* (Routledge 2001) 113. See also Paul Thagard, *Mind: Introduction to Cognitive Science* (2nd edn, MIT Press 2005) 4 et seq.

[16] Gordon Moskowitz, *Social Cognition: Understanding Self and Others* (1st edn, Guilford 2005) 64. See also Stanislas Dehaene, *Consciousness and the Brain* (Penguin 2014) 60–62.

[17] Asia Friedman, *Blind to Sameness* (University of Chicago Press 2013) 20.

[18] See, eg, Eviatar Zerubavel, *Hidden in Plain Sight: The Social Structure of Irrelevance* (OUP 2015) 2–3.

[19] Fiske and Taylor (n 13) 15, 195–96; Daniel Kahneman, *Thinking Fast and Slow* (Penguin 2012) 98. See also Hans Eysenck and Mark Keane, *Cognitive Psychology* (7th edn, Psychology Press 2015), 141–42, 441–42; Jens Rydgren, 'The Power of the Past: A Contribution to a Cognitive Sociology of Ethnic Conflict' (2007) 25 Sociological Theory 225, 228.

[20] See, eg, Kathleen Galotti, *Cognitive Psychology: In and Out of the Laboratory* (6th edn, SAGE 2018) 314; Kahneman (n 19) 130; Fiske and Taylor (n 13) 206.

### 3.2. Cognition and society

Human cognition is influenced by neurological, psychological, socio-cultural, and other factors. Cognitive science literature (heavily influenced by psychological research work)[21] has tended to focus on *individual* cognition and implicitly assumed universal elements of human cognition. As a result, it has generally neglected interactions between individuals and their social environment.[22] Recent social cognition literature generally acknowledges cultural effects on human cognition, but socio-cultural issues are not centre stage in this literature.[23] As to the sociological literature, since the path-breaking publications of Zerubavel[24] and DiMaggio[25] in the late 1990s, interest in cognition has grown exponentially within sociological scholarship, and sociologists increasingly seek to explain how cultures and cognition interact.[26] The cognitive-sociological literature emphasizes that socio-cultural factors affect how humans acquire and process information. While not ignoring universal or personal cognitive processes (such as certain elements of neural processing), cognitive sociologists highlight that cultural patterns often undergird individuals' cognitive process.[27]

### 3.3. Unconscious processes and blind spots

One of the important distinctions in social cognition studies concerns the division between automatic and deliberate processes. Automatic cognitive processes can occur below the level of consciousness while deliberate thought demands consciousness.[28] Cognitive sociology scholarship relies on the above dual-process model[29] to explain various sociological concepts and processes (such as 'culture'

[21] See, eg, Clark Barret, 'Towards a Cognitive Science of the Human: Cross-Cultural Approaches and Their Urgency' (2020) 24 Trends in Cognitive Science 620, 620–23.

[22] Karen A Cerulo, 'Establishing a Sociology of Culture and Cognition' in Karen A Cerulo (ed), *Culture in Mind: Toward a Sociology of Culture and Cognition* (Routledge 2022) 1, 2; Thagard (n 15) 205; Barret (n 21) 623.

[23] See, eg, Paul Thagard, *Mind: Society* (OUP 2019) 80; Barret (n 21) 623. It is noteworthy that cross-cultural psychology studies often highlight the interactions between culture and cognitive processes; see, eg, Richard Nisbett and Ara Norenzayan, 'Culture and Cognition' in Douglas Medin (ed), *Stevens' Handbook of Experimental Psychology* (vol 2, 3rd edn, Wiley 2002) 561, 562; Michael Cole and Martin Packer, 'Culture and Cognition' in Kenneth D Keith (ed), *Cross-Cultural Psychology: Contemporary Themes and Perspectives* (2nd edn, Wiley Blackwell 2019) 243.

[24] Eviatar Zerubavel, *Social Mindscapes: An Invitation to Cognitive Sociology* (Harvard UP 1997).

[25] Paul DiMaggio, 'Culture and Cognition' (1997) 23 Annual Review of Sociology 263.

[26] See, eg, Vanina Leschziner and Gordon Brett, 'Have Schemas Been Good to Think With?' (2021) 36 Sociological Forum 1207. See also Kaidesoja, Hyyryläinen, and Puustinen (n 1) 529.

[27] Eviatar Zerubavel, 'Cognitive Sociology: Between the Personal and the Universal Mind' in Wayne H Brekhus and Gabe Ignatow (eds), *The Oxford Handbook of Cognitive Sociology* (OUP 2019) 31, 34–38; Karen A Cerulo, 'Representation and Integration: An Introduction' in Karen A Cerulo (ed), *Culture in Mind: Toward a Sociology of Culture and Cognition* (Routledge 2002) 113.

[28] On several degrees of automatic processing, see Fiske and Taylor (n 13) 36.

[29] See, eg, Stephen Vaisey, 'Motivation and Justification: A Dual-Process Model of Culture in Action' (2009) 114 American Journal of Sociology 1675, 1687; Karen A Cerulo, Vanina Leschziner, and Hana

and acquisition of cultural patterns).[30] While socio-cultural features permeate both automatic and deliberate cognitive processes,[31] automatic processes rely heavily on culturally available mental structures providing default assumptions about the characteristics of people, places, objects, or events.[32] Thus, individuals often hold cultural world views below their conscious level,[33] unconsciously conforming to moral values or automatically classifying someone's gender or race upon first meeting.[34]

Individuals and societies display varying degrees of awareness concerning cultural features; with some cognitive sociologists exploring radical cases characterized by a total or almost complete lack of awareness. On the societal level, Friedman labels such cases as 'cultural blind spots' marked by unconscious social patterns of *in*attention.[35] Because of their embeddedness in a social group, people in such cases fail to notice the group's cultural patterns or are unaware that there are alternative cognitive patterns. Cultural blind spots are primarily generated by two mechanisms: habituation and focusing attention. Habituation occurs when people are unaware of some objects or social features that are constantly around them. Focusing attention on a particular item often involves ignoring some other items located outside of people's field of attention, thus facilitating a cultural blind spot.[36]

## 3.4. Cultural schemas

The concept of schema has significantly influenced the development of cognitive sociology literature, particularly following DiMaggio's seminal article on culture and cognition (1997).[37] Schemas are both highly generalized structures

Shepherd, 'Rethinking Culture and Cognition' (2021) 47 Annual Review of Sociology 63, 70–71; Omar Lizardo and others, 'What Are Dual Process Models? Implications for Cultural Analysis in Sociology' (2016) 34 Sociological Theory 287.

[30] See, eg, Cerulo, Leschziner, and Shepherd (n 29) 64–65; Karen A Cerulo and Janet M Ruane, 'Future Imaginings: Public and Personal Culture' (2021) 36 Sociological Forum 1345, 1346, 1350. See also Yuki Shimi, Hajin Lee, and James S Uleman, 'Culture as Automatic Processes for Making Meaning: Spontaneous Trait Inferences' (2017) 69 Journal of Experimental Social Psychology 79.

[31] Malia Mason and Michael Morris, 'Culture, Attribution and Automaticity: A Social Cognitive Neuroscience View' (2010) 5 Social Cognitive and Affective Neuroscience 292, 293, 300–02.

[32] DiMaggio (n 25) 269; Karen Cerulo, 'Mining the Intersections of Cognitive Sociology and Neuroscience' (2010) 38 Poetics 115, 117–19. See also Shimi, Lee, and Uleman (n 30) 79.

[33] On cultural repertoires about morality and automatic cognition, see Michèle Lamont and others, 'Bridging Cultural Sociology and Cognitive Psychology in Three Contemporary Research Programmes' (2017) 1 Nature: Human Behaviour 866, 869–70.

[34] Cerulo, Leschziner, and Shepherd (n 29) 64–65.

[35] Asia Friedman, 'Cultural Blind Spots and Blind Fields: Collective Forms of Unawareness' in Wayne H Brekhus and Gabe Ignatow (eds), *Oxford Handbook of Cognitive Sociology* 467, 471. See also Zerubavel (n 18) 5 et seq.

[36] Zerubavel (n 18) 27; Friedman (n 35) 471–72.

[37] DiMaggio (n 25) 263.

of existing knowledge as well as information-processing mechanisms.[38] One of the prominent types of schemas are 'event schemas'; after participating in several classrooms, one develops a general notion of classrooms—a schema constructed from the various attributes of the different classrooms one has experienced.[39] As DiMaggio explained, cognitive schemas are closely related with culture;[40] they are often constructed through repeated exposures to cultural patterns, and the presence of certain socio-cultural features (such as religious symbols) can activate stored schemas.[41] Culturally infused schemas do not only cluster multiple socially shared representations that are stored in memory[42] but also constitute cognitive lenses through which people (largely unconsciously) perceive incoming information.[43] Thus, for example, racial stereotypes are considered as one type of cultural schemas (a schema about a group of people) and such mental structures filter people's attention, fill in the gaps in perceived information, assist in understanding new experience, and affect memory.[44] Cultural schemas, and prominently racial or gender stereotypes, have the potential to bias attention and interpretation, and may set the stage for various forms of discriminatory treatment.[45]

### 3.5. Social-cognitive interaction

Most cognitive sociology studies do not pay significant attention to the *emergence* of socially shared cognitive processes, but some studies suggest that certain social interactions tend to engender qualitatively different cognitive outcomes. Some experimental studies indicate that when people belonging to a social group simultaneously attend the same external stimulus (and know that others also focus on this stimulus), they direct more cognitive resources towards the processed stimulus.[46] Thus, co-attending members of the group are inclined to prioritize collectively attended objects and promote cognitive alignment, while reducing doubt about

[38] ibid 269. See also Perry R Hinton, *The Perception of People: Integrating Cognition with Culture* (Routledge 2016) 31.

[39] Cerulo (n 32) 125.

[40] DiMaggio (n 25) 269.

[41] Cerulo, 'Storage and Retrieval' in Karen A Cerulo (ed), *Culture in Mind: Toward A Sociology of Culture and Cognition* (Routledge 2002) 201, 204; Zerubavel (n 24) 88–89.

[42] Leschziner and Brett (n 26) 1209; Andrei Boutylinea and Laura K Soter, 'Cultural Schemas: What They Are, How to Find Them, and What to Do Once You've Caught One' (2021) 86 American Sociological Review 728, 730; Cerulo, Leschziner, and Shepherd (n 28) 66.

[43] Vaisey (n 28) 1686–87; Hinton (n 37) 31–32.

[44] Boutyline and Soter (n 41) 733–34; Cerulo, Leschziner, and Shepherd (n 29) 125–26.

[45] Deva Pager and Hana Shepherd, 'The Sociology of Discrimination: Racial Discrimination in Employment, Housing, Credit, and Consumer Markets' (2008) 34 Annual Review Sociology 181, 193.

[46] Cerulo, Leschziner, and Shepherd (n 29) 72; Garriy Shteynberg, 'A Silent Emergence of Culture: The Social Tuning Effect' (2010) 99 Journal of Personality and Social Psychology 683, 687. On the impact of sense of belonging on socially shared understanding, see Fiske and Taylor (n 13) 54 et seq.

shared knowledge.[47] As for memory, consistent with the hypothesis that stimuli experienced by one's social group are more prominent in both cognition and behaviour,[48] such shared stimuli are also more likely to result in better memory (and more extreme evaluations towards the recalled object).[49] The evidence indicating that individuals pay preferential attention and better remember information that similar others simultaneously have access to can explain some processes involved in collective memory. For example, the above resultant collective attention can clarify why people exposed to some descriptions of a past event (eg through the media) develop a similar selective representation of that past event,[50] and why interactions between individuals within their social network results in greater overlap in memory between the group members.[51]

## 4. Sociological Analysis of International Law and the Cognitive Turn

### 4.1. Sociological theory and major streams in cognitive sociology

Contemporary sociology is marked by theoretical pluralism with no single theory dominating the discipline.[52] Among numerous sociological theories, three broad traditions are widely recognized as the most central: the structural-functional perspective, the symbolic-interactionist approach, and the social conflict perspective. While there are many streams in *cognitive* sociology, the two major streams in this field are the *embodied-cognitive* approach (inspired by Bourdieusian scholarship) and the *cultural-cognitive* perspective (prominently influenced by Zerubavel's pioneering writings).[53] Bourdieu's embodied-cognitive approach echoes some core elements of the social conflict tradition in general sociological theory and the *cultural-cognitive approach* resonates with some key assumptions of the symbolic-interactionist tradition in general sociological theory. As elaborated below, these two principal streams in cognitive sociology influence the recent

[47] Garriy Shteynberg and others, 'Shared Worlds and Shared Minds: A Theory of Collective Learning and a Psychology of Common Knowledge' (2020) 127 Psychological Review 918, 921–23.

[48] Shteynberg (n 46) 687.

[49] Cerulo, Leschziner, and Shepherd (n 29) 72; Garriy Shteynberg, 'Shared Attention' (2015) 10 Perspectives on Psychological Science 579, 583.

[50] Alin Coman, 'Collective Memory, Psychology of' in *International Encyclopaedia of the Social & Behavioural Sciences* (2nd edn, vol 4, Elsevier 2015) 188, 190.

[51] Cerulo, Leschziner, and Shepherd (n 29) 72; Alin Coman and others, 'Mnemonic Convergence in Social Networks: The Emergent Properties of Cognition at a Collective Level' (2016) 113 Proceedings of the National Academy of Sciences 8171, 8175.

[52] See, eg, Giddens and Sutton (n 5) 24–25.

[53] On additional theoretical streams in cognitive sociology, see Wayne H Berkhus and Gabe Ingnatow, 'Cognitive Sociology and the Cultural Mind: Debates, Directions, and Challenges' in Wayne H Brekhus and Gabe Ignatow (eds), *The Oxford Handbook of Cognitive Sociology* (OUP 2019) 1, 3–6; Wayne H Berkhus, *Culture and Cognition* (Polity 2015) 9–18.

cognitive-sociological analysis of international law and suggest some changes in the ways we conceive the international legal system and its institutions.

#### 4.1.1. The embodied-cognitive approach

The embodied-cognitive approach is considerably influenced by Bourdieu's writings which significantly resonate with some central features of the social conflict tradition in general sociological theory. The social conflict perspective highlights the role of social hierarchies, power relations, politics, and the need for social change.[54] From this perspective, society is characterized by regular patterns of inequality and the uneven distribution of resources engenders struggle between rival groups, with each interested in advancing its own interests.[55] An important source of conflict is a group's sense of relative deprivation, which leads to class consciousness.[56]

Turning to *cognitive sociology*, Bourdieu also focused on social hierarchies[57] and struggles in society,[58] emphasizing not only economic struggles but also cultural ones.[59] Bourdieu's influential scholarship posits that culture is expressed and located not only in cultural symbols, values, and socialization, but primarily in the individual involving sensory perception, bodily schemas, and practical action. Cultural patterns are initially instilled via routine elements of bodily conduct (including specific ways of sitting, gazing, etc), and only later elaborated in terms of high level of symbolic representations. Cognition is primarily grounded in the features of the human bodies (which feel, see, hear, smell, taste, and touch) and they relate to the material environment from which they collect information. Bourdieu understands action as habituated, and related to unconscious reproduction of external social fields.[60] Thus, cognitive processes emerge from an entwined system that includes neural operations, bodily experiences, and the environment in which they are embedded.[61]

[54] David K Brown, *Social Blueprints: Conceptual Foundations of Sociology* (OUP 2004) 76; Jonathan H Turner, *Contemporary Sociological Theory* (SAGE 2013) 217.

[55] Kenneth Allan, *The Social Lens: An Invitation to Social and Sociological Theory* (2nd edn, SAGE 2011) 253; Randall Collins, *Conflict Sociology* (Routledge 1975) 59–60.

[56] Allan (n 55) 237.

[57] On Bourdieu's critical approach to law and courts, see Section 4.2.3.

[58] See, eg, Pierre Bourdieu, *The Logic of Practice* (Stanford UP 1990) 23, 136, 139–40. See also Michelle Dillon, *Introduction to Sociological Theory* (3rd edn, Wiley Blackwell 2020) 394 et seq.

[59] See, eg, Bourdieu (n 58) 16, 136, 180, 240.

[60] Kleio Akrivou and Lorenzo Todorow Di San Giorgio, 'A Dialogical Conception of Habitus: Allowing Human Freedom and Restoring the Social Basis of Learning' (2014) 8 Frontiers in Human Neuroscience 432 et seq.

[61] See, eg, Bourdieu (n 58) 66–79; Berkhus and Ignatow (n 53) 11; Omar Lizardo, 'Pierre Bourdieu as Cognitive Sociologist' in Wayne H Berkhus and Gabe Ignatow (eds), *The Oxford Handbook of Cognitive Sociology* (OUP 2019) 65, 71; Karen A Cerulo, 'Embodied Cognition: Sociology's Role in Bridging Mind, Brain, and Body' in Wayne H Berkhus and Gabe Ignatow (eds), *The Oxford Handbook of Cognitive Sociology* (OUP 2019) 81.

Bourdieu's renowned concept of the 'habitus'[62] is intimately linked with the above notion of cognitive schema.[63] 'Habitus' refers to general and durable socially produced cognitive structures that are deeply internalized (largely below the below the unconscious level), composed of bodily operations that generate people's practices, and constitute the basis for the perception and appreciation of human experiences. Habitus structures are extensively influenced by humans' history (such as schooling); and they tend to generate behaviours considered as 'reasonable' or reflecting 'common sense'.[64] As for cognitive schemas, Bourdieu explains that the habitus produces people's actions in accordance with schemas of perception, thought, and action that tend to ensure the 'correctness' of practices and their 'constancy over time'.[65]

### 4.1.2. The cultural-cognitive approach

The symbolic-interactionist tradition in general sociological literature includes some seeds of the recent cultural-cognitive approach in cognitive sociology. This is particularly notable with regard to Goffman's seminal writings regarding frames as 'schemata of interpretation' (1974)[66] and the influential treaties of Berger and Luckmann on the 'social construction of reality' (1966).[67] The symbolic-interactionist tradition in sociological theory emphasizes interactions between individuals and society (primarily in small groups) and places particular emphasis on explanations of everyday social experiences, frequently from the point of view of a certain individual or types of individuals. This sociological theory also underlines the *inter-subjective aspects* of individuals' interactions, such as the meaning of a particular object (or social phenomenon) shared among the members of a group.[68] The interpretations that individuals confer upon social patterns are important because they significantly influence their behaviour. Meanings shared by members of social groups emerge from social interactions; and in certain cases,

[62] On the concept of habitus, see Chapter 10 by Mikael Rask Madsen and Salvatore Caserta in this volume.

[63] On cognitive schemas, see Section 3.4.

[64] Bourdieu (n 58) 52 et seq; Omar Lizardo, 'The Cognitive Origins of Bourdieu's Habitus', (2004) 34 Journal for the Theory of Social Behaviour 375, 393–94; Berkhus and Ignatow (n 53) 11; Yves Dezalay and Mikael Rask Madsen, 'The Force of Law and Lawyers: Pierre Bourdieu and the Reflexive Sociology of Law' (2012) 8 Annual Review of Law and Social Science 433, 442.

[65] Bourdieu (n 58) 54.

[66] According to Goffman, these 'schemata of interpretation' allow people to locate, perceive, identify, and label their occurrences, thus 'rendering what would otherwise be a meaningless aspect of the scene into something that is meaningful'. Erving Goffman, *Frame Analysis: An Essay on the Organization of Experience* (Northwestern UP 1974) 21. See also at 10–11.

[67] Peter L Berger and Thomas Luckmann, *The Social Construction of Reality: A Treatise in the Sociology of Knowledge* (Penguin 1966, reprinted 1991) 15 et seq. See also Berkhus and Ignatow (n 53) 4–5.

[68] Ritzer and Stepnisky (n 6) at 350–51. See also Norman K Denzin, *Symbolic Interactionism and Cultural Studies* (Wiley Blackwell 1992) 23.

such interpretations are contested by the community's members.[69] From this perspective, humans live in a physical-objective reality and in a social reality. They do not sense the objective environment directly but rather socially define the situation they are in. The latter definitions result from ongoing social interactions and they strongly influence people's reactions to reality.[70]

Turning to *cognitive sociology*, the cultural-cognitive approach posits that the way people perceive and think about their environment is significantly related to their social groups. Criticizing cognitive individualism (that underlines unique personal factors) and cognitive universalism (that highlights cognitive commonality among human beings), the cultural- cognitive approach emphasizes the significant influence of communities on individuals' perceptions of reality.[71] Zerubavel (a key figure in this theoretical stream) emphasizes that '[s]ociety . . . plays a major role in organizing our "optical" predispositions. Indeed, many of the mental lenses through which we come to "see" the world are actually *socio*mental lenses grounded in particular social environments'.[72]

Scholars belonging to the cultural-cognitive approach apply some core concepts of 'classical' sociology to explain acquiring and enacting socio-cognitive patterns. For example, individuals' socialization includes learning different cognitive norms (such as conventions of attention, categorization or memory), with social control mechanisms exerting pressure on groups' members to follow such cognitive patterns.[73] Consequently, similar 'thought communities' follow similar patterns of attention, classification, memory, and additional cognitive processes.[74] While emphasizing cognitive similarities within social groups, the cultural-cognitive stream also highlights socio-cognitive variances between different communities (and across different periods).[75] This perspective promotes greater awareness of cognitive diversity and is generally averse to the view that humans belonging to different social groups think alike.[76]

As discussed below, the above major streams in cognitive sociology generate some changes in the way the new cognitive-sociological approach to international law conceives the international legal system and its institutions.

[69] Malcolm Waters, *Modern Sociological Theory* (SAGE 1994) 12, 15; Denzin (n 68) 49, 25.

[70] Charon (n 14) 28, 43.

[71] Zerubavel (n 27) 31–33.

[72] Zerubavel (n 24) 31, 22, 42. See also Brekhus (n 53) 33, 25; Karen Cerulo, 'Discrimination and Classification' in Karen Cerulo (ed), *Culture in Mind: Toward A Sociology of Culture and Cognition* (Routledge 2002) 57, 60.

[73] See, eg, Zerubavel (n 27) 35–36.

[74] Berkhus and Ignatow (n 53) 6–7; Zerubavel (n 27) 32–33.

[75] Berkhus and Ignatow (n 53) 6–7; Kaidesoja, Hyyryläinen, and Puustinen (n 1) 529–31; Zerubavel (n 24) 11–21; Berkhus (n 53) 13–14.

[76] Zerubavel (n 27) 34–35.

## 4.2. Sociological analysis of international law and the cognitive turn

The formation, interpretation, and implementation of international law interact with diverse socio-cognitive processes. Thus, for example, negotiations leading to international treaties are affected by socially constructed cognitive frames,[77] and legal classification of social groups (such as indigenous peoples or racial groups) interact with widely held social categorizations.[78] As for implementation, recent behavioural international law scholarship has amply shown that international legal decision-makers are susceptible to the influence of certain cognitive biases.[79] Cognitive-behavioural studies can also shed light on the way many people conceive international law. Significant changes in social theory often herald changes in international legal theory. Such changes may not only influence the way we understand the role of international law but also suggest potential patterns of interpretation or desirable legal strategies to be adopted by international law policy-makers. The remaining parts of this section addresses four primary implications of cognitive studies for the new cognitive-sociological approach to international law.

### 4.2.1. Mind, society, and legal decision-making

The most prominent implication of cognitive literature for the sociological approach to international law concerns the influence of socio-cultural factors on international legal decision-makers. As discussed above, recent social-cognitive studies pay increasing attention to the influence of culture on human cognition.[80] Fiske and Taylor explain in their famous book on social cognition that '[m]any of the central assumptions about how people think about other people turn out to be culturally bound'.[81] Tapping into this relatively recent wave in cognitive literature, cognitive-sociological studies expand and deepen the analysis of societal influence on individuals' mental processes.

Cognitive sociologists underline that human information processing varies cross-culturally, historically, and within cultures.[82] A series of cross-cultural

[77] See, eg, Margherita Melillo, 'Labels as the Visible Part of International Law's Invisible Frames: The Case of the Framework Convention on Tobacco Control as an "Evidence-Based" Treaty' in Andrea Bianchi and Moshe Hirsch (eds), *International Law's Invisible Frames: Social Cognition and Knowledge Production in International Legal Processes* (OUP 2021) 141.

[78] On socio-cognitive categorization and international law, see, eg, Moshe Hirsch, 'Cognitive Sociology, Social Cognition and Coping with Racial Discrimination in International Law' (2019) 30 EJIL 1319, 1325–26, 1328.

[79] Anne van Aaken, 'Behavioral International Law and Economics' (2014) 55 Harvard International Law Journal 421, 439 et seq; Tomer Broude, 'Behavioral International Law' (2015) 163 University of Pennsylvania Law Review 1099, 1136 et seq; Shiri Krebs, 'The Invisible Frames Affecting Wartime Investigations: Legal Epistemology, Metaphors, and Cognitive Biases' in Andrea Bianchi and Moshe Hirsch (eds), *International Law's Invisible Frames: Social Cognition and Knowledge Production in International Legal Processes* (OUP 2021) 124, 129–33.

[80] See Section 3.2.

[81] Fiske and Taylor (n 13) 28.

[82] See, eg, Zerubavel (n 24) 22, 31; Cerulo, Leschziner, and Shepherd (n 29) 63, 64 et seq; Brekhus (n 53) 31, 22.

experiments has shown that people from different cultural systems have different attention patterns. These studies point out, for example, that East Asians and Westerners perceive reality and think about it in different ways.[83] It is worth emphasizing that socio-cognitive patterns vary not only across distinct cultures but also within cultures, for example according to historical periods, sub-cultures, social networks, and in accordance with social roles (like gender or professional roles).[84] Such socio-cognitive characteristics are transmitted to new members of society via social mechanisms, such as socialization or language, and are enforced via social control mechanisms.[85]

The above social-cognitive studies confirm and reinforce the key argument of the sociological approach to international law that social groups significantly influence the behaviour and normative choices of international legal decision-makers (including international organizations' officials or national policy-makers). The new cognitive-sociological perspective underscores that socio-cultural factors affect not only the beliefs and behaviour of legal decision-makers but also their deeply ingrained cognitive patterns through which they perceive reality. Thus, for example, cognitive patterns (such as certain behavioural bias) prevailing in the social group of the particular adjudicator or military commander can affect legal decisions undertaken by such a legal decision-maker; and different patterns of categorization or cognitive schemas can lead them to respond differently to the same factual situations.

### 4.2.2. Deep sociology, unconscious process, and diminished agency

The second implication of cognitive studies for the new sociological approach to international law concerns the dual-process model in social cognition. While the common sociological analysis of international law implicitly assumed a deliberate-conscious legal decision-making process (influenced by socio-cultural factors), the recent cognitive-sociological perspective turns the spotlight to the deeper unconscious layer of social influence. Cultural features pervade both conscious and unconscious mental processes, but the social-cognitive literature emphasizes that processes undertaken below the level of awareness heavily rely on culturally available mental structures.[86] Thus, the recent cognitive-sociological approach

[83] Nisbett and Masuda conclude from a series of studies that East Asians attend to the entire field and background features more than do Westerners, and that Westerners pay more attention to focal objects. Richard Nisbett and Takahiko Masuda, 'Culture and Point of View' (2003) 100 PNAS 1163, 1169. See also Shinobu Kitayama and Ayse Uskul, 'Culture, Mind, and the Brain' (2011) 64 Annual Review of Psychology 419, 435–36; Suparna Choudhury and Ian Gold, 'Mapping the Field of Cultural Neuroscience' (2011) 6 BioSocieties 271, 274. On additional cross-cultural cognitive studies, see Cole and Packer (n 23) 253 et seq.

[84] Eg Zerubavel (n 24), 33; Asia Friedman, 'Toward a Sociology of Perception: Sight, Sex, and Gender' (2011) 5 Cultural Sociology 187.

[85] Eg Zerubavel (n 18) 62–66; Zerubavel (n 24) 14–15; Rydgren (n 19) 228. On learning mental representations, see Augoustinos and others (n 14) 20–21.

[86] See Section 3.3.

to international law alerts us that socio-cognitive patterns (like stereotyped schemas) enter individuals' minds not only through the traditional social channels (eg socialization) but also via less visible mechanisms, such as constant exposure of decision-makers to certain cultural patterns, regular bodily movements, or language.

International legal decision-makers (including adjudicators) are often unaware that their thinking and decisions are affected by culturally infused cognitive structures, like schemas, patterns of categorization, or memory. Once habituated by their social groups to follow some cognitive patterns, legal decision-makers often do not pay attention to alternative cognitive patterns (such as different norms of attention). The new cognitive-sociological conception of legal decision-making tends to underline the constraining force of socio-cognitive patterns on individuals, and corollary points out to the limited freedom of individual decision-makers vis-à-vis their social groups. As elaborated below, coming to terms with this inference concerning the restricted freedom of legal decision-makers may suggest some interpretations of international legal rules.

International criminal behaviour occasionally involves some socio-cognitive patterns. For example, launching an attack where it would knowingly cause excessive incidental loss of life or injury to civilians (compared to the anticipated military advantage) constitutes a war crime.[87] Military commanders' calculations of the expected collateral damage to civilians (and civilian targets) are susceptible to the influence of several cognitive heuristics,[88] prominently 'availability bias'.[89] Accordingly, military commanders' assessments of probabilities are often influenced by their prior experience and familiarity with or memories of previous events (affected, eg, by the mass media's coverage of certain events).[90] The latter factors and risk perceptions are likely to be influenced, inter alia, by the particular decision-maker's distinctive culture concerning the specific risk.[91] Consequently, proportionality assessments undertaken by different military commanders can be influenced by their distinctive cultural systems.[92]

[87] Art 8(2)(b)(iv) of the Rome Statute of the International Criminal Court (adopted 17 July 1998, entered into force 1 July 2002) 2187 UNTS 90 (hereafter 'ICC Statute').

[88] On cognitive biases that are occasionally involved in proportional analysis, see Anne van Aaken, 'The Decision Architecture of Proportionality Analysis: Cognitive Biases and Heuristics' 7–8, 17 et seq (28 March 2019) <http://dx.doi.org/10.2139/ssrn.3364553> accessed 3 December 2023.

[89] Luke A Whittemore, 'Proportionality Decision Making in Targeting: Heuristics, Cognitive Biases, and the Law' (2016) 7 Harvard National Security Journal 577, 619–20. On availability bias, see also Chapter * by Shiri Krebs in this volume.

[90] See, eg, Fiske and Taylor (n 13) 200–01.

[91] Cass R Sunstein, 'Precautions against What? The Availability Heuristic and Cross-Cultural Risk Perception: Risk and the Law' (2005) 57 Alabama Law Review 75, 87–93. See also Chapter 7 by Regina Jefferies in this volume, Section 3.1.

[92] See, eg, Jonathan Hasson and Ariel Slama, 'IHL's Reasonable Military Commander Standard and Culture: Applying the Lessons of ICL and IHRL' (2023) 58 Tulsa Law Review 184, 190–91.

The considerable emphasis placed by international criminal law doctrine on *individual* liability implicitly assumes a substantial measure of human agency and free will.[93] On the other hand, the emphasis placed by cognitive sociology (and particularly the embodied cognition approach) on the constraining influence of deeply entrenched socio-cognitive structures points out that at least in some normative situations, human choice is significantly limited. Such socio-cognitive constraints on individuals' freedom bring to the fore the dilemma regarding the role of the defendant's socio-cognitive background at the sentencing stage. From this perspective, where it is credibly proven that a particular crime directly and significantly involves socio-cognitive patterns dominating the defendant's cultural system (such as a culturally infused bias), one of the primary rationales for criminal punishment—personal retribution—is weakened.[94] In such 'hard cases', tribunals may adopt a broad interpretation of some legal provisions[95] to mitigate the punishment.[96]

### 4.2.3. Critical cognition and tribunals' limited neutrality

The third implication of cognitive studies arises from the considerable role played by Bourdieu's scholarship in cognitive sociology and the critical perspective characterizing his writings. This combination suggests that the new cognitive-sociological approach to international law inclines towards critical international legal theory. Bourdieu's critical attitude and the critical approach to international law share some core assumptions, notably paying special attention to hidden structures, viewing societies as riddled with persistent hierarchies and struggles over different kinds of resources, as well as underscoring intimate links between law, power relations, and politics.[97]

[93] See, eg, Carsten Stahn, *A Critical Introduction to International Criminal Law* (CUP 2019) 157, 419–20. On the links between free will and general criminal responsibility, see Alan Brudner, *Punishment and Freedom: A Liberal Theory of Penal Justice* (OUP 2009) 59.

[94] International criminal tribunals generally consider the objectives of deterrence and personal retribution as the primary objectives of punishment. The jurisprudence of these tribunals also discusses the justifications of public condemnation ('expressivism') and rehabilitation. Sergey Vasiliev, 'Punishment Rationales in International Criminal Jurisprudence: Two Readings of a Non-Question' in Florian Jeßberger and Julia Geneuss (eds), *Why Punish Perpetrators of Mass Atrocities? Purposes of Punishment in International Criminal Law* (CUP 2020) 45, 54–73; Mirko Bagaric and John Morss, 'International Sentencing Law: In Search of a Justification and Coherent Framework' (2006) 6 International Criminal Law Review 191, 206 et seq; Barbora Hola, 'International Sentencing', *Encyclopedia of Criminology and Criminal Justice* (vol 5, Springer 2014) 20643, 2647–48.

[95] The prominent provisions of the ICC law relating to sentencing are Article 78(1) of the Statute, and Rule 145 of the Rules of Procedures and Evidence.

[96] It is worth emphasizing that even in such cases, where tribunals are convinced that the objective of deterrence is paramount, they may consider the defendant's socio-cognitive background and still impose the full penalty.

[97] See, eg, Andrea Bianchi, *International Legal Theories: An Inquiry into Different Ways of Thinking* (OUP 2016) 140 et seq; Fleur Johns, 'Critical International Legal Theory' in Jeffrey L Dunoff and Mark A Pollack (eds), *International Legal Theory: Foundations and Frontiers* (CUP 2022) 133, 140 et seq.

According to Bourdieu, the legal field is a site of confrontation in which interpretative struggles are held and courts choose between the interests of the rival parties.[98] Law presents some cognitive features, including its 'quasi-magical power' related to conferring a particular meaning upon reality, frequently through the production of official categories and schemas of perception.[99] The 'legal habitus'—involving the posture of judges as simply applying the law—is shaped through legal studies and practices of members of the legal profession.[100] Judges conventionally cling to a formalist presentation of the juridical field as a neutral space, in which courts are independent of the rival social groups.[101] In reality, however, judges possess a significant freedom in interpreting legal texts and retain only partial autonomy from politics. Ultimately, they are linked with political and economic power, and their rulings are not likely to disadvantage dominant groups. Judicial interpretations also result from struggles between professional lawyers possessing unequal technical skills and social influence. Thus, law and tribunals not only register the existing structure of power relations but also lock and legitimize it.[102]

The Bourdieusian critical-cognitive approach exposes some weaknesses of international adjudication, turning our attention to often invisible links between international tribunals, global stratification, and socio-cognitive processes. International tribunals are anxious to project an image schema of independent actors engaged in an objective determination of facts and legal interpretation. From the Bourdieusian perspective, however, tribunals are viewed as only partially independent, and are often influenced by dominant international actors; thus, they tend to legitimize existing asymmetric power relations. For example, global courts are inclined to disproportionally protect the dominant position of Western countries and their cultural-cognitive structures (such as categories and language).[103] The dominance of Western 'schemas of perception' in international law can be explained (at least partially) by the privileged position of Western countries in the composition of international tribunals[104] and the relatively inferior

[98] Pierre Bourdieu, 'The Force of Law: Towards Sociology of the Juridical Field' (1987) 38 Hasting Law Journal 814, 817–18, 826, 841–43.

[99] ibid 838–40.

[100] ibid 823.

[101] ibid 819, 823–24, 830, 843–44. See also Dezalay and Madsen (n 64) 443–44.

[102] Bourdieu (n 98) 816–17, 826–27, 841–43.

[103] On the tendency of the ICC to take local cultural knowledge and force it to fit into typical Western concepts and categories, see Joshua Isaak Bishay, 'Cultural Experts at the International Criminal Court (ICC): The Local and the International' (2021) 11 Nordic Journal of International Law and Social Research 103, 115–17, 119. On Western language, categories of thought, and norms that underpin international law, see Salvatore Caserta, 'Western Centrism, Contemporary International Law, and International Courts' (2021) 34 LJIL 321, 324–25.

[104] According to longstanding tradition (and with some few notable exceptions), each of the five permanent members of the Security Council may a have judge in the ICJ (and three out of the five are powerful Western countries); Shabtai Rosenne, 'International Court of Justice (ICJ)'. *Max Planck Encyclopaedia of Public International Law* (June 2006) para 17; S Gozie Ogbodo, 'An Overview of the Challenges Facing the International Court of Justice in the 21st Century' (2012) 18 Annual Survey of International and Comparative Law 93, 106–07, 110.

resources (including expertise) available to weaker countries in international legal proceedings.[105] This cognitive dominance is also facilitated by the disproportionate role of Western universities in the education of international judges,[106] and international lawyers appearing before international courts,[107] as well as the fact that the two working languages in many significant international tribunals are English and French.[108]

The above cognitive-critical approach is conducive to harsh criticism of international tribunals and tends to undermine their legitimacy. Some legal strategies may mitigate power asymmetries in international legal proceedings. From this perspective, tribunals are called, for example, to deviate from their traditional habitus and openly acknowledge in their decisions the asymmetric positions of the rival litigating parties. Deviating from the backgrounded norm of (in)attention that guides tribunals to overlook the parties' asymmetric positions can facilitate the application of special legal rules to reduce such inequalities in legal proceedings. For example, tribunals adjudicating a dispute in a considerably asymmetric setting that involves unclear evidence may apply a special rule of evidence and grant the benefit of the doubt to the weaker party. As for the interpretation of treaty provisions, tribunals encountering such asymmetric settings may adopt the interpretation favouring the disadvantaged party.[109]

### 4.2.4. Cognitive variety and deeply fragmented community

The fourth implication of cognitive studies emerges from the above cultural-cognitive stream and indicates that the new cognitive-sociological approach on international law gravitates towards the pluralist approach in international legal theory. The cultural-cognitive stream in cognitive sociology underlines that different cultures tend to develop different cognitive patterns (eg different norms of attention or memory). Individuals belonging to social groups are socialized and socially pressured to follow cognitive patterns predominating in their social groups.[110] Thus, this approach sensitizes us to the fact international legal decision-makers from different communities often use different lenses (occasionally biased

[105] See, eg, with regard to the World Trade Organization (WTO) tribunals and the ICJ, Vitalius Tumonis, 'Adjudication Fallacies: The Role of International Courts in Interstate Dispute Settlement' (2014) 31 Wisconsin International Law Journal 35, 47–49.

[106] Caserte (n 103) 326.

[107] ibid.

[108] Odile Ammann, 'Language Bias in International Legal Scholarship: Symptoms, Explanations, Implications and Remedies' (2022) 33 EJIL 821, 832–33.

[109] A principle of interpretation that prefers the weaker party is inconsistent with existing customary principles of international treaty law, but certain rules of interpretation resonate with this method. Thus, for instance, the rule of interpretation against the drafter *(contra proferentem)* that commonly has the stronger bargaining position during the negotiations is not new to international law. See, eg, Lord McNair, *The Law of Treaties* (OUP 1961) 464–65; Robert Jennings and Arthur Watt, *Oppenheim's International Law* (9th edn, Longman 1996) 1279.

[110] See Section 4.1.2.

ones) and perceive differently the same factual or normative situation.[111] This vision of international law resonates with some prominent elements of the pluralist approach to international law, referring not only to the multiplicity of legal orders and informal norms in the international system but also to socio-cultural diversity[112] and the plurality of ways to understand reality (that undergird legal pluralism).

Assuming that the international legal systems is deeply fragmented along socio-cognitive lines foregrounds the risk of inter-cultural misunderstandings and cognitive biases in international adjudication. International adjudicators are socialized into different cultures and occasionally employ certain cognitive devices (eg categorization or schema) to perceive evidence, at times to the detriment of a particular litigating party.[113] It is noteworthy that while many national legal systems operate in multi-cultural settings, the international legal system is characterized by intensified multi-cultural characteristics. The above risks of socio-cognitive misunderstandings and biases may undermine the legitimacy of tribunals, and it is particularly acute in the sphere of international criminal law. Judges of international criminal courts are frequently required to process large volumes of information, selectively focus their attention on the 'relevant' facts, and attach a particular meaning to evidence, including the defendants' behaviour from different societies. Applying a particular set of culturally infused lenses may lead to misinterpretations; for example, with regard to discerning the defendant's intention, interpreting interactions between the defendant and the prosecution or judges (eg during cross-examination), or detecting the meaning of a gaze (direct or averted) of a witness socialized in a different cultural system.[114] Although the

[111] PLP Rau and others, 'The Cognitive Bias in Cross-Cultural Design' in E Vanderheiden and CH Mayer (eds), *Mistakes, Errors and Failures across Cultures* (Springer 2020) 455, 458 et seq. On differences regarding negative bias, see Stuart Sorokaa, Patrick Fournierc, and Lilach Nir, 'Cross-National Evidence of a Negativity Bias in Psychophysiological Reactions to News' (2019) PNAS 1888, 1889. See also Jenny Yiend and others, 'Biased Cognition in East Asian and Western Cultures' (2019) Plos One <https://journals.plos.org/plosone/article?id=10.1371/journal.pone.0223358> accessed 3 December 2023.

[112] Frédéric Mégret, 'International Law as a System of Legal Pluralism' in Paul Schiff Berman (ed), *The Oxford Handbook of Global Legal Pluralism* (OUP 2020) 533, 533–36, 541; Bianchi (n 97) 238 et seq. See also Boaventura de Sousa Santos, 'A Map of Misreading: Toward a Postmodern Conception of Law' (1987) 14 Journal of Law and Society 279, 295–98; Nico Krisch, 'Global Legal Pluralism' in Jeffrey L Dunoff and Mark A Pollack (eds), *International Legal Theory: Foundations and Frontiers* (CUP 2022) 240. See also Anthea Roberts, *Is International Law International?* (OUP 2017) xxi et seq.

[113] See, eg, with regard to biases related to attributing mental states (such as intention) to other people, Kevin J Heller, 'The Cognitive Psychology of Mens Rea' (2009) 99 Journal of Criminal Law and Criminology 317, 326; Cristiano Castelfranchi, 'Mind Reading: How and for What?' (2019) 3 Annals of Cognitive Science 86, 105.

[114] On the perception of eye contact by people from different cultural backgrounds, see Jari K Hietanen, 'Eye Contact Perception in the West and East: A Cross-Cultural Study' (2015) 10 Plos One <https://journals.plos.org/plosone/article?id=10.1371/journal.pone.0118094> accessed 3 December 2023. On emotion perception in different cultures, see Xia Fang, Magdalena Rychlowska, and Jens Lange, 'Cross-Cultural and Inter-Group Research on Emotion Perception' (2022) 6 Journal of Cultural Cognitive Science 1, 1–3.

involvement of distinct socio-cognitive styles is visible to some observers, it may constitute a blind spot for some international criminal decision-makers who habitually function in a multi-cultural environment.[115] Non-criminal tribunals (eg the International Court of Justice (ICJ) or International Tribunal for the Law of the Sea (ITLOS)) are also susceptible to some cultural-cognitive misunderstandings and biases.

The above perils pertaining to the functioning of inter-cultural tribunals emphasize the need for legal strategies to cope with such risks. Diversifying the composition of international tribunals (including the prosecutorial or secretarial staff) and constantly reminding adjudicators to use multi-focal lenses may mitigate cultural-cognitive misinterpretations. Having at least one adjudicator socialized into the particularly relevant cultural system is likely to decrease the risk of such deficiencies. A judge from the relevant cultural background may direct the attention of the other judges to the distinctive socio-cognitive patterns occasionally located in other judges' cultural blind fields. The need to apply more responsive multi-focal lenses may involve additional practices, such as frequently inviting cultural expert opinions to shed light on the socio-cognitive features of the particular community.

The above conception of the international system as deeply divided along socio-cognitive lines generates some implications for the structure of international legal regimes. Global legal regimes are much more susceptible to misinterpretation of culturally infused legal provisions and people's behaviours. Controversies related to such differences frequently cannot be resolved in a satisfactory manner and may inhibit international cooperation. These comparative disadvantages of global legal regimes suggest that in many cases, it would not be desirable to promote worldwide governance frameworks that include a unified set of legal rules applied to all member states. The cultural-cognitive perspective suggests that wherever possible, it is advantageous to promote international cooperation in frameworks involving culturally similar state societies ('like-minded states'), often in regional or sub-regional instruments. In cases where global cooperation is essential (eg climate change), it is desirable to establish a global legal regime that combines some uniformly applicable rules with adequate culturally-sensitive provisions (such as 'cultural exceptions', reservations, or 'margin of appreciation').[116]

[115] On the link between habitual behaviour and cultural blind spots, see Section 3.3.

[116] Some further implications of cognitive studies for the sociological approach to international law are briefly discussed in the following section.

## 5. Concluding Remarks and Some Limits of Socio-Cognitive Analysis of International Law

Cognitive-behavioural studies introduce diverse changes into the sociological approach to international law and the discussion above highlights four principal implications. Cognitive studies reinforce the key assumption regarding the influence of socio-cultural factors on international legal decision-makers, revealing that social groups guide not only decision-makers' behaviour but also their perception of factual and normative situations. Furthermore, new social-cognitive studies reveal that people's unconscious processes rely heavily on culturally available mental structures (such as schemas) and international law decision-makers are often unaware of this social influence. The vital role played by Bourdieu's embodied scholarship in cognitive sociology and the critical perspective characterizing his writings indicate that the new cognitive-sociological perspective on international law inclines towards critical approaches in international legal theory (highlighting, eg, cognitive hegemony in international adjudication). Finally, the important role played by cultural-cognitive scholars in the development of cognitive sociology suggests that the new cognitive-sociological analysis of international law gravitates towards legal pluralism in international legal theory (exposing, eg, the risks arising from socio-cognitive differences for the international legal system).

Cognitive studies provide valuable insights that enrich our understanding of the ways international law is constructed and implemented but the above discussion also exposes some weaknesses of the new cognitive-sociological perspective on international law. While the 'conventional' sociological approach examines both the impacts of society on individuals (top-down processes) and the influence of individuals and small groups on society (bottom-up processes), the new cognitive-sociological approach to international law (and prominently, the embodied-cognitive stream) is largely concerned with the first type of social (top-down) processes. The tendency to focus on the influence of social groups on individual legal decision-makers (and mainly on how culture inters into individual minds) can be explained by the leading role of cognitive-psychological studies in the cognitive literature,[117] and the traditional emphasis placed in psychological literature on the individual level.[118] Future research work may deviate from this current tendency and explore bottom-up processes shedding light, for example, on the role of individuals or social movements in constructing widespread cognitive patterns that interact with international law (relating, eg, to gender categorization or cognitive schemas of intellectual property).

[117] See, eg, Barret (n 21) 620.

[118] Social psychology is also focused on the individual level and explores how individuals think, feel, and behave in a social context. See, eg, Saul Kassin, Steve Fein, and Hazel Rose Markus, *Social Psychology* (7th edn, Houghton Mifflin 2008) 5, 8.

The second weakness of the emerging cognitive-sociological approach to international law concerns socio-cognitive change. Socio-cognitive patterns are not immune to change but the new cognitive-sociological perspective is largely orientated towards static analysis, mostly focused on the impacts of existing cognitive features (eg biases) on international legal decision-makers. This static inclination is arguably linked to cognitive psychology literature, suggesting long-term processes of adaptational-functional change.[119] Future studies may engage with dynamic cognitive processes, such as changing schemas (eg relating to race) or evolving categorization of international crimes or legal entities that interact with international law.

Finally, the new cognitive-sociological perspective on international law (and particularly the cultural-cognitive stream) projects an image of the international legal system as profoundly fragmented along cognitive lines, highlighting different perceptions of reality that prevail in different communities. While this literature reveals a significant challenge to international law, it tends to undervalue some similar socio-cognitive patterns prevalent in many regions of the international community. It is worth emphasizing that international law itself also plays a role in fostering widely shared cognitive features and meaning. Thus, for example, international legal rules and institutions occasionally contribute to promoting similar (but not unified) patterns of categorization of or attention to certain activities (such as international crimes) and actors in significant parts of the global system. Future research work may examine developments in different directions; both the impact of socio-cognitive fragmentation on international law and the role of international legal rules and institutions in promoting internationally shared socio-cognitive features (eg through international socialization or social pressure).

[119] In the cognitive-psychological literature, such changes are often aimed at managing external challenges relating, eg, to self-protection or disease avoidance. Steven Neuberg and Mark Schaller, 'Evolutionary Social Cognition' in Eugene Borgida and John Bargh (eds), *APA Handbook of Personality and Social Psychology* (vol 1, APA 2015) 2; Cecilia Heyes, 'New Thinking: The Evolution of Human Cognition' (2012) 367 Philosophical Transactions of the Royal Society 2091, 2093–94. See also Galotti (n 20) 21.

# 10

# International Judicial Habitus

## Pierre Bourdieu and the Cognitive Turn

*Mikael Rask Madsen and Salvatore Caserta*

### 1. Introduction

Pierre Bourdieu's sociology and analytical tools have become increasingly central to international law scholarship. This has notably been the case in the context of studies of law and globalization,[1] where they have inspired works on the rise of international commercial arbitration,[2] the European Union,[3] European human rights,[4] international criminal law,[5] and the authority of the international judiciary.[6] Many of these studies employ the Bourdieusian notions of field and capital to depict how new social spaces of law are created. However, one key concept of the Bourdieusian sociological toolbox remains underused in most law-related projects: *habitus*. There are many reasons for this, but the main one is that the existing literature has been mainly interested in developing structural analysis of the emergence of the new spaces of law and less focused on cognitive dimensions.

This chapter is a first stab at remedying this gap, while contributing to the broader project of applying insights from cognitive sociology and behavioural studies to international legal theory.[7] The sociology of Bourdieu indeed has strong relations to cognitive sociology,[8] particularly for the part in which it develops a

[1] See, among others, Didier Bigo and Mikael R Madsen, 'Introduction to the Symposium "A Different Reading of the International": Pierre Bourdieu and International Studies' (2011) 5 International Political Sociology 219; Rebecca Adler-Nissen (ed), *Bourdieu in International Relations: Rethinking Key Concepts in IR* (Routledge 2013).

[2] Yves Dezalay and Bryant G Garth, *Dealing in Virtue: International Commercial Arbitration and the Construction of a Transnational Legal Order* (University of Chicago Press 1996).

[3] Antoine Vauchez, 'The Force of a Weak Field: Law and Lawyers in the Government of the European Union (For a Renewed Research Agenda)' (2008) 2 International Political Sociology 128.

[4] Mikael R Madsen, 'Reflexivity and the Construction of the International Object: The Case of Human Rights' (2011) 5 International Political Sociology 259.

[5] Mikkel Jarle Christensen, 'The Creation of an Ad Hoc Elite: The Value of International Criminal Law Expertise on a Global Market' in Kevin Jon Heller and others (eds), *The Oxford Handbook of International Criminal Justice* (OUP 2020); John Hagan, *Justice in the Balkans: Prosecuting War Crimes in the Hague Tribunal* (University of Chicago Press 2003).

[6] See, generally, Karen J Alter, Laurence R Helfer, and Mikael Rask Madsen (eds), *International Court Authority* (OUP 2018).

[7] See Anne van Aaken and Moshe Hirsch's Introduction to this volume.

[8] See Omar Lizardo, 'Pierre Bourdieu as Cognitive Sociologist' in Wayne H Brekhus and Gabriel Ognatow (eds), *The Oxford Handbook of Cognitive Sociology* (OUP 2019) 65.

Mikael Rask Madsen and Salvatore Caserta, *International Judicial Habitus* In: *International Legal Theory and the Cognitive Turn*. Edited by: Anne van Aaken and Moshe Hirsch, Oxford University Press.
 DOI: 10.1093/9780198909293.003.0011

theory of embodied cognition, for which bodily structures and experiences (i.e., perceptions, categorizations, morality, social interactions, and forms of reasoning) are considered central elements of the cognitive activity of human beings.[9]

We are particularly interested in, firstly, clarifying the notion of habitus and, secondly, exploring its potential uses in international legal theory and empirical analysis as a form of embodiment of the cognitive unconscious.[10] In this view, the body constitutes the site through which individuals internalize the external world, thus transforming the inputs coming from the environment into dispositions that implicitly and unconsciously guide behaviour.[11] This is part of the broader theory of action characterizing the sociology of Bourdieu for which human behaviour is largely driven by habits and directly linked to the unconscious reproduction of behavioural patterns and/or schemes deemed appropriate within the context of the social fields in which action takes place. This, in turn, means that in order to understand the behaviour of international legal actors, one must examine the cognitive patterns characterizing certain legal communities and the social schemes unconsciously influencing behaviour and decisions.[12]

More specifically, we approach habitus as an analytical tool to interpret and explain the operations of the international *homo juridicus*, using the case of international judges. Accordingly, we develop a particular object of inquiry, *international judicial habitus*, as a distinct, yet socially constructed, type of legal behaviour which influence international judicial practices. To conduct this analysis, the chapter proceeds as follows. Section 2 outlines the trajectory of Bourdieusian sociology in studies of international law and politics. Section 3 defines habitus, explaining its cognitive origins and how it can be used to understand the international judiciary. Section 4 illustrates some central issues related to how to study international judicial habitus in practice. Section 5 concludes by summarizing the main findings of the chapter.

## 2. Bourdieu and International (Legal) Scholarship

Compared to other fields of study, where Bourdieusian sociology had a rapid and significant impact, it took much longer for Bourdieu's insights to gain a foothold in international legal and political studies. This was partly due to Bourdieu's overwhelming focus on French society and the French state, as well as the then-limited

[9] Karen A Cerulo, 'Embodied Cognition: Sociology's Role in Bridging Mind, Brain, and Body' in Wayne H Brekhus and Gabriel Ognatow (eds), *The Oxford Handbook of Cognitive Sociology* (OUP 2019) 81.

[10] Lizardo (n 8) 7.

[11] Michael Strand and Omar Lizardo, 'Beyond World Images: Belief as Embodied Action in the World' (2015) 33 Sociological Theory 1, 44–70.

[12] See also Chapter 9 by Mosche Hirsch in this volume.

role played by international political sociology both in law and international relations (IR) approaches.[13] As concerns law specifically, Bourdieu's outline of a sociology of law initially had a limited effect as it was constructed around a civil law conception of law, which did not travel well to the common-law world where courts and lawyers, rather than state bureaucracies, were the central objects of inquiry. Some IR scholars discovered Bourdieu in the late 1980s using Bourdieusian insights in a central debate between positivists and post-positivists.[14] This debate chiefly revolved around questions of epistemology, and Bourdieusian insights were employed to challenge the then-dominant realist worldview of an international anarchical society constituted by antagonistic sovereign states.[15] Bourdieu was also instrumental in operationalizing the so-called 'practice turn' in IR,[16] according to which international phenomena are understood as bundles of individual and collective practices which produce specific outcomes, and ultimately constitute social reality.[17] To this day, a branch of IR practice theory largely relies on Bourdieu.[18] In addition, the now booming field of international political sociology builds in part on Bourdieusian approaches.[19]

It is, however, in the field of the sociology of law and globalization that Bourdieu has contributed most significantly to developing a novel research paradigm. In 1996, Yves Dezalay and Bryant Garth paved the road with their seminal book *Dealing in Virtue*, in which they studied the emergence of a new elite of transnational legal professionals in the area of international commercial arbitration. They used Bourdieusian theory to depict both the composition of this new elite, using the notion of *capital*, and the social space of oppositions in which they developed their practices, using the notion of a *transnational field*.[20] Building on Dezalay and Garth's

[13] For a more detailed explanation of this initial weak reception, see Mikael R Madsen and Yves Dezalay, 'The Force of Law and Lawyers: Pierre Bourdieu and the Reflexive Sociology of Law' (2012) 8 Annual Review of Law and Social Sciences 433.

[14] Adler-Nissen (n 1) 7.

[15] Didier Bigo and Rob BJ Walker, 'Political Sociology and the Problem of the International' (2007) 35 Millennium 725, 728.

[16] Vincent Pouliot, 'Methodology: Putting Practice Theory into Practice' in Rebecca Adler-Nissen (ed), *Bourdieu in International Relations: Rethinking Key Concepts in IR* (Routledge 2013), 45–58; Vincent Pouliot, 'The Logic of Practicality: A Theory of Practice of Security Communities' (2008) 62 International Organization 257.

[17] Jérémie Cornut, 'The Practice Turn in International Relations Theory' in *Oxford Research Encyclopedia of International Studies* (OUP 2015), 467–605.

[18] See, for instance, Jens Meierhenrich, 'The Practice of International Law: A Theoretical Analysis' (2013) 76 Law and Contemporary Problems 1.

[19] Bigo and Madsen (n 1).

[20] Dezalay and Garth (n 2). Subsequent works also relied on Bourdieusian sociology when explaining the battles for power and democratization in Latin America and Asia. See Yves Dezalay and Bryant G Garth, *The Internationalization of Palace Wars: Lawyers, Economists, and the Contest to Transform Latin American States* (University of Chicago Press 2002); Mikael R Madsen, *La Genèse de l'Europe des Droits de l'Homme: Enjeux Juridiques et Stratégies d'Etat (France, Grande-Bretagne et Pays Scandinaves, 1945-1970)* (Presses Universitaires de Strasbourg 2010); Yves Dezalay and Bryant G Garth, *Asian Legal Revivals: Lawyers in the Shadow of the Empire* (University of Chicago Press 2010).

interpretations of Bourdieu, a next generation of scholarship focused on the formation of more institutionalized international legal orders such as the European Union and European human rights.[21] In 2012, a broad programme was outlined in the article *The Force of Law and Lawyers: Pierre Bourdieu and the Reflexive Sociology of Law*, which emphasized the idea of studying international legal fields through the lens of the agency of international and transnational law.[22] A large set of studies followed, many focused on international organizations and courts.[23]

Notwithstanding this interest and surge in publications using variations of Bourdieusian sociology to critically study international law and the international judiciary, the notion of habitus is yet to be fully unpacked in the context of studies of law and legal theory. Some attempts have been made in the area of legal philosophy to revitalize legal realism.[24] More recently, we ourselves built a theory of international judging as characterized by situated and bounded rationality using Bourdieusian insights.[25] In this work, we outlined an interpretative framework theory of judicial behaviour which conceives international judicial action and institutional practices as a consequence of the interplay between the internal and external dynamics of the international judiciary.[26] More specifically, the theory proposes that the internal (legal/institutional) and external (contextual) aspects of international adjudication cannot be studied in separation; and that, accordingly, international courts and judges are constrained by their social contexts, while influencing and shaping such contexts through judicial practices.[27] This, in turn, means that, while formally independent, international courts are never

[21] See generally Antoine Vauchez, *Brokering Europe: Lawyers and the Formation of a Transnational Polity* (CUP 2015).

[22] Madsen and Dezalay (n 13).

[23] For example, John Hagan and Ron Levi, 'Justiciability as Field Effect: When Sociology Meets Human Rights' (2007) 22 Sociological Forum 372; Antonin Cohen and Mikael R Madsen, 'Cold War Law: Legal Entrepreneurs and the Emergence of a European Legal Field (1945–1965)' in Volkmar Gessner and David Nelken (eds), *European Ways of Law: Towards a European Sociology of Law* (Hart Publishing 2007), 175–201; Guillaume Sacriste and Antoine Vauchez, 'The Force of International Law: Lawyers' Diplomacy on the International Scene in the 1920s' (2007) 32 Law and Social Inquiry 83; Julie Bailleux, *Penser l'Europe par le Droit: l'Invention du Droit Communautaire en France (1945–1990)* (Dalloz 2014); Mikkel Jarle Christensen, 'The Emerging Sociology of International Criminal Courts: Between Global Restructurings and Scientific Innovations' (2015) 63 Current Sociology 825; Salvatore Caserta, *International Courts in Latin American and the Caribbean: Foundations and Authority* (OUP 2020); Nicholas Haagensen, 'Legal Strategies at the Governance Precipice: Transnational Lawyers in the European Union's Sovereign Debt Crisis (2010–2012)' [2023] Law and Social Inquiry 1.

[24] Jakob VH Holtermann and Mikael R Madsen, 'European New Legal Realism and International Law: How to Make International Law Intelligible' (2015) 28 LJIL 211.

[25] Salvatore Caserta and Mikael R Madsen, 'The Situated and Bounded Rationality of International Courts: A Structuralist Approach to International Adjudicative Practices' (2022) 35 LJIL 931.

[26] ibid.

[27] ibid 934. This goes back to the idea put forward by Alf Ross, for whom doctrinal law and practices are rationalized ideology, and who posits that in order to understand such ideology, researchers need to explain both the internal and external perspectives. See Alf Ross and Henrik Palmer Olsen, 'The 25th Anniversary of the Pure Theory of Law' (2011) 31 Oxford Journal of Legal Studies 243.

entirely autonomous. They are instead marked by a situated and bounded rationality, which influences how they articulate the world into a legal language that can be understood and accepted in given historical and socio-political contexts.[28]

The underlying epistemological logic of the argument relies on Bourdieu, particularly for the part that argues that international courts can only be made intelligible if one shifts the object of study from the normativity of law to the operationalization of law within one or more specific legal fields. In other words, we have argued that what researchers must study are the very conditions that make the production of legal normativity in society possible through, for instance, courts.[29] Following these ideas, the research focus changes from judicial behaviour as such to the study of judicial practices and their making. This entails transgressing the conventional distinction between institutions and their context,[30] between the internal and external dimensions of law and institutions,[31] and between agency and structure.[32] Put simply, it is a call for a basic reflexive study of agents, institutions, and broader historical and cultural dynamics to understand judicial habitus and the resulting practices.[33]

## 3. International Judicial Habitus and International Legal Theory

The cited programme for understanding the situated and bounded rationality of courts has primarily been outlined so far as a theoretical one; and the articulation of how to empirically approach such judicial practices has not yet been fully worked out, particularly for what concerns habitus. Therefore, in what follows we further unpack the notion of international judicial habitus and explain how this can be employed in empirical explorations of international judges and how their practices come about.

Our theory builds on the basic assumption that international adjudication is shaped by both social and psychological processes that operate as a form of double structuration of judicial practices. It also suggests that judicial practices can be further understood through the notion of international judicial habitus. Habitus, however, is one of the most complex notions in the Bourdieusian theoretical arsenal. Since its initial formulations, it seemed capable of contributing to

28 Caserta and Madsen (n 25). On the limited independence of international tribunals, see Chapter 9 by Hirsch in this volume (Section 4.2.3).

29 As argued in Pierre Bourdieu, 'The Force of Law: Toward a Sociology of the Juridical Field' (1987) 38 Hastings Law Journal 817.

30 Alter, Helfer, and Madsen (n 6).

31 HLA Hart, *The Concept of Law* (OUP 2012).

32 Keith Dowding, 'Agency and Structure: Interpreting Power Relationships' (2008) 1 Journal of Power 21.

33 The notion of reflexivity in this regard has a specific meaning. See Mikael R Madsen, 'Reflexivity and the Construction of the International Object: The Case of Human Rights' (2011) 5 International Political Sociology 259.

theoretical debates about action and identity, yet it nevertheless remains somewhat underexplained. While Paul DiMaggio defined it as a 'kind of theoretical *deus ex machina*',[34] others dismissed it as too fuzzy an idea[35] and/or as part of an overly deterministic and static conception of social action.[36] In what follows, we try to first clarify what habitus actually seeks to explain; and then show how it can be used by international legal scholars to study judicial and, more generally, legal practices.

Probably the best definition of habitus was provided by Bourdieu in his book *Logic of Practice*, where he defined habitus as:

> Systems of durable, transposable dispositions, *structured structures* predisposed to function as *structuring structures*, that is, as principles which generate and organize practices and representations that can be objectively adapted to their outcomes without presupposing a conscious aiming at ends or an express mastery of the *operations* necessary in order to attain them. Objectively 'regulated' and 'regular' without being in any way the product of obedience to rules, they can be collectively orchestrated without being the product of the organizing action of a conductor.[37]

A simpler, yet still precise and helpful, definition was provided in the introduction to the English translation of *La force du droit* (*The Force of Law*), where habitus is defined as:

> the habitual, patterned ways of understanding, judging, and acting which arise from our particular position as members of one or several social fields, and from our particular trajectory in the social structure.[38]

What emerges from these definitions is that habitus is more than an intellectual structure of perception. Rather, it is a semi-conscious and embodied set of points of orientation acquired through long processes of practical engagement and other psychological processes related to making sense of the world from the perspective of agents' personal trajectories through one or more fields.[39] The logic is that action is possible but within limits set by pre-constituted sensibilities, embodied schemes of perception, and broader social structures.[40] In other

[34] Paul DiMaggio, 'Review Essay: On Pierre Bourdieu' (1979) 6 American Journal of Sociology 1460.
[35] Dennis H Wrong, 'The Oversocialized Conception of Man in Modern Sociology' in NJ Smelser and WT Smelser (eds), *Personality and Social System* (John Wiley & Sons 1963), 183–93.
[36] Richard Jenkins, 'Pierre Bourdieu and the Reproduction of Determinism' (1982) 16 Sociology 270.
[37] Pierre Bourdieu, *The Logic of Practice* (Stanford UP 1990) 53. Other definitions are provided in earlier works. See, for instance, Pierre Bourdieu, *Outline of a Theory of Practice* (CUP 1977) 72.
[38] Bourdieu (n 29) 811.
[39] C Michael Williams, 'Culture: Elements toward an Understanding of Charisma in International Relations' in Rebecca Adler-Nissen (ed), *Bourdieu in International Relations: Rethinking Key Concepts in IR* (Routledge 2013), 131–47.
[40] Bourdieu, *The Logic of Practice* (n 37).

words, habitus disposes actors towards certain structures of recognition and action.[41]

Another angle from which to understand habitus is through the ideas of embodiment and/or embodied cognition briefly introduced in Section 1 of this chapter. Habitus allows researchers to explore both how the body inhabits the social world and how the social world infiltrates the body, shaping action and beliefs. In Bourdieu's own words, the habitus constitutes 'a socialised body. A structured body, a body which has incorporated the immanent structures of the world or of a particular sector of that world—a field—and which structures the perception of that world as well as action in that world'.[42] This is perhaps the most direct linkage between habitus and cognitive sociology, namely the embodiment of broader social structures in the individual, often expressed through ways of 'standing, speaking, walking, and thereby feeling and thinking'.[43] Similarly, we argue, *judging* is an expression of social structures embodied in the practices of the judge.

From all this, it follows that individual action can only be made intelligible by investigating how such action is produced through social structures and schemes of perception that sub-consciously influence actors. In this way, habitus becomes an objective structure in itself. As Bourdieu put it, habitus is 'the objectivity of the subjective'.[44] Yet, habitus is not merely an objective *structured structure* but also a *structuring structure*, as it has broader (external) effects on the social world. In this regard, habitus is a structure that generates practical action in itself.[45] This is because the objective structures in which action takes place are themselves a product of historical practices that have been produced, reproduced, and transformed by other historical practices, which in turn were produced by the structures that habitus tends to reproduce.[46] This is at the core of the reflexivity advocated by Bourdieu in terms of the co-constitutive nature of structure and agency in making and shaping society.

It is from here that Bourdieu's notion of habitus contributes to discussions about agency in international society. Habitus is transformative and/or generative of potential actions, which themselves are often constrained through social demands indirectly imposed upon individuals by society. In other words, habitus is a transformative cognitive 'tool' that allows individuals to reproduce the social conditions for their behaviour: it shapes behaviours, fitting them to particular social settings, while maintaining unpredictability. Habitus is, in fact, more than mere mechanical

[41] Vincent Pouliot, *International Security in Practice: The Politics of NATO-Russia Diplomacy* (vol 113, CUP 2010).

[42] Pierre Bourdieu, *Practical Reason: On the Theory of Action* (Stanford UP 1998) 81.

[43] Bourdieu, *The Logic of Practice* (n 37) 70.

[44] See Bourdieu, *The Logic of Practice* (n 37).

[45] Rooted in the genetic structuralism of Jean Piaget and thus in (post-Kantian) neo-structuralism, as argued in Omar Lizardo, 'The Cognitive Origins of Bourdieu's Habitus' (2004) 34 Journal for the Theory of Social Behaviour 375, 380.

[46] Bourdieu, *The Logic of Practice* (n 37) 83.

reproduction of existing structures.[47] Yet, while allowing for individual agency and therefore change, habitus also predisposes individuals towards certain structured forms of behaviour as it is 'an objective basis for regular modes of behaviour, and thus for the regularity of modes of practices, and if practices can be predicted ... this is because the effect of the habitus in the agents who are equipped with it will behave in a certain way in certain circumstances'.[48] It must, however, be underlined that the logic of habitus is not one of predictable regularity of behaviour but 'of vagueness, of the more-or-less, which defines one's ordinary relation to the world'.[49]

What Bourdieu is proposing is, therefore, a holistic theory of social action marked by co-constitutive processes that result in what he termed 'a practical sense' of social life. Seen from this dual perspective, habitus is thus the result of both social (external) and psychological (internal) processes, which are—and cannot be—separate processes. In other words, habitus reflects the dialectic processes of '*internalization of externality*' and '*externalization of internality*'.[50]

This in turn means that social practices—even those that seem straightforward and enacted through presumably rational decisions—are only partially determined by the rational will of agents. Practices are in part determined by the (past) objective structures in which they are produced.[51] In other words, practices are constructed and enacted 'in relation to a system of objective potentialities, immediately inscribed in the present, things to do or not to do, to say or not to say, in relation to a *forthcoming* reality which ... puts itself forward with an urgency and a claim to existence excluding all deliberations'.[52] This further means that practices are a result of the relation between socially constituted systems of cognitive structures (habitus) and the socially structured context in which the interests of agents are defined. It is this interaction between internal and external factors—'history turned into nature'[53] and/or 'the forgetting of history which history itself produces by incorporating the objective structures it produces'[54]—that generate regularities, rules, and appropriate behaviours. As Bourdieu put it: 'habitus is the universalizing mediation which causes an individual agent's practices, without either explicit reason or signifying intent, to be none the less "sensible" and "reasonable"'.[55]

Further constraining individual action are the interactions with other individuals in specific settings. Relevant for our purpose is what Bourdieu refers to as the *hysteresis effect* of social interaction. This is implied in the logic constituting habitus

[47] Pierre Bourdieu, *Sociology in Question* (vol 18, SAGE 1993) 87.
[48] Pierre Bourdieu, *In Other Words: Essays toward a Reflexive Sociology* (Stanford UP 1990).
[49] ibid 78.
[50] Bourdieu, *The Logic of Practice* (n 37) 72.
[51] ibid.
[52] ibid 76.
[53] ibid 79.
[54] ibid.
[55] ibid.

and it entails that practices receive a somewhat negative sanction if they are too distant from the overall logic of the field in which they are enacted.[56] Habitus is, in some ways, a social skill-set, as it partly reproduces existing structures, while being enacted in a social setting. Put differently, the logic of habitus sheds light on the legitimating processes of practices constituted of 'the production of a commonsense world endowed with the *objectivity* secured by consensus on the meaning (*sens*) of practices',[57] an element of key importance to understand the international judiciary and its functioning. To give an example, a judge continuously and consistently dissenting with the majority on the bench will inevitably be marginalized over time. However, a judge who only occasionally does not adapt to the dominant positions will be able to dissent without being marginalized. Here, the combination of hysteresis and legitimation becomes obvious.[58]

This does not mean that habitus necessarily leads to an increasing degree of social uniformity. Bourdieu acknowledges the possibility of differences and diversity among the members of a given social grouping.[59] Habitus differs to the extent that individual trajectories differ: 'Just as no two individual histories are identical so no two individual habituses [*sic*] are identical.'[60] What, however, becomes a central element of sociological analysis is the collective nature of habitus in terms of socialization processes at international courts, for example, where the individually, socially acquired viewpoints are challenged and potentially transformed in the specific interactions taking place in the deliberation room. However, rather than simply assuming that the individual will succumb to a dominant culture, the analytical interest is to explore how the individual fits within past and present social structures, while at the same time shaping new structures of thought by the combination of cognitive structures accumulated in the past and the effects of interaction.

These interlinkages between the past, the present, and the future are a reason for cautioning against deploying habitus as a stand-alone concept. It is necessary to integrate it with the rest of the Bourdieusian toolkit to discover the *modus operandi* from which habitus itself arises. Only in this way is it possible to understand this (at first glance obscure) principle of action, which in Bourdieu's own words 'lies neither in structures nor in consciousness, but rather in the relation of immediate proximity between objective structures and embodied structures in

56 ibid 78.

57 ibid 80.

58 This question concerns a much broader debate in psychology about how dominant narratives can influence, and even control, decision-making. Part of the explanation is the fear of isolation when confronting dominant narratives or perception. See, for instance, Burton M Atkins, 'Judicial Behavior and Tendencies towards Conformity in a Three Member Small Group: A Case Study of Dissent Behavior on the US Court of Appeals' (1973) 54 Social Science Quarterly 1, 41.

59 Diane Reay Diane, '"It's All Becoming a Habitus": Beyond the Habitual Use of Habitus in Educational Research' (2004) 25 British Journal of Sociology of Education 4, 434.

60 Bourdieu (n 48) 46.

habitus'.[61] While this is true for any study of habitus, we argue that it becomes particularly pronounced when dealing with judicial habitus at international courts. The ordinary collective socialization into legal thinking and logic is complicated at the international level of law by the fact that international legal actors have different national and professional backgrounds, languages, legal cultures, and social networks.[62] Although they come together as jurists, their ways of becoming jurists have been marked by different, mostly national, pathways.

A study by Madsen explores the educational capital of international judges in order to understand the extent to which certain visions of international law produced at leading academic centres such as Oxbridge, Paris, and US Ivy League universities dominate.[63] Conducting a comparative analysis of the judges at nine international courts based in Africa, Europe, Latin America, and the Caribbean and operating in three different domains—human rights, market law, and global law—the analysis demonstrates that Western judges typically are nationally trained and endowed with particular perceptions of international law from those states and legal cultures. Yet, global south judges tend to have their highest degrees from leading Western universities and thereby reinforce an imbalance in understandings of international law. At global courts, jurists can come together as international judges, particularly because a dominant and socially constructed set of ideas of international law prevails. At Western regional courts like the European international courts of the Council of Europe and the European Union, however, the interaction is marked more strongly by different national traditions.

It is, however, not sufficient to only explore educational capital. We need to understand other forms of capital and the status of that capital—how it is capitalized in different fields, for example legal fields. A brief comment on the notions of field and capital is necessary for further unpacking habitus. Conceptually, a Bourdieusian field is a space of practice marked by an internal division of labour that reflects both the various positions of the actors at play in it and the actors' different ties to other fields. The actors' relationships within a field can be characterized as a network of objective relations between positions, which provide both social continuity and the possibility of the construction of new practices. The positions within the field are objectively defined by the occupants' present and potential situation in the structure of the distribution of power, a positioning in part determined by their capitals.[64]

[61] Pierre Bourdieu, *The State Nobility* (Polity Press 1996) 38.

[62] Leigh Swigarth and Daniel Terris, 'Who Are International Judges?' in Cesare Romano and others (eds), *The Oxford Handbook of International Adjudication* (OUP 2014), 619–38.

[63] See Mikael R Madsen, 'Who Rules the World: The Educational Capital of the International Judiciary' (2018) 3 UC Irvine Journal of International, Transnational and Comparative Law 97.

[64] Pierre Bourdieu and Loic JD Wacquant, *An Invitation to Reflexive Sociology* (University of Chicago Press 1992).

Such a field approach emphasizes how international legal practices are shaped by conflicting social interests, classes, networks, and cultures, and thus by socio-legal struggles over domination and meaning. Put differently, the creation of autonomous spaces of international law practice entails examining legal agents as part of transnational power elites;[65] that is to say, agents embedded in national and international society directly or indirectly battling over the structuration of a given field of law.[66] While this opens the door to a broader analysis, in this chapter we only explore the more subjective level. But, at this more subjective level, habitus and capital are particularly linked as it is the capital of the actor that allows for their visions to be put forward in the field.

The analytical challenge of studying international legal fields is that agents are rather schizophrenic, as noted by Dezalay and Garth.[67] International elites, like international lawyers and judges, are marked by a certain (objectively speaking) double or triple agency, as they pursue both national and international careers and thus adopt multiple strategies to impose themselves among and across fields. It is for these reasons that we suggest using habitus in combination with the Bourdieusian notion of capital to compare the habitus of different actors and explore how they nevertheless form a collective at international courts.

Bourdieu viewed capital(s) as objectively valorized competences in given social fields. For example, international judges have juridical capital, which is a particular form of objectified and codified capital providing jurists with the symbolic power to interpret and practise law.[68] Yet, different international judges have relatively different types of capital acquired prior to joining the international bench. Some have chiefly legal academic capital; others have capital derived from engagement in diplomacy and politics or from engagement in legal practice as judges or attorneys prior to being appointed.

All of the above means that the social space in which international judges operate is shaped by how the holders of these relatively different types of capital compete for dominance in their interpretation of the law and production of 'juristic truth'. In this regard, we hypothesize a clear correlation between the accumulation of capital through individual trajectories and the positions taken by international judges on given issues when acting as judges. This argument is based on the premise that the accumulation of resources and capital, together with the professional position occupied by given judges within a field, ultimately shape the habitus and schemes

[65] Niilo Kauppi and Mikael R Madsen, 'Transnational Power Elites: The New Professionals of Governance, Law and Security' in Niilo Kauppi and Mikael R Madsen (eds), *Transnational Power Elites: The New Professionals of Governance, Law and Security* (Routledge 2013) 1.

[66] Madsen and Dezalay (n 13).

[67] Yves Dezalay, 'Les Courtiers de l'International: Héritiers Cosmopolites, Mercenaires de l'Impérialisme et Missionnaires de l'Universel' (2004) 151–52 Actes de la Recherche en Sciences Sociales 5.

[68] Caserta and Madsen (n 25).

of individual judges in terms of their legal views and orientations. As cognitive schemes form a mental heuristic to reduce the load of cognitive process and increase decision-making efficiency,[69] the above learned or accumulated cognitive schemas of international judges make the difficult mental tasks involved in adjudication more doable. For these reasons, it is likely that the way an international judge or a lawyer will, for instance, view a legal problem is influenced by their social and professional background.

This idea is corroborated by previous empirical studies on the international judiciary. For instance, Shai Dothan and Gregor Maučec have shown that former diplomats are generally softer on states. This suggests that in adjudicatory practices of judges who have a diplomatic trajectory, the understanding of what is reasonable state behaviour differs from other judges who, for example, have a background in the judiciary or academia.[70] Madsen has found that courts lacking judges with a background in politics and diplomacy often lose sight of the political fragility of their institution and tend to overreach and trigger pushback or backlash.[71] Somewhat similar to Dothan and Maučec, this suggests that an appreciation of the interplay of international law and politics is greater among judges with a background in diplomacy. They simply have a heightened interest in this matter and a different concept of the relationship to politics. Ezgi Yildiz has noted how individual characteristics of judges can lead them to take on different roles in the collective decision-making process, distinguishing between judges as arbitrators, entrepreneurs, and delineators.[72] Within her categories, former diplomats are more likely to take on an arbitrational role due to their shared experiences and perception of the necessity of compromising in diplomacy.

The outcome of the competing visions of international judges in terms of international judicial practices is ultimately the result of a power play. Bourdieu's notion of symbolic power helps to explain this game and how competition among actors structures international legal fields and outcomes. Symbolic power is the power of transforming the world by changing the words naming it, and thus producing new categories and visions of the world within a given field.[73] In other words, symbolic power is part of the struggle to define reality itself, in our case law, in which agents invest time and resources in their battle with other actors to impose their own

[69] See Chapter 13 by Ruti G Teitel and Shreya Shankar in this volume.

[70] Gregor Maučec and Shai Dothan, 'The Effects of International Judges' Personal Characteristics on Their Judging' (2022) 35 LJIL 887.

[71] Mikael R Madsen, 'The Legitimization Strategies of International Courts: The Case of the European Court of Human Rights' in Michal Bobek (ed), *Selecting Europe's Judges: A Critical Review of the Appointment Procedures to the European Courts* (OUP 2015), 259–78.

[72] Ezgi Yildiz, 'A Court with Many Faces: Judicial Characters and Modes of Norm Development in the European Court of Human Rights' (2020) 31 EJIL 73.

[73] Bourdieu, 'The Force of Law' (n 29).

socially inherited visions of the world, which themselves are cognitive categories of perception.[74]

The distribution of symbolic power within a given field is linked to the capital held and positions occupied by its agents, a fact that in turn means that the actual configuration of any legal field is historically contingent. In other words, international law and politics are sites of continuous power struggles where the stakes (both symbolic and material) are in constant evolution. Judicial habitus results from these various interactions. The outcomes of this analysis relate directly to symbolic power as it is an attempt by agents to define the world, building on their socially acquired points of orientation in law and life; that is, their habitus.

## 4. International Legal Habitus in Practice

While the previous section attempted to delineate the multifaceted notion of habitus, in this section we turn to the more practical and methodological dimensions of using habitus in empirical legal studies. As an empirical object of inquiry, the notion of judicial habitus requires the development of an analysis able to capture the double nature of judicial practices in terms of positional and dispositional logics. In other words, there is a need to understand the correlation between positions and dispositions. In both cases, this can be done by examining the social and professional trajectories of the individuals that populate given social fields since individual and structural developments are inscribed in these trajectories. The goal must be to understand the 'complicity between two states of the social ... between history objectified in the forms of structures and mechanisms ... and the history incarnated in bodies'.[75] The objective is to produce 'a science of the social world that cannot be reduced either to a social phenomenology or to a social physics'.[76] The goal, basically, is to create a single analysis considering both social structures and the actions taking place within those structures. As already suggested, what links these two dimensions is the notion of habitus.

At the positional level, the sociology of Bourdieu is often used to create a social topology in terms of an analysis of relative positions and objective relations between different positions in the field.[77] The approach of Bourdieu—explicated in the notion of the field—is fundamentally relational as it is the relations that constitute social spaces. To convert the theoretical claim into empirical approaches, a number of methods have been developed to capture social relations and

[74] Vincent Pouliot and Frederic Merand, 'Bourdieu's Concepts: Political Sociology in International Relations' in Rebecca Adler-Nissen (ed), *Bourdieu in International Relations: Rethinking Key Concepts in IR* (Routledge 2013) 24.
[75] Pierre Bourdieu, *Pascalian Meditations* (Polity 2000) 150.
[76] Bourdieu, 'The Force of Law' (n 29) 25.
[77] Pierre Bourdieu, 'Social Space and Symbolic Power' (1989) 7 Sociological Theory 14.

correlations.[78] The best-known quantitative approach in this regard is Multiple Correspondence Analysis (MCA), which is a statistical model for mapping the dimensions of social spaces (fields) against the types of capitals (i.e., economic, cultural, educational, social, political, and juridical) that agents possess in the space.[79] MCA helps to visualize relations among agents in a social field as objective relations determined by the distribution of particular resources (capital). The model seeks thereby to discover relational social structures that, while *prima facie* hidden by the dominant narrative (*doxa*) of given fields, are central to explaining social dynamics.

While an MCA of the international judiciary has not yet been published, Mikkel Jarle Christensen has used MCA to map the elites that populate the field of international criminal justice. He finds, among other things, that dominant elites rely on positions of proximity to the states, while those dominated have different trajectories, often linked to personal commitments to international justice and therefore working in non-state organizations. This, in turn, leads to a division of labour within the field between these two groups, with different legitimating effects.[80] In short, such a quantitative examination of the positions of agents of the field of international justice sheds light on the development (if not imposition) of legitimating agendas and discourses, as well as the construction of what is taken for granted as the orthodoxy of the field. In other words, the method helps us understand the different worldviews in terms of schemata of perception which agents bring to the field and how the differences in habitus ultimately contribute to the structuring of the field.

Other approaches have been developed, for example by Kauppi and Madsen who have conceptualized the international judiciary in terms of a 'transnational power elite'; that is, a transnational social grouping of agents characterized by a collective and transnational form of knowledge-based (legal) capital and by their connections to national legal and political sites of power.[81] Using this approach to depict the social space of international courts, Madsen, as mentioned above, has investigated the educational capital of international judges from several international courts to provide an analysis of their internationalization and elitism, finding that, while international judges from European and global courts tend to be nationally educated, those from Africa, Latin America, and the Caribbean have more international profiles.[82] In all these cases, the point is not to predict how judges will rule but to make the international judiciary intelligible and to better

[78] Frédéric Lebaron, 'How Bourdieu "Quantified" Bourdieu: The Geometric Modelling of Data' in Karen Robson and Chris Sanders (eds) *Quantifying Theory: Pierre Bourdieu* (Springer 2009) 11.

[79] ibid 13.

[80] Mikkel Jarle Christensen, 'State Nobility in the Field of International Criminal Justice: Divergent Elites and the Contest to Control Power over Capital' (2023) 102 Social Forces 753.

[81] Kauppi and Madsen (n 65).

[82] Madsen (n 63).

understand how it operates through the schemata of perceptions employed by different judges.

In addition to the above-mentioned approaches of MCA and transnational elites, we find more qualitative analyses of agents' dispositions in given fields in terms of the mapping of embodied inclinations acquired through exposure and experience in various positions. Conducting such an analysis requires gaining access to the practices by digging into the dynamics of the field.[83] This can be done through ethnographic participant observation; that is, the researcher's direct participation in a particular social setting. When participation is not feasible (for reasons of secrecy, for instance), the best way to access the embodied inclination is to talk about such inclinations with the actors involved. This can be done through qualitative semi-structured interviews in which the researcher asks the interviewees to recount and describe their practices against the background of their professional trajectories. Fieldwork in the form of ethnographic observation and qualitative interviews can be used to reconstruct the dispositional logic of actors and thus their habitus within given fields. This is chiefly done by following the agents and their activities to empirically document their movements and strategies, considering their trajectories.[84]

An ideal method to do this is, again, to observe the agents in the practical enactment of their dispositions. It is through this approach that one can observe and interpret the tacit know-how on which they rely in their work.[85] Also in this case, when access is not possible, one can study the relational networks and professional trajectories of the agents of the field through interviews. Here the main challenge is to contrast the representational knowledge of the actors, which is especially strong in the legal field. The suggested solution here is 'to focus less on what interviewees talk *about* than what they talk *from*—the stock of unspoken assumptions and tacit know-how that ought to be presumed in order to say what is being said'.[86] The differences in presumptions—which again are sets of perceptions—could also be revealed by other means, for instance by feeding interviewees information that is presumed to trigger certain perceptions. Very often, small bits of information inserted in the context of questioning, for instance a judgment, will make the interviewee highlight certain prepositions.

Interviews can also be used to conduct prosopographical analysis; that is, the gathering of the collective relational biographies of the agents in a field followed by an analysis of how these trajectories form social patterns and relationships. This exercise consists of studying common patterns in group members' biographies (i.e., professional trajectories and educational background) and the origins of the

[83] Madsen and Dezalay (n 13).
[84] ibid.
[85] Diane Vaughan, 'Bourdieu and Organizations: The Empirical Challenge' (2008) 37 Theory and Society 65, 70.
[86] Pouliot (n 16).

agents' dispositions, and inquiring into the relationships between individuals. In this regard, the researcher can take advantage of the potential mobility in the field given by their external position to the practices in order to observe and contrast the positions within the field. As Madsen and Dezalay put it:

> the many and different accounts being presented throughout the research provide critical data for interrogating the agents and escaping their neutralizing and naturalizing discourses ... In practice, and very different from the agents' maneuvering capabilities, the research can interview the opposing camps, if not at the same time then immediately after each other, following a research logic that breaks with the logic of the practices of the respective agents ... What we suggest here is basically to turn the logic of the field inside out as a means for deconstructing social practices and reconstructing them in terms of fields.[87]

A leading example of scholarship using such a research approach is the work of Dezalay and Garth on international commercial arbitration.[88] By relying on more than 250 interviews, the authors mapped the emergence and evolution of the field of commercial arbitration largely relying on the social capital and personal trajectories of the individuals involved in that area of practice. In their words, their research aimed to explore 'what they [the individuals] bring concretely to international arbitration, as well as the principles and ideas underlying the field in the minds and strategies of the people who operate in and around it'.[89]

In the field of international criminal law, the works of John Hagan, Ron Levi, and Sara Dezalay exploit the notion of habitus to explore the origins and developments of some of the leading institutions in the field, with a particular focus on how different prosecutorial practices played a central role in this enterprise.[90] Particularly interesting are the findings of the authors, according to which the initial authority of the International Military Tribunal at Nurenberg was largely built on the prosecutorial approaches led by a community of US-based antitrust lawyers.[91] This was, in turn, instrumental for the Tribunal to build a constituency of support in the United States and the United Kingdom where, at that point, there were opposite views concerning criminally prosecuting Nazi leaders.[92] Using

[87] Madsen and Dezalay (n 13).

[88] Dezalay and Garth (n 2). See also Yves Dezalay and Bryant Garth, 'Merchant of Law as Moral Entrepreneurs: Constructing International Justice from the Competition for Transnational Business Disputes' (1995) 29 Law and Society Review 1, 27.

[89] ibid 33.

[90] See, among other works, Ron Levi, John Hagan, and Sara Dezalay, 'International Criminal Tribunals: Prosecutorial Strategies in Atypical Political Environments' in Karen J Alter, Laurence R Helfer, and Mikael R Madsen (eds), *International Court Authority* (OUP 2018) 342; John Hagan and Ron Levi, 'Crimes of War and the Force of Law' (2005) 83 Social Forces 4, 1500.

[91] Levi, Hagan, and Dezalay (n 90) 347–48.

[92] ibid.

similar approaches, the three authors explain the different stages in the evolution of the International Criminal Tribunal for the Former Yugoslavia by looking at the professional background and dispositions (habitus) of the three prosecutors that alternate themselves at the institution, Justice Richard Goldstone from South Africa, Louise Arbour from Canada, and Carla del Ponte from Switzerland.[93] More specifically, they argue that Goldstone's diplomatic background and approach was instrumental in allowing the Tribunal to impose itself as a legitimate institution vis-à-vis the broader public and international community of lawyers.[94] Conversely, Arbour brought to the court her extensive training in criminal law to open new avenues and support among criminal lawyers and investigators and securing state support for the indictment and prosecution of several individuals.[95] Finally, Del Ponte, who had inherited an established and globally recognized institution, focused on prosecuting complex cases by relying on her previous experience as Swiss attorney general, a position in which she came to be known as the investigator of bankers and organized-crime individuals.[96] In other words, there was one institution and three different prosecutors, whose professional backgrounds affected their dispositions regarding the perceiving and therefore framing of the various cases to prosecute, ultimately setting different paths in the process of giving the Tribunal authority and legitimacy.

Using similar research logics, the work of Salvatore Caserta on international courts in Latin America and the Caribbean has explored judicial outcomes through a combined analysis of the collective biography of the judges of these courts and the evolving social space in which these courts operate. He finds that, for example, the Caribbean Court of Justice (CCJ)—a regional economic and constitutional court with jurisdiction over the Member States of the Caribbean Common Market—has been deeply marked by a tension between two social groupings of Caribbean legal elites: an old, English-educated legal and political elite, largely sceptical of the CCJ due to their post-colonial connections with England and its system of justice, and a younger, locally educated legal and political elite, which welcomed the establishment of the new court and was willing to pursue Caribbean integrationist agendas.[97] Importantly, the professional trajectories of the judges selected to sit on the bench of the CCJ mirrored these battles, thus constituting a judicial microcosm of the broader Caribbean legal field. This, in turn, allowed the court to navigate the intricacies of the field and issue a set of rulings which, although at times

[93] ibid 352–57.
[94] ibid 353.
[95] ibid 354.
[96] ibid 356.
[97] Salvatore Caserta and Mikael R Madsen, 'Between Community Law and Common Law: The Rise of the Caribbean Court of Justice at the Intersection of Regional Integration and Post-Colonial Legacies' (2016) 79 Law and Contemporary Problems 89.

bold, balanced these competing interests.[98] What essentially was at stake in the early institutionalization of the CCJ were different perceptions and conceptions of the Caribbean: a local version produced through regional integration institutions, notably common university and law programmes, on the one hand, and a vision of the Caribbean emerging in Caribbean debating societies at Oxbridge, on the other. These differences had a major impact on how these agents envisaged the court.

Another international court studied using these approaches is the Central American Court of Justice (CACJ), the judicial arm of the Central American System of Integration. In order to explain the relative failure of this institution, Caserta provided an analysis of the particular legal and political elites who have influenced the direction of the court: a close-knitted network of domestic supreme court judges who wanted to vest the court with powers to enforce democracy in the Member States, and a more technocratic elite which envisioned the court as an economic regional institution to foster functional integration and market liberalization.[99] The fundamental differences among these groupings have critically impacted the institution and impaired its ability to deliver viable judgments. Again, we note that institutionalization of the court is marked—and in this case hampered—by differences in perception which are then translated into different institutional strategies with far-reaching consequences.

Both these studies approach the evolution of international courts by looking at the underlying battles that structure their field of operation, using the agents (notably but not only judges) as a starting point in order to show which types of capital and resources have been used at different moments of structuring the field. The structural insights gained from this analysis allow for a consideration of the judicial practices of these institutions. Following the same approach, a study of the European Court of Human Rights has demonstrated that the institution evolved from being a more diplomatic institution of the post-war period into a de facto supreme court in the area.[100] This transformation was enabled by both structural changes in its field of operation, which increasingly favoured rights litigation, and a change in the socio-professional profiles of the appointed judges. In other words, the legal practices of the court could be correlated to both change in broader social structures and the agency of the court. All this resulted in a court with changing institutional rationalities because of how the habitus of the judges connected with structural changes. These gradual changes, the study suggests, are visible at the agentic level of the institutions. The changes in the recruitment

[98] Salvatore Caserta and Mikael R Madsen, 'Consolidating Supranational Authority: The Caribbean Court of Justice Decisions in the Tomlinson Cases' (2016) 110 AJIL 533.

[99] Salvatore Caserta and Mikael R Madsen, 'The World's Most Powerful International Court? The Central American Court of Justice and the Quest for De Facto Authority (1907–2020)', (2022) 35 American University International Law Review 483.

[100] Mikael R Madsen, 'From Cold War Instrument to Supreme European Court: The European Court of Human Rights at the Crossroads of International and National Law and Politics' (2007) 32 Law and Social Inquiry 137.

patterns—themselves reflective of changes in operational context—transform the courts; for instance, from being more diplomatic institutions to undertaking a process of judicialization in which a different institutional rationality is reinforced by the recruitment of agents with very significant judicial experience but with little or no diplomatic experience.

## 5. Conclusion

As these last examples drawn from empirical research on international courts in the Caribbean, Central America, and Europe suggest, the outlined approaches are most fruitfully used to conduct a more structural analysis of judicial practices. While most research in the field of judicial behaviour seeks to explain the microcosm of adjudication by identifying factors which possibly influence a judicial decision's direction, the outlined approaches to judicial habitus are taking on a different, more structural project. Part of the reason for this difference is the resolutely sociological approach that studying judicial habitus involves. This is not a theory of psychology or rational actors but rather the study of the structures enabling legal practices to take place in terms of both broader social structures and structures of agency. Thereby, it contributes to a more structural cognitive sociology of international law.

In this structural analysis, habitus becomes an analytical tool for connecting the different levels of analysis. Rather than a goal in itself, the study of judicial habitus helps us to see how individual trajectories towards an institution—in our case, an international court—form collective spaces where dispositions have taken place in terms of judicial decision-making and judging. These decisions are structured by the 'psychological baggage' that each judge brings to the bench in terms of lived and learned experiences and resulting preferences and viewpoints. Yet, the collective biography and psychology of the bench is in itself insufficient for explaining judicial practices. As shown, practices have always taken place in given social contexts and fields. To paraphrase Bourdieu, dispositions correlate with positions. Judicial practices are also often a sort of compromise. While the individuals forming the microcosm where international judicial decisions are made interact, balance out their viewpoints, and share legal training, they also bring different types of capital to the fore, ranging from judicial experience from other courts to diplomatic or academic experience. These different types of capital reflect different individual trajectories and resulting habitus. The capitalization of these resources and resultant symbolic capital within the court are largely structured by the broader field in which the court is situated. The judicial exercise is thus both bounded and situated, with the notion of habitus helping us connect structure and agency when we seek to analyse those practices.

The outlined structural approach obviously has some limitations. If the goal is a predictive analysis of judicial behaviour, this kind of interpretative sociology is not the most promising avenue. Likewise, if the analytical goal is a fine-grained micro-psychological analysis of behaviour on the bench, the outlined approach is not the most suitable. However, in both cases the approach can help better contextualize action and provide the structural dimensions to, for example, judicial decision-making. After all, judges operate in institutions and judicial practices are institutional outputs. The cognitive schemata which habitus refers to make it initially appear as merely a cognitive sociological tool and it is only fully appreciated as a more structural sociological concept. It connects to cognitive sciences but remains a tool for structural sociological analysis.

# 11

# Critical Legal Geography, Spatial Cognition, and International Law

*Sofia Stolk*

## 1. Introduction

How do people experience and make sense of places of international law? How does space affect behavior and attitudes toward international law and, vice versa, how does the behavior and attitude of individuals affect the space, and the law? These questions are put on the table when we start to examine the interplay between cognitive studies and legal geography. The intimate connection between law and space has been extensively explored in this by now well-established field of legal geography.[1] In international law, too, scholars are increasingly embracing space as a key component or a lens to understand what international law is and does; and what people do with it beyond its written texts, as evidenced by international law's spatial, aesthetic, and material turns.[2] In this context, critical international lawyers have become interested in the physical presence of international law and its local and tangible geographical embedment. For example, following a more established field of law and (courthouse) architecture in domestic legal systems,[3] we now witness a growing appreciation of the importance of the concrete

[1] Just a few seminal examples are Irus Braverman and others (eds), *The Expanding Spaces of Law: A Timely Legal Geography* (Stanford UP 2014); David Delaney, *The Spatial, the Legal and the Pragmatics of Place-Making: Nomospheric Investigations* (Routledge 2010); Nicholas Blomley, *Law, Space, and the Geographies of Power* (Guilford Press 1994); Andreas Philippopoulos-Mihalopoulos, 'Law's Spatial Turn: Geography, Justice and a Certain Fear of Space' (2011) 7 Law, Culture and the Humanities 2, 187–202; Luke Bennett and Antonia Layard, 'Legal Geography: Becoming Spatial Detectives' (2015) 9 Geography Compass 406; Alex Jeffrey, *The Edge of Law: Legal Geographies of a War Crimes Court* (CUP 2019).

[2] Just a few examples: Nikolas Rajkovic, 'The Visual Conquest of International Law: Brute Boundaries, the Map, and the Legacy of Cartogenesis' (2018) 31 LJIL 267; Hyo Yoon Kang and Sara Kendall, 'Special Issue on Legal Materiality' (2019) 23 Law Text Culture, 1–15; Jessie Hohmann and Daniel Joyce (eds), *International Law's Objects* (OUP 2018); Daniel Quiroga-Villamarín, 'Domains of Objects, Rituals of Truth: Mapping Intersections between International Legal History and the New Materialisms' (2020) 8 International Politics Reviews 129.

[3] Linda Mulcahy and Emma Rowden, *The Democratic Courthouse: A Modern History of Design, Due Process and Dignity* (Routledge 2019); Connie Zhang, 'Spatial Cognition in the Courtroom: A Quasi-Experimental Study of the Influence Canadian Courtroom Design Has on Jury Cognition' (2019) 3 The Young Researcher 33; Piyel Haldar, 'In and Out of Court: On Topographies of Law and the Architecture of Court Buildings—A Study of the Supreme Court of the State of Israel' (1994) 7 International Journal for the Semiotics of Law 185; Emma Rowden and Diane Jones, 'Design, Dignity and Due Process: The Construction of the Coffs Harbour Courthouse' (2018) 14 Law, Culture and the Humanities 317.

Sofia Stolk, *Critical Legal Geography, Spatial Cognition, and International Law* In: *International Legal Theory and the Cognitive Turn*. Edited by: Anne van Aaken and Moshe Hirsch, Oxford University Press. © Sofia Stolk 2025.
DOI: 10.1093/9780198909293.003.0012

spaces in which international law resides for the shaping of its power, authority, identity, and legitimacy.[4] From a more critical angle, these buildings have been studied as vessels that (re)produce international law's fundamental biases and hierarchical structures. However, the influence of space on the experiences of and attitudes toward international law by individuals and the cognitive processes involved have until now only been a very marginal part of these investigations.

If the key focus of legal geography is on the co-constitution between people, space, and law, adding the cognitive dimension draws attention to the crucial question of how people perceive and behave in spaces of law and, thereby, contribute to the (re)construction of law and space. Especially if we think of the importance of the notion of "justice" in both critical international law and the legal geography discourse, it is appealing to turn to cognitive studies in an attempt to better understand the inherently subjective character of this notion and its important psychological dimension. Such engagements allow us to start seeing how making sense of international law and justice and our attitudes toward them entails the mental processing of space. In this chapter, I explore what happens to a legal geographical study of international law if we add the question of cognition and look into the mental process involved in how spaces of international law are experienced, interpretated, and (re)produced; and how this affects what we think, feel, and do about or with international law. The chapter carves out points of connection between the fields as well as the limits of their convergence.

Our mental conceptualization of space forms a significant part of how we understand the world. Drawing on literature on spatial cognition and behavioral geography, the chapter investigates how space shapes our perception and understanding of international law and (in)justice. The chapter starts from the central idea in legal geography that space is never neutral and static but rather always subjective and relational. The chapter investigates the meaning of this idea if seen from the perspective of international legal theory and cognition. This lens shifts our focus to the co-construction of people, space, and law and the mediating function of cognition in the perception and appreciation of the legal environment. Moreover, in the context of *international* law, it provides a novel angle on the meaning and importance of localness and embeddedness. More specifically, I explore whether the field of spatial cognition can offer a complementary perspective on the everyday (re)production of systemic patterns of in- and exclusion in

[4] Miriam Bak McKenna, 'Designing for International Law: The Architecture of International Organizations 1922–1952' (2021) 34 LJIL 1; Renske Vos and Sofia Stolk, 'Law in Concrete: Institutional Architecture in Brussels and The Hague' (2020) 14 Law and Humanities 57; Tanja Aalberts and Sofia Stolk, 'Building (of) the International Community: A History of the Peace Palace through Transnational Gifts and Local Bureaucracy' (2022) 10 London Review of International Law 169. Institutional Architecture blog series, Legal Sightseeing Blog, December 2022 <https://legalsightseeing.org/2022/12/06/institutional-architecture-mini-blog-series> accessed 16 April 2024.

international law that have been observed in critical international legal studies and critical legal geography alike.

In what follows, I will first elaborate on the study of the intimate relation between (international) law and space in the field of legal geography and the subfield of *critical* legal geography (Section 2). Next, I will elaborate on the interaction between this work and cognitive-behavioral studies, with a focus on spatial cognition and behavioral geography. Here, I particularly draw attention to the interplay between space, cognition, and emotion (Section 3). In Section 4, I use a concrete case study to illustrate this interplay in the context of the courthouses design of the International Criminal Court (ICC). In the conclusion, I will tease out the potential and limits of the cognitive-behavioral perspective—particularly the spatial, visual, and emotional aspects—for the understanding of international law and its actors (Section 5).

## 2. Legal Geography, Critical Legal Geography, and International Law

### 2.1. From legal geography to critical legal geography

The field of legal geography has rapidly grown in the past decades.[5] One of the most comprehensive and straightforward definitions of legal geography is provided by Bennett and Layard, who state that: "[L]egal Geography investigates the co-constitutive relationship of people, place and law."[6] Or in the words of one of the key figures in the field, David Delaney, legal geographers are interested in "how place matters to the legal and how the legal is implicated in the production (or destruction) of place(s)."[7]

Studying law and geography together has not always been self-evident. Bennett and Layard describe the often-invoked tension between overly abstract law on the one hand and detail-focused geography on the other.[8] This is, however, as they argue, a caricature depiction of the two fields. Legal geography sets out to show the intertwinement rather than the differences between law and space. As one of the pioneers in legal geography, Nicholas Blomley, notes: "by reading the legal in terms of the spatial and the spatial in terms of the legal, our understanding of both 'space' and 'law' may be changed."[9] In this endeavor, the "spatial turn" in

[5] Matteo Nicolini, *Legal Geography: Comparative Law and the Production of Space* (Springer Nature 2022) 134.

[6] Bennett and Layard (n 1) 406.

[7] David Delaney, 'Legal Geography III: New Worlds, New Convergences' (2017) 41 Progress in Human Geography 668.

[8] Bennett and Layard (n 1).

[9] David Delaney, Nicholas Blomley, and Richard Thompson Ford (eds), *The Legal Geographies Reader: Law, Power, and Space* (Blackwell Publishers 2001) xvii.

human geography has been crucial, providing an understanding of space as a social product[10] that was relational in nature.[11] This idea of space paved the way for a deeper investigation of law's spatial characteristics too. Legal geography endeavors to show how law is always locally enacted and how the materiality of a place gives "life to law."[12] Law *is* always somewhere. This view on the entanglement of law and space underlines the importance of understanding *where* the law happens in order to understand *how* the law happens and to whom.[13]

In the past decades, work in legal geography has taken different directions; from an interest in the effects of space on legal implementation and drafting, to investigations into the role of law in constituting place, to an engagement with jurisdiction and scale.[14] One specific branch of legal geography of interest to this particular chapter has focused on courts as spaces where all of the issues mentioned above play a role. In his 2019 "progress report" on the field of legal geography, Jeffrey pays specific attention to the growing interest in court materiality. In his analysis, he distinguishes two approaches to geography and trials. One strand of research looks into the spatial attributes of trials, considering "the situatedness of legal practice and, in different ways, look to emphasize the significance of place, embodiment and performance in the accomplishment of law."[15] This work includes, for example, the architecture of courtrooms,[16] the implications of new technologies,[17] and the performance of trial participants.[18] The other strand shows an interest in sociomaterial practices, seeking "to deepen our understanding of how reality is encountered, understood and theorized, challenging established binaries through which the world is apprehended—for example, nature/society, material/immaterial, or human/non-human."[19] Interestingly, some of the latter studies into the

[10] Edward W Soja, *Postmodern Geographies: The Reassertion of Space in Critical Social Theory* (Verso 1989); Henri Lefebvre, *The Production of Space* (Blackwell 1991).

[11] Doreen Massey, *For Space* (SAGE 2005).

[12] Bennett and Layard (n 1) 214.

[13] Braverman and others (n 1) 1.

[14] Bennett and Layard (n 1) 410.

[15] Alex Jeffrey, 'Legal Geography 1: Court Materiality' (2019) 42 Progress in Human Geography 566.

[16] Clare Graham, *Ordering Law: The Architectural and Social History of the English Law Court to 1914* (Routledge 2003); Linda Mulcahy, *Legal Architecture: Justice, Due Process and the Place of Law* (Routledge 2011); Jonathan D Rosenbloom, 'Social Ideology as Seen through Courtroom and Courthouse Architecture' (1997) 22 Columbia Journal of Law and the Arts 463.

[17] Christian Licoppe, CMaud Verdier, and Laurence Dumoulin, 'Courtroom Interaction as a Multimedia Event: The Work of Producing Relevant Videoconference Frames in French Pre-Trial Hearings' (2013) 23 The Electronic Journal of Communication 1; Emma Rowden, 'Virtual Courts and Putting "Summary" Back into "Summary Justice": Merely Brief, or Unjust?' in Jonathan Simon, Nicholas Temple, and Renee Tobe (eds), *Architecture and Justice: Judicial Meanings in the Public Realm* (Ashgate 2013) 101.

[18] See, eg, Shoshana Felman, *The Juridical Unconscious: Trials and Traumas in the Twentieth Century* (Harvard UP 2002); Rachel Hughes, 'Ordinary Theatre and Extraordinary Law at the Khmer Rouge Tribunal' (2015) 33 Environment and Planning D: Society and Space 714.

[19] Jeffrey (n 15) 566. See Sarah Whatmore, 'Materialist Returns: Practising Cultural Geography in and for a More-Than-Human World' (2006) 13 Cultural Geographies 600; Ben Anderson and John Wylie, 'On Geography and Materiality' (2009) 41 Environment and Planning A 318; Divya P

realm of the non-human explicitly move away from a human-centered focus, which potentially provides a tension with the field of cognition.[20] I will return to this point in the final section.

Where legal geography thus investigates the co-constitutive relationship of people, place, and law, *critical* legal geography throws power into the mix; or, as Nicolini puts it, "the dialectics between domination and critique."[21] When the school of critical legal studies put the question of power on the table in the field of law, new interdisciplinary connections between the fields of critical geography and law were easily forged since both have an interest in unpacking the "ideological underpinnings of the law."[22] Both fields were engaging with similar questions, sharing "a concern with social, economic, and political inequality and seek to demonstrate how legal institutions, conventions, and practices reinforce hierarchical social relationships."[23] Seen from this perspective, the co-constitution between people, place, and law becomes entangled with the production of (in)justice.[24] Critical legal geography shares connections with, for example, postcolonial and feminist legal theory, similar to critical international law, as I will explore in the next section.[25]

## 2.2. (Critical) legal geography and international law

International law and its preoccupation with territory—which is undeniably "space"—seems to provide ample ground for reflections of law and space. However, engagements with (critical) legal geography in international law have been limited. Perhaps even on the contrary, the ideal of sovereign, equal states that has long formed the backbone of international legal thinking significantly flattened and simplified the geographical imagination of international law's space. In this

Tolia-Kelly, 'The Geographies of Cultural Geography III: Material Geographies, Vibrant Matters and Risking Surface Geographies' (2013) 37 Progress in Human Geography 153.

[20] Unless cognition is defined more broadly such as in N Katherine Hayles' cognitive assemblages. N Katherine Hayles, 'Cognitive Assemblages: Technical Agency and Human Interactions' (2016) 43 Critical Inquiry 32.

[21] Nicolini (n 5) 134.

[22] Nicolini (n 5) 136.

[23] Benjamin Forest, 'Legal Geography' (2017) in Douglas Richardson and others (eds), *International Encyclopedia of Geography: People, the Earth, Environment and Technology* (Wiley-Blackwell 2017) 8. See also Daniela Palacio-Rodirquez, 'Spatializing International Law: A Legal Geography Approach' (2020) Universidad de los Andes <http://hdl.handle.net/1992/50856> accessed 24 April 2024.

[24] David Delaney, 'Legal Geography III: New Worlds, New Convergences' (2016) 41(5) Progress in Human Geography 268.

[25] Surprisingly, feminist legal geography is still a relatively small subfield. For a good overview, see Dand Cuomo and Katherine Brickell, 'Feminist Legal Geographies' (2019) 51 Environment and Planning A: Economy and Space 1043. On feminism and cognitive studies, see Chapter 5 by Veronika Fikfak in this volume.

scenario, "international" space is taken as a given; as an apolitical, ahistorical, static reality. Critical international lawyers operating in the intersection of critical legal studies, feminist approaches, Third World Approaches to International Law (TWAIL), and science and technology studies have started to shake international law's static spatial foundations by incorporating insights from legal geography. Typically, these approaches entail an emphasis on reflexivity, shifting attention to our own positionality in a theoretical, social, political, and physical sense.

The intertwinement of law, space, and power on the international plane has been interrogated most prominently by Mahmud and Rajkovic.[26] They have shown the inextricable historical interdependence of cartography, imperialism, and the rise of international law, and highlight international law's complicity in neutralizing contested space and, in so doing, perpetuating injustice and inequality. Another area of engagement is the study of war and international humanitarian law from the angle of legal geography, questioning, for example, how space is crucial for imagining the civilian/combatant distinction and the material placement thereof in a specific environment; and vice versa, how this legally relevant distinction affects the constitution of space.[27] Furthermore, and of particular relevance to this chapter, critical international legal scholars display a growing interest in legal materiality and international law's everyday life, zoning in on "the artefacts, practices, formats and settings in and through which law acts and is enacted."[28] Studies in this area shed light on international law's very concrete worldmaking power and the—often very material—ways in which it "disciplines its subjects" through physical objects.[29] In this research, legal geography's emphasis on the localness of the law gains a new dimension. As convincingly shown by, for example, Luis Eslava and Juan Amayo-Castro, even international law is eventually situated and enacted locally.[30]

In this vein, international lawyers have become interested in the physical spaces where international law operates and the way in which it becomes visible and tangible to its subjects and/or constituencies. These "beacons" of international law and the tension between global aspirations and local rootedness are particularly

[26] See, eg, Tayyab Mahmud, 'Law of Geography and the Geography of Law: A Post-Colonial Mapping' (2010) 3 Washington University Jurisprudence Review 64; Rajkovic (n 2). On the use of maps in the courtroom, see also Sofia Stolk, 'Imagining Scenes of Mass Atrocity from Afar: Maps and Landscapes at the International Criminal Court' (2017) 5 London Review of International Law 425. On critical legal geography and the study of boundary drawing, see also Nicolini (n 5) 125–26.

[27] Craig Jones and Michael Smith, 'War/Law/Space: Notes toward a Legal Geography of War' (2015) 33 Society and Space 581; Margo Kleinfeld, 'Too Difficult to Protect: A History of the 1934 Monaco Draft and the Problem of Territory for International Humanitarian Law' (2015) 33 Society and Space 592.

[28] Kendall and Kang (n 2) 3.

[29] Hohmann and Joyce (n 2) 2.

[30] Juan Amaya-Castro, 'Teaching International Law: Both Everywhere and Somewhere' in Juan Carlos Sainz Borgo and others (eds), *Liber Amicorum in Honour of a Modern Renaissance Man Gudmundur Eiríksson* (University of Peace 2017) 521; Luis Eslava, *Local Space, Global Life* (CUP 2015).

visible in the spaces of international courthouses. As Bennett and Layard note, courtrooms consist of "a geographic and a spatial set of meanings that are both legally and spatially distinguishable from other sites."[31] In international courthouses specifically, reflections on space, materiality, and hierarchy are accompanied by questions of visuality and aesthetics. As argued by Miriam Bak McKenna, "[international law is] dependent upon aesthetics and spatial dynamics to elicit faith in its ideals and principles, and to project international legal discourse to the outside."[32] This has sparked an emerging interest in the architecture of the buildings in which international institutions reside.[33] Buildings are powerful vessels to materialize and communicate ideals and principles.[34] Ideas about transparency, security, and inclusion fostered by democratic institutions such as courthouses transpire not only through their proceedings but also through the aesthetic and functional choices in their architectural design.[35] The emphasis on the public nature of democratic courthouses affects the requirements of the courthouse design (eg it needs to include a public gallery) and its access and security.

Exploring the architecture of international legal institutions can generate insight into the material ways in which international courts communicate with their constituencies and affect how they, cognitively, make sense of what international law and justice is. Beyond that, studying the spatial arrangements of courthouses provides insight into the everyday practices of movement, access, and in- and exclusion of legal institutions. Feminist studies in courtroom geography have drawn attention to the deep entanglement between movement, space, politics, and emotion in courthouses.[36] This is echoed in the work of Jeffrey and Jakala who investigate the war crimes court in Bosnia and Herzegovina as a "hybrid legal geography," drawing attention to the significance of (imaginaries of) space and place in "the plural material, bodily, and imagined practices through which legal processes assert their authority."[37]

The intersection of material, bodily, and *imagined* practices is where I see a potential point of connection between legal geography and cognitive studies. The

[31] Bennett and Layard (n 1); see also Antonia Layard, 'Freedom of Expression and Spatial (Imaginations of) Justice' in Dimitry Kochenov and Gráinne de Burca (eds), *Europe's Justice Deficit?* (Hart Publishing 2015) 417–34.

[32] Bak McKenna (n 4) 6.

[33] Eg Bak McKenna (n 4); Vos and Stolk (n 4); Aalberts and Stolk (n 4).

[34] See, eg, Thomas F Gieryn, 'What Buildings Do' (2002) 31 Theory and Society 35.

[35] Judith Resnik and Dennis Edward Curtis, *Representing Justice: Invention, Controversy, and Rights in City-States and Democratic Courtrooms* (Yale UP 2011); Linda Mulcahy and Emma Rowden, *The Democratic Courthouse: A Modern History of Design, Due Process and Dignity* (Routledge 2019).

[36] Caroline Faria and others, 'Embodied Exhibits: Toward a Feminist Geographic Courtroom Ethnography' (2020) 110 Annals of the American Association of Geographers 1104. As Faria and others note: "The courtroom is a space where global political and economic systems infused with dominant legal discourse manifest materially and where legal subjects are enlivened, forced to navigate the personal and intimate felt experience."

[37] Alex Jeffrey and Michaelina Jakala, 'The Hybrid Legal Geographies of a War Crimes Court' (2014) 104 Annals of the Association of American Geographers 652, 658.

important relationship between spaces of law and *experiences* of law and justice that is brought to the fore in critical legal geography forms a good starting point for the further exploration of an interdisciplinary dialogue between (spatial) cognitive studies and a critical legal geography with a focus on international law, to which I turn in the next section.

## 3. Space, International Law, and Cognition

### 3.1. Cognition and critical legal geography: common interests and methodological challenges

What happens if we infuse the already interdisciplinary field of critical legal geography and international law with insights from cognitive and behavioral studies? Cognition seems in different ways a good companion for studies in international legal geography, especially because of the shared interest in the relationship between people and their surroundings. As Van Aaken and Hirsch note in the Introduction to this volume, one of the fundamental ideas of cognitive studies is that "[p]eople do not directly sense their physical environment, and cognitive processes mediate between sensory input from the external environment and human behaviour."[38] This mediation between people and environments is of relevance to legal geography too. Moreover, legal geography and cognitive-behavioral studies share a strong interest in knowledge production.[39] How people know, perceive, and enact (international) law is a question of cognition as well as a question of law's spatiality. If we look at critical legal geography specifically, cognitive studies could shed light on questions of space, law, and power, for example when investigating how certain hierarchies are entrenched in spaces of law and how this translates into individual experiences of international law's power and speaks to one's cognitive schemata and behavior.

In this context, the notions of identity, belonging, and attachment are key to, quite literally, "localizing" experiences of (in)justice. In the Introduction, Van Aaken and Hirsch note how "[p]eople's cognitive processes (such as interpretation) are affected by their identity, and identity can trigger automatic processes." In this light, combining space, cognition, and *international* law potentially sheds new light on the local enactment of the global. Taking a cognitive perspective, this could become a question of how international law travels and transforms on the micro-localized level of the *mind* of individuals and how this affects behavior, cognitive processes, and, on a broader level, social relations. Here, I see a striking overlap—as well as a tension to which I will come back later—between feminist

[38] See Anne van Aaken and Moshe Hirsh's Introduction to this volume, p 4.
[39] Nicolini (n 5).

legal geography and the focus of cognition on individual processes of sense-making in spaces of law. This allows for a different iteration of the question of *where* the law happens (in order to understand *how* the law happens) because one could argue that it "happens" in the physical space as well as in the mental representation and processing of such spaces in the mind of individuals. A cognitive "turn" of legal geography invites an exploration of how certain "spaces of law" affect human behavior in certain ways and how such spaces shape cognitive process—such as attention, categorization, and memory—and, vice versa, how cognition shapes the perception of spaces of law. This can entail investigating how the co-constitution of space and cognition affects human decision-making in specific environments as well as how these environments are emotionally experienced—and how this again affects decision-making processes.[40] This emotional experience of space is deeply connected to the notion of "justice," a concept that takes a central place in critical geography and critical legal studies alike.

Methodologically, however, the approaches of (critical) legal geography and cognition diverge. Where cognitive studies lean heavily on experimental research, legal geographers extensively rely on ethnographic fieldwork. Legal geographers often position themselves as "insiders" in the legal world, deploying anthropological strategies of "studying up," "multi-sited," "engaged," and "para"-ethnographies.[41] In critical legal geography, as mentioned above, the subjectivity of the researcher is a key feature in the research design and the notions of reflexivity and positionality take a central place in the analysis. This can be at odds with an experimental approach that takes the neutrality of scientific methods as its point of departure.

Despite the shared interest in the relation between people, law, and their environment, the two approaches seem to employ different epistemologies, ask different questions, and look for different answers. Cognitive studies often seek to expose and explain certain assumptions, mental processes, and phenomena following a problem-solving rationale, whereas critical legal geography mainly seeks to problematize or even unsettle these processes.[42] Additionally, the move from studying individual cognitive biases to an investigation of systemic bias, or vice versa, is not without problems. One challenge to such an engagement is the fallacy of psychologism, occurring when "social phenomena are explained purely in terms of facts and doctrines about the mental characteristics of individuals," obscuring "the objective economic and social conditions that operate independently of the

[40] See Norbert Schwarz, 'Emotion, Cognition, and Decision-Making' (2000) 14 Cognition and Emotion 433.

[41] Irus Braverman, 'Who's Afraid of Methodology? Advocating a Methodological Turn in Legal Geography' in Irus Braverman and others (eds), *The Expanding Spaces of Law: A Timely Legal Geography* (Stanford UP 2014) 120–21.

[42] Jeffrey and Jakala (n 37) 665.

individual."[43] This is obviously in tension with a critical legal geography approach to international law, which aims to expose power dynamics, ideologies, and *systemic* inequality instead. The latter approach is linked with cognitive sociological and constructivist studies that highlight the social dimension of cognitive processes and may provide a fruitful conversation.[44]

## 3.2. Interdisciplinary opportunities: behavioral geography and spatial cognition

Nevertheless, despite some clear tensions and differences between the two fields, it is worth exploring how scholars in each field can learn from and complement one another, even if only to better understand their own disciplinary boundaries. There are two strands of behavioral-cognitive studies that are particularly informative when exploring the interdisciplinary opportunities to study the relations between space, cognition, international law, and emotion: behavioral geography and spatial cognition. This section will briefly discuss both and link them to potential points of connection in international legal theory and critical legal geography.

### 3.2.1. Behavioral geography

Combining critical legal geography with cognitive-behavioral studies draws from the scholarly endeavors in the field of behavioral geography. Gold distinguishes two streams within this subfield of behavioral geography: "humanistic (interest in understanding imagination) and cognitive (examining regularities in human spatial cognition and behavior and using their findings as a basis from which to generate theories about how people make decisions and act in geographic space)."[45] The latter builds on ideas of discrepancies between perception and actuality; between objective environments and behavioral environments. Convergence between the two streams can be found in attention to the *attachment to place* as an important starting point for exploring how emotion, space, and cognition are interrelated. Here, we speak of issues such as belonging, identity, security, territory, and perhaps justice.

This brings us back to the important notion in legal geography that law is embedded in the real world, embodied by people and places. If we consider people to be "vectors" of law who "carry it through space and time, performing both spatiality and legality as they travel,"[46] their mental processes while doing this matter if we want to understand the intertwinement of law and space on a cognitive level.

[43] John R Gold, 'Behavioural Geography' in Audrey Kobayashi (ed), *International Encyclopedia of Human Geography* (2nd edn, vol 1, Elsevier 2009) 290.
[44] See Chapter 3 by Ian Johnstone and Arun Mohan Sukumar in this volume.
[45] Gold (n 43).
[46] Bennett and Layard (n 1) 415.

Particularly the study of international law's everyday practices and legal imagination can be enriched by an appreciation of their cognitive-behavioral dimensions. A focus on the "daily world-making of individual actors"[47] through the lens of behavioral geography and international law can deepen our understanding of the mutually constitutive relationship between people, place, power, and law and the role of cognition and emotion therein.

#### 3.2.2. Spatial cognition

Another subfield that provides specific insights into the link between space and cognition is, not unexpectedly, called spatial cognition. Spatial cognition can, in short, be described as "the mental faculty that takes in information about the spatial surroundings, transmitted via the senses—especially vision—and assembles it into a subjective percept that lets a person experience, understand and use the space optimally."[48] Importantly, there is a close link between the spatial-cognitive system and the emotional processing system.[49] Spatial cognition can enrich the critical evaluation of international legal spaces for it helps to move away from a focus on its "static morphology" to international law as an embodied process of interpretation and experience.[50]

There are some ancient brain circuits involved in the emotional processing of space, since the attribution of positivity or negativity to a certain space has always been crucial to survival.[51] Exploring and orienting is a cognitive priority when entering a new environment. Cognitive mapping, action, and emotional processing work together in shaping the experience of a space. On the one hand, positive experience is related to a satisfaction of curiosity, being able to orient oneself, and the freedom of movement. Spatial unease, on the other hand, arises when insufficient orientation is provided and not all parts of the space are available for visual or actual exploration. There is increasing evidence of the importance of "affordance of movement"[52] in the shaping of a mental map and the attached emotions. The term "affordance" was famously coined by Gibson and is widely used in the cognitive sciences and beyond: "[t]he affordances of the environment are what it offers the animal, what it provides or furnishes, either for good or ill."[53] Space offers affordances for actions such as escape, concealment, surveillance, and wandering

[47] ibid 417.

[48] Kate Jeffery, 'Urban Architecture: A Cognitive Neuroscience Perspective' (2019) 22 The Design Journal 853. See also Neil Burges, 'Spatial Cognition and the Brain' (2008) 1124 Annals of the New York Academy of Sciences 77.

[49] Jeffery (n 48). See also Heini Saarimäki and others, 'Discrete Neural Signatures of Basic Emotions' (2016) 26 Cerebral Cortex 2563.

[50] Anna Schliehe and Alex Jeffrey, 'Investigating Trial Spaces: Thinking through Legal Spatiality beyond the Court' (2023) 48 Transactions of the Institute of British Geographers 9.

[51] Jeffery (n 48) 861.

[52] Jeffery (n 48) 866–67.

[53] James J Gibson, *The Ecological Approach to Visual Perception: Classic Edition* (Psychology Press 2015) 119.

and, in so doing, shapes emotions.[54] There obviously is a direct connection between the affordance of movement and the design of, for example, a courthouse.[55] Also in less obvious or more complex "legal spaces" such as border areas, a spatial cognition lens could provide interesting perspectives on, for example, movement, decision-making processes, and questions of identity and identification. Moreover, specifically in the wake of the increasing use of AI in, for example, the military, the meaning of cognition and making sense of space gains yet another layer of complexity when we think of categorization, interpretation, and agency.[56]

Another related spatial concept that is of key concern to both international law and cognition is that of territoriality. Territoriality as spatial and social emotion entails the "sense of ownership and mastery of a space ... requiring knowledge not just of the space in one's territory, and the boundaries, but also of which other individuals belong there and their relative places in the dominance hierarchy."[57] The fundamental intertwinement of social and spatial relationships is of relevance to a critical reflection on international law that wants to understand how its fundamental hierarchies are constructed and reproduced. The insights from spatial cognition shed light on the importance of space to the experiences of justice, equality, hierarchies, power, and patterns of in- and exclusion.

A related spatial dimension that is of particular concern to legal geography and international law alike is that of distance, specifically in terms of the abovementioned global/local conundrum. However, thinking of space in terms of spatial cognition and emotion also requires a move beyond a criticism of distance in absolute terms. As Philippopoulos-Mihalopoulos forcefully argued, thinking in terms of space should not be reduced to a discussion on distance in terms of local, regional, and global without an eye on the fluid, dynamic, parallel, relational qualities of space.[58] Theories of legal geography, in that way, can potentially enrich thinking through the connection between (spatial) cognition and international law by offering a conceptualization of justice as a subjective, embodied experience rooted in space. This enables us to rethink "distance" and "physical connection" without romanticizing physical space. It offers insight into the possibilities of feeling estranged and disconnected even in physical space or, vice versa, feeling connected despite distance.

[54] Jeffery (n 48) 866.
[55] Jonathan RA Maier, Georges M Fadel, and Dina G Battisto, 'An Affordance-Based Approach to Architectural Theory, Design, and Practice' (2009) 30 Design Studies 393.
[56] Shiri Krebs, 'Through the Drone Looking Glass: Visualization Technologies and Military Decision-Making' (Lieber Institute West Point, February 11, 2022) <https://lieber.westpoint.edu/visualization-technologies-military-decision-making> accessed February 8, 2024; Klaudia Klonowska, 'Military Surveillance Practices: What Machines See and Algorithms Know', 2023, on file with author.
[57] Jeffery (n 48) 863.
[58] Andreas Philippopoulos-Mihalopoulos, 'Law's Spatial Turn: Geography, Justice and a Certain Fear of Space' (2011) 7 Law, Culture and the Humanities 187.

Finally, an important notion in spatial cognition and legal geography alike is that of the "cognitive map." In the neurosciences, the cognitive map theory has been extensively explored, trying to locate where spatial information is processed in the brain and how so-called "place cells" work. Research on animals reveals that place cells can act differently in similar spatial contexts, depending on contextual information.[59] The concept of the cognitive map has been adopted in the social sciences too, which brings us back to behavioral geography and its interest in spatial imagination.[60]

The shared interest of legal geography and spatial cognition in the impact of space on law (and vice versa) clearly converges in the space of the courtroom. In domestic settings, studies have been conducted on the impact of courtroom design on the cognition and behavior and perception of trial participants, which could possibly be transposed to the international level. For example, experimental research shows how courtroom design influences jury cognition. In one of these experiments, the courtroom layout that was ranked as most comfortable by the participants also turned out to contain a higher rate of innocent verdicts.[61] The influence of the courtroom design on the perception of the defendant is further confirmed in studies on the positioning of the defendant either in an open/closed/guarded dock or at a bar table.[62] These are important considerations for critical reflections on inequality and bias as well as more procedural evaluations of due process or human rights concerns regarding dignity and fair trial rights.[63] Research into spatial cognition can illuminate how arrangements of space that are often taken for granted can actually have a far-reaching impact on trial participants and experiences of justice. In this context, the concept of the mental map could enhance our understanding of how legal space—for example, a courthouse—is processed and navigated differently by different people on different occasions, shedding further light on the experience of "justice" as a fluid, changing, individual process.

With this in mind, and in line with the concrete aim of legal geographers "to identify what work law and spatiality are doing at any particular place and time,"[64] let us now see how combining insights from cognitive-behavioral studies with critical legal geography could play out at a *specific* site of international law: the ICC.

[59] Jeffery (n 48).

[60] Gold (n 43).

[61] Connie Zhang, 'Spatial Cognition in the Courtroom: A Quasi-Experimental Study of the Influence Canadian Courtroom Design Has on Jury Cognition' (2019) 3 The Young Researcher 33.

[62] Blake M McKimmie, Jillian M Hays, and David Tait, 'Just Spaces: Does Courtroom Design Affect How the Defendant Is Perceived?' (2016) 23 Psychiatry, Psychology and Law 885.

[63] See Emma Rowden and Diane Jones, 'Design, Dignity and Due Process: The Construction of the Coffs Harbour Courthouse' (2018) 14 Law, Culture and the Humanities 317.

[64] Bennett and Layard (n 1) 409.

## 4. The Premises of the International Criminal Court: A Spatial-Cognitive Analysis

### 4.1. International criminal law, architecture, and cognition

Arguably, international criminal law (ICL) is one of the branches of international law that is most visibly anchored in the physical space of the courthouse. The origins of ICL are often traced back to the International Military Tribunal in Nuremberg. Some decades later, two regional United Nations (UN)-mandated tribunals were established to prosecute war crimes, crimes against humanity, and genocide committed in the 1990s in the Balkans (the International Criminal Tribunal for the former Yugoslavia) and Rwanda (the International Criminal Tribunal for Rwanda). Different types of international and regional criminal courts and tribunals have been established since, for example the hybrid courts in Cambodia and Sierra Leone and the Special Tribunal for Lebanon. In 2002, the permanent ICC began its operation in The Hague. As the first and only permanent international criminal court, it consolidated the place of ICL in the international legal landscape, which was also physically affirmed by the opening of its newly designed and built permanent premises in 2015.

The insight that the physicality of international justice matters to the understanding of and attitudes toward ICL is an idea that is shared by ICL's proponents and critics alike. The phrase "justice must be seen to be done" has become one of ICL's most prominent mantras. In this spirit, the architectural design of international courts has taken up a specific place in ICL's continuous battle for legitimacy, both as a materialization of democratic values and as a symbolic, communicative device.[65] In turn, the lack of visibility and accessibility has been criticized; many of the courthouses in which "justice is done" are out of reach, both physically and metaphorically, to the people whose justice is at stake. The importance attached to the act of "seeing" as a necessary precondition to satisfy the experience of "justice" opens up many ways to engage with the role of cognition and legal geography in this process.

Although ICL is often presented as an inclusive, universal endeavor, benefiting humanity as a whole, all ICL institutions have faced criticism of bias, exclusion, selectivity, and stigmatization.[66] Most prominently, TWAIL scholars have identified

[65] Bak McKenna (n 4); Vos and Stolk (n 4).

[66] See, eg, Christine Schwöbel (ed), *Critical Approaches to International Criminal Law: An Introduction* (Routledge 2014).; Frédéric Mégret, 'Practices of Stigmatization' (2013) 76 Law and Contemporary Problems 287; Sarah MH Nouwen and Wouter G Werner, 'Doing Justice to the Political: The International Criminal Court in Uganda and Sudan' (2010) 21 EJIL 941; Kamari Clarke, 'Refiguring the Perpetrator: Culpability, History and International Criminal Law's Impunity Gap' in Cathy J Schlund-Vials and Samuel Martínez (eds), *Interrogating the Perpetrator* (Routledge 2018) 56; Sofia Stolk, 'A Sophisticated Beast? On the Construction of an "Ideal" Perpetrator in the Opening Statements of International Criminal Trials' (2018) 29 EJIL 677; Randle C DeFalco, *Invisible Atrocities* (CUP 2022).

the Eurocentric, Western, colonial foundations of international law in general and ICL specifically.[67] These scholars argue how inequality is deeply anchored in the foundational structures of ICL institutions and reproduced by its practices. The ICC, for example, has been accused of an "African bias" because, especially in its first decade of operation, its cases predominantly featured African nationals, reproducing racial stereotypes and a problematic North–South division in which the "civilized" North saves the "savage" South.[68] These practices of selectivity and exclusion have affected how the justice done by these institutions has been experienced by trial participants and how it is perceived by the general public. Structural bias and practices of stereotyping and exclusion in ICL institutions on a macro level have been rendered even more tangible in studies of its micro everyday operations. Critical legal geography and the study of courthouse architecture and spatial cognition have something to contribute to both levels. The buildings play a role in the macro-narrative of ICL's legitimacy and authority as well as the everyday life of ICL in which the relation between architecture, law, and cognition becomes tangible.

The following discussion focuses on the courthouse as a place where different audiences gather and where ideas of what international law is and does are shaped *beyond* the courtroom. I aim to trace how visiting international courthouses brings about certain psychological connections between space, emotion, and the perception of justice. By focusing on "the significance of individual interpretation in creating meaning in court space,"[69] a spatial analysis moves beyond a static evaluation of the physical court space into the subjective experiences of its users. I particularly focus on the everyday reality of entering the courthouse and the primary cognitive process of making sense of the space itself—before the process of making sense of a specific trial or courtroom behavior. I approach this process of sense-making from the legal geography perspective of embodiment, and explore if and how this can be enriched or challenged by insights drawn from cognitive-behavioral studies. In so doing, I aim to show how these approaches take an interest in similar scenes and questions, but often find their answers in different ways.

[67] Anthony Anghie and BS Chimni, 'Third World Approaches to International Law and Individual Responsibility in Internal Conflicts' (2003) 2 Chinese Journal of International Law 77; Asad Kiyani, 'Third World Approaches to International Criminal Law' (2015) 109 AJIL Unbound 255; John Reynolds and Sujith Xavier, 'The Dark Corners of the World, TWAIL and International Criminal Justice' (2016) 14 Journal of International Criminal Justice 959.

[68] Kamari Clarke, *Affective Justice: The International Criminal Court and the Pan-Africanist Pushback* (Duke UP 2019); Adam Branch, 'International Justice, Local Injustice' (2004) 51 Dissent 22; Christine Schwöbel-Patel, 'The "Ideal" Victim of International Criminal Law' (2018) 29 EJIL 703.

[69] Schliehe and Jeffrey (n 50) 3. This starting point assumes a relational understanding of space; see Doreen Massey, *For Space* (SAGE 2005).

### 4.2. Cognition and emotion at the ICC's permanent premises

In 2008, the ICC launched an international architectural design competition for the construction of its permanent premises.[70] Next to the technical specifications, the ICC provided the competitors with a set of key values to be reflected in the design that strikingly resemble some of the concepts that are key in critical legal geography and spatial cognition: Justice, Human Dignity, Openness, Credibility, Safety, Global, and Icon. The ICC and actors around it were very aware of the potential impact of the design. The Coalition for the ICC (CICC), an international network of non-governmental organizations (NGOs) advocating for the Court and monitoring its work, emphasized the importance of having a building that engages audiences and embodies cultural, social, and historical meaning and authority. The CICC showed itself to be very aware of the psychological dimension of space and conceptions of justice. In their statement to the jury of the ICC's design competition, the CICC emphasized the role between architecture and emotion, emphasizing that "Justice is a very emotive experience for these participants; how the architecture 'feels' to them will be particularly significant."[71]

This statement echoes insights from research into democratic architecture and principles of legal design that are also influenced by cognitive and behavioral psychology.[72] Legal design entails a human-centered approach to law with "a designerly focus on lived experience; how we do things, how things look and feel to us, how things serve us."[73] In line with this focus, inclusivity was put forward as a central feature to be integrated into the design of the ICC building. In the words of the architect: "It is important that a formal institution like the ICC does not constitute barriers for people. On the contrary, it expresses the very essence of democratic architecture."[74] This ambition speaks to the notion of comfort in spatial cognition theory and appeals to a satisfaction of an individual's preference for curiosity, easy orientation, and freedom of movement. From a legal geography perspective, it is interesting that this statement engages with the idea of a courtroom visit as an embodied experience that is more than its technical procedures.

The main design feature in the ICC building that corresponds with inclusivity and a comfortable spatial and bodily experience is its appeal to transparency, a

[70] For a more comprehensive analysis of the ICC's architectural design its aesthetic and functional challenges, see Vos and Stolk (n 4).

[71] Coalition for the ICC, 'Architectural Design Competition for the Permanent Premises of the ICC: Statement to Jury' (October 30–31, 2008), on file with author.

[72] On legal design in general, see, eg, Margaret Hagan, 'Legal Design as a Thing: A Theory of Change and a Set of Methods to Craft a Human-Centered Legal System' (2020) 36 Design Issues 3.

[73] ibid.

[74] International Criminal Court, 'The Permanent Premises of ICC by Schmidt Hammer Lassen architects', video uploaded on December 7, 2010 <www.youtube.com/watch?v=Uu6oZZQ8vzU> accessed February 8, 2024.

value that has been important to the design of courthouses for decades.[75] A sense of transparency in the ICC building is established through, for example, the "playful facade" that mainly consists of a pattern of forward- and backward-tilting windows and a wide public plaza "as a natural way of approaching the building" (Figure 11.1).[76] Security features are hidden in the landscape: "The perimeter security concept offers both a high level of security and an unobstructed view to the ICC building. The surrounding landscape is designed to support the security level of the building and in addition it offers beautiful scenery." Natural elements and gardens in- and outside of the premises are a central feature in the design, appealing to the creation of a sense of belonging, recognition, and attachment to place.[77]

In sum, the main design idea is to have an open, transparent, accessible building. The architects proposed a building "that conveys the eminence and authority of the ICC, while at the same time relating on a human scale."[78] However, the ambition to combine human-centeredness with a reflection of eminence and authority is challenging, especially in light of the criticism of ICL identified earlier: the authority of the court arguably arises from a system that is structurally unequal and the trials take place in a type of building, a courthouse, that is intrinsically segregated. Exclusion and inaccessibility are key features in the design too, as can be observed when actually moving through the premises. The features that spatial cognition theories identify as key in creating spatial unease, such as obstruction and restricted movement, are prominently present in the design on multiple levels. Our critical legal geography lens makes us attentive to the political and social arrangement that permeate the ostensible transparent design. While cognitive studies could point us to design features that may make the spatial experience more comfortable in general, critical legal geography aims to expose the way in which space and architectural design manipulate emotions with regards to law and justice as well as the limits thereof.[79]

[75] Katherine Fischer Taylor, 'The Festival of Justice: Paris, 1849' in Costas Douzinas and Lynda Nead (eds) 137–77, *Law and the Image: The Authority of Art and the Aesthetics* (University of Chicago Press 1999).

[76] International Criminal Court, 'Permanent Premises of the ICC', public information leaflet <www.icc-cpi.int/sites/default/files/NR/rdonlyres/075EA925-13F6-4C02-8FC7-2FB0C528EDB9/0/IccBuilding0110EngWeb.pdf> accessed February 8, 2024.

[77] According to the architect: "Gardens have always existed as part of all cultures and all religions. The parterre gardens rise up as a green landmark and a symbol of unity, regardless of nationality and culture." International Criminal Court, 'The Permanent Premises of ICC by Schmidt Hammer Lassen architects', video uploaded on December 7, 2010 <www.youtube.com/watch?v=Uu6oZZQ8vzU> accessed February 8, 2024.

[78] International Criminal Court, 'The Permanent Premises of ICC by Schmidt Hammer Lassen architects', video uploaded on December 7, 2010 <www.youtube.com/watch?v=Uu6oZZQ8vzU> accessed February 8, 2024.

[79] For recent insights into the cognitive dimension of moving through buildings and the relation between architecture, cognition, and emotion see, eg, Alex Coburn, Oshin Vartanian, and Anjan Chatterjee, 'Buildings, Beauty, and the Brain: A Neuroscience of Architectural Experience' (2017) 29 Journal of Cognitive Neuroscience 1521; Juan Luis Higuera-Trujillo, Carmen Llinares, and Eduardo Macagno, 'The Cognitive-Emotional Design and Study of Architectural Space: A Scoping Review of

**Figure 11.1** The ICC permanent premises.
Source: Photo by author.

On a meta level, the choice for The Hague as the home for the ICC necessarily implies exclusion. All current situations and cases that are investigated or prosecuted before the ICC focus on areas outside of the Netherlands—most of them even from outside of Europe. The issue of local justice versus international justice and the problematic distance between the ICC and the affected communities over which it rules has been heavily debated since its inception, especially in light of the criticism of ICL's Eurocentrism.[80] Traveling to The Hague is out of reach for many; it requires time, money, and a recognized passport.[81] This distance in the physical sense undoubtedly also impacts the imagined distance. Interestingly, the move to virtual hearings accelerated by the Covid-19 pandemic has sparked a discussion on

Neuroarchitecture and Its Precursor Approaches' (2021) 21 Sensors 2193; Guopeng Li, 'The Dynamics of Architectural Form: Space, Emotion and Memory' (2019) 7 Art and Design Review 187.

[80] Nesam McMillan, *Imagining the International: Crime, Justice, and the Promise of Community* (Stanford UP 2020); Branch (n 68); Christian de Vos, 'Investigating from Afar: The ICC's Evidence Problem' (2013) 26 LJIL 1009; Sativa January, 'Tribunal Verité: Documenting Transitional Justice in Sierra Leone' (2009) 3 International Journal of Transitional Justice 207.

[81] On the exclusionary power of passports, see Mahmoud Keshavarz, 'Material Practices of Power—Part I: Passports and Passporting' (2015) 13 Design Philosophy Papers 97.

what we lose and what we gain when we get rid of the physical courtroom.[82] One aspect that is often mentioned is the loss of legitimacy of trials and decisions due to a diminished physical connection to the community on whose behalf justice is dispensed.[83] The move to the virtual raises questions about how virtual trials enhance participation and the democratic character of trials, but also how they may (dis) advantage certain groups. Experimental and empirical research has shown how a lack of physical participation could potentially disproportionally affect already-disadvantaged groups, but could also, under the right technical circumstances, improve the impression of the defendant on a jury, for example.[84] Remarkably, in ICL, the absence of this physical connection has always been problematic, even without the move to the virtual space. One could in this context even wonder if the move to the virtual space bridges some of the perceived distance or at least partially remedies unequal levels of accessibility.

Even when trial participants or audiences manage to travel to The Hague, the question of distance does not evaporate. Firstly, the ICC is not located centrally in The Hague. It is placed on the outskirts of the city. Although on paper it is part of The Hague's "international zone," this zone stretches out over a wide area and the ICC is located on its very border, rather isolated from the city and not very well connected to, for example, the public transportation network. The embeddedness of a courthouse within the city affects not only its physical but also its psychological accessibility. As Haldar notes, "law has at once been designated a separate, formal and distinct site and has been located within reach of an urban environment."[85] In contrast to this central location where we often find domestic courthouses, the ICC building is removed from that urban environment, enhancing its image of being a "distanced" court. A trip to this court then entails encountering many psychological markers signaling this distance.

Once we move on to entering the actual building (Figure 11.2), the actions afforded by the space are dominated by surveillance and control mechanisms. Despite the architect's ambition to conceal security by "ingenious" use of the landscape, the tension between security and accessibility is everywhere present, visible, and tangible. The building itself is transparent and opaque at the same time. Its façade of trapezoidal windows is intended "to create a feeling of movement and

[82] Meredith Rossner, David Tait, and Martha McCurdy, 'Justice Reimagined: Challenges and Opportunities with Implementing Virtual Courts' (2021) 33 Current Issues in Criminal Justice 94; João Ilhão Moreira and Liwen Zhang, 'Assessing Credibility in Online Arbitration Hearings: Determining Facts and Justice by Zoom' (2023) International Journal for the Semiotics of Law <https://doi.org/10.1007/s11196-023-10046-7> accessed April 16, 2024; Susan A Bandes and Neal Feigenson, 'Empathy and Remote Legal Proceedings' (2021) 51 Southwestern Law Review 20.

[83] Emma Rowden, 'Distributed Courts and Legitimacy: What Do We Lose When We Lose the Courthouse?' (2018) 14 Law, Culture and the Humanities 263; Jo Hynes, Nick Gill, and Joe Tomlinson, 'In Defence of the Hearing? Emerging Geographies of Publicness, Materiality, Access and Communication in Court Hearings' (2020) 14 Geography Compass 5.

[84] See David Tai and Vincent Tay, 'Virtual Court Study: Report of a Pilot Test' (Western Sydney University 2018) <https://courtofthefuture.org/publications-category/reports> accessed February 8, 2024; Bandes and Feigenson (n 82); Hynes, Gill, and Tomlinson (n 83).

[85] Haldar (n 3) 193.

**Figure 11.2** ICC entrance.
Source: Photo by author.

reflection, but also designed to defeat sniper targeting."[86] The tilted windows also create deflection: one cannot *actually* look inside, but there is an optical illusion of transparency. Before entering the main court building, visitors and trial participants alike have to pass through a gatehouse where the first security check is

[86] Christine Murray, 'Transparency, Democracy, High-Security: Schmidt Hammer Lassen's International Criminal Court' (*The Architectural Review*, February 5, 2016) <www.architectural-review.com/buildings/transparency-democracy-high-security-schmidt-hammer-lassens-international-criminal-court> accessed February 8, 2024.

performed. A valid ID is required and all persons and their belongings are scanned. This seemingly formal scene of entering the courthouse security check is loaded with socio-technical arrangements that interfere with privacy and may produce inequalities.[87] In terms of spatial cognition, the constraint of movement and access restrictions may, on the one hand, feed spatial unease. On the other hand, the rapid spread of such security measures at all sorts of sites has made the presence of security checks more predictable and expected.[88] Hence, a cognitive process of recognition and memory may be at work during security checks, appealing to routine behavior and stabilizing anxiety. Cognitive studies could shed light on how passing through a security check may trigger normalized, internalized behavior in some individuals, while in others it may induce stress and activate fearful or hostile attitudes. Critical legal geography lends us tools to criticize the broader social-political structures and implications thereof.

Thinking of courthouses in terms of navigation, orientation, and "affordance of movement" of specifically non-regular visitors provides a picture in which spatial unease and bodily discomfort constantly lurk. Spatial cognition studies show how a different system of cognitive mapping is activated in familiar spaces where movement is more routine-based.[89] ICC staff who walk through the security entrance regularly rely on route-based navigation, which probably entails a difference in the processing of space and emotion distinct from the one-time visitor. As Mulcahy notes, a sophisticated form of "segmentation and segregation" is common to modern courthouses.[90] This segregation is intentional and one of the intrinsic features of courthouse architecture.[91] Concerns of privacy are balanced with those of transparency. Spatial unease in those who are excluded seems unavoidable and can possibly only be remedied by violating the spatial comfort of others.

After passing the security check, the route to the main entrance leads over a small bridge. The courthouse is surrounded by water. If we look at this scene from a behavioral-cognitive lens, we can see at least two possible schemes of interpretation. One echoes a comparison with a castle moat, an imaginary that cognitively signals another layer of inaccessibility and perhaps even danger.[92] It limits and directs movement, a factor in creating spatial unease. At the same time, seeing water

[87] Govert Valkenburg and Irma van der Ploeg, 'Materialities between Security and Privacy: A Constructivist Account of Airport Security Scanners' (2015) 46 Security Dialogue 326; Anthony Amicelle, Claudia Aradau, and Julien Jeandesboz. 'Questioning Security Devices: Performativity, Resistance, Politics' (2015) 46 Security Dialogue 293; Marieke de Goede, 'The Chain of Security' (2018) 44 Review of International Studies 24.

[88] Stephen Graham, 'The Urban "Battlespace"' (2009) 26 Theory, Culture and Society 278.

[89] Russel A Poldrack and others, 'Interactive Memory Systems in the Human Brain' (2001) 414 Nature 546.

[90] Mulcahy (n 16) 48.

[91] Julienne Hanson, 'The Architecture of Justice: Iconography and Space Configuration in the English Law Court Building' (1996) 1 Architectural Research Quarterly 50.

[92] Murray (n 86).

can also bring about associations with comfort or even activate primary survival circuits.[93] The inside of the building itself clearly separates public space from areas with authorized access.[94] This reflects a key challenge of courtroom design to find "the most efficient way to move bodies round a succession of parallel private and public zones."[95] Through a carefully constructed network of corridors, different parties—staff, audience, judges, defendants—will never coincidently run into each other. Staff and visitors can meet in a cafeteria or in the hall that features an exhibition about the work of the ICC, but the other doors are secured and only accessible with a pass. And although the galleries are open to the public, the movement and behavior of visitors inside the space is restricted, monitored, and policed. All belongings must be stored in the lockers in the basement, including mobile phones. Before entering the public gallery, visitors have to pass through another security check. In the gallery, visitors are supervised by guards who strictly follow the Rules of Decorum: visitors are requested to be silent, pay attention, and dress suitably.[96] Security guards observe the behavior of visitors, emphasizing strict hierarchies and institutional control. The gallery is separated from the courtroom by a thick glass wall.

Thinking of the space of the courthouse as a subjective space in which individuals make sense of the space depending on their different cognitive dispositions reminds us of the importance of the stark differences between the individuals who enter the space. Regular visitors and newcomers draw on distinct brain circuits, and witnesses also process the space differently from, say, a defendant. The design of the ICC seems to reinforce the latter individual process by differentiating the spatial experiences between groups of people. The defendants enter the building through a distinct vehicle entrance, separating them from other trial participants and visitors. This entrance brings them directly to the holding cells. There is a striking contrast in the design choices between these holding cells and the other areas of the courthouse. The light in the overall design and its warm atmosphere was lauded by the jury of the design competition, for it provides psychological support to the witnesses and victims. But, as Murray writes,

> If soothing daylit spaces are intended to psychologically strengthen the witness, the dark grey holding cell complete with steel table and chair bolted to the floor, a slab for a bed, seatless stainless-steel prison toilet and sink are surely intended to bring the accused down a notch. This is no different from any other court, but it does say something about the idiom, "innocent until proven guilty." Certainly, the

93 See Veronica Strang, *The Meaning of Water* (Berg Publishers 2004).

94 See also Jeanne Gaakeer and others, 'Carey Young's Palais de Justice' (2018) 12 Law and Humanities 278.

95 Mulcahy (n 16) 49–50.

96 International Criminal Court, 'Rules of Decorum' <www.icc-cpi.int/sites/default/files/iccdocs/PIDS/publications/ICCRODEngLR.pdf> accessed February 8, 2024.

> architecture has already chosen sides. One can't really imagine a Western leader being held here.[97]

Entering a courthouse as a defendant will activate certain cognitive-emotional processes that are different from those of witnesses or lawyers. Beyond that, if we look at the courthouse as a hybrid geography, we can note how the design, the space, embodies certain patterns of hierarchy, stereotyping, and stigmatization. This separation between groups and individuals who share yet not entirely share a building reflects hierarchies that are forged by the design. It also creates clear boundaries between staff (those who "belong" in the building), visitors (those who are passing through voluntarily), and trial participants (those who do not entirely belong but have to be there). These hierarchies are of interest both from a cognitive perspective (which cognitive processes engage in this spatial experience of belonging? How do they affect attitudes and behavior?) and a critical legal geography perspective (how are these hierarchies sustained and reproduced? How does this affect the sense of justice experienced?).

Cognitive studies can shed light on the behavior of different visitors of the building in terms of identification and categorization of space and making sense of (in)accessibility and its relation to emotional processing. If we were to further explore these initial observations, empirical methods borrowed from the area of behavioral geography could dig deeper into the meaning of spatial cognition and spatial decision-making in the context of international courtrooms. Next to that, experimental cognitive research could provide tools to study and measure the perception of justice and conceptualization of spaces of international law, for example experiments to test the effects of specific design choices in international courthouses on the different participants in international justice, or the use of a method that combines cognition with affective or aesthetic valuation.[98] Moreover, thinking of spatial cognition and mental maps is not limited to those who can physically access the court. In neuroscience, there is evidence that seeing photos of places activates the brain in similar ways to the actual visit of places.[99] These insights as well as experiments with, for example, virtual reality trials[100] invite a reconfiguration

[97] Christine Murray, 'Transparency, Democracy, High-Security: Schmidt Hammer Lassen's International Criminal Court' (*The Architectural Review*, February 5, 2016) <www.architectural-review.com/buildings/transparency-democracy-high-security-schmidt-hammer-lassens-international-criminal-court> accessed February 8, 2024.

[98] See, eg, Lisa Reuter and others, 'Direct Assessment of Individual Connotation and Experience: An Introduction to Cognitive-Affective Mapping' (2022) 41 Politics and the Life Sciences 131; Anjan Chatterjee and Oshin Vartanian, 'Neuroscience of Aesthetics' (2016) 1369 Annals of the New York Academy of Sciences 172.

[99] Russell A Epstein and others, 'The Cognitive Map in Humans: Spatial Navigation and Beyond' (2017) 20 Nature Neuroscience 1504.

[100] See, eg, Renske Vos and Sofia Stolk, 'Courtroom 600: The (Virtual) Reality of Being There' (2022) 22 International Criminal Law Review 308.

of the meaning of concepts such as "imagination," "distance," and "connection" in the context of international law and reinforce the importance of international law's spatial life. Cognitive studies can enhance our understanding of how space is processed and how this leads to certain behavior by individuals or groups, with the aim of enhancing inclusion, accessibility, and comfort for all participants. Critical legal geography, however, will point to the complexity of these experiences that go beyond design features and beyond procedural rules. Such a perspective can account for the multilayered navigation between personal, political, social, and legal that makes up the embodied experience of a court visit. It can destabilize promises of inclusion and universality in ICL and possibly also point to the limits of what can be fixed by repairing spatial inequality in terms of accessibility and comfort.

## 5. Conclusion

This chapter explored the overlap and difference between theories of critical legal geography and spatial cognition in the context of international law. Moving through spaces of law and studying spatial cognition and the affordance of movement in such spaces gives a sense of the deep intertwinement between international law, space, emotion, and experiences of justice. The chapter offers a promise rather than results. It is an invitation for critical international lawyers who embark on the study of law's materiality to see what happens if spatial cognition is thrown into the mix. It is also an exercise in testing the boundaries between two already interdisciplinary fields of study that share an interest in the relation between people and their environments.

On a more critical note, colliding cognitive-behavioral studies with critical legal geography could potentially result in clashing fundamental premises. Critical legal geography embraces a research attitude of reflexivity and self-criticism. When adding cognition, one has to navigate the discomfort that could arise when introducing elements of functionalism that can be found in some strands of cognitive and behavioral theories into the field of critical legal geography that has resisted such elements from its very inception. The problem-solving aim that is more common in cognitive-behavioral studies does not always match the problematizing aims of critical legal geography studies. One of the aims of certain branches of cognitive psychology, to call out and "repair" individual biases, is not easy to reconcile with the exposure of systematic bias and the call for more radical reconceptualization of, in this case, the international legal system. Enhancing the comfort of courthouses by taking cognitive factors on board in design choices is promising. But if we look at the issues raised by critical legal geographers, the practices of boundary drawing and spatially embedded inequalities run much deeper. This is not, however, a reason to stay away from cognitive inquiries as a legal geographer altogether; a resort to cognitive-behavioral studies may also entail the necessary "step back" to get a deeper understanding of the problems flagged by critical legal geography studies. Moreover, such an interdisciplinary endeavor may entail a quest to dive deeper and to investigate how practices of boundary drawing in international legal spaces are not only socially but also psychologically constructed and reproduced.

Cognitive-behavioral studies and critical legal geography are mutually supportive in their interest in human beings as subjects who live the law and make sense of it in their own ways. They both rely on precise and localized lenses in order to grasp the bigger picture of what international law is (not) and does (not), and where and how it happens. The challenge, as well as the promise, in my view, lies in studying how the bodily, material, and cognitive are entangled; how the spatial, social, legal, and psychological are interdependent. It is in studying and understanding this entanglement in hybrid spaces such as international courthouses that we may gain a deeper understanding of the life and limits of international law.

# 12

# Marxism and the Cognitive Turn in International Law

## Exploring an Uneasy Relationship

*Kanad Bagchi*[*]

### 1. Introduction

Bringing into conversation Marxism and socio-cognitive approaches is an admittedly difficult task. I do not consider myself nearly as prolific as the other contributors of this book, many of whom have compellingly demonstrated that disparate traditions can be fruitfully brought together.[1] My task is further complicated given that Marxism has rarely, if ever, conformed to a singular tradition. As Matt McManus in an excellent review of Søren Mau's new book *Mute Compulsion* jestingly writes, 'Ask any two Marxists to define Marxism, and you will likely get at least three answers.'[2] Cognitive-behavioural studies have also evolved considerably over the decades, multiplying into many schools of thought, even when some core underlying assumptions have remained.

But even if one can effectively tease out some core underlying insights from what are contested and non-monolithic approaches, speaking of a certain 'interaction' between them, as the editors hope to do with the book, brings me back to my initial difficulty. Marxism and cognitive-behavioural approaches operate on very different planes and contain within them very different sets of theoretical positions, methodological choices, and, of course, ideological and political positions. To speak of them in the same project comes with a certain danger that we effectively might lose much of the explanatory potential of either frameworks.

* I would like to particularly thank the editors of this volume, Anne van Aaken and Moshe Hirsch, for their very generous feedback and comments. Also, many thanks to Ntina Tzouvala for directing me to some important literature and close engagement with the text. I also thank the readers of the Law and Marxist Methods Spring School 2024 and especially Fernando Quintana for his comments on the draft. All errors are my own.

[1] See, for instance, Chapter 4 by Shiri Krebs and Chapter 5 by Veronika Fikfak in this volume, respectively.

[2] Matt McManus, 'An Introduction to Marxism Unlike Any Other' (*The Nation*, 25 December 2023) <www.thenation.com/article/culture/soren-mau-marx-mute-compulsion> accessed 17 April 2024.

Kanad Bagchi, *Marxism and the Cognitive Turn in International Law* In: *International Legal Theory and the Cognitive Turn*. Edited by: Anne van Aaken and Moshe Hirsch, Oxford University Press. © Kanad Bagchi 2025.
DOI: 10.1093/9780198909293.003.0013

We have another point to consider. This book is situated in a conversation about international law and the way it interacts with the social, cultural, political, and material world around us. In this, the way we perceive the structuring role of international law and what international law is in the first place will determine what forms our enquiry will take. Indeed, international law is not a singularly self-evident system but a complex array of different sensibilities, argumentative patterns, and an assemblage of multiple traditions. Neither of the approaches considered in this chapter can claim to provide a complete picture of the work that international law does in this world. At best, we are working with partial sensibilities, an insight that is also at the heart of this volume.

But thinking through two different streams of thought and their attending ideational frameworks need not mean that they ought to be necessarily and immediately proven to work in complementarity. Critical approaches, inasmuch as they have attended to similar dispositions, have evolved both in parallel and sometimes even thinking through and against other approaches.[3] Something similar, I submit, is at work in the present chapter. It makes little sense to force upon a conversation where there might be little common ground. Instead, I propose to think through these two approaches in terms of an 'uneasy relationship' where it might well be that they are difficult to reconcile. This is neither a loss for the project of 'theory' in general nor one for this book. Sometimes theoretical tensions reflect the most contested aspects of social formations and open radically different imaginations of how it can be different. There is much to gain in capturing these different worldviews within a single project that the editors have so carefully curated.

Therefore, what follows is a discussion of the 'uneasy relationship' between Marxism and cognitive-behavioural sciences. I argue that this relationship cannot be one of straightforward synthesis. The divides between these two approaches remain far and wide. At a basic level, cognitive approaches (at least in its cruder versions) still operate within the over schema of behavioural studies, with its empiricist and positivist assumptions going against the very basis of the Marxist tradition which eschews a positivist conception of social reality. Moreover, the Marxist *problematique* with its emphasis on structural critique, historical analysis, and the idea of 'social totality' challenges the underlying assumptions of cognitive-behavioural studies and the kind of subject making and transformation it does. Instead, I find it useful to think about how Marxist insights in international law might help us prod, nudge (pun intended), and introspect some of the explanatory frameworks prevalent within cognitive-behavioural approaches. The idea is not to

[3] For an indicative list, see Tendati Achiume and Devon W Carbado (2021) 'Critical Race Theory Meets Third World Approaches to International Law' (UCLA School of Law, Public Law Research Paper No 21-05); Akbar Rasulov, 'CLS and Marxism: A History of an Affair' (2014) 5(4) Transnational Legal Theory 622–39; Samuel Moyn, 'Reconstructing Critical Legal Studies' (Yale Law School, Public Law Research Paper, 4 August 2023); Devon W Carbado and Daria Roithmayr, 'Critical Race Theory Meets Social Science' (2014) 10 Annual Review of Law and Social Sciences 149–67.

replace one framework with another, but to identify how each entail and inhabit different professional commitments, ideological structures, and cognitive spaces.

Following this introduction, in Section 2, I provide a snapshot of cognitive-behavioural approaches drawing largely from the editors of this book. In Section 3, I situate Marxism in international legal theory and scholarship, mindful of the fact that it is necessarily going to be hopelessly incomplete and partial. That then brings me to a direct relationship between the two approaches, which can sometimes be rather messy, inexhaustive, and of course 'uneasy'. This is covered in Section 4. Having considered this relationship, in Section 5 I move on to a specific iteration of how the two approaches throw up different questions, modes of enquiry, and strategies for action. I illustrate this through the example of race and racialization in international law and how these approaches come to understand the nature of the problem. Drawing from this discussion, in Section 6 I 'revisit' the relationship between Marxism and cognitive-behavioural approaches and think about how one might be able to work with these two traditions, despite their evidently different starting positions and sensibilities. I argue that Marxism brings three sets of propositions to cognitive-behavioural approaches, namely the importance of ideology, the influence of history in determining preferences and intentions, and, finally, a critical reflection on the empiricist and voluntarist assumptions of the field. Section 7 concludes.

## 2. The Cognitive 'Turn': A Snapshot

International legal scholarship is not bereft of 'turns'. We have had the linguistic turn,[4] historical turn,[5] postcolonial turn,[6] political economy turn,[7] materialist turn,[8] and many others. The self-description of international law and its multiple turns says something about our discipline and the scholarly environment it is embedded within. Perhaps it speaks to a deep sense of disciplinary anxiety, the innate sense of how international law matters, and yet it does not. Scholarly 'turns' evoke a sense of disciplinary progress, a continuous adaptation, perhaps even a story of re-articulation, in the light of its repeated failures. Turns in academia are problematic

[4] Benedikt Pirker and Jennifer Smolka, 'International Law and Linguistics: Pieces of an Interdisciplinary Puzzle' (2020) 11(4) Journal of International Dispute Settlement 501–21.

[5] George Rodrigo Bandeira Galindo, 'Martti Koskenniemi and the Historiographical Turn in International Law' (2005) 16(3) European Journal of International Law 539–59.

[6] Antony Anghie, 'Towards a Postcolonial International Law' in Prabhakar Singh and Benoît Mayer (eds), *Critical International Law: Postrealism, Postcolonialism, and Transnationalism* (OUP 2014).

[7] John Haskell and Akbar Rasulov, 'International Law and the Turn to Political Economy' (2018) 31(2) Leiden Journal of International Law 243–50.

[8] Daniel Ricardo Quiroga-Villamarín, 'Beyond Texts? Towards a Material Turn in the Theory and History of International Law' (2020) 23(3) Journal of the History of International Law 466–500.

in that they can easily turn into fiefdoms, with their own ritualistic practices, in which one is either in or out.

Academic turns also raise the question of positionality and power. Many of the turns that international law has witnessed have emerged from institutional spaces with a certain pedigree, endowed with institutional prestige and power and located within universities in the Global North. In this sense, turns are preceded by academic stature, positions, the location of the academic, the journal(s) where the specific iteration appears, and the infrastructural power of the institution. The ability to host and fund conferences, book projects, workshops, symposiums, and the like all contribute to whether a particular scholarly intervention transforms into a paradigm of thought and a universalized set of conversations. In other words, the question of scholarly turns has a very material component.

For these reasons, I remain sceptical of 'turn talk' in academia. Thinking alongside Akbar Rasulov and John Haskell, one must be cautious of what a certain turn really means, and to question whether there has been any turn at all[9] and from whose standpoint. The effect of the cognitive turn to broader scholarship is difficult to predict. But we will leave that question aside for now. Suffice it to say that attributing a turn to a scholarly endeavour must not prevent critique of what the turn stands for and whether it advances our sensibilities to work towards a set of institutional norms and practices better than what we found them to be. Fortunately, the editors of this book remain open to that thought.

This book brings together a challenging but remarkably erudite set of propositions to international law. It is a study how international law is to be found in the multiple cognitive spaces of different actors but at the same time a push towards more interdisciplinary thinking in terms of sociology, psychology, and so on. Indeed, much of the groundwork for this project has been laid together by the editors themselves, in a number of their prior works,[10] which I will be referencing throughout this chapter.

Overall, the crux of the argument is that international lawyers do not operate within a vacuum, but rules, interpretations, and professional practice transpire within a certain cognitive context and through a range of cognitive processes. These cognitive processes are guided by perceptions and behaviour which not only shape the background conditions of the actors but also make these actors 'susceptible to diverse biases'.[11] The recognition of human actors operating within cognitive frames and mental processes has implications for how international law is theorized, the range of possible outcomes it prescribes, and the kind of work[12]

[9] Haskell and Rasulov (n 7).

[10] For a selective indication, see Anne van Aaken and Tomer Broude (eds), 'The Psychology of International Law', Special Issue (2019) 30(4) European Journal of International Law; Moshe Hirsch, *Invitation to the Sociology of International Law* (OUP 2015) 99 et seq.

[11] See Van Aaken and Hirsch's Introduction to this volume.

[12] Monica Hakimi, 'The Work of International Law' (2017) 58(1) Harvard International Law Journal 1–46.

that international law is meant to do. Indeed, when international legal actors make, interpret, or apply international law, they operate within a diverse set of cognitive frameworks, much of which ultimately influences their judgement and attitude.

Crucially, though, these knowledge *schemas*, cognitive representations, and the multiple sets of mental assumptions that go into decision-making and theorizing are often hidden away or decontextualized. One of the purposes of the cognitive turn is to make explicit what is often implicit in international legal thinking and provide programmatic ways to change such perceptions. In other words, the cognitive turn in international legal thought is argued to inform and unearth the many silences, invisible frames,[13] and legal consciousness of its actors so as to turn the mirror inwards, and perhaps even imbue a much-needed reflexivity in the discipline.[14]

The literature on cognitive processes that typically affect decision-making, including the application and interpretation of international law, has proliferated significantly. Scholars have mapped the multiple mental frames, heuristics, and cognitive biases that operate in the background. These includes hindsight bias, confirmation bias, and automation bias.[15] Specific legal relationships and institutional design evoke difference responses from states and international institutions depending on the kind of *framing* effects they create.[16] International actors are likely to react differently to different types of cognitive impulses and information systems. All these point to the necessary role of cognitive-behavioural science in supplementing and creating infrastructures of coordination and collective action in international relations.

Situated within two further turns in international legal scholarship, namely the interdisciplinary turn[17] and the empirical turn,[18] cognitive approaches draw from social psychology, cultural cognition, microeconomics, and philosophy.[19] The methods employed are equally eclectic. Scholars in this tradition have incorporated rationalist perspectives, constructivist thinking, and behavioural insights in law and economics. It is perhaps more appropriate, then, to think of 'cognitive-behavioural' approaches as a combined effort into exploring the multiple

[13] Andrea Bianchi and Moshe Hirsch (eds), *International Law's Invisible Frames: Social Cognition and Knowledge Production in International Legal Processes* (OUP 2021).

[14] Farnush Ghadery and others, 'A Self-Reflexive Rebellion: Of Universality and False Empowerment of the Global South' (Opinio Juris Blog, 17 March 2022).

[15] See Van Aaken and Hirsch's Introduction to this volume; also Chapter 4 by Krebs in this volume.

[16] Anne van Aaken and Jan-Philip Elm, 'Framing in and through Public International Law' in Andrea Bianchi and Moshe Hirsch (eds), *International Law's Invisible Frames: Social Cognition and Knowledge Production in International Legal Processes* (OUP 2021) 35–54.

[17] Jeffrey L Dunoff and Mark A Pollack, *Interdisciplinary Perspectives on International Law and International Relations: The State of the Art* (CUP 2020).

[18] Gregory Shaffer and Tom Ginsburg, 'The Empirical Turn in International Legal Scholarship' (2012) 106(1) American Journal of International Law 1–46.

[19] See here Moshe Hirsch, 'Social Cognitive Studies, Sociological Theory, and International Law' in Bianchi and Hirsch (n 13).

relationalities between *internal* organization of knowledge and perception within the human mind and *externally* observed human behaviour. The task is to study what kind of motivations and heuristic conceptions influence actors towards particular choices, argumentative practices, and behavioural patterns.

Apart from recognizing the growing importance of cognitive-behavioural approaches to the work of international institutions as well as in international legal scholarship, the contributions to this volume have an additional objective. This is to understand how different *theoretical* approaches to international law, as organizing bodies of knowledge, schemas, and information interact with and impact upon conditions of mental cognition. It proposes to understand the role and significance of cognitive sciences to the 'descriptive and explanatory premises'[20] of different theoretical approaches to international law.

This research is not without significance. Any theoretical approach comes with its own set of assumptions about the world, the role of specific actors within it, and the importance they assign to law as a means for change and transformation. When it comes to critical scholarship, including Third World Approaches to International Law (TWAIL) and feminist and Marxist work, the question of who benefits and what systems of thought uphold the existing order of things requires an analysis of the law's social effects and to some extent its world-making functions. Cognitive-behavioural approaches confront and bring to bear a number of critical questions to the Marxist framework, including that of human subjectivities, historical method, and how they classify, organize, and categorize human behaviour.

## 3. Situating Marxism in International Legal Theory

At the outset, it is important to recognize that the Marxist tradition does not represent a cohesive, uncontested set of prescriptions. Instead, Marxist thought remains highly splintered and disaggregated and includes a diverse set of propositions. Even within this diversity of Marxist thought, a few key themes feature prominently. These include Marxism's preoccupation with 'totality', 'ideology', 'class struggle', and 'commodification', alongside its approach to human subjectification as grounded in historical materialism. Even though Marx did not expound a theory of law, it would be remiss to suggest that law played no role in Marx's thinking.[21] Moreover, generations of Marxist scholars have drawn from Marx's larger insights into history and political economy to bear on the role of law in society. Marxist international legal theory has argued that international law is deeply implicated

[20] Van Aaken and Hirsch's Introduction to this volume.

[21] Marx intended to write on both the state and international trade and other topics, but did not manage to get there during his lifetime. <https://wikirouge.net/texts/en/Letter_to_Ferdinand_Lassalle,February_22,_1858> accessed 17 April 2024.

in the imperial and global capitalist project based on a system of exploitation of labour power, ecological extractivism, land dispossession, and endless accumulation of surplus value.

In mainstream international law scholarship, Marxist approaches have had a steady revival in the last two decades.[22] Clearly, this has something to say about the discipline of international law trying to grapple with ever more systemic questions of injustice and oppression. The reigning ecological disaster, imperialist wars, settler colonial violence, forced migration, and structural inequality all point to the inevitable nature of capitalist expropriation and its intimate connection with international law. It also exposes the nature of capitalism as uneven and inherently prone to crisis. Marxism has provided a useful lens to study the structural relationship between capitalism and imperialism and how international law creates conditions of crisis, unequal distribution, and material subordination for the vast majority of the world's population.

At least four important Marxist perspectives on international law are important to note.[23] First, Marxist accounts have located the history of international law to the birth and spread of global capitalism which also coincided with the period of colonial expropriation and imperial expansion. In this, international law was crucial to the violent process of *primitive accumulation*, both at home and in the colonies entailing the 'extirpation, enslavement and entombment' of the native population.[24] The imperial thrust of international law manifested not only in the large scale expropriation of native land but also the wholesale transformation of non-capitalist societies into the image of capitalist modernity.[25] International law, including its rules on trade and commerce, the doctrine of territory, sovereignty, statehood, and 'civilization', became central to this imperial project of domination.[26]

In other words, Marxist accounts have offered a historical-materialist critique of the discipline where violence and expropriation are by default part of international law's systemic logic. Importantly, this logic is not merely part of the history of international law but continues to the present day. It allows us to witness modern international law as a continuation of past practices of 'exclusion and conditional

[22] An interesting conversation on the topic can be found here. See 'Revival and Renewal of Marxist Approaches' (LPE Blog) <https://lpeproject.org/conferences/revival-and-renewal-of-marxist-approaches> accessed 17 April 2024.

[23] Elsewhere, I have elaborated on each of them in greater detail. This section draws from that earlier piece. See Kanad Bagchi, 'Marxist Approaches to International Law: An Outline' (Max Planck Institute for Comparative Public Law and International Law (MPIL) Research Paper No 2022-16) <https://papers.ssrn.com/sol3/papers.cfm?abstract_id=4155411> accessed 17 April 2024.

[24] Karl Marx, *Capital: A Critique of Political Economy*, vol 1, 'Chapter Thirty-One: Genesis of the Industrial Capitalist' (1867) <www.marxists.org/archive/marx/works/1867-c1/ch31.htm> accessed 17 April 2024.

[25] Mark Neocleous, 'International Law as Primitive Accumulation; Or, the Secret of Systematic Colonization' (2012) 23(4) European Journal of International Law 941–62.

[26] Ntina Tzouvala, *Capitalism as Civilisation: A History of International Law* (CUP 2020).

inclusion' of the non-Western world.[27] The constitution of the United Nations, the battle for self-determination,[28] and the quest for an international human rights framework did not fundamentally change the erstwhile colonial relationships but marked the beginning of 'imperialism without colonies'.[29] This has ensured that even while international law has proffered a limited framework for political emancipation, international economic institutions continue to tie the 'Third World' to the economic dependence of former colonial powers. Important work in this regard has highlighted how bilateral investment treaties (BITs) entrench the power of foreign capital, the rules of the World Trade Organization and its Agreement on Trade-Related Aspects of Intellectual Property (TRIPS) prevent access to life-saving drugs, and financial institutions such as the World Bank and International Monetary Fund discipline states and political communities into austerity, multiplying sovereign debt and market liberalization.[30]

A second important contribution of Marxist international legal theory has been to imagine international law as a terrain of class antagonism in which legal structures enable, reflect, and reify the competing interests of different classes. International law, therefore, is not an empty vessel or a neutral instrument but is crucial to how capital accumulation acquires a global dimension characterized by the international division of labour. Marxist international law scholars such as Chimni and Rasulov have argued for a class approach to international law which visibilizes the role of different classes which materially influence the formation and interpretation of international law.[31] They have cautioned against theorizing the state and international institutions as a monolithic black box. Instead, locating them under the present conditions of globalization as mediating the rise of two competing social fractions—what has been loosely referred to as the transnational capitalist classes (TCCs) (that is, those who control the means of production and capital accumulation) and an emerging transnational oppressed class (TOC) composed of social groups who are disenfranchised from the means of production. In

[27] ibid 2.

[28] Jochen von Bernstorff and Philipp Dann (eds), *The Battle for International Law: South-North Perspectives on the Decolonization Era* (OUP 2019).

[29] BS Chimni, *International Law and World Order: A Critique of Contemporary Approaches* (CUP 2017) 496.

[30] Amaka Vanni, 'On Intellectual Property Rights, Access to Medicines and Vaccine Imperialism' (TWAILR Reflections, 23 March 2021); Pratyush Nath Upreti, 'A TWAIL Critique of Intellectual Property and Related Disputes in Investor-State Dispute Settlement' (2022) 25(1) The Journal of World Intellectual Property 220–37; Kate Miles, *The Origins of International Investment Law: Empire, Environment and the Safeguarding of Capital* (CUP 2013); John Linarelli, Margot Salomon, and Muthucumaraswamy Sornarajah, *The Misery of International Law: Confrontations with Injustice in the Global Economy* (OUP 2018).

[31] Akbar Rasulov, 'The Nameless Rapture of the Struggle: Towards a Marxist Class-Theoretic Approach to International Law' (2008) 19 Finnish Yearbook of International Law 243–94; BS Chimni, 'Prolegomena to a Class Approach to International Law' (2010) 21(1) European Journal of International Law 57–82.

this sense, the state emerges as the crystallization of class struggle[32] and its function is not simply to entrench and stabilize the interests of the capitalist class but to ensure that the long-term interests of capital are protected, even if that means, in the short term, the state might as well facilitate working-class interests.[33] A Marxist class analysis allows us to comprehend the material struggles on the ground—climate change, biodiversity protection, development-related displacement—as primarily a struggle between the interests of transnational capital and that of the rights of labour, indigenous communities, and agricultural workers. What role international law plays in the organization of this struggle has been an important object of Marxist legal thinking.

An understanding of the class structure of international law begs the question of how certain ideas, interests, and values become more dominant than others. Drawing from the concept of 'ideology', Marxist international legal scholars have argued that supposedly 'universal' values such as democracy, human rights, the rule of law, or economic development are susceptible to selective interests and open to co-option by dominant classes.[34] Here, law (including international law) acts as an 'ideological form'[35] which domesticates resistance and invisibilizes class conflict by presenting particular interests as universal ones. This has been most visible with respect to humanitarian intervention, the 'war on terror', and economic conditionalities imposed by international financial institutions—all invoking international law in the pursuit of freedom, liberation, and economic prosperity.[36] Each of these notions carry with them prescriptions for a particular kind of legal-institutional/bureaucratic-state transformation of the 'Third World', in which transnational capital must be kept safe from local interference. Susan Marks has spent considerable efforts to show how ideology operates to legitimize exploitation, by masking the oppressive system of capitalist social relations as natural and permanent.[37] Ideology through international law is mobilised through abstract legal concepts, the repeated use of 'ideas and rhetorical processes', and the

[32] Umut Özsu, 'The Necessity of Contingency: Method and Marxism in International Law' in Ingo Venzke and Kevin Jon Heller (eds), *Contingency in International Law: On the Possibility of Different Legal Histories* (OUP 2021) 60–76, 68.

[33] See here the contribution by Antonios Tzanakopoulos, 'The Master's Tools and the Master's House: Marxist Insights for International Law' in Anne van Aaken, Pierre d'Argent, Lauri Mälksoo, and Johann Justus Vasel (eds), *The Oxford Handbook of International Law in Europe* (OUP online edn, Oxford Academic, 20 June 2023) <https://academic.oup.com/edited-volume/46846/chapter-abstract/440490116?redirectedFrom=fulltext> accessed 14 May 2024.

[34] Susan Marks, *The Riddle of All Constitutions: International Law, Democracy, and the Critique of Ideology* (OUP 2003).

[35] Karl Marx, 'Preface to a Contribution to the Critique of Political Economy' (1859) <www.marxists.org/archive/marx/works/1859/critique-pol-economy/preface.htm> accessed 17 April 2024.

[36] See, for instance, Hilary Charlesworth, 'Feminist Reflections on the Responsibility to Protect' (2010) 2(3) Global Responsibility to Protect 232–49; Ntina Tzouvala, 'TWAIL and the Unwilling and Unable Doctrine: Continuities and Ruptures' 109 AJIL Unbound 266–70.

[37] Susan Marks, 'Exploitation as an International Legal Concept' in Susan Marks (ed), *International Law on the Left: Re-examining Marxist Legacies* (CUP 2008) 281–307.

mystification and abstraction of individual harms and conduct, even while leaving untouched the deeper structures of political economy which makes violence part of the ordinary.[38]

The law's propensity to create abstractions in which individuals and their social relationships are removed from concrete material conditions squarely follows capital's inherent tendency to commodify everything, but most crucially labour power.[39] Labour produces surplus value but itself is alienated from the very means of production. Capital and law in the Marxist tradition therefore exhibits a *structural* relationship. Soviet jurist Evgeny Pashukanis, one of the most influential Marxist theorists of law, analysed the abstracting and commodifying tendency of the law most astutely. He argued, in what has come to be known as the 'Commodity form theory of law', that in capitalist societies individuals holding property rights backed by contract law are homologous to abstract commodities. Just as commodities which are traded in the market are abstracted from their specific historical context, individuals through legal relations are similarly separated from their material conditions. For him, the 'legal subject is thus the abstract commodity owner elevated into the heavens'[40] and the legal form mirrors this commodity form. One consequence of such commodification is that individuals are then treated as equal bearers of rights and exchange is permitted as transpiring between two equals. By doing so, Pashukanis argues that law invisibilizes, hides, and 'permits real inequality' among individuals.[41] The task, then, is to 'know the real historical substratum of our cognitive abstractions'.[42]

Applying this logic to international law produces the insight that states operate precisely as owners of property with each bearing equal rights. The problem, however, is that this formal equality fundamentally disguises 'that they are unequal in their significance and their power'.[43] It is when conflicts arise that the veneer of sovereign equality gives way to brute force and domination. China Miéville extended Pashukanis's commodity form theory to questions of international law to bring home the point that exchange implies ownership, largely exercised through legal means and with the objective of excluding others. In the realm of international law,

[38] Susan Marks (ed), *International Law on the Left: Re-examining Marxist Legacies* (CUP 2008) 7. She talks about five different ways in which ideology works. Ideology works through (1) universalization, (2) reification, (3) naturalization, (4) rationalization, and (5) narrativization.

[39] For an illustrative discussion, see China Miéville, 'The Commodity-Form Theory of International Law' in Susan Marks (ed), *International Law on the Left: Re-examining Marxist Legacies* (CUP 2008) 107.

[40] Evgeny Pashukanis, *The General Theory of Law and Marxism*, chapter IV: Commodity and the Subject (1924) <www.marxists.org/archive/pashukanis/1924/law/ch04.htm> accessed 17 April 2024.

[41] Evgeny Pashukanis, *International Law* (1925) <www.marxists.org/archive/pashukanis/1925/xx/intlaw.htm> accessed 17 April 2024.

[42] Evgeny Pashukanis, 'The General Theory of Law and Marxism: Methods of Constructing the Concrete in the Abstract Sciences' www.marxists.org/archive/pashukanis/1924/law/ch01.htm.

[43] Evgeny Pashukanis, *International Law* (1925) <www.marxists.org/archive/pashukanis/1925/xx/intlaw.htm> accessed 17 April 2024.

where a centralized enforcement system is absent, sovereign entities themselves resolve disputes related to rule interpretation. In a deeply unequal global landscape, this translates to powerful states shaping the order and substance of legal norms through economic and military influence. It is in this context that China Miéville argued 'coercion is at the heart of the commodity form',[44] and since international law mediates commodity exchange, *violence* is central to it—'Between Equal Rights, force decides'.[45] Miéville's reconstruction of Pashukanis found both acclaim as well as drawing criticism.[46] For Miéville, any Marxist conception of international law must acknowledge the very *legal form* as imbricated in violence, imperialist rivalry, and domination. As he most remarkably put it, 'The chaotic and bloody world around us is the rule of law.'[47]

Marxist international legal scholarship has reflected on several important questions in the field. Chimni has uncovered that foundational doctrines such as that of 'sources', particularly customary international law and the law of jurisdiction, have been historically enmeshed with the consolidation and expansion of capitalism and imperialism.[48] Drawing from Pashukanis, Grietje Baars has situated the historical role of 'corporations' in the struggle for imperialist rivalry.[49] Tor Kevor[50] and Christine Schwoebel-Patel[51] have worked with the concept of ideology to reveal the individualizing and abstracting character of international criminal law as well as how the idea of global justice is itself commodified, sold, and marketed through international criminal law processes, courts, and tribunals. Ruth Fletcher and Mai Taha have both extended the Marxist critique to issues of gender and social reproduction within notions of value in commodity exchange.[52]

[44] China Miéville, *Between Equal Rights: A Marxist Theory of International Law* (Brill 2005) 126.

[45] Karl Marx, *Capital Vol. I*: 'Chapter Ten: The Working-Day' (1867) <www.marxists.org/archive/marx/works/1867-c1/ch10.htm> accessed 17 April 2024.

[46] Grietje Baars, *The Corporation, Law and Capitalism: A Radical Perspective on the Role of Law in the Global Political Economy* (Brill 2019); A Claire Cutler, 'New Constitutionalism and the Commodity Form of Global Capitalism' in Stephen Gill and A Claire Cutler (eds), *New Constitutionalism and World Order* (CUP 2014) 45–62. For criticism, see Chimni (n 29) 473–77.

[47] Miéville (n 44) 319.

[48] BS Chimni, 'Customary International Law: A Third World Perspective' (2018) 112(1) American Journal of International Law 1–46; BS Chimni, 'International Law of Jurisdiction: A Third World Perspective' (2022) 35(1) Leiden Journal of International Law 29–54.

[49] Grietje Baars, *The Corporation, Law and Capitalism: A Radical Perspective on the Role of Law in the Global Political Economy* (Brill 2019).

[50] Tor Krever, 'International Criminal Law: An Ideology Critique' (2013) 26(3) Leiden Journal of International Law 701–23.

[51] Christine Schwöbel-Patel, *Marketing Global Justice: The Political Economy of International Criminal Law* (CUP 2021).

[52] Ruth Fletcher, 'Legal Form, Commodities and Re-production: Reading Pashukanis' (2013) Queen Mary School of Law Legal Studies Research Paper No 158 <https://papers.ssrn.com/sol3/papers.cfm?abstract_id=2359140> accessed 17 April 2024; Mai Taha, 'Reading "Class" in International Law: The Labor Question in Interwar Egypt' (2016) 25(5) Social and Legal Studies 567–89. The works cited here are only representative. For an extended reading list of Marxist work in international law, see Robert Knox, 'Marxist Approaches to International Law Bibliography' (2018) Oxford Bibliographies <www.oxfordbibliographies.com/view/document/obo-9780199796953/obo-9780199796953-0163.xml> accessed 17 April 2024.

To bring it all together, Marxism provides a framework to think about social relations, including international law and capitalism, as an 'integrated whole'.[53] It probes us to think about international law not as a detached body of rules but as part of a larger social and economic infrastructure with its own operating logic. Capital for its very reproduction requires endless accumulation, expropriation, and extraction which international law makes possible. As Rosa Luxemburg argued, 'Capitalism must always and everywhere fight a battle of annihilation against every non-capitalist form that it encounters.'[54] International law creates new markets, feeds labour to the production process, and stabilizes local political and economic structures to make it amenable for capitalist production, inevitably through violent dispossession and extraction. In other words, international law, capitalism, and the imperialist project go hand in hand.

A Marxist critique of international law is aimed at uncovering precisely the many idealistic portrayals of the discipline as denouncing war and promoting peace or human rights. In this sense, alongside a structural critique, it is also an 'internal' critique of the system that exposes the inner contradictions of its operating logic, with the hope that it invites radical political action to change existing structures of political economy.[55]

## 4. Marxism and Cognitive-Behavioural Studies: An Uneasy Relationship

The relationship between Marxism and cognitive sciences (broadly understood)[56] has been a subject of lively debate in the past.[57] Some have suggested that Marxism and cognitive studies are the closest when it comes to rejecting narrow disciplinary boundaries, drawing instead from a wide range of intellectual frameworks including social anthropology, psychology, and economic theory. One can cite

[53] Andrea Bianchi, *International Law Theories: An Inquiry into Different Ways of Thinking* (OUP 2016) 84.

[54] Rosa Luxemburg, *The Accumulation of Capital*, 'The Struggle Against Natural Economy' (1913) <www.marxists.org/archive/luxemburg/1913/accumulation-capital/ch27.htm> accessed 17 April 2024.

[55] Paul Mattick, *Theory as Critique: Essays on Capital* (Brill 2018). Also, as Marx himself put it, 'Philosophers have hitherto only interpreted the world in various ways; the point is to change it' (Karl Marx, 'Eleven Theses on Feuerbach' <www.marxists.org/archive/marx/works/1845/theses> accessed 17 April 2024).

[56] See the definition provided by Moshe Hirsch: 'Cognitive science is the interdisciplinary study of mental processes involved in acquiring, classifying, and interpreting knowledge in human environment, and in deciding what action might be appropriate.' See Moshe Hirsch, 'Social Cognitive Studies, Sociological Theory, and International Law' in Bianchi and Hirsch (n 13).

[57] For example, see John E Roemer, 'Rational Choice Marxism: Some Issues of Method and Substance' (1985) 20(34) Economic and Political Weekly 1439–42; Stephen Eric Bronner, 'Politics and Judgment: A Critique of Rational Choice Marxism' (1990) 52(2) The Review of Politics 242–64.

here the important yet contested tradition of analytical Marxism emerging in the 1970s and 1980s, which combined Marxist insights and social science methods, including that of rational choice and game theory models and neoclassical economics.[58] Much like their cognitive-behavioural counterparts, analytical Marxists were particularly interested in studying the relationship between social structures and individual behaviour. Yet, the popularity of analytical Marxism and indeed its relationship to classical Marxist scholarship began to wane because of fundamental methodological disagreements including the latter's rejection of Marxist dialectics and the embrace, sometimes unequivocally, of programmatic empirical solutions. Several Marxist as well as non-Marxist scholars critically noted in analytical Marxism, an 'unconditional surrender to mainstream liberal philosophical and political process'.[59]

Having said that, it must be emphasized that classical Marxism and cognitive-behavioural studies share perhaps one key feature, in that both traditions view empirical observation and inquiry as an important tool of critique.[60] Yet, in the Marxist tradition, empirical observation is not a given but needs to be further investigated as against the 'totality' of material social relations which then shapes both the content and form of how knowledge and observation is gathered and produced. In other words, even while accepting the scientificity of the empirical method, Marxism broadly rejects the 'empiricism' prevalent in some cruder versions of cognitive-behavioural approaches,[61] which suggests that 'reality' is based on 'facts' which can be objectively accessed through observation and perception.[62] For Marxism and critical theory in general, taking the road to empiricism leads to unquestioned positivism. This is because in the Marxist tradition facts are not a given, waiting to be discovered, governed by immutable laws, but are made in the dynamic process of class and social struggles.

The significance of the concept of 'totality' in Marxist thought comes from the fact that Marxism is primarily concerned with a *structural* analysis of social relations, locating them, as Marx had explained, in the 'material conditions of life'.[63] To view things in totality means to view the world as an endless set of interrelationships, where one phenomenon is always connected to the other. Here,

[58] GA Cohen, *Karl Marx's Theory of History: A Defence* (Princeton UP 2000); H Gintis, *Analytical Marxism*, edited by John Roemer (CUP 1986). See also 'Analytical Marxism' (Stanford Encyclopedia of Philosophy) <https://plato.stanford.edu/entries/marxism-analytical> accessed 17 April 2024.

[59] Marcus Roberts, *Analytical Marxism: A Critique* (New York: Verso 1997).

[60] See, for instance, Georg H Fromm, 'Empiricism, Science, and Philosophy in the German Ideology' (2015) 27(1) Rethinking Marxism 9–32.

[61] Probodh Dhor Chakrabarti, 'Behavioralism: A Challenge to Marxism?' (1976) 4(9) Social Scientist 55–59.

[62] Geoffrey Pilling, 'The Concepts of Capital in Marx's "Capital"' (Routledge 2015, originally published in 1980) <www.marxists.org/archive/pilling/works/capital/pilling2.htm> accessed 17 April 2024; see, for a fuller description, David M Trubek, 'Where the Action Is: Critical Legal Studies and Empiricism' (1984) 36(1/2) Stanford Law Review 575–622.

[63] Karl Marx, 'Preface to a Contribution to the Critique of Political Economy' (1859) <www.marxists.org/archive/marx/works/1859/critique-pol-economy/preface.htm> accessed 17 April 2024.

structures represent '(unobservable) sets of internally related elements'[64] that are neither static nor everlasting but take shape from the imperatives of a particular mode of production. For Marxists, it is the capitalist mode of production which determines the relationship of individuals to each other, to society, and to nature and thus also limits human agency in a historically specific way. The political, economic, and social structures of capitalism create the conditions for its constant reproduction. Any analysis of social phenomenon, then, must adopt a concrete historical mode of enquiry in which the given phenomena must be considered as against the entire 'social organism'.[65]

A predisposition to structures must not be understood in the simplistic sense of the *base* determining the legal and political *superstructure*. To the contrary, the relationship of the 'base/superstructure' is highly continent, co-constitutive, and even contradictory—a point that is routinely forgotten.[66] Far from economic determinism, for Marx, cultural and social aspects of human interaction need to be understood as part of the larger edifice of structural relations of power.

Cognitive-behavioural approaches, on the other hand, largely operate within what is termed as 'methodological individualism' that places individuals as the 'unit of analysis'.[67] The framework of methodological individualism (MI) posits that social phenomenon and structural relations can and ought to be explained through individual motivations, (self-)interests, ideas, beliefs, and biases.[68] Flipping the Marxist framework, MI argues that social wholes are composed of individuals, each with their own set of behavioural patterns and cultural eccentricities. That we must be able to analyse the 'micro' foundations of social relationships, individual motivations, and cognitive frames within which they operate. It is for this reason that cognitive-behavioural approaches, even while they seek to challenge the 'rationalist' paradigm, nonetheless do not reject it entirely. Bounded rationality, which is presented as a corrective to rational choice theory, holds on the individualist framework, tweaking it ever so slightly to account for circumstances of irrational behaviour. The argument goes that if we could unearth and mitigate the

[64] Jutta Weldes, 'Marxism and Methodological Individualism: A Critique' (1989) 18(3) Theory and Society 353–86, 368.

[65] Pyotr Kondrashov, 'Reflections on Lenin's Dialectics' (*Monthly Review*, 1 January 2023) <https://monthlyreview.org/2023/01/01/reflections-on-lenins-dialectics> accessed 17 April 2024.

[66] In fact, Engels himself had pointedly rejected the interpretation that the 'base' is the ultimate determining factor. In a letter to J. Bloch in 1980, Engels writes: 'According to the materialist conception of history, the ultimately determining element in history is the production and reproduction of real life. Other than this neither Marx nor I have ever asserted. Hence if somebody twists this into saying that the economic element is the only determining one, he transforms that proposition into a meaningless, abstract, senseless phrase.' <www.marxists.org/archive/marx/works/1890/letters/90_09_21.htm> accessed 17 April 2024.

[67] Hirsch (n 56). This is, however, not to suggest that important streams within cognitive-behavioural studies do not focus on social groups. Yet, as I argue below, this focus on social groups and identities does not necessarily take cognitive-behavioral approaches out of its methodological inclinations.

[68] See also 'Methodological Individualism' (Stanford Encyclopedia of Philosophy) <https://plato.stanford.edu/entries/methodological-individualism> accessed 17 April 2024.

multiple biases, heuristics, and sensibilities of individual actors taking into consideration their social, economic, and cultural circumstances, law and legal intervention might help us construct a better world.

The thrust of MI presents an obvious problem for the Marxist thinker, and this relates to how human subjectivities are formed and change. From a Marxist perspective, individual sensibilities, beliefs, and consciousness take form and shape based on the function of such individuals in relation to the means of production. It is this relationship that 'constitute[s] individuals; they confer onto them definite characteristics, motives for action'.[69] As Louis Althusser would go on to say, 'individuals are always-already subjects' and are assigned a specific role and rationality in the system of capitalist production.[70] It is this system that governs property among private parties and assigns workers to the necessity of selling their labour and capitalists to the exploitation of land, labour, and resources. Thus a 'worker' is a worker not in isolation but in relation to the capitalist class and vice versa. Similarly, Jutta Weldes writes:

> capitalists exist, form intentions, and possess and exercise power as capitalists only in relation to the working class and in virtue of their position in the particular mode of production in which they are embedded.[71]

Individuals are not simply a product of their class relationship but are also exemplified by their relationship to gender, sexuality, and race. A Marxist theoretical framework, however, implores us to think about these relationships in materialist terms, eschewing their identarian connotations. Marx himself had posited that it is not the 'consciousness of men that determines their existence, but their social existence that determines their consciousness'.[72]

Cognitive-behavioural studies, even with their emphasis on group dynamics,[73] are unable to explain how social identity within a particular group is historically formed or relates to the *systemic* logic of material relations. As Marx had insightfully noted in his *Theses on Feuerbach*, 'the human essence is no abstraction inherent in each single individual. In its reality it is the ensemble of the social relations'[74] This exposes cognitive-behavioural studies to the critique of abstracting

[69] Weldes (n 64) 373.

[70] Louis Althusser, 'Ideology and Ideological State Apparatuses (Notes towards an Investigation)' (1970) <https://mforbes.sites.gettysburg.edu/cims226/wp-content/uploads/2018/09/Week-3b-Louis-Althusser.pdf> accessed 17 April 2024.

[71] Weldes (n 64) 365.

[72] Karl Marx, 'A Contribution to the Critique of Political Economy: Preface' (1859) <www.marxists.org/archive/marx/works/1859/critique-pol-economy/preface.htm> accessed 17 April 2024.

[73] On group dynamics, see Van Aaken and Hirsch's Introduction to this volume.

[74] Karl Marx, 'Thesis on Feuerbach' (1845) <www.marxists.org/archive/marx/works/1845/theses/thses.htm> accessed 17 April 2024.

individuals from 'full historical complexity'[75] and flattening them out. To put it somewhat differently, Marxism proposes a theory of history and not so much individual action, whereas cognitive-behavioural approaches are a theory of individual action without a theory of history.[76]

The two approaches also hold diametrically opposite assumptions about the role of power, neutrality, and universality in scientific enquiry. Cognitive-behavioural approaches squarely operate within the positivist tradition with its emphasis on empirical data, commitment to realism, and a quest towards objectivity and neutrality.[77] In this, certain epistemological frameworks and modes of analysis become normative standpoints for methodological intervention. Human subjectivities are viewed from the prism of universally accepted patterns of behaviour comprising common cognitive characteristics which, once identified, can be remoulded into specific actions.

A Marxist perspective would push us to exercise caution regarding the false universality of the scientific method, especially the claim that human subjectivity can be objectively observed, patterned, and programmatically altered. Instead, as the discussion in the previous section highlights, a Marxist analysis points to the ideological apparatus through which legal norms and scientific claims operate to depoliticize existing social conflicts and class contradictions inherent to the scientific schema. In the Marxist tradition, ideology serves the function of establishing, stabilizing, and interpreting social phenomenon as objective and natural. Ideology works through several different planes, most notably through universalization, reification, and abstraction.[78] A Marxist ideology critique, then, would find that what is presented as universal is in fact an expression of a particular ideology and value system in which power is often embedded within notions of objectivity and value-free methodology and research.

Ideology also has a material effect and takes shape from the numerous socio-legal practices and institutional customs which govern everyday life. Cognitive-behavioural approaches, then, are not without ideology of a particular kind that deflects responsibility to individual actions, neglecting the structural ways in which the system operates. It has real-world consequences in terms of how people are governed and categorized, but it also plays a crucial role in the 'mystification' of social relations.[79]

[75] Ruey-Chyi Wang, 'Methodological Individualism, Rational Choice and Marxism: Jon Elster's Reconstruction of Marxism' (1992) 33 Tunghai Journal 477–504.

[76] ibid.

[77] This is also a point made in Chapter 4 by Krebs in this volume.

[78] See Susan Marks, 'Big Brother Is Bleeping Us: With the Message That Ideology Does Not Matter' (2001) 12(1) European Journal of International Law 109–23.

[79] Robert Knox and Ntina Tzouvala, 'International Law of State Responsibility and COVID-19: An Ideology Critique' (2021) 39(1) The Australian Year Book of International Law Online 105–21. See also Louis Althusser, *On the Reproduction of Capitalism: Ideology and Ideological State Apparatuses* (GM Goshgarian tr, Verso 2014).

Cognitive-behavioural approaches situate socio-mental biases as primarily inhering in the legislator, the judge, and the academic and international institutions tasked with formulating, interpreting, and applying legal norms. Thus much of the emphasis remains on how law might correct such biases, as we will see in the next section. A Marxist ideological perspective would argue that biases are inherent to the legal form, encoding, systematizing, and legitimizing a system of beliefs, which then attributes specific characteristics to individual behaviour. In this sense, a Marxist perspective understands individual and social behaviour as already historically constituted and determined.

## 5. International Law, Racial Discrimination, and Racialization

The tension between cognitive-behavioural approaches and Marxism comes into sharp relief especially in the light of how these approaches view the role of international law in the struggle towards a more just and equal society. In this section, I take the example of race as it features within Marxist accounts of international law and counterpose it to accounts of racial discrimination, prevalent within cognitive studies. What I hope to achieve by studying these approaches alongside each other is to appreciate the peculiar argumentative patterns, ideological standpoints, and theoretical premises they employ to the work of international law in producing and mitigating racism and racialization.

In an important contribution, Moshe Hirsch, one of the editors of this volume, set out to think about how social cognitive and cultural factors, including cognitive biases, 'feed and reproduce racially discriminatory behaviour'.[80] Hirsch argues that discriminatory behaviour is deeply ingrained within the idea of racial groups and is not easily abandoned. Social groups influence their members' behaviour towards other social groups through several mental classifications, forms of stereotyping, perception, and information dissemination but also through reinforcing individual and collective memory. Social groups construct collective knowledge, set the contours of acceptable behaviour, and establish parameters for individuality and identity. Personality traits and racial attributes such as skin colour trigger perception which ultimately fits into a particular 'schema about a group of people'. In other words, socio-mental lenses group, categorize, and conform individuals to certain distinct spaces in society, thus reproducing a 'fertile ground for further racially discriminatory practices'.[81]

If we understand racial discrimination as significantly influenced by cognitive-cultural factors that synthesize, process, and disseminate certain kinds of

[80] Moshe Hirsch, 'Cognitive Sociology, Social Cognition and Coping with Racial Discrimination in International Law' (2020) 30(4) European Journal of International Law 1319–38, 1321.
[81] ibid 1331.

information about other groups, effective strategies towards mitigating these cognitive biases becomes the obvious answer. As Hirsch optimistically posits, 'biased mental processes, however, are not inevitable and may change over time'.[82] His proposition is that international law might play a role in that process, especially given that the prohibition of racial discrimination is a fundamental principle of international human rights law.[83] What follows, then, is a set of procedural proposals and legal strategies which might alleviate negative racial attitudes towards marginalized and racial groups. These prescriptions rely on international institutions, adjudicatory bodies, non-governmental organizations, and states to use their legal instruments towards encouraging, nudging, and shaping the cognitive-social infrastructure that enables and sustains discrimination. The list includes involving external (impartial) actors within the local context, dissemination information concerning racially harmful practices, exposing negative stereotypes, participation of mass media in international regimes, and, finally, employing less demanding standards of proof and evidentiary burden regarding particular acts of discrimination.[84] While none of these measures are expected to miraculously end racial discrimination, Hirsch believes that they might influence socio-cognitive biases by making them visible and thus undesirable.

In other words, racism is understood to be about discrimination, mental schemas, and constellations, a set of ideas and a construction that primarily exists in one's mind, unconnected to, or perhaps existing independently of, the concrete material relations within which race is produced. The racism as 'discrimination' lens gathers attention to the inter-personal relations among individuals as they respond to the 'other'.[85] Racism becomes about prejudice,[86] an aberration from an otherwise non-racist social and legal infrastructure, and, most importantly, a cognitive failure which can be corrected. Insofar as law and, in this case, international law can be programmed towards altering or changing these mental tendencies, it becomes a tool for emancipation.

A Marxist account would be diametrically opposed to this understanding of race and racism. From a Marxist perspective, how we explain race acquires an important place. So does the question of why certain 'races' are at the receiving end of domination and discrimination. In this, race and racism are not about expressing difference alone but principally about why certain differences have historically acquired prominence, and which set of social relations has made that possible. Put differently, Marxist international legal scholars have offered a sustained account of

[82] ibid 1321.

[83] For instance, the International Convention on the Elimination of All Forms of Racial Discrimination 1969.

[84] Hirsch (n 80) 1331–37.

[85] See Carbado and Roithmayr (n 3).

[86] See Ntina Tzouvala, 'Invested in Whiteness: Zimbabwe, the von Pezold Arbitration, and the Question of Race in International Law' (2022) 2(2) Journal of Law and Political Economy 226–51.

race as a historically contingent and materially conditioned phenomenon which continues to the present day. Even though forms of racism change over different historical periods, it is marked by an exploitative and violent continuity. The central focus of Marxist analysis on race is not so much discrimination as understanding racism as rooted in the process of 'racialization'.[87]

From a historical-materialist perspective, race is neither a natural fact nor a pre-exiting category in which different groups of people can be neatly summarized. Instead, race is socially produced in the process of capitalist accumulation and has historically been accompanied by imperial expansion and colonial violence. Early Third World Marxists, especially Franz Fanon, Eric Williams, and Walter Rodney, located racism precisely within this matrix, where race and capital co-produce each other through the extractive (international) division of labour and dispossession of land in the non-Western world.[88] They understood racialization as a process of abstraction through which different communities are systematically put into a hierarchy characterized by the place and role that a certain community acquires in the capitalist mode of production.[89] Racism, then, is intimately connected to the ways in which 'difference' is manifested through the subordination of some communities embedded within historical processes of economic and wealth extraction. Race is not simply a cultural phenomenon, and neither is it tied to particular identifies, but is intimately co-constituted through the structures of global political economy.[90]

If we understand race and racism through the perspective of 'racialization', then it becomes clear that physical attributes such as skin colour and the like are not what distinguishes communities and groups from each other but that these attributes relate to how groups navigate and manage the relationship of domination and hierarchy. Law generally and international law specifically are tools for such differentiated management and have historically structured institutions and rules of the 'global order including slavery, colonialism and empire'.[91] International law, then, is deeply implicated in the process of justifying, stabilizing, and juridifying racialization. It is part of the problem and not the solution.

[87] See here Robert Knox, 'International Law, Race and Capitalism: A Marxist Perspective' (2023) 117 AJIL Unbound 55–60.

[88] For a good account of how race interacts with capital, see Robert Knox and Ashok Kumar, 'Reexamining Race and Capitalism in the Marxist Tradition: Editorial Introduction' (2023) 31(2) Historical Materialism 25–48; Robert Knox, 'Valuing Race? Stretched Marxism and the Logic of Imperialism' (2016) 4 London Review of International Law 81.

[89] Robert Knox again explains it much better: 'Rather, racism is about the systematic *abstraction* of difference, its systematisation and its insertion into a hierarchy.' Notes for the workshop on Gender and Race in Law and Political Economy (University of Amsterdam, 7 December 2023). On file with the author.

[90] James Thuo Gathii and Ntina Tzouvala, 'Racial Capitalism and International Economic Law: Introduction' (2022) 25(2) Journal of International Economic Law 199–206.

[91] James Thuo Gathii, 'Studying Race in International Law Scholarship Using a Social Science Approach' (2021) 22(1) Chicago Journal of International Law 71–86, 74.

Race making and empire are visible in the different modes of international governance and within institutional regimes that (coercively) bind communities across the North–South divide. International economic institutions which perpetuate the global debt trap, rules of intellectual property that limit access to life-saving medicines, privatization of climate finance, and rules concerning humanitarian intervention all rearticulate the racialized 'dynamic of difference'.[92] Underlying these interventions is an unending transformation of the non-Western world into the image of European capitalist modernity, where the myth of equal sovereignty is precisely used to create and sustain perpetual bonds of subordination and dependency between the core and a racialized periphery. In this logic, the process of racialization and the project of constructing race makes the very 'DNA of international law' a 'capitalist, commercial and coercive enterprise'.[93] The shift from colonialism to formal independence did not fundamentally alter the global racial infrastructure of inequality and unfreedom, even while transmuting the contours of racism to conform to the present needs of capitalist social relations. In this sense, racism is integral to the maintenance and preservation of global capitalist expansion and cannot be studied in isolation from it.[94]

Unmaking this paradigm would require a fundamental restructuring of the global political economy. Law perhaps is not even the most important site of battle, imbricated as it is in the imperial project all the way down. This also means that from a Marxist perspective, prescriptions for more transparency, information, and rearticulating social preferences are unlikely to challenge the 'root cause'[95] of racial subjugation, and worse still, might end up legitimizing those very structures which engender the problem in the first place. Locating and mitigating racism through the prism of individualized discrimination, or repurposing faith in the transformative potential of the human rights regime, ignores the multiple material sites of race production in international law. Race, then, must be located within a globalized system of racialized exploitation in which race operates to stratify communities based on their potential for extraction and profit making.[96]

Finally, and relatedly, locating racism in individual relationships of the everyday discrimination also reinforces the binary and separatedness between race, gender, and sexuality as co-constitutive in the production of capitalist social relations. The relationship between capitalist patriarchy and the racial division of labour have been prominent in the work of many materialist black feminists who have argued

[92] Antony Anghie, *Imperialism, Sovereignty and the Making of International Law* (CUP 2005).

[93] John Linarelli, Margot Salomon, and Muthucumaraswamy Sornarajah, *The Misery of International Law: Confrontations with Injustice in the Global Economy* (OUP 2018) 22.

[94] Cedric J Robinson, *Black Marxism: The Making of the Black Radical Tradition* (3rd edn, University of North Carolina Press 2000). See also Walter Rodney, *How Europe Underdeveloped Africa* (Verso 2018, originally published in 1982).

[95] Susan Marks, 'Human Rights and Root Causes' (2011) 74(1) The Modern Law Review 57–78.

[96] Carmen G Gonzalez and Athena Mutua, 'Introduction: Special Issue on Racial Capitalism and Law' (2023) 2(1) Journal of Law and Political Economy 121–26.

that gender and racial hierarchy form part of capitalism's violent process of surplus creation. For Marxist international lawyers, accounting for race without accounting for gender, sexuality, or class is meaningless,[97] especially given that human subjectivities and the location of communities within the material, cultural, and political structures are deeply linked to the totality of capitalist social relations.

## 6. Revisiting the Relationship

A fundamental insight that emerges from the discussion above is that mitigating cognitive and socio-mental biases without embedding those within a specific historical moment in which they originate and take shape risks segregating human action from the determining elements of the larger material structures. This has the effect of naturalizing social relations and prefiguring them into chains of actions disconnected from the reality of concrete conditions. Consequently, Marxism and cognitive-behavioural approaches construct differently not only the kind of questions that one can ask about justice, change, and emancipation through international law but also offer radically different answers to how to go about it. How are we to think about the relationship between the two?

Marxism, even while it is tied to a materialist conception of history, is neither deterministic nor mechanical. Instead, Marxist thought is based on the idea that history itself is messy, complex, and imbued with contradictions. Class struggle, imperialist rivalry, technological advancement, and the like all point to the dynamism of capitalist social relations. Social structures are in perpetual motion, constantly produced, reproduced, and transformed through individual and collective action. Social structures, however, cannot be deduced to individual action alone. As Marx insightfully pointed out: 'Men make their own history … but they do not make it just as they please … but under circumstances directly encountered, given and transmitted from the past.'[98]

What this means is that even though social structures pre-determine individual agency, beliefs, and intentions, they are neither inevitable nor necessary. Perhaps, then, a useful way to think about Marxism and behavioural-cognitive approaches is through the contingency of legal struggles. Importantly, Marx himself was not against the liberal regime of right-based agitation, despite what popular contention might hold. In his work 'On the Jewish Question', which is often cited to bring home the point that Marx was disillusioned with the potential of equal

[97] Aytak Dibavar, 'Reclaiming Gender: A Case for Feminist Decolonial and Social Reproduction Theory' (2022) Global Constitutionalism 11(3) 450–64.

[98] Karl Marx, 'The Eighteenth Brumaire of Louis Bonaparte' (1852) <www.marxists.org/archive/marx/works/1852/18th-brumaire/ch01.htm> accessed 17 April 2024.

rights, Marx had only advanced a limited critique of *formal* legal equality. For him, political emancipation through law and legal rights was deeply 'individualizing' and 'alienating' and thus cannot be an end but only a means towards engendering larger social changes beyond what the law could provide.[99] This is also evident from Marx's extensive discussion on the length of the working day, which was won on a legal terrain.[100] Umut Özsu illustrates this point from Marx's work where he situates contingency within the contradictions of capitalist totality, arguing that the law and the state are crucial sites of continuing class struggle, opening, albeit in a limited way, the possibilities of change and transformation.[101] The point about contingency is to find and augment those 'pockets of freedom' that are often overshadowed by powerful designs.[102]

Marxism brings at least three sets of propositions to the study of socio-cognitive approaches to international law. First, Marxist conception of ideology exposes the false contingency of international law, the idea that even though historical relations are contingent, they are not always susceptible to change. As Susan Marks writes, 'just as things do not have to be as they are, so too history is not simply a matter of chance and will', meaning that human agency, while paramount for resistance and change, always operates within the 'logics of a system'.[103] The work of ideology points to the multiple ways in which dominant paradigms of thought, ideas, and institutional processes, even when they create conditions of injustice and oppression, are made to be seen as natural, mundane, and part of the ordinary. Ideology shows why certain argumentative patterns and belief systems are singled out, separated, and rejected and why others 'stick'. International law remains complicit in this process, as it naturalizes legal relationships and domesticates class conflicts. It also plays a significant role in propagating seemingly neutral concepts, such as 'development', 'rule of law', and 'fair and equitable treatment', even as it hides the multiple distributive contestations within them. Ideology critique exposes the larger

[99] A good starting point for discussions around Marxism and international human rights discourse is Rob Knox and Ntina Tzouvala, 'Marxist Approaches to International Law' in Christina Binder and others (eds), *Elgar Encyclopedia of Human Rights* (Elgar 2022) 447–50.

[100] For a good description, see Igor Shoikhedbrod, *Revisiting Marx's Critique of Liberalism: Rethinking Justice, Legality and Rights* (Palgrave 2019).

[101] Umut Özsu (n 32); see also Umut's interview on the Volkerrecht blog where he notes: 'Far from being relegated to an epiphenomenal sphere of merely derivative structures, Marx and Engels therefore accord law a significant degree of constitutive power in regard to the production and reproduction of capitalist social relations. This means that the juridico-political order encodes and formalizes the limited victories won by the working classes, and that the resulting rights should not be dismissed out of hand. It also means, though, that law is integral to the operation, legitimation, and conservation of capitalist societies and states alike—in other words, that law is, as the conventional "critical legal studies" lingo has it, "part of the problem".' <https://voelkerrechtsblog.org/on-marx-marxism-and-international-law> accessed 17 April 2024.

[102] Ingo Venzke, 'Situating Contingency in the Path of International Law' in Ingo Venzke and Kevin Jon Heller (eds), *Contingency in International Law: On the Possibility of Different Legal Histories* (OUP 2021) 3–21, 4. Another good reference to further explore some of these questions is Paul O'Connell and Umut Özsu (eds), *Research Handbook on Law and Marxism* (Elgar 2021).

[103] Susan Marks, 'False Contingency' (2009) 62(1) Current Legal Problems 1–21, 10.

interpretative framework within which one can locate the formation of identities, preferences, and belief systems, as well as socio-cognitive biases.

Second, and relatedly, a Marxist historical-materialist framework can provide a general theory of how preferences and intentions are historically determined and how they change. The question of 'why do we act in the way we do?' eschews a simplistic answer. Although we are moved by socio-mental inclinations, these very same inclinations form identifiable and concrete expressions depending on the location of individuals within the totality of social relations, but also, most importantly, the place one occupies in relation to the prevalent mode of production. A capitalist is exploitative towards workers not because of individual greed or some sense of individual moral bankruptcy but because of the necessity of survival within the capitalist system itself. A key insight of Marxist thought is that relations of exploitation and class domination are 'impersonal' under capitalism. In this sense, class consciousness, group dynamics, and identity politics do not provide an immediate answer to social behaviour but only nudge us to probe further and uncover the many contestations within these purportedly monolithic social formations. Marxist approaches can provide a basis for a more grounded theory of political economy within cognitive-behavioural studies.[104]

A third point of learning between Marxism and cognitive-behavioural approaches is that the former can temper some of the hardcore empiricist and voluntarist assumptions of the latter. This would mean adopting a scientific approach that is not overtly reductionist and mechanistic. It would also mean that readily argued 'programmatic' prescriptions do not prefigure the nature of the problem and the kind of questions that can be asked. Marx had himself cautioned against prescribing detailed pathways for making the world better, what he called 'recipes … for the cook-shops of the future'.[105] One need not necessarily take Marx's statement to heart. The larger point is that cognitive-behavioural work is motivated by an approach which perceives the tensions, biases, and faulty mental processes as deviations from an otherwise valid and equitable political and legal process. The effort is to 'isolate problems and propose remedial action, on the footing of a framework of ideas and practices which are not in itself in question'.[106] This approach of finding managerial and legal fixes to what are profoundly structural problems risks validating and legitimizing the same system it is meant to correct.

Going back to our discussion on race and racialization in the previous section, a crucial point that was missed amidst the elaborate presentation of legal

[104] For instance, Anne van Aaken acknowledges this when she posits that 'behavioralist approaches would need a more refined theory of behavioral political economy'. See Anne van Aaken, 'Rationalist and Behavioralist Approaches to International Law' in Jeffrey L Dunoff and Mark A Pollack (eds), *International Legal Theory: Foundations and Frontiers* (CUP 2022) 261–81.

[105] Karl Marx, 'Afterword to the Second German Edition' (*Capital Volume I*) <www.marxists.org/archive/marx/works/1867-c1/p3.htm> accessed 17 April 2024.

[106] Marks (n 78) 118.

strategies to mitigate racial discrimination was that the most unrelenting forms of racialization perhaps occur within regimes which have no apparent connection to race in the first place. The international regime for reparations, cancellations of sovereign debt, and equitable climate transition and adaptation are among the most pressing battlegrounds for racialized justice. Any consequential agenda for the fight against racialization must go beyond strategies to merely influence 'social attitudes' or, for that matter, free us from a certain realm of inherited consciousness about the world. Instead, one must be able to contest and unsettle the deeply racialized normativity and materiality of international law.

## 7. Conclusion

I end with a caveat. My argument is that not Marxism offers a uniquely superior alternative to socio-cognitive approaches and thus must be replaced by the former. Rather, I submit that a Marxist framework provides a way to reflect on some of the core presuppositions of socio-cognitive approaches. It offers a basis for self-reflexivity within the discipline and a foundation for critical research that does not collapse the political into the legal and the possible to the inevitable. Certainly, the Marxist tradition cannot claim to provide comprehensive answers to the multiple and unfolding contradictions of capitalist crisis. Cognitive-behavioural interventions, whether through courts, public advocacy, legislative acts, or administrative strictures, are crucial in that they constantly shift the balance of power between dominant and less dominant groups. Similarly, debiasing techniques within institutional norms and processes has the potential to introduce multiple cognitive impulses that might mitigate implicit biases.[107] One might argue that Marxist theory holds much space for such short-term, 'tactical' legal intervention but caution that our 'tactics' must not apprehend our larger 'strategic' commitments to fundamentally transform existing society.[108] In this, cognitive-behavioural approaches might supplement a Marxist structural enquiry through detailed analysis of individual agency and situated freedom, mindful of the 'false contingency' and limits of the legal form. In the process we might have to reckon with the realization that international law is not even the answer or only a small part of the solution and that a struggle for a more just order must play out in other forums, as they always have.

[107] Sergio Puig, 'Debiasing International Economic Law' (2019) 30(4) European Journal of International Law 1339–57.

[108] Robert Knox, 'Marxism, International Law, and Political Strategy' (2009) 22 Leiden Journal of International Law 413–36, 433. See also Bill Bowring, 'What Is "Radical" in Radical International Law?' (2011) 22 Finnish Yearbook of International Law 2–29 and Rob Knox's response to Bill Bowring in the same issue: Robert Knox, 'What Is to Be Done (with Critical Theory)?' (2011) 22 Finnish Yearbook of International Law 32–47.

# 13

# Transitional Justice and Cognitive-Behavioural Studies

*Ruti G Teitel and Shreya Shankar*

## 1. Introduction

Transitional justice (TJ) processes involve psychological and cognitive processes; but TJ scholarship of international law has yet to meaningfully incorporate cognitive-behavioural insights. This chapter aims at presenting the four pillars and a genealogy of TJ involving international legal processes, as well as shedding light on the potential role of cognitive-behavioural studies in understanding and improving TJ processes. This endeavour can also narrow the gap between the increasing incorporation of behavioural science by the United Nations (UN) which has not yet reached TJ, in spite of the internationalization of TJ processes.

We will begin by briefly presenting the genealogy of transitional justice[1] and its main foundational 'pillars' which offer a useful heuristic, linking up different TJ dimensions associated with the *acqui* that has evolved over time through the stages of transitional justice. Highlighting the TJ four pillars—namely truth-seeking, prosecution (or 'accountability'), reparations, and institutional reforms or guarantees of non-repetition (including memorialization),[2] we submit that cognitive-behavioural science may constitute a useful lens to explore and enrich our understanding of some successes and failures of TJ processes. Cognitive and behavioural studies can also offer some suggestions regarding the design of better TJ institutions.

TJ broadly refers to the 'full range of processes and mechanisms associated with a society's attempt to come to terms with a legacy of large-scale past abuses, in order to ensure accountability, serve justice and achieve reconciliation'.[3] From the very beginning, the UN has embraced an integrated approach cautioning that

[1] Ruti G Teitel, 'Transitional Justice Genealogy' (2003) 16 Harv Hum Rts J 69.

[2] UN Secretary General, Guidance note of the Secretary-General: United Nations approach to transitional justice, ST/SG(09)/A652 (2010); Economic and Social Council (1997) 'Question of the impunity of perpetrators of human rights violations (Civil and Political)', UN Doc E/CN.4/Sub.2/1997/20 (Joint Principles) <www.refworld.org/docid/3b00f1a124.html>.

[3] ibid.

Ruti G Teitel and Shreya Shankar, *Transitional Justice and Cognitive-Behavioural Studies* In: *International Legal Theory and the Cognitive Turn*. Edited by: Anne van Aaken and Moshe Hirsch, Oxford University Press.
 DOI: 10.1093/9780198909293.003.0014

in situations of post conflict, TJ processes must balance between a variety of goals and that the 'strategies must be holistic'.[4]

Diverse cognitive-behavioural studies spotlight a plethora of interactions between the two fields as well as some practical implications for TJ processes. The cognitive-behavioural literature examines why people think and behave in a certain way; while TJ often attempts to influence the thoughts and behaviours of people in societies that recently experienced conflict in a way that prepares it for peace and development. More specifically, below we analyse how existing cognitive schemas impact expectations regarding future truth commissions, the influence of witnesses' memories on prosecutions, the impact of group identity on the perception of reparations, and how certain framing may affect guarantees of non-repetition. The discussion of these four issues is accompanied by some recommendations concerning the design of TJ processes, as well as some observations regarding the potential limitations of using cognitive-behavioural sciences to shape TJ processes. The specific links between different TJ pillars and cognitive-behavioural concepts should be read as examples of the broad range of possible relationships between these two fields. Furthermore, we supplement the theoretical argumentation with empirical examples where appropriate.

We proceed as follows: Section 2 sets out to present the principal TJ pillars as well as a genealogy of the history and development of TJ concepts; including international legal processes and goals. Section 3 turns to interactions between cognitive-behavioural studies and each of the main TJ pillars. Drawing on cognitive-behavioural studies, the discussion here highlights certain factors that may undermine the effectiveness of TJ processes and institutions. Finally, Section 4 concludes by offering some cautionary notes relating to how insights drawn from cognitive-behavioural literature can also be misused in designing TJ initiatives, and offers some concrete suggestions regarding enhancing TJ processes.

## 2. Transitional Justice in International Law

TJ has been defined by Teitel in the foundational scholarship as 'the conceptualization of justice in periods of radical political change'.[5] By now, TJ reflects an interdisciplinary field with an established connection to international law. This section highlights some principal stages in the development of TJ as reflected in international law; that is, the emergence and consolidation of the above-mentioned four TJ pillars and related goals, prominently prosecution

[4] The rule of law and transitional justice in conflict and post-conflict societies, Report of the Secretary-General, UN Doc S/2004/616 (23 August 2004) 9.

[5] Ruti G Teitel, *Transitional Justice* (OUP 2002) 3–4; Ruti Teitel, 'Transitional Jurisprudence: The Rule of Law in Political Transformation' (1997) 106 Yale LJ 2009.

(or 'accountability'), truth-seeking, reparations, and non-repetition involving long-term peacebuilding.[6] In contemporary developments, state commitments involving 'memorialization'[7] are also included in these pillars.

The four phases in the evolution of TJ we propose below are not linear but cumulative in terms of increase in the state's obligations where addressing past wrongs. The core norm of accountability was initially instantiated in the Nuremberg Trials as well as the following occupation era and national trials. The second phase relates to post-military transitions of the twentieth century that shaped significant international legal developments in the move to rights and reparatory justice in many instances of national transitions. These developments involve civil society (including victims) as well as societal claims to truth and reparations established in international jurisprudence. The third phase sees the global developments and the emergence of new actors and institutions involved in TJ measures; particularly during war and or post-conflict periods (where states lack capacity), there is an evident increasing density of TJ in its global practices. Finally, there is the contemporary political context associated with democratic backsliding which has raised significant concerns about the need for consolidation of the gains in justice which in turn give rise to new state obligations under international law to commitments to 'non-recurrence' and related states' duties to education and memorialization reflected in international conventions as well as caselaw. These recent international law commitments are grounded in various assumptions explored and evaluated in Section 3.

***Phase 1: Post-War Trials and the Norm of Individual Accountability:*** From the post-World War II moment, TJ was associated with post-war justice; that is, the law and norms relating to *jus post bellum* and related international humanitarian law.[8] While post-war trials have a long pedigree in international law, these post-World War II trials represented an innovation in the aims and means of justice: first by asserting forward-looking aims of rule of law as well as in the form of punishment processes with contemplated individual attribution even for crimes hitherto attributed to states. The second element is the transnational dimension of the offences prosecuted as articulated in the 'crime against humanity' which would lay a basis for transnational criminal law into the next century.

These core ideas constitute the legacy of Nuremberg and have become central elements in the international law of TJ.[9] The Nuremberg Charter itself is an

[6] See UN Report (2010). On memory and transitional justice, see Iavor Rangelov and Ruti Teitel, 'The Justice Archive: Transitional Justice and Digital Memory' (2023) 11(1) Lond Rev Int Law 83–109.

[7] 'International legal standards underpinning the pillars of transitional justice: Report of the Special Rapporteur on the promotion of truth, justice, reparation and guarantees of non-recurrence', UN Doc A/HRC/54/24 (21 June 2023) paras 67–69.

[8] See Ruti Teitel, 'Rethinking Jus Post Bellum in an Age of Global Transitional Justice: Engaging with Michael Walzer and Larry May' (2013) 24 EJIL 335.

[9] Ruti Teitel, 'Transitional Justice: Postwar Legacies (Symposium: The Nuremberg Trials: A Reappraisal and Their Legacy)' (2006) 27 Cardozo L Rev 1615.

international document and together with the UN Charter reflected international law agreements on the settlement of conflict and post-war justice at the time—all of which constituted landmark establishment of the international law of international security as reflected in the United Nations Charter. Ensuing normative developments in accountability would include the Genocide Convention, and international humanitarian law agreements (such as the Geneva Conventions), and their relevance given their connection to post-conflict situations.[10] Subsequently, other global human rights instruments followed in time (such as the International Covenants), as well as regional instruments, particularly in the Americas which have been important in laying the basis for the societal claims to truth and reparatory justice vis-à-vis the state.[11]

With the shift in political alliances after World War II associated with the rise of the Soviet Union, the historical phase of enforcement of post-war justice would be necessarily brief. Nevertheless, these international legal developments endured and became a basis for international justices' return following the Cold War's end with ethnic persecution in Yugoslavia's collapse, prosecution of the Rwandan genocide, and related judicial projects.[12] These normative developments' impact is later reflected in the establishment of a number of international criminal tribunals many decades after Nuremberg, dedicated to the similar purposes of accountability and witnessed in the statutes of the International Criminal Tribunal for the former Yugoslavia (ICTY) and the International Criminal Tribunal for Rwanda (ICTR) established by the United Nations Security Council. A full half-century after the post-World War II trials, in 2002, we witness the entrenchment of the Nuremberg paradigm in the international system with the return of international tribunals; this time outside of a particular military conflict through the establishment of the permanent International Criminal Court (ICC) (now 124 state parties). The UN Secretary Gneral reports on transitional justice highlight the reiteration and exhortation of the critical importance of the justice pillar to meaningful transition.[13] Moreover, as was key from the start, the purposes of such tribunals' punishment are asserted to be forward-looking aims of TJ: including

[10] 'Convention on the Prevention and Punishment of the Crime of Genocide', signed 9 December 1948. Entry into force 12 January 1951, 78 UNTS 277. See also The Geneva Conventions and Their Commentaries <www.icrc.org/en/law-and-policy/geneva-conventions-and-their-commentaries>.

[11] 'International Covenant on Economic, Social, and Cultural Rights, International Covenant on Civil and Political Rights and Optional Protocol to the International Covenant on Civil and Political Rights' (UN Doc A/RES/2200(XXI) 1967) Protocol; Ruti Teitel, 'Human Rights Genealogy' (1997) 66 Fordham L Rev 301.

[12] 'Statute of the International Tribunal for the Prosecution of Persons Responsible for Serious Violations of International Humanitarian Law Committed in the Territory of the Former Yugoslavia since 1991' (UN Doc S/25704, Annex (1993), as amended by UN Doc S/RES/1166 (1998), reprinted in 32 ILM 1192 1993); 'Statute of the International Tribunal for Rwanda' (UN Doc S/RES/955 (1994), reprinted in 33 ILM 1598 1994).

[13] See 'International Legal Standards Underlying the Pillars of Transitional Justice, Report of the Special Rapporteur on Truth, Justice, Reparations, and Non-Recurrence', Fabian Salvioli A/HRC/54/24 10 July 2023.

rule of law and peace-making pursued through the focus on individual accountability for egregious wrongs.

***Phase 2: The Evolving Mandate of Transitional Justice under International Law—Truth-Seeking and Reparations:*** The next phase was characterized by a surge in transitions out of authoritarian rule in the Americas and post-communist regimes of the former Soviet Bloc. The surge gives rise to an interest in shared knowledge: as more countries were undergoing political transition, TJ emerges as a field of knowledge which began essentially as a comparative study of national experiments. This field started in the late 1980s with predecessor military regimes struggling with their authoritarian pasts in periods of political change; reflecting diverse resolutions to the problem of reckoning with the past in political transition.[14] At this still relatively early stage in the field, scholarly attention focused primarily on the significance of national differences across an array of political contexts, such as which institutions and actors were relevant in shaping responses at that crucial time for transitional societies. While starting in the Global South, with countries emerging out of military rule, this phenomenon extended to the Soviet collapse and included post-communist developments involving significant political and economic change. At that time, the focus of the field concentrated on constitutional change and comparative analysis of transitional constitutionalism, in addition to other regional societal responses emphasizing international measures.[15]

The foundational conception of TJ is often characterized in terms of the punishment/amnesty debate, connected to the related pillar of accountability (prosecution). In this regard the 1980s debate was largely associated with the developments in the Global South regarding TJ processes that shared some dimensions with the foundational Nuremberg precedent. Yet, the emergence of a number of local experiments presented varying balances between peace and justice. Accordingly, at this time, throughout the Americas, there were robust debates about amnesty versus punishment, and the extent to which there was an obligation under international law to bring to justice those responsible for grave crimes in the predecessor regime, which in turn would give rise to broader obligations towards victims and society.[16] When many countries in Latin America adopted amnesty arrangements, it gave rise to judicial review of the protection of human rights by combatting 'impunity', including in the United Nations Secretary-General (UN SG) reports suggesting limiting amnesties.[17] International institutions and actors, such as regional

[14] See Teitel (n 5).

[15] See Ruti Teitel, 'Paradoxes in the Revolution of the Rules of Law' (1994) 19 Yale J Intl L 239. See also Jon Elster, *Closing the Books: Transitional Justice in Historical Perspective* (CUP 2004).

[16] See 'Accountability: Prosecuting and Punishing Gross Violations of Human Rights and Serious Violations of International Humanitarian Law in the Context of Transitional Justice Processes: Report of the Special Rapporteur on the Promotion of Truth, Justice, Reparation and Guarantees of non-Recurrence', Fabian Salvioli UN Doc A/HRC/48/60 (9 July 2021) 29–30.

[17] Diane Orentlicher, 'Impunity: Note by the Secretary-General', UN Doc E/CN.4/2004/88 (27 February 2004).

human rights courts, got involved as umpires in deciding on the legitimacy of the local TJ experiments.

Accordingly, fundamental developments in TJ would inform international law and in particular identify the foundations of what has become known in shorthand as the 'pillars' of TJ.[18] Significant caselaw emerged regarding the Latin American legacy aiming to reconcile the Nuremberg justice paradigm with the local-societal demands of peace. While different balances between peace and justice were struck in a range of countries in the region , these compromises would prove to be controversial, giving rise to litigation and appeals to the regional human rights courts. In a landmark case, *Barrios Altos v Peru*, the Inter-American Court of Human Rights (IACtHR) struck down a blanket amnesty and called for a norm of a modicum of accountability, of 'justice', as one of the foundations of TJ.[19] Moreover in related jurisprudence, this regional human rights court evaluated Peru's amnesty law concluding that where multiple victims' human rights were at stake , considerations of impunity and prevention as well as of access to investigations and right to truth were critically importantt.[20]

This period highlights important normative developments undertaken in Latin America that have significantly contributed to the international law of TJ; most notably we see a clear nexus between the crime of forced disappearances (associated with twentieth-century military repression) and the recognition of international law rights of victims to truth and reparations. In a landmark case, the IACtHR concluded that instances of forced disappearances constitute complex offences characterized as ongoing wrongs where there were systemic denials and failure to prevent, investigate, and punish.[21] Thus, from its earliest days, relying on the American Convention of Human Rights, the Inter-American Court would adjudicate cases involving TJ establishing related international responsibility relating to the context of 'conditions of impunity'.[22] *Velasquez-Rodriquez v Honduras* remains a landmark in jurisprudence establishing rights for the disappeared and their kin to truth and other reparatory measures.[23] In *Velasquez-Rodriquez*, the Court asserted that:

> [t]he duty to investigate the facts of this type ... continues as long as there is uncertainty about the fate of the person who has disappeared. Even in the hypothetical

[18] Eleonora Mesquita Ceia, 'The Contributions of the Inter-American Court of Human Rights to the Development of Transitional Justice' (2015) 14 The Law and Practice of International Courts and Tribunals 457. See Ruti Teitel and Valeria Vegh Weis, 'Transitional Justice and Human Rights' in Tamar Herzog and Thomas Duve (eds), *The Cambridge History of Latin American Law in Global Perspective* (CUP 2024) 468, 469.

[19] *Barrios Altos v Peru*, Judgment of 14 March 2001, [2001] IACtHR (Ser C) No 75.

[20] ibid 42.

[21] See *Velasquez Rodriguez v Honduras*, Judgment of 29 July 1988, [1988] IACtHR (Ser C) No 4, 147.

[22] *Goiburu et al v Paraguay*, judgment on merits, reparations and costs of 22 September 2006, [2006] IACtHR (Ser C) No 153, 89.

[23] *Velasquez Rodriguez v Honduras* (n 21) 153.

> case that those individually responsible for crimes of this type cannot be legally punished under certain circumstances, the State is obligated to use the means at its disposal to inform the relatives of the fate of the victim.[24]

In *Gomes Lund v Brazil*, the IACtHR addressed Brazil's disappearance practices, emphasizing that the 'right to truth' is inherent in Article 13 of the American Convention on Human Rights, particularly when it deals with gross human rights violations. In international precedents, the Court would squarely place responsibility on the state not just for the original disappearance but also for the state's apparent ongoing failure to 'acknowledge the detention and to reveal the situation' which comprised human rights to truth and to reparations.[25]

Thus, changes in the law of state responsibility developed, establishing critical elements of TJ, such as investigatory obligations occurring primarily through the emergence of alternative justice practices such as 'truth commissions'. These national institutions were convened at first in Latin America. For example, Argentina's landmark truth commission involved an open-ended inquiry resulting in a related report *Nunca Mas*[26] (or *Never Again*); the latter investigation led to the trials of perpetrators as well as reparations for victims. Other investigatory commissions were dedicated to additional TJ purposes beyond truth, such as reconciliation.[27]

In this phase the focus is on broader restorative justice, leading to increasing recognition of reparations as a matter of victims' rights under international law (including tribunals' caselaw).[28] In *Velasquez-Rodriquez*, the IACtHR put it succinctly: '[t]he objective of international human rights law is not to punish those individuals who are guilty of violations, but rather to protect the victims and to provide for the reparation of damages resulting from the acts of the States responsible'.[29] This can be considered by now as customary international law affirmed by the UN General Assembly statement of victims' rights to reparations as set out in the Basic Principles and Guidelines on the Right to a Remedy and Reparation for Victims of Gross Violations of International Human Rights Law and Serious Violations of International Humanitarian Law.[30]

***Phase 3: Transitional Justice Globalized—The Consolidation of the Normative Mandate on Transitional Justice in International Law:*** The consolidation of the normative paradigm in international law leads to the evolution of TJ as a field

[24] ibid 181.

[25] See *Gomes Lund et al v Brazil*, Judgement of 24 November 2010, [2010] IACtHR, 103.

[26] *Nunca más: The Report of the Argentine National Commission on the Disappeared; with an Introduction by Ronald Dworkin* (Farrar, Straus, and Giroux 1986).

[27] See, eg, Chile's Truth and Reconciliation Commission and South Africa's Truth Commission discussed in Teitel (n 5).

[28] Pablo De Greiff, *The Handbook of Reparations* (OUP 2008). In the case of *Gomes Lund et al. ('Guerrilha do Araguaia') v Brazil*, IACHR Judgment of 24 November 2010.

[29] See *Velasquez-Rodriguez v Honduras* (n 21) 134.

[30] UN Doc A/RES/60/147 (12 September 2005). See UNSG, *Guidance Note of the Secretary-General United Nations Approach to Transitional Justice* (March 2010).

where the relevant questions are being posed—*beyond the state* and *beyond the transition* with evident implications for TJ law and policy.[31] Relatedly, at this time, the scholarly project of TJ shifts from a comparative focus on national policies to what might be considered a *global* phase that engages multiple actors—beyond the state- and consequently involving an often diverse array of aims, institutions, and processes.

Starting in the 1990s with the proliferation of relevant dedicated international actors and institutions, there is a greater density of phenomena relating to the international law of TJ, often but not exclusively associated with political transition. During this phase, the UN becomes a significant actor in TJ, a dynamic site of norm production. The emergence of a special UN unit dedicated to TJ and rule of law is witnessed in the establishment of a UN Special Rapporteur, reflecting the understanding that TJ is part of the UN's agenda and mandate.[32] The UN Special Rapporteur plays a sui generis role in articulating the normative developments in terms of 'pillars of transitional justice'.

In one of its first reports in the area, the UN recognized the close relationship between the context of conflict, peace-making, and TJ.[33] Indeed, these issues are entwined:

> [o]ur experience in the past decade has demonstrated clearly that the consolidation of peace in the immediate post-conflict period, as well as the maintenance of peace in the long term, cannot be achieved unless the population is confident that redress for grievances can be obtained through legitimate structures for the peaceful settlement of disputes and the fair administration of justice.[34]

The UN also recognized that various approaches were being utilized in conflict and post-conflict:

> The notion of 'transitional justice' ... comprises the full range of processes and mechanisms associated with a society's attempts to come to terms with a legacy of large-scale past abuses, in order to ensure accountability, serve justice and achieve reconciliation. These may include both judicial and non-judicial mechanisms, with differing levels of international involvement (or none at all) and individual prosecutions, reparations, truth-seeking, institutional reform, vetting and dismissals, or a combination thereof.[35]

[31] Ruti G Teitel, *Globalizing Transitional Justice* (OUP 2014).

[32] 'The Rule of Law and Transitional Justice in Conflict and Post-Conflict Societies: Report of the Secretary-General', UN Doc S/2004/616 (23 August 2004); 'Special Rapporteur on the Promotion of Truth, Justice, Reparation, and Guarantees of Non-Recurrence: Resolution/adopted by the Human Rights Council', UN Doc A/HRC/RES/18/7 (13 October 2011); 'Guidance Note of the Secretary-General: United Nations Approach to Transitional Justice' (UN Doc ST/SG(09)/A652 2010).

[33] 'The Rule of Law and Transitional Justice in Conflict and Post-Conflict Societies' (n 32).

[34] ibid 3.

[35] ibid 4.

Thereafter the above elements are summarized in terms of a framework of foundations or 'pillars', when possible working synergistically.

TJ's global phase is associated with transnationalism in international law as well as with a growing interest in the development of best practices at the international level. The distinctive practices that evolved during this time associated with TJ largely take the form of national commissions of inquiry and international tribunals. These bodies relate to longstanding schema of thought regarding practices concerning judicial or judicial like inquiry. In particular, one can see that the preference for international justice is informed by the successful post-war trials, and prominently the paradigmatic International Military Tribunal convened at Nuremberg in Germany after World War II.

In the global phase, the 1990s post-Cold War politics at the time gave rise to similar associated TJ and international judicial interventions and the erection of specialized tribunals by the UN. A justice mechanism in the form of an international criminal tribunal was deemed to be the path to peace.[36] As the Statute of the International Criminal Tribunal for the Former Yugoslavia would provide,[37] the asserted notion here is that international tribunals can advance truth and reconciliation—connecting the above pillars of justice and truth-seeking.[38] This schema of thought became clearer as the field developed in its global phase, creating a basis for heightened expectations in a way that set such institutions possibly up for failure and led to growing interest in the need to consider justice in context.

***Phase 4:The Contemporary Political Context, Democratic Regression and the Evolution of the Transitional Justice Mandate for Non-Recurrence and Memorialization:*** Of late, we see concerns about the preservation of the aforementioned political and legal gains in light of the phenomenon of international human rights backlash,[39] as well as pressures on democracy impacting human rights in more than one region. Hence, there is an emerging concern for more than one temporality regarding transitional justice—that is, the asserted justice aims are not merely responding to the past and to amelioration of the present—but also implicate anxieties about protection of justice and rights in the future. This is what gives rise to the notion of a TJ right or claim to 'non-recurrence' taken up in phase 4 of the development of the field above.

The development of the above TJ pillars reflects a holistic and comprehensive approach to TJ. The UN has also recognized the limits of tribunals as well as of truth commissions. Accordingly, it is now elaborating the comprehensive 'duty

[36] Statute of the ICTY (n 12); UNSC, 'On Establishment of International Tribunal for the Prosecution of Persons Responsible for Violations of International Humanitarian Law Committed in the Territory of the Former Yugoslavia', UN Doc S/RES/808 (22 February 1993). See Ruti Teitel, *Globalizing Transitional Justice* (OUP 2014) chapter 5.

[37] See ICTY Preamble (n 12).

[38] See Teitel (n 36) 81–94.

[39] See Leslie Vinjamuri, 'Human Rights Backlash' in Stephen Hopgood, Jack Snyder, and Leslie Vinjamuri (eds), *Human Rights Futures* (CUP 2017) 114–34.

to non-recurrence' that engages more than one institution or actor, and with a wider concern for the society as a whole. As highlighted in the recent 2018 UN Report, the 'updated set of principles for the protection and promotion of human rights through action to combat impunity ... [outlined that] guarantees of non-recurrence are an integral part of reparation and redress for victims'.[40]

In this vein, the UN has called for a 'pro-active approach to non-recurrence'. Here, the UN has underscored the relevance of context for guarantees of non-recurrence: 'the institutional context, its characteristics, capacities and history all matter, as do the cultural circumstances and individual dispositions'.[41] Subsequently, the UN has also critically underlined that 'transitional justice and preventive initiatives centred on institutions ... have hardly ever reached the level of the broader society, let alone the grass-roots level'.[42] The UN has exhorted states not to 'exclude parts of society that are crucial to efforts to re-establish truth, including at the local community level'.[43] Yet, in spite of turning to behavioural science in other fields of international law, the UN has yet to meaningfully take behavioural studies into account in the TJ field.

In the latest phase of normative developments, we see the emergence of an extended fourth pillar of TJ supported by customary international law as well as articulated in UN report of 14 July 2023 (by Fabian Salvioli).[44] The Special Rapporteur observes that there is a connection between the concern for the dimension of nonrecurrence to t to education and memorialization of past wrongs and that is, in turn, the sine qua non for non-recurrence: without the memory of the past, there can be no right to truth, justice, reparation, or guarantees of non-recurrence. The discussion here on the cognitive process of memory is linked with serious violations of human rights, with international humanitarian law enriching all pillars of TJ.[45] Furthermore, the UN concludes that memory 'is a vital tool for enabling societies to emerge from the cycle of hatred and conflict and begin taking definite steps toward building a culture of peace'.[46] This support for

[40] Report of the Special Rapporteur on the Promotion of Truth, Justice, Reparation and Guarantees of Non-Recurrence, UN Doc A/HRC/39/53 (25 July 2018) 40.

[41] Pablo de Greiff, 'Report of the Special Rapporteur on the Promotion of Truth, Justice, Reparation and Guarantees of Non-Recurrence', UN Doc A/HRC/30/42 (7 September 2015) 30; see also 28–32.

[42] Report of the Special Rapporteur on the Promotion of Truth, Justice, Reparation and Guarantees of Non-Recurrence UN Doc A.HRC/39/53 (25 July 2018) 44.

[43] ibid.

[44] Fabian Salvioli, 'Report of the Special Rapporteur on the Promotion of Truth, Justice, Reparation and Guarantees of Non-Recurrence, on his visit to Serbia' UN Doc A/HRC/54/24/Add.2 (10 July 2023).

[45] See 'Report of the Special Rapporteur, Memorialization Processes in the Context of Serious Violations of Human Rights and International Humanitarian Law: The Fifth Pillar of Transitional Justice', UN Doc A/HRC/45/45 (2023) 21. We resume memorialization here under the fourth pillar because of its strong connections to non-recurrence. Yet, as the Report holds, 'It is both a stand-alone and a cross-cutting pillar, as it contributes to the implementation of the other four pillars and is a vital tool for enabling societies to emerge from the cycle of hatred and conflict and begin taking definite steps towards building a culture of peace.'

[46] ibid.

memorialization is also reflected in the Inter-American Commission on Human Rights website and the establishment of the Rapporteurship on Memory, Truth and Justice.[47]

While in theory the notion of commitments to establishing collective memory of the past is significant and entwined with the fulfilment of the other pillars—such as justice, truth and reparations, and non-recurrence—the UN has cautioned that in times of conflict 'memorialization is extremely difficult'.[48] Moreover, as in the pursuit of truth, these questions are often dependent on victims' and societal expectations, and as we explain in Section 3, this aim of TJ would benefit from greater knowledge of the cognitive-behavioural bases of those expectations.

It is worth observing that one country that has exemplified the links between memorialization and other pillars is Germany whose TJ policies reflect a holistic approach. Justice as in the Nuremberg Trials (but also subsequent national trials) was justified as forward looking and as a matter of moral education. Likewise, the trials were contextualized with follow-on responses of reparations and memorialization. For some time now, the accepted wisdom is that the post-war paradigm of justice, along with education, promoted democratization in Germany.

In sum, the evolving international law regarding TJ appears to recognize diverse methods and processes; while displaying at the same time gaps regarding the impact of its application. This question of the impact of these pillars—namely truth-seeking, accountability (prosecution), reparation, and non-recurrence (including memorialzation)—has given rise to evaluative scholarship and attempts to critically review the success of TJ initiatives. In this regard, there is already recognition of the significance of the *context* for the evaluation of the impact of TJ. While the tribunals for the Former Yugoslavia and Ruanda were justified in terms of the UN Charter Chapter VII's stated purposes of international peace and security, the question of their significance and impact would ultimately be a complex matter. Thus far, the studies regarding these tribunals' impact points to the importance of context and reception. Significant scholarly literature in political science and international relations emerged based on surveys of population data targeted at different groups to assess the impact of international judicial intervention. That impact seemed to depend on a variety of factors. Several qualitative analyses of case studies on mass violence and repression[49] show comprehensive

[47] Inter-American Commission on Human Rights, 'Rapporteurship on Memory, Truth, and Justice' <www.oas.org/en/iachr/jsForm/?File=/en/IACHR/r/MVJ/relator.asp#:~:text=Rapporteur%20on%20Memory%2C%20Truth%2C%20and,Inter%2DAmerican%20Human%20Rights%20System> accessed 25 August 2024.

[48] ibid para 44.

[49] Laurel E Fletcher and Harvey M Weinstein, 'Violence and Social Repair: Rethinking the Contribution of Justice to Reconciliation' (2002) 24 Hum Rts Q 573; Laurel E Fletcher and Harvey M Weinstein, 'Justice, Accountability and Social Reconstruction: An Interview Study of Bosnian Judges and Prosecutors' (2000) 18 Berkeley J Intl L 102; Laurel E Fletcher and Harvey M Weinstein, 'How Power Dynamics Influence the North-South Gap in Transitional Justice' (2018) 36 Berkeley J Intl L

appreciation of the dynamic system in which TJ interventions occur, where each system component can influence the outcome of these interventions. More optimistic conclusions emerged from Lara Nettelfield's *Courting Democracy* surveying the impact of the ICTY in advancing democratic developments through its exclusion of war criminals from politics as well as in constructing a space countering historical denial.[50] Other scholarly research examining the role of particular actors in the judicial processes and/or in the field has illuminated other effects of international judicial interventions; such as Eric Stover's research on witnesses offering a cautionary note about the gap in victims' expectations that trials raise[51] and Jelena Subotic's study of local communities concluding that in the Balkans, international justice had a 'backlash' effect, in some cases worsening political divisions and exacerbating ethno-nationalist historical narratives.[52] Similar concerns about the imposition of international trials were raised in the aftermath of the Rwandan genocide.[53] While by now there have been a handful of evaluative studies,[54] these did not generally go beyond the current framing and associated TJ measures. And yet, a new database under construction[55] would help to add quantitative data and match this with the cognitive-behavioural insights as elaborated below. In sum, while best understood as a heuristic—the 'pillars' framing of TJ processes and mechanisms renders it possible to test various assumptions associated with these distinctive modalities or virtues of justice. Yet what remains underexplored are the cognitive-behavioural bases behind those findings to which the chapter now turns.

190; Laurel E Fletcher and Harvey M Weinstein, 'Context, Timing and the Dynamics of Transitional Justice: A Historical Perspective' (2009) 31 Hum Rts Q 163.

[50] Researching and evaluating outcomes regarding the ICTY in terms of the variables of time as well as of outreach. Lara Nettelfield, *Courting Democracy in Bosnia and Herzegovina: The Hague Tribunal's Impact in a Postwar State* (CUP 2010).

[51] Evaluating witness testimony to atrocities and their disappointments in the process. Eric Stover, *The Witnesses: War Crimes and the Promise of Justice in The Hague* (U Penn 2007).

[52] Jelena Subotic, *Hijacked Justice: Dealing with the Past in the Balkans* (Cornell UP 2009), argues that international transitional justice becomes 'hijacked' by domestic actors—for such local political strategies, it fosters domestic backlash, deepens political instability, and politicizes versions of history. On the 'backlash' phenomenon in human rights, see Stephen Hopgood, Jack Snyder, and Leslie Vinjamuri (eds), *Human Rights Futures* (CUP 2017).

[53] See Jose Alvarez, 'Crimes of States/Crimes of Hate: Lessons from Rwanda' (1999) 24 Yale J Intl L 365.

[54] Eg Tricia D Olsen, Payne A Leigh, and Andrew G Reiter, 'The Justice Balance: When Transitional Justice Improves Human Rights and Democracy' (2010) 32 Hum Rts Q 980.

[55] Transitional Justice Evaluation Tools (TJET); see <www.transnationaljudicata.com> accessed 25 August 2024.

## 3. Cognitive-Behavioural Studies for the Development of Transitional Justice

As noted above, TJ's development has progressed through several phases, each foregrounding different aims principles, means, and scope. The application of TJ strategies has been successful to varying degrees in different contexts.[56] While several factors[57] may explain inconsistent performances of TJ processes, existing scholarship has largely elided the role of cognitive-behavioural psychology in devising TJ strategies to fulfil its aims concerning reconciliation, anti-impunity, and structuring of the state under transition.[58] Since TJ is aimed at impacting thinking and behaviour of individuals and groups within society, cognitive psychological mechanisms underlying individual and group behaviour can be significant in designing better TJ interventions. Cognitive-behavioural sciences generally study how cognitive processes mediate between sensory inputs that an individual is exposed to, and the perception of these inputs, as well as their mental organization in mind (as knowledge about an event, person, or abstract idea). This knowledge is used by individuals while making decisions or performing actions.[59] Cognitive-behavioural theory challenges the assumption that human beings or communities act rationally at all points. Instead, it identifies consistent patterns of bounded rationality and biases in human behaviour.[60] As for TJ, the perception of a particular event by a particular community or individual is mediated through cognitive-behavioural processes that shape the perception, memory, and expectations of these persons or communities with respect to engagement with the particular TJ pillar (such as a truth commission or courts). Thus, analysing cognitive-behavioural process that premediate and influence interactions between the relevant actors and the TJ processes may enable us to better understand people's reactions to TJ and possibly enhance their effectiveness.[61]

Before diving into each pillar of TJ, it is useful to provide an example of why cognitive-behavioural sciences can be instrumental in shaping better TJ initiatives. To illustrate this relationship, we refer to the studies on emotions in relation to TJ. An important study in this area is Doak's study on 'cognitive emotions' arising from and due to an individual's involvement in a human conflict. He points out that TJ models often do not consider the individual cognitive emotions of the

[56] Olsen, Payne, and Reiter (n 54).

[57] Briony Jones, 'The Performance and Persistence of Transitional Justice and Its Ways of Knowing Atrocity' (2021) 56 Coop Confl 163; Kiran Kaur Grewal, 'The Epistemic Violence of Transitional Justice: A View from Sri Lanka' (2023) 17 IJTJ 322.

[58] There are a handful of exceptions, eg the scholarship of Brandon Hamber (n 83).

[59] See Anne van Aaken and Moshe Hirsch's Introduction to this volume.

[60] Mohammad Sadegh Montazeri, 'Rationality in the Cognitive Psychology' in Mohammad Sadegh Montazeri, *Psychotherapist's Guide to Socratic Dialogue* (Springer 2022) 185.

[61] See Naomi Roht-Arriaza and Javier Mariezcurrena (eds), *Transitional Justice in the Twenty-First Century: Beyond Truth versus Justice* (CUP 2006).

victims interacting with systems of TJ. However, TJ processes, specifically trials and truth commissions, have the potential of addressing the cognitive emotions experienced by individuals.[62] Taking account of the cognitive emotions present in individuals can help design court and truth commission processes that maximise the therapeutic benefit for each individual. Doak proposes considering four antecedents, namely truth finding, account-making, justice, and deliberative encounter, in managing the cognitive emotions of individuals interacting with courts and truth commissions. While the exact modality of how these antecedents are used lies outside the scope of this chapter, Doak's conclusion on the importance of addressing cognitive emotions through TJ mechanisms can be extrapolated to cognitive-behavioural processes in general.[63]

We learn from this example that cognitive processes can be considered and managed in order to increase the efficacy of a TJ system. For example, cognitive psychological processes such as rationalization of unethical behaviour[64] or biases and heuristics may explain crimes committed during the conflict and inform strategies to cope with atrocities and crimes committed during the transitional period.[65] Therefore, interventions need to consider how they are being perceived by different stakeholders to address the underlying emotional and psychological processes through TJ in a way that can lead to long-term peace. Cognitive-behavioural sciences provide a process through which this can be accomplished.

This section analyses interactions between four cognitive-behavioural concepts and each of the four pillars of TJ, namely: truth-seeking and cognitive schemas, prosecutions and memory, reparations and group identity, and guarantees of non-repetition and framing. We do so by considering the different aims of TJ as the background for what might constitute a behavioural analysis of a TJ pillar, enhancing the understanding of TJ. For example, truth-seeking is often aimed at preserving memory, peacebuilding, and reconciliation within a transitional society. Similarly, as mentioned above, prosecutions are often aimed at minimizing impunity, creating generational change, and creating education in society. Reparations aim to rebuild societal infrastructure and help reconciliation, while non-repetition guarantees aim to prevent recurring atrocities and promote peacebuilding. We capture the framework of the pillars of TJ, the aims of each of the pillars, the institutions

[62] David B Wexler and Bruce J Winick, *Law in a Therapeutic Key: Developments in Therapeutic Jurisprudence* (Carolina Academic Press 1998).

[63] Jonathan Doak, 'The Therapeutic Dimension of Transitional Justice: Emotional Repair and Victim Satisfaction in International Trials and Truth Commissions' (2011) 11 Intl Crim L Rev 263.

[64] Francesca Gino, Shahar Ayal, and Dan Ariely, 'Self-Serving Altruism? The Lure of Unethical Actions That Benefit Others' (2013) 93 J Econ Behav Organ 285; Dan Ariely, *The (Honest) Truth about Dishonesty* (HarperCollins Publishers 2012).

[65] Ezzat Fattah, 'Is Punishment an Appropriate Response to Gross Human Rights Violations?' ('The Politics of Restorative Justice in Post-Conflict South Africa and Beyond' conference, Cape Town, 21–22 September 2006) <www.csvr.org.za/docs/crime/fatahreport.pdf> accessed 25 August 2024.

**Table 13.1** Relationship between pillars of transitional justice, aims, and cognitive-behavioural concepts

| **Pillar of TJ** | **Aims encapsulated within the pillar** | **Institutions used to operationalize the pillar** | **Relation to a cognitive-behavioural concept** |
|---|---|---|---|
| Truth-seeking | Preserving memory, reconciliation, peacebuilding | Truth commissions, investigative bodies | Cognitive schemas |
| Prosecutions | Minimizing impunity, education, generational change | International tribunals, domestic courts, local justice systems | Memory |
| Reparations | Rebuilding, construction of societal infrastructure | Memorial building, monetary compensation | Group identity |
| Guarantees of non-repetition | Prevention of atrocities from recurring | Institutional reforms, vetting | Framing |

through which they are operationalized, and the cognitive-behavioural science concept that we relate it to in this chapter through Table 13.1.

## 3.1. Truth commissions and cognitive schemas: the line between imagination and reality

In this section, we link the cognitive-behavioural concept of cognitive schemas with the TJ institution of truth commission. We are interested in how the perception of the function of a truth commission influences the cognitive schema of the communities affected by the pre-transitional period.[66] Understanding their cognitive schemas is important to discern how truth commissions work and whether they are successful. We argue that in a transitional society, cognitive schemas that are contrary to reality will likely influence cognition and behaviour far beyond the functioning of a truth commission negatively.

[66] Beatrice E Mayans-Hermida, Barbora Holá, and Cartien Bijleveld, 'Between Impunity and Justice? Exploring Stakeholders' Perceptions of Colombia's Special Sanctions (Sanciones Propias) for International Crimes' (2023) 17 Intl J of Transitional Justice 192.

Truth commissions may perform diverse functions, including offering a process to report and share trauma as well as acting as repositories of different narratives to preserve accounts of the traumatic experiences of affected communities (therapeutic function).[67] They also act as investigative mechanisms that are limited in ambit and scope (investigative function). While several cognitive schemas are likely to operate when considering the functioning of a truth commission, we focus on one particular cognitive schema of the affected community, namely the truth commission's therapeutic function.

Cognitive schemas can be defined as clusters of existing knowledge through which an individual perceives and synthesises the world.[68] This cluster can be about oneself and the self's relation to others.[69] Schemas form a mental shortcut (heuristic) to reduce the load from cognitive processing and increase decision-making efficiency.[70] Cognitive schemas affect several cognitive behaviours such as perceptions, language usage, expectations, and memory.[71] Specifically, cognitive schemas perform an important role in recording memories during the conflict and recounting them afterwards, both on an individual level and a collective level,[72] at a time when cognitive resources were likely used to support constant vigilance.[73]

The cognitive schema regarding truth commissions held by affected communities is mostly comprised of two components. First, truth commissions are likely to allow an individual's narratives to be heard and acknowledged; and secondly, this hearing, understanding, and acknowledgement may result in a process equivalent to a therapeutic process, benefiting victims of atrocities. Given that these two dimensions form an interconnected cluster of information that allows an individual to process information about a truth commission, it can be considered a cognitive schema about the role of a truth commission. This schema then generates expectations on the role of a truth commission.[74] Yet, this cognitive schema and the

[67] Doak (n 63); Onur Bakiner, 'Truth Commission Impact on Policy, Courts and Society' (2021) 17 Annu Rev Law Soc Sci 73.

[68] For a discussion on cognitive schemas and their interactions with legal theory, see Anne van Aaken and Moshe Hirsch's Introduction to this volume.

[69] Ian Andrew James, Lesley Southam, and Ivy Marie Blackburn, 'Schemas Revisited' (2004) 11 Clin Psychol Psychother 369.

[70] Ian James, Helen Todd, and F Katharina Reichelt, 'Schemas Defined' (2009) 2 Cogn Behav Ther 1.

[71] Christina E Webb and Nancy A Dennis, 'Memory for the Usual: The Influence of Schemas on Memory for non-Schematic Information in Younger and Older Adults' (2020) 37 Cogn Neuropsychol 58.

[72] Cognitive schemas can be divided into highly individualistic schemas and those that are widely shared among certain stakeholders, called collective schemas. See Joshua Harold and Eric Fong, 'Mobilizing Memory: Collective Memory Schemas and the Social Boundaries of Jews in Toronto' (2018) 41 Ethn Racial Stud 343.

[73] Jace Flanagan and Dan Nathan-Roberts, 'Theories of Vigilance and the Prospect of Cognitive Restoration' (2019) 63 Proc Hum Factors Ergon Soc Annu Meet 1639.

[74] As recounted above, cognitive schemas affect several other cognitive behaviours other than expectations, such as perceptions, language usage, and memory. In this chapter, we specifically focus on the expectation dimension. For more on the impact of cognitive schemas on memory processes, see Webb and Dennis (n 71).

resulting expectations can be subverted by reality. The pre-existing schemas of different members of an affected community may affect their perception of the truth commission at varying levels and may be resistant to change to varying degrees. The engagement of affected communities is instrumental in the success or failure of the TJ system itself. These communities are often linked together with other stakeholders such as members of a truth commission or governmental institutions in the transitional period through a complex web of economic, political, and social dependencies such as social acceptance or reputation; and their interactions are mediated by cognitive schemas held collectively or individually. These schemas may or may not be congruent with each other. We argue that the message on how a truth commission is supposed to perform a therapeutic function by hearing or acknowledging individual narratives forms a part of the cluster of information that enters a cognitive schema of affected communities. This schema in turn helps understand and process information about a truth commission. It involves two pieces of information: first, that the truth commission's work is cathartic in nature, and second that this catharsis is a result of hearing and acknowledging the victim's narratives. We arrive at this cognitive schema by looking at the works of scholars as well as the messaging of truth commissions, in order to understand the possible preconceived notions regarding a truth commission that an affected community may have. Incongruence between schema and reality can influence the effectiveness of a truth commission negatively.

In relation to the cathartic nature, several scholars argue that taking account of human rights violations and allowing a victimized individual or community to share their narrative and experience can be individually beneficial.[75] For example, in Chile, during the transitional period, individuals who survived torture were given twelve 'therapy sessions' where they recounted their stories. These were subsequently shared with the community or made part of archives. Participants often found the process beneficial, especially the component of sharing with the community or archiving. In fact, scholars observe that the process undertaken within a truth and justice commission may mirror a therapeutic process.[76] Yet, despite some evidence pointing to the accuracy of the cathartic nature of a truth commission's work, some studies also point out that truth commissions may function in ways that are harmful to an individual's mental health, due to the process of recounting past abuses.[77]

In spite of the impact of a truth commission as a therapeutic tool being contested, the notion that truth-telling and acknowledgement is necessarily helpful, often forms the messaging of truth commissions. For example, the South African

[75] Nora Sveaass and Nils Johan Lavik, 'Psychological Aspects of Human Rights Violations: The Importance of Justice and Reconciliation' (2000) 69 Nord J Intl L 35.

[76] Tina Rosenberg, *The Haunted Land: Facing Europe's Ghosts after Communism* (Vintage 1995).

[77] Etienne Mullet, Lonzozou Kpanake, and Felix Neto, 'Lay People's Views about Truth Commissions' (2012) 24 Peace Rev 359.

Truth and Reconciliation Commission (SATRC) used the phrase 'healing is revealing' as its slogan.[78] Similarly, the Sierra Leone Truth and Reconciliation Commission mentioned 'healing' within its mandate. Television and radio skits used phrases such as 'come blow your mind, come clear your chest'.[79]

We will now examine this particular cognitive schema, namely that truth commissions allow participants to share their experiences and that this sharing is therapeutic, to analyse the SATRC. As noted earlier, the SATRC banner highlights the pervasiveness of the cognitive schema by proclaiming 'revealing is healing'. Despite this proclamation lending support to the cognitive schema discussed earlier, the SATRC did not uniformly allow the revealing of experiences during apartheid. The original structure of SATRC allowed a more extensive narrative formation accounting of experiences. However, this structure changed throughout the SATRC lifetime, eventually resulting in vastly different types of account taking, some featuring therapeutic interventions and others featuring police interrogations, a stark deviation from the cognitive schema attached to truth commissions.[80] Therefore, the cognitive schema regarding the truth commission as therapeutic was not always validated in reality: we can observe that the first element of providing acknowledgement did not uniformly occur in the SATRC. Aside from SATRC, we see examples of other truth commissions, such as the Commission Nationale de Vérité et de Justice in Haiti, that did not allow for a consistent space for participants to share their stories.[81] We also see cases, such as the Salvadoran truth commission, where the institution in question is labelled as a truth commission but is tasked with an investigative role, thereby fully negating the schema that a truth commission is meant to provide a platform for recounting narratives by the victimized community.[82] Therefore, this component of the cognitive schema is often divergent from reality.

With regard to the second component or the element of healing, in his seminal work on the experience of victims in SATRC, Hamber also found that even in cases where recounting a traumatic incident was possible, it is not uniformly helpful or cathartic for every individual. Healing from a traumatic event is a complex process that is not adequately addressed by a singular interaction with a truth commission.[83] Therefore, the expectation of group individuals to collectively benefit

[78] Debra Kaminer and others, 'The Truth and Reconciliation Commission in South Africa: Relation to Psychiatric Status and Forgiveness among Survivors of Human Rights Abuses' (2001) 178 British J of Psychiatry 373.

[79] Rosalind Shaw, 'Rethinking Truth and Reconciliation Commissions Lessons from Sierra Leone' (US Institute of Peace special report 130, February 2005) <www.usip.org/sites/default/files/resources/sr130.pdf> accessed 26 August 2024.

[80] Kaminer and others (n 78).

[81] Joanna R Quinn, 'Haiti's Failed Truth Commission: Lessons in Transitional Justice' (2009) 8 J of Hum Rts 265.

[82] Margaret Popkin and Naomi Roht-Arriaza, 'Truth as Justice: Investigatory Commissions in Latin America' (1995) 20 LSI 79.

[83] Brandon Hamber, *Transforming Societies after Political Violence: Truth, Reconciliation and Mental Health* (Springer 2009).

from therapeutic healing in a 'one-size-fits-all' approach as a part of this cognitive schema is unlikely to be met. This is exemplified by the difference in experience between Hamber's study and the Chilean therapeutic intervention study. The Chilean study's starting point was akin to a therapy session, whereas the SATRC did not consider therapeutic principles in its operation. At the same time, we saw that the Chilean intervention was perceived to be especially useful when accompanied by sharing with the community. This component was also not uniformly present in the SATRC. Furthermore, the intersectional position of each affected individual often plays a significant role in determining how the pre-transitional period is experienced and what interventions are necessary to support the mental health of the victim community.[84]

This fracture between a cognitive schema and individuals' reality has several adverse effects, specific to the concept of cognitive schemas.[85] Cognitive schemas generally impact memory processes by heightening memory of an event that corresponds with the existing schema while leading to worsened memory if the event falls outside the schematic system.[86] This means that a truth commission, even if advertised as purely investigative, may not be sufficient to alter a pre-existing schema substantially. In such a situation, it might be useful to extend the logic of accurate messaging to cover the way a particular institution is labelled. For example, a purely investigative body should be clearly labelled as such.

In what is often a fledgling society, dissonances between cognitive schemas and reality can cause disillusionment with the processes set up by the governing system. This is further exacerbated by the 'halo effect', where disillusionment with the truth commission leaks into opinions about other transitional/post-conflict institutions[87] and can affect the process of constitution building.[88] In other words, since collective cognitive schemas constitute interpretative tools[89] to make sense of the processes of truth commissions, the failure of a truth commission to meet the expectations derived from a collective schema may lead to a negative interpretation of other TJ institutions. Parts of the original schema, such as the idea that the victim community will receive its share of public space to share its narrative, may

[84] Carolyn Shimmin and others, 'Moving towards a More Inclusive Patient and Public Involvement in Health Research Paradigm: The Incorporation of a Trauma-Informed Intersectional Analysis' (2017) 17 BMC Health Services Research 1.

[85] The divergence of a cognitive schema from reality is different from the divergence of expectations not based on a cognitive schema since as noted earlier, the cognitive schema impacts other cognitive-behavioural processes in a pervasive manner, whereas having expectations not met often only affects the impression of the institution.

[86] Webb and Dennis (n 71).

[87] Libing Nie and others, 'Halo Effect of University: The Reputation and Technology Cross-Regional Commercialisation in China' (2024) 32 Asian J of Tech Innovation 221. This article applies the same logic to universities and technology transfer.

[88] See Section 2 for comparative constitutionalism in TJ systems.

[89] Sharon J Derry, 'Cognitive Schema Theory in the Constructivist Debate' (1996) 31 Educ Psychol 163.

be extinguished entirely, also leading to distrust in the institutions that are 'supposed' to guarantee this space.[90]

The expectations derived from a cognitive schema are merely an example of the possible implications of cognitive schemas yet point to the importance of managing expectations with appropriate messaging. Ensuring that accurate information with adequate disclaimers are provided in order to form cognitive schemas in line with reality can improve several other experiences such as memory formation during the transitional period.

### 3.2. Memories and trials: prosecutions to establish peace

Prosecutions form an essential pillar of TJ. As traced in Section 2, trials and prosecutions can be considered one of the earliest components of TJ.[91] The aims of prosecution stem from the anti-impunity principle but encompass a wide range of other aims, such as education and generational change.[92] Similar to truth commissions, prosecutions are also often considered a platform to present historical narratives and offer cathartic experiences to the individual.[93] Prosecutions may play a role in increasing respect for domestic and international law,[94] may help deter potential perpetrators of violence, or may be reparative in nature.[95] Therefore, prosecutions are meant to fulfil several goals of TJ at once.

Several cognitive concepts impact the prosecution process. Here, we explore the relationship between memory and prosecutions. We do so for two reasons. First, because courts and tribunals operating in the context of a transitional society, extensively rely on the memory recall of individual victims and witnesses[96] without adequately addressing memory errors.[97] This makes for a dangerous combination in an already fragile post-conflict context. Second, because cognitive structures such as political opinions and attitudes[98] or trauma responses often influence

[90] Yury S Dodonov and Yulia A Dodonova, 'Basic Processes of Cognitive Development: Missing Component in Piaget's Theory' (2011) 30 Procedia Soc Behav Sci 1345.
[91] See Section 2.
[92] See Section 2.
[93] Claire Garbett, 'The International Criminal Court and Restorative Justice: Victims, Participation and the Processes of Justice' (2017) 5 RJ 198.
[94] Jovana Davidovic, 'Finding Space for Criminal Prosecutions Post-Conflict' (2015) 33 J of Applied Philosophy 53.
[95] Paul Christoph Bornkamm, *Rwanda's Gacaca Courts: Between Retribution and Reparation* (OUP 2012) 91.
[96] ICTY, *Prosecutor v Karadžić*, Judgment, Case No IT-95-5/18-T, Trial Chamber, 24 March 2016, 17.
[97] ICTY, *Prosecutor v Tadić*, Opinion and Judgment, Case No IT-94-1-T, Trial Chamber, 7 May 1997, 550.
[98] Gabriele Chlevickaitė, Barbora Holá, and Catrien Bijleveld, 'Judicial Witness Assessments at the ICTY, ICTR and ICC: Is There "Standard Practice" in International Criminal Justice?' (2020) 18 JICJ 185.

an individual's memory.[99] Therefore, an incorrect assessment of the strength of memory of a witness may derail the prosecution process.

Before discussing the implications of individuals' memory on prosecutions, it is useful to outline the different stages of memory briefly. Memory is generally understood to have three distinctive stages. The first stage of memory is the encoding stage, where information is perceived and encoded into the knowledge system of an individual. The second stage is storage, which involves the maintenance of a particular sequence of information about an event or idea. The last stage is called retrieval, where the information is recalled when needed at a temporally different time.[100] Memory lapses can occur due to disruptions in any one of these stages. Furthermore, repeated intervening information during the memory process may result in unconsciously storing incorrect memories for future recall.[101] This process itself has significant implications for prosecutions, especially to the extent it relies on memory recall by witnesses.[102]

In a prosecution, it is difficult to ascertain whether or not an eyewitness's statement is accurate.[103] This is further complicated by instances of the eyewitness themselves being unaware of the incorrectness within their statements. Research suggests that falsehoods may enter a narration under two circumstances, both common in prosecution cases in TJ frameworks. These two situations are, first, the experience of trauma during the construction of the memory[104] and, second, the time delay between the encoding of the memory and recall interspersed by incidents of recall in the intervening period.[105] In understanding the impact of memory on courtroom proceedings, it is critical to consider the impact of trauma and delay as mutually interactive variables.

Given the purpose of a post-conflict trial to reckon with the worst atrocities committed during the conflict, it follows that witness testimonies often deal with traumatic events.[106] Research on the memory of traumatic events recalled after a delay finds that the central details of a traumatic event, that is directly responsible

[99] Deryn Strange and Melanie KT Takarangi, 'Memory Distortion for Traumatic Events: The Role of Mental Imagery' (2015) 6(27) Front Psychiatry 1; Ana Catarino and others, 'Failing to Forget' (2015) 26 Psychol Sci 604.

[100] Swaleha Mujawar and others, 'Memory: Neurobiological Mechanisms and Assessment' (2021) 30(Supp 1) Ind Psychiatry J S311.

[101] David R Ross and others, 'Unconscious Transference and Mistaken Identity: When a Witness Misidentifies a Familiar but Innocent Person' (1994) 79 J of Applied Psychology 918.

[102] See, for information on the unreliability of eyewitness testimonies, Philip U Gustafsson, Torun Lindholm, and Fredrik U Jönsson, 'Eyewitness Accuracy and Retrieval Effort: Effects of Time and Repetition' (2022) 17 PLOS ONE e0273455 <https://doi.org/10.1371/journal.pone.0273455> accessed 26 August 2024. See Robin L Kaplan and others, 'Emotion and False Memory' (2016) 8 Emotion Rev 8.

[103] Geeta Singh and others, 'Does Cognitive Therapy Change the Early Maladaptive Schemas in Individuals with Alcohol Dependence? Evidence from a Randomized Controlled Trial' (2023) 45 Indian J Psychol Med 124.

[104] Strange and Takarangi (n 99).

[105] Ross and others (n 101).

[106] ICC, *Prosecutor v Lubanga*, Judgment pursuant to Article 74 of the Statute, Case No ICC-01/04-01/06-2842, Trial Chamber I, 5 April 2012, 105.

for emotional arousal,[107] may be resistant to wear and tear.[108] Peripheral details of the event, specifically identification of the perpetrator and the time and place, are more likely to be inaccurate.[109] In light of this, a trial chamber of the ICTY stated that any inaccuracy in 'peripheral details' should not affect the weight that must be accorded to witness testimonies.[110] Furthermore, those experiencing post-traumatic stress disorder are more likely to hold on to a wider variety of retrieval cues for the trauma memory and may have better recall of the core memory in question.[111]

Especially in the aftermath of a conflict, alongside the role played by trauma, both individual and collective memories impact recall. Assmann outlines the relationship between individual and collective memory by positioning the individual's existence in both singular and plural senses.[112] She finds that the individual is also part of a collective (through group membership) and, therefore, personalizes the collective memory while simultaneously existing as an individual with episodic or semantic memories that are individual in nature.[113] This means that collective memories shaped during atrocities may appear as individual memories in trials.

Furthermore, in a TJ process, trials are often conducted years after the relevant events ,[114] because setting up a fair judicial system in the immediate aftermath of the conflict is often challenging. In this period, victims and witnesses are likely to recall the memory of the incident repeatedly to describe their experiences to friends and family or to provide an account to the media. In this era of internet access, it is also likely that these events are recounted by the media and discussed on social media platforms. The extended delay between the event and the initial interview may lead to unconscious transference, where the memory of the original event is tainted with any inaccuracies that occur during each subsequent recall process.[115] This process of unconscious transference may lead to inaccurate eye-witness testimonies during prosecutions.

[107] Martin Safer and others, 'Tunnel Memory for Traumatic Events' (1998) 12 App Cog Psychol 99.

[108] Catarino and others (n 99).

[109] Birgit Kleim and Anke Ehlers, 'Reduced Autobiographical Memory Specificity Predicts Depression and Posttraumatic Stress Disorder after Recent Trauma' (2008) 75 J of Consulting and Clinical Psychology 231.

[110] ICTY, *Prosecutor v Brđanin*, Judgment, Case No IT-99-36-T, Trial Chamber II, 1 September 2004, 25.

[111] Catarino and others (n 99).

[112] Aleida Assmann, 'Memory, Individual and Collective', in Robert E Goodin and Charles Tilly (eds), *The Oxford Handbook of Contextual Political Analysis* (OUP 2006) 211.

[113] Aleida Assmann, 'Memory, Individual and Collective' in Robert E Goodin and Charles Tilly (eds), *The Oxford Handbook of Contextual Political Analysis* (OUP 2006) 213–16. Episodic memory refers to memory of events from the past, whereas semantic memory refers to factual information. See Endel Tulving, 'Episodic and Semantic Memory: Where Should We Go from Here?' (1986) 9 BBS 573.

[114] Birju Kotecha, 'The International Criminal Court's Selectivity and Procedural Justice' (2020) 18 JICJ 107.

[115] Ross and others (n 101).

These insights from cognitive-behavioural studies help us exercise caution within courtrooms. Since not each subsequent recall is created equal, it is useful to consider the use of psychologically valid interview techniques to maximise accuracy. Aggressive and suggestive interviews often perpetuate suggestibility among the participants, inserting false memories into the testimonies.[116] In contrast, a supportive, non-repetitive interview structure can help maximise accuracy. The use of these techniques during the investigation as well as the trial stage within a prosecution can help maximise the accuracy of the court's decision-making.[117]

In sum, prosecutions within the TJ framework may require a different approach, with trained psychologists leading examinations at least when it comes to witnesses. It may involve studying the witness statements for signs of inaccuracies or confusion and a more expansive timeline for prosecutions. Given that trauma memories are more resilient to external influence and forgetting, courts located in TJ environments may accept evidence arising from the central details of a trauma memory. The use of eyewitness accounts can also be corroborated with data derived from digital evidence, to ensure accurate decision-making.[118]

### 3.3. The impact of social identity on reparations

Research in the field of psychology indicates that different people need different interventions to heal after a traumatic incident.[119] However, TJ structures often do not consider the variability of each victim's requirements in determining the design of the TJ framework. Although individualized reparations may not be possible, one method to analyse what kind of TJ initiative is appropriate is to understand group identities as a shorthand to see what type of interventions, such as reparations, may be more or less valuable to each group.

This section deals with the third dimension or pillar of TJ: reparations, perhaps TJ's most broadly defined pillar, encompassing any material or symbolic measures after large-scale human rights violations. The United Nations Office of the High Commissioner has repeatedly highlighted the extent of the impact of 'genuine' reparations on affected communities.[120] According to the UN guidelines on the right to a remedy and reparation for victims of gross violations of international human

[116] Malwina Szpitalak and Romuald Polczyk, 'Reducing Interrogative Suggestibility: The Role of Self-Affirmation and Positive Feedback' (2020) 7 PLOS ONE e0236088 <https://journals.plos.org/plosone/article?id=10.1371/journal.pone.0236088> accessed 26 August 2024.

[117] David La Rooy and others, 'Do We Need to Rethink Guidance on Repeated Interviews?' (2010) 16 Psychol Pub Policy and L 373.

[118] See Leiden Guidelines on Digitally Derived Evidence.

[119] Guerda Nicolas, Anna Wheatley, and Casta Guillaume, 'Does One Trauma Fit All? Exploring the Relevance of PTSD across Cultures' (2015) 8 Intl J of Culture and Mental Health 34.

[120] OHCHR, 'Statement by Michelle Bachelet, UN High Commissioner for Human Rights' (16 December 2020) <www.ohchr.org/en/statements/2020/12/15th-anniversary-basic-principles-and-guidelines-right-remedy-and-reparation> accessed 26 August 2024.

rights law and serious violations of international humanitarian law, reparations include four categories of interventions: restitution, compensation, rehabilitation and satisfaction.[121]

The design of a reparative intervention must consider the needs of specific communities. One cognitive-behavioural tool that can be used in this context is group identity theory. This section defines group identity as the component of an individual's identity that is tied to membership in a social group located in a specific social, economic or political context.[122] Group identity affects common perceptions, attitudes, and concerns that a significant number of individuals belonging to the group might share. Group identity leads members to favour their in-group members, thus discriminating against out-group members.[123] At the same time, not every situation or interaction between different groups or individuals is based on social identity to the same extent. The concept of identity salience captures this differential role of identity in different interactions. It posits that the qualitative strength of a particular identity and the number of people or groups tied to an entity determine the extent to which the particular identity is salient.[124] The role of group identity in designing reparations is exemplified by research around mental health support as a reparative intervention.

In recent years, a popular form of reparations is providing psychological or mental health care for individuals affected by conflict.[125] However, these interventions are often heavily medicalized in nature, locating trauma within the constraints of a victim/survivor narrative.[126] Trauma is often also physically

[121] UNGA, *Basic Principles and Guidelines on the Right to a Remedy and Reparation for Victims of Gross Violations of International Human Rights Law and Serious Violations of International Humanitarian Law*, UN Doc A/RES/60/147 (21 March 2006). Satisfaction is a broadly defined form of reparations that may include symbolic acts such as public apologies for the construction of memorials. It also includes elements of the other pillars of transitional justice such as truth-seeking (the first pillar) and cessation of violations (closely associated with guarantees of non-repetition or institutional reform). Therefore, reparations can be classified as the most broad-reaching TJ intervention. The wording of this pillar itself indicates its role as mainly a reconciliatory mechanism designed to allow a previously conflict-ridden society to experience peace.

[122] John C Turner, Rupert J Brown, and Henri Tajfel, 'Social Comparison and Group Interest in Ingroup Favouritism' (1979) 9 Eur J of Social Psychology 187.

[123] See Moshe Hirsch, 'Social Cognitive Studies, Sociological Theory, and International Law' in Andrea Bianchi and Moshe Hirsch (eds), *International Law's Invisible Frames: Social Cognition and Knowledge Production in International Legal Processes* (OUP 2021) 21, 22 for a discussion of social identity theory.

[124] See Moshe Hirsch, *Invitation to the Sociology of International Law* (OUP 2015) 91 (on 'Social Identity, International Groups and International Law'). This section deals with several results that occur as a result of identity salience such as depersonalization where people are viewed less in individualistic terms and more in terms of their group identity and perceptions, where a greater degree of homogeneity is perceived among members of the in-group. Each of these cognitive processes arising from identity can have significant impacts on the transitional justice process.

[125] International Rehabilitation Council for Torture Victims, *Rehabilitation of Torture Victims: Global Directory of Centres and Programmes 2003–2004* (IRCT 2003).

[126] M Brinton Lykes and Marcie Mersky, 'Reparations and Mental Health' in Pablo de Greiff (ed), *The Handbook of Reparations* (OUP 2006) 593.

materialized and can be seen in the brain through magnetic resonance imaging.[127] The implicit assumption that this type of victim's narrative carries is the universality of the experience of trauma among all those who have experienced conflict, irrespective of other factors such as gender[128] and social position.[129] Several authors and researchers have challenged this assumption. Trauma, these authors argue, is located in the intersection between the individual, and the groups to which they belong.[130] The trauma of experiencing a conflict is located in an individual's psyche. However, a person's psyche has individual and collective elements,[131] often bolstered by the polarising effect of the conflict itself. This model challenging the universality of trauma as a biomedical response locates the trauma response within cultural discourses prevalent within a specific community.[132] The trauma itself is often caused by dehumanizing social relationships, spurring violence that persists during the conflict.[133] Which cultural patterns are important and how psycho-social responses to a traumatic event can be structured thus often depends on individuals' particular group identity. Therefore, the experience of group identity (and, by extension, the person's identity) is dynamic during and post-conflict, depending on the responses of different stakeholders.[134] It is difficult to construct a linear relationship between collective and individual traumas. However, one possible relationship between these two concepts is that collective identity mediates the experience that an individual has, impacting the type of individual trauma.

Thus, a non-medicalized community view of mental health that takes into account an individual's social identity is more likely to lead to constructive reparations compared with individual therapeutic interventions. These can be exemplified by community-based reparations, such as rebuilding physical infrastructure, or constructing memorials to enable community participation and create distance from the pre-transitional period or even work on supporting the livelihoods of community members previously engaged in economic activities revolving around the conflict.[135] Even more importantly, a decision on what form

[127] Akira Kunimatsu and others, 'MRI Findings in Posttraumatic Stress Disorder' (2020) 52 J Magn Reson Imaging 380.

[128] See Chapter * by Shiri Krebs in this volume for a discussion on feminist and Third World Approaches to International Law (TWAIL) positionality in perceiving the law.

[129] Patrick J Bracken, 'Hidden Agendas: Deconstructing Post-Traumatic Stress Disorder' in Patrick J Bracken and Cella Petty (eds), *Rethinking the Trauma of War* (Free Association Books 1998) 40–43.

[130] Elizabeth Lira Kornfeld, 'The Development of Treatment Approaches for Victims of Human Rights Violations in Chile' in Rolf J Kleber, Charles R Figley, and Berthold PR Gersons (eds), *Beyond Trauma: Cultural and Societal Dynamics* (Plenum Press 1995) 118.

[131] Raija-Leena Punamaki, 'Political Violence and Mental Health' (1989) 17 Intl J of Mental Health 3.

[132] Maurice Eisenbruch, 'From Post-Traumatic Stress Disorder to Cultural Bereavement: Diagnosis of Southeast Asian Refugees' (1991) 33 Soc Sci Med 673.

[133] Ignacio Martín-Baró, 'War and Mental Health' in Ignacio Martín-Baró, *Writings for a Liberation Psychology* (Harvard UP 1994) 109–11.

[134] See Hirsch (n 124).

[135] Rama Mani, 'Rebuilding an Inclusive Political Community after War' (2005) 36 Secur Dialogue 511.

of mental health-based intervention as a reparation should be provided should be based on community considerations instead of operating from a medicalized perspective.

Therefore, reparative measures should consider social structures that often position different groups in opposition to each other in terms of social status relative to access to economic and social resources or public spaces. This also often determines each group's attitude in the post-conflict period.[136] For example, Hakim, Branscombe, and Schoemann indicate that when the victim group is an indigenous community, the relationship between group-based guilt and support for reparations is stronger than when the victim community is not an indigenous community.[137]

While it is unclear from the study why this effect exists, these attitudes derived from the social identity of an individual, similar to cognitive schemas discussed previously, have significant impacts on the social perception of a particular measure as well as the resultant behaviour.[138] A strongly negative attitude towards a certain mode of reparations is unlikely to lead to lasting social change or help the peacebuilding process, even if public institutions force such a change, unless there is a change in attitude towards the measure. Therefore, reparative policies within TJ institutions must be mindful of targeting the underlying group identities and the collective insecurities or fears the group faces in designing reparative measures.[139] This consideration of group identity should also apply to the design of mental health-based reparative services. In summary, as seen in Table 13.1, since reparations are aimed at rebuilding societal infrastructures, it must consider the social context in the form of group identity, that forms the constraints within which reparations operate.

### 3.4. Framing and memory in transitional justice processes

The above sections have mainly addressed how cognitive-behavioural studies may provide insights into designing better interventions in TJ systems. Cognitive-behavioural studies merely offer a window into human behaviour in different contexts and can be used to better institutional design. Insights from cognitive-behavioural studies may, however, also point to some potential negative effects.

[136] Lasse Lykke Rørbæk, 'Killing in the Name of...? Types of Ethnic Groups and Armed Conflict' (2017) 52 Coop Confl 537.

[137] Nader Hakim, Nyla Branscombe, and Alexander Schoemann, 'Group-Based Emotions and Support for Reparations: A Meta-Analysis' (2021) 2 Affect Sci 363.

[138] Paula M Niedenthal and others, 'Embodiment in Attitudes, Social Perception, and Emotion' (2005) 9 Personality and Social Psychology Rev 184.

[139] For more on the specific impacts of inter-group conflict on perceptions and cognition and ways to reduce such bias, see Fabian MH Schellhaas and John F Dovidio, 'Improving Intergroup Relations' (2016) 11 Curr Opin Psychol 10.

This will be illustrated by linking the framing effect to the pillar of guarantees of non-repetition.

Guarantees of non-repetition constitute the fourth pillar of TJ. It is defined as interventions targeted at dismantling social and political structures that led to large-scale human rights violations to allow people and communities to feel safe in post-conflict peace.[140] One possible means of executing guarantees of non-repetition is through institutional reforms.

The framing effect refers to a change in decision based on how the problem is 'framed'.[141] The equivalence framing effect is often studied in relation to the impact of phrasing an intervention positively or negatively. Tversky and Kahneman found that phrasing the same intervention positively led to more participants choosing the intervention than when presented negatively.[142] This effect is potent since the language used to market a TJ intervention can be manipulated to generate support without genuinely attempting to make the intervention useful for the involved communities. The effect of manipulating the language particularly affects institutional reforms. This is because transitional governmental institutions are often inherited from the conflict period.[143] Furthermore, governments often prioritize economic growth and consolidation of political power in the aftermath of a conflict. Therefore, it is easy for public authorities to use the framing effect to assuage the local population or change the narratives around institutional reform.[144]

In the TJ literature, Kochanski argues that regimes often use framing to change the discursive dialogue around conflicts such that pre-existing institutions are often left out of the discussion regarding their role in the conflict and the atrocities committed.[145] He calls this 'distortional framing' based on Snow and Benford's preventative and persuasive framing model.[146] Distortional framing is

[140] Commission on Human Rights, 'The Administration of Justice and Human Rights of Detainees', *Sub-commission on Prevention of Discrimination and Protection of Minorities*, UN Doc E/CN.4/Sub.2/1997/20/Rev.1 (2 October 1997) <http://hrlibrary.umn.edu/demo/RightsofDetainees_Joinet.pdf> accessed 26 August 2024.

[141] Pooya Tabesh, Parnian Tabesh, and Kaveh Moghaddam, 'Individual and Contextual Influences on Framing Effect: Evidence from the Middle East' (2019) 45 J of Gen Management 30.

[142] Amos Tversky and Daniel Kahneman, 'The Framing of Decisions and the Psychology of Choice' (1981) 211(4481) Science 453.

[143] Marginalization, discrimination, and social exclusion are considered significant risk factors for atrocities or mass human rights violations. For more on the link between these risk factors and atrocities, see presentation by Savita Pawnday, Deputy Executive Director of the Global Centre for the Responsibility to Protect, on 26 May 2020 for the Organization for Security and Co-operation in Europe's Supplementary Human Dimension Meeting on Addressing All Forms of Intolerance and Discrimination during a session entitled 'From Early Warning to Early Action Prevention of Discrimination from Escalation into Tensions or Conflict'.

[144] Janelle Sylvester and others, 'A Rapid Approach for Informing the Prioritization of Degraded Agricultural Lands for Ecological Recovery: A Case Study for Colombia' (2020) 58 J for Nature Conservation 125921.

[145] Adam Kochanski, 'Framing, Truth-Telling, and the Limits of Local Transitional Justice' (2021) 47 Rev of Intl Studies 468.

[146] David A Snow and Robert D Benford, 'Ideology, Frame Resonance, and Participant Mobilization' (1988) 1 Intl Soc Movement Research 197.

fundamentally discursive. It is constructed using different co-acting processes such as framing the timeline of a conflict in a narrow manner so that certain events are collectively excluded from consideration, personifying the regime to occupy a victim/liberator character to frame the conflict in black and white (without acknowledging the shades of grey), especially backgrounding crimes committed by the regime itself.[147] The saliency bias affects this type of framing where some information is highlighted while others are neglected.[148] Kochanski argues that this type of framing impacts local actor's behaviour by drawing boundaries on what is acceptable within the discourse and what one can acquire through TJ. This type of framing may also significantly impact the memorialization process, an important component of TJ.[149] For example, Ricoeur views framing as a tool to intentionally engage collective memories, either to construct an event in a specific way or to forget to mention certain events entirely.[150] The newly constructed frame concerning the events and experiences during the conflict may exclude subversive experiences, making memorialization necessarily subjective and selective in a way that benefits those constructing the frame.

Additionally, research suggests that stimuli framed to suggest a gain for the person, if recollected, are more likely to be remembered; while stimuli that if recalled may lead to fewer benefits or a loss are more likely to be forgotten. Since the socially constructed version of the events that occurred grants social acceptability, memories that do not correspond to this specific framing of the event may become prone to memory lapses.[151]

It is difficult to predict the extent of the impact of this type of exclusion of events and information on reconciliation and peacebuilding in the long run. However, we argue that this inappropriate memorialization is a form of institutional epistemic injustice.[152] Therefore, in some senses, cognitive-behavioural sciences can inform how framing can undermine the TJ project by guiding/determining the construction of certain memories for people and communities about what they are allowed to ask for and what remains outside their reach. As Table 13.1 indicates, framing actively affects collective memory during TJ processes. Therefore, it is helpful to use cognitive-behavioural studies to draw attention to this problem.

[147] Sarah Kenyon Lischer, 'Narrating Atrocity: Genocide Memorials, Dark Tourism, and the Politics of Memory' (2019) 45 Rev of Intl Studies 805, 825.

[148] Debraj Ray and Joan Esteban, 'Conflict and Development' (2017) 9 Annual Rev of Econ 263, 286 et seq.

[149] UN, 'Promotion of Truth, Justice, Reparation and Guarantees of Non-Recurrence: Note by Secretary-General', UN Doc A/67/368 (13 September 2012); UN, 'Promotion of Truth, Justice, Reparation and Guarantees of non-Recurrence: Note by Secretary-General', UN Doc A/HRC/34/62 (27 December 2016).

[150] Paul Ricoeur, *Memory, History, Forgetting* (University of Chicago Press 2004).

[151] Dillon H Murphy and Barbara J Knowlton, 'Framing Effects in Value-Directed Remembering' (2022) 50 Mem Cogn 1350.

[152] Miranda Fricker, *Epistemic Injustice: Power and the Ethics of Knowing* (OUP 2007).

Indeed recognizing the problem here offers a first step in finding ways to mitigate or ameliorate it.

## 4. Conclusion: Ways Forward in Applying Cognitive-Behavioural Sciences to Transitional Justice Systems

Throughout this chapter, we have explored the link between the different pillars of TJ and the insights derived from cognitive-behavioural sciences. Often, the conclusions derived from cognitive-behavioural sciences draw attention to what may be problematic in TJ processes given their goals, and offer the possibility of designing more detailed interventions that help meet the aims of TJ mechanisms. Thereby they illuminate the means of achieving the goals of TJ, contributing to the theory of the same.

For example, if the aim of truth-seeking as a foundational dimension of TJ is to ensure long-term peacebuilding in society by acknowledging the truth of different experiences during the commission of atrocities, one might conclude that there is an imperative to establish a truth commission that accurately describes its aims and process. This helps create an accurate cognitive schema that leads to expectations of a truth commission that can be met. Similarly, considering the potential lapses in memory due to both delay and trauma may increase the credibility of prosecutions within a TJ judicial process. In turn, this may aid in arriving at the aims of prosecutions in TJ, such as increasing respect for law and initiating generational change. Moreover, when significant resources are often spent on reparations, considerations regarding what reparations are likely to be welcomed by a community and create a basis for reconciliation in society are important. These considerations can be made based on the group identity and social relationships prevalent in the transitional society. Furthermore, as exemplified by the discussion on framing and guarantees of non-repetition, cognitive-behavioural insights can help paint a picture of the potential problems that may arise while designing and implementing TJ. Those are just some examples of how cognitive-behavioural studies can inform TJ theory which needs to grapple with the question of under what conditions TJ processes are most successful. The insights gained from cognitive-behavioural sciences can offer TJ theory insights into human behaviour which is at the heart of TJ processes. Simultaneously, the relationships can be considered with greater nuance through empirical research into this area.

Moreover, as a matter of best practice within TJ systems, it may be useful to consider some basic principles based on the discussion in this chapter. Firstly, the description of each intervention must be as clearly and unambiguously published as possible, along with the intervention's process. Furthermore, the anticipated result of each intervention should be publicly available upfront. This information may help challenge any existing schemas or aid in creating new ones that accurately represent a TJ initiative. Secondly, misinformation or exaggeration of facts within the media should be mitigated as much as possible to preserve accurate memories for truth commissions or prosecutions. Furthermore, courts, tribunals or truth commissions in TJ systems must equip themselves with psychologists or social workers to help conduct witness interviews. Thirdly, interventions in TJ systems should consider the needs of different social groups to analyse what type of intervention might best suit the group's needs. Finally, TJ theory should address the role of intentional framing in public messaging. In the initial setting-up period of transitional processes, it would be important to use care regarding rhetoric to reduce the risk of violence and potential vulnerability among implicated groups and communities. Achieving the overarching goal of justice in TJ requires a closer inquiry into the minds and behaviour of the relevant stakeholders Doing this would go some way to addressing the current gap between internationalized TJ and the turn to behavioural science of the UN in other areas. As AO Hirschman said: 'The architect of social change can never have a reliable blueprint ... what can be most usefully conveyed by the builders of one house is the understanding of the experience that made it at all possible to build under these trying circumstances.'[153]

[153] Albert O Hirschman, *A Bias for Hope* (Yale 1971) 360.

# Index

*For the benefit of digital users, indexed terms that span two pages (e.g., 52–53) may, on occasion, appear on only one of those pages.*